SCHOLAR Study Guide
Higher Psychology

Authored by:

Isobel Mullarkey (Ayreshire College)

Lynn Findlay (Borders College)

Reviewed by:

Marie Morrison (Edinburgh College)

Previously authored by:

Andrea Walsh

Joe Walsh

Heriot-Watt University

Edinburgh EH14 4AS, United Kingdom.

First published 2018 by Heriot-Watt University.

This edition published in 2018 by Heriot-Watt University SCHOLAR.

Distributed by the SCHOLAR Forum.

SCHOLAR Study Guide Higher Psychology

Higher Psychology Course Code: C863 76

ISBN 978-1-911057-52-9

Print Production and Fulfilment in UK by Print Trail www.printtrail.com

Acknowledgements

Thanks are due to the members of Heriot-Watt University's SCHOLAR team who planned and created these materials, and to the many colleagues who reviewed the content.

We would like to acknowledge the assistance of the education authorities, colleges, teachers and students who contributed to the SCHOLAR programme and who evaluated these materials.

Grateful acknowledgement is made for permission to use the following material in the SCHOLAR programme:

The Scottish Qualifications Authority for permission to use Past Papers assessments.

The Scottish Government for financial support.

The content of this Study Guide is aligned to the Scottish Qualifications Authority (SQA) curriculum.

Contents

Unit 1: Research

Unit 1 Topic 1

Stages in the research process

Contents

Prerequisites

You can undertake this course if your school/college thinks you are ready to do so. However, it will be useful if you have any of the following:

- National 5 Psychology Course or area of studies;

- National 5 Biology Course or area of studies;

- Social Studies or Social Sciences Courses or area of studies at National 5 level.

Learning objective

By the end of this topic, you should be able to:

- describe the stages of the research process:

    1. Choose topic
    2. Review literature
    3. Form hypothesis
    4. Design study
    5. Collect data
    6. Examine data
    7. Reach conclusion
    8. Report findings

- explain that a hypothesis is a testable statement of what we think will happen in our research and gives us a clear starting point;

- describe the different types of hypothesis: experimental, correlational, null, alternative, directional and non-directional;

- explain qualitative and quantitative data, and understand the difference between them;

- explain measures of central tendency (mean, median and mode) and know how to calculate them;

- explain measures of dispersion (range and standard deviation).

1.1 Introduction

We all have an idea of what we think psychologists do, usually from TV and films. This is good entertainment, but doesn't reflect what they really do.

What do psychological researchers do? This is the subject of this area of study: "Research".

Before we move on, consider the following questions.

Introduction: Questions Go online

Q1: Explain/define the term 'objectivity'.

....

Q2: Explain/define the term 'subjectivity'.

....

Q3: Which of the two approaches to research outlined above should psychologists take, and why?

In this area of study, the major themes of area of study 2 and area of study 3, such as sleep and dreams, stress, conformity etc. are used as context for the research methodologies involved in investigating behaviour.

For example, if you study the topic about memory, you may be asked to consider one of the models of memory and to investigate in a scientific manner the theory behind one or more aspect of the memory model.

What the research area of study does is to help you to tackle this sort of investigation in a logical, systematic and scientific manner.

Also, as you will see later in the area of study, you have to carry out your own investigation using scientific methodology and then produce a report on your work - this will be used as part of the course assessment.

1.2   Stages in the research process

Learning objective

By the end of this section, you should be able to:

- describe the stages of the research process:
    1. Choose topic
    2. Review literature
    3. Form hypothesis
    4. Design study
    5. Collect data
    6. Examine data
    7. Reach conclusion
    8. Report findings

Researchers use a systematic approach to research, called the research process, which is cyclical.

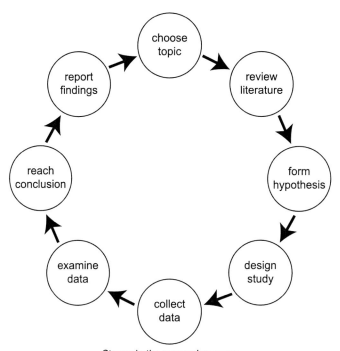

Stages in the research process

1.2.1 Choosing a topic

The first step in the **research** process is to decide on an area of interest. What kinds of things interest you about human behaviour? What would you like to know more about?

Topics may include general questions, such as:

- what steps can be taken to reduce online 'trolling'?
- does short-term memory decline with age?
- does creativity reach a peak at age 30?
- does sleeping less than seven hours per night affect driving ability?

1.2.2 Reviewing the literature

Once an area of interest has been chosen, the researchers must then conduct a thorough review of the existing literature on the subject. What do we mean by 'literature'? These are publications of important studies that have been carried out previously into the topic chosen in the previous step of the **research** process.

Why do researchers conduct a literature review? There are three main reasons:

1. to improve their understanding of the topic they have chosen to study;
2. to demonstrate their knowledge to others conducting research in a similar area;
3. to bring the reader up-to-date with findings in the topic area.

The findings from a literature review will be presented in the Introduction section of the report of the research (you will do this yourself when writing up your Research Investigation). This process also helps the researcher with the next step of the research process - formulating a **hypothesis**.

1.2.3 Formulating a hypothesis

Learning objective

By the end of this section, you should be able to:

- explain that a hypothesis is a testable statement of what we think will happen in our research and gives us a clear starting point;
- explain that there are different types of hypothesis: experimental, correlational, null, alternative, directional, and non-directional.

The researcher can now make specific predictions about the study he/she is planning. It is important to note that **hypotheses** should be as specific as possible since you are trying to find valid and reliable results, and the more vague your hypotheses, the more vague your conclusions.

For example, if I am conducting a study on whether short-term memory declines with age how can I test this to find out if this prediction is a valid one? A good hypothesis is required, such as:

Participants over the age of 70 will score less on a test of short-term memory than participants under the age of 70.

A hypothesis is a testable statement of what we think will happen in our research, and gives a clear starting point.

To discover whether the prediction is correct, factual data is gathered (scores on a memory test) which will help to support the hypothesis or otherwise. If the hypothesis has generated supporting evidence (e.g. if participants over 70 do indeed score less on a test of short-term memory than participants under the age of 70), this gives a measure of confidence in accepting any theory from which the hypothesis came (that short-term memory declines with age).

There are two types of research hypothesis used in psychology, the **experimental hypothesis** and the **correlational hypothesis**.

You will come across both of these in subsequent topics when we look at the experimental method and the correlational technique.

Both types share the feature of the **null hypothesis**.

1.2.3.1   The null hypothesis

The **null hypothesis** is a statement that you want to test. In general, the null hypothesis is that things are the same as each other, or the same as a theoretical expectation. For example:

> *There will be **no difference** in scores on a memory test between participants over the age of 70 and participants under the age of 70.*

Finding that participants over the age of 70 score lower on memory tests might lead to all kinds of exciting discoveries that will help improve memory in older people (and others). Finding that there is no difference in memory ability between the two groups wouldn't lead to anything much.

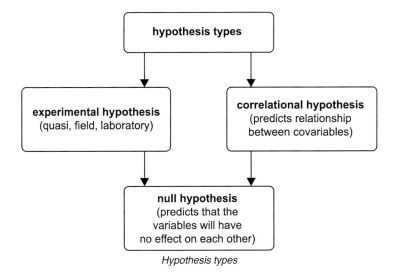

Hypothesis types

The null hypothesis predicts that one variable will have no effect on the other. This is the hypothesis that will be tested by the researcher, e.g. if we use the hypothesis given earlier, a null hypothesis would be:

There will be no difference in scores on a memory test between participants over the age of 70 and participants under the age of 70.

The null hypothesis: Notebook exercise

You will need your psychology notebook for this activity.

Change the research aims in the following table into experimental/alternative hypotheses and null hypotheses.

- Hypothesis: a testable statement which makes a prediction of what the outcome of the research will be.

- Experimental Hypothesis: states that there will be a difference between the two sets of scores.

- Null Hypothesis: states that there will not be a difference between the two sets of scores.

Aim	Hypothesis (alternative or experimental)	Hypothesis (null)
To find out if keeping a sleep journal helps you sleep better.		
To see if regular exercise affects personal wellbeing.		
	Eating brown bread will increase scores on an arithmetic test.	Eating brown bread will have no effect on scores on an arithmetic test.
	Lack of sleep makes you eat more.	
		There will be no difference in the number of words remembered when they are processed visually compared to when they are processed acoustically.
	People under the age of 15 will conform more in a group situation than those over 15.	
To find out if a large workload makes people more stressed.		

Before moving on, we'll find out about different types of experimental/**alternative hypotheses**: directional and non-directional.

1.2.3.2 Directional and non-directional hypotheses

A **directional hypothesis** is one that makes a prediction in a particular direction, e.g. that one variable will increase, or decrease. For example, the one we gave earlier:

Participants over the age of 70 will score less on a test of short-term memory than participants under the age of 70.

This is making a prediction that short-term memory ability will decrease with age, so is directional (sometimes called one-tailed). If we however, state the following:

There will be a difference in memory scores between those aged over 70 and those aged under 70.

This predicts that there will be a change in memory scores, but not in what direction. It is a **non-directional hypothesis** (sometimes called two-tailed).

Directional and non-directional hypotheses: Questions   Go online

Choose which of these hypotheses are *directional* and which are *non-directional*.

Q4: Students studying Higher Psychology are much happier than those studying Higher English.

a) Directional
b) Non-directional

....

Q5: There will be a difference between males and females in the number of times that they give their coats to a shivering child at a bus stop.

a) Directional
b) Non-directional

....

Q6: People who eat fish once a week score more highly on IQ tests than people who eat fish less than once a week

a) Directional
b) Non-directional

....

Q7: There will be a difference between American and Scottish participants on scores of extraversion/introversion.

a) Directional
b) Non-directional

....

Q8: S4 pupils are more likely to conform to a teachers' incorrect response in a test than S6 students.

a) Directional
b) Non-directional

....

Q9: Introverts will cough more times when asked to sit in silence, than extraverts.

a) Directional
b) Non-directional

....

Q10: Participants will have a slower reaction time on a computer game after consuming one area of study of alcohol.

a) Directional
b) Non-directional

....

Q11: Students who wear designer labels will score lower on scales of agreeableness than students who do not.

a) Directional
b) Non-directional

Next we set up the research to support or disprove the null hypothesis.

1.2.4 Designing the study

There are a number of methods that we can choose from for the design of the research study, which fall into two broad categories:

1. experimental;

2. non-experimental.

These, in turn, have subcategories.

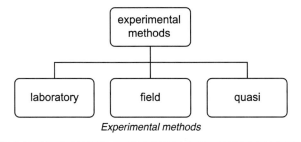

Experimental methods

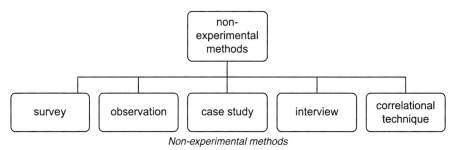

Non-experimental methods

Designing the study: Notebook exercise

You will need your psychology notebook for this activity.

It will be useful for you to draw these two hierarchies out and then add to them as you learn more about each method (which you will do in Topic 2: Experimental methods and Topic 3: Non-experimental methods). This will help you remember the details better, and with less effort!

You will learn more about experimental and non-experimental research methods in Topics 2 and 3.

1.2.5   Collecting data

Learning objective

By the end of this section, you should be able to:

- explain qualitative and quantitative data, and understand the difference between them.

Research methods can gather two different types of data: qualitative and quantitative.

Qualitative data is descriptive detail about an issue.

Example 1 - Qualitative data

Detail about people's opinions about their memory ability, in comparison with others.

Quantitative data on the other hand is a count or measurement of some kind concerning the behaviour under investigation.

Example 2 - Quantitative data

In the experiment on age and memory mentioned before, people's scores on memory tests were counted.

In psychology, quantitative data is often also called empirical data, i.e. those facts about our world achieved through sensory experience.

The experimental, observational, and survey methods of research often derive quantitative data.

Collecting data: Notebook exercise

You will need your psychology notebook for this activity.

You now have some detail to add to the hierarchies that you drew in the *Designing the study: Notebook exercise* activity about which methods collect quantitative data and which methods collect qualitative data. Make your hierarchies colourful, personal and visual. This will enhance your chances of remembering information. Give your memory a treat!

1.2.6 Examining the data

Learning objective

By the end of this section, you should be able to:

- explain measures of central tendency (mean, median and mode), and know how to calculate them;

- explain measures of dispersion (range and standard deviation).

So, you have carried out a piece of research, you have your results, but now what? Obviously, you need to put that data into some sort of form from which you can draw conclusions.

Measures of central tendency

Averages inform us about central or 'typical' values for a set of data, providing a useful description of a data set. There are three different ways to show an average.

1. **Mean** - calculated by adding up all of the numbers and dividing by how many numbers there are, a strength of which is that it makes use of all of the data. However, if there are extreme values, the mean may not be representative.

2. **Median** - calculated by putting all of the data in order and finding the middle number, which has the advantage of not being effected by extreme scores. If there are two or more middle scores, the mean of these scores is calculated. However, it is not as sensitive as the mean as it does not take into account all of the numbers.

3. **Mode** - the number that appears the most often in a set of data, which is useful when the data is in categories. However, it is not as useful if there is more than one mode.

Measures of dispersion

Measures of dispersion inform us about the spread of scores. There are two ways to show dispersion.

1. **Range** - this tells us what the highest and lowest values are, and what the difference between these two is. For eaxmple, if the highest number in a set of data was 57 and the lowest was

43, the range would be 14. The range is easy to calculate therefore, and provides direct information. However, it is easily effected by extreme values, and does not take into account all of the data in a set.

2. **Standard deviation** - this is a measure of dispersion which, like the mean, takes all of the values in a set of data into account when it is calculated. It is also like the mean in that we must assume that we have a normal distribution before it is reasonable to use it.

Note that you won't need to calculate a standard deviation, either in the exam or in the Research Investigation, but you do need to know what they can tell a researcher about a data set.

Examining the data: Calculating the range   Go online

Calculate the range in the following sets of data (it's easier if you rank them in order first, lowest to highest):

Q12: 5, 7, 2, 9, 3, 2, 5, 4

....

Q13: 33, 768, 57, 22, 43, 23

We will revisit measures of central tendency and dispersion when we look at "Calculating and presenting data using descriptive statistics", in Topic 3 of this area of study.

Once this data has been examined, usually using statistics like the above, researchers can summarise the data, analyse the results, and then draw conclusions based on this evidence.

1.2.7   Reaching a conclusion

So how does a researcher decide what the results of a study mean? They do this by using statistical analyses, which can support (or refute) the researcher's hypothesis. You will need to draw conclusions from your data when you have conducted your research for the Research Investigation. The use of inferential statistics (which you do not need to learn for Higher (CfE) Psychology) can tell the researcher if the results are statistically significant or if they are due to chance (should results suggest that the null hypothesis cannot be rejected).

1.2.8   Reporting the findings

Researchers in psychology hope that their research will be published in an academic journal, to be read by their peers, and to re-establish the research cycle by prompting some other researcher to choose their topic of interest, so they must write up an account of their research, findings and conclusions in a specific format.

1. Title page

2. Contents page

3. Abstract: this is a summary of the entire piece of research, from beginning to end. It is written last, but appears first in the report.

4. Introduction: this introduces the reader to the background studies chosen during the literature

review (Step 2), then to the researcher's own aims and hypotheses.

5. Method: this takes the reader through the research procedures, to the extent that they should be able to replicate the study quite easily. As such, it includes information about participants, sampling, materials/apparatus, as well as any confounding variables that were controlled for.

6. Results: here the findings are presented, displayed and explained. They are discussed in more detail in the next section of the report.

7. Discussion: here, the results are related to the background studies described in the Introduction, any problems with the research that occurred are explained.

8. Conclusion: the aims and hypotheses are restated here, along with the main research results.

9. References: provided in a standard form (e.g. Harvard).

10. Appendices: all 'raw' data goes in here, e.g. copies of any questionnaires used, instructions to participants, calculations of statistics and tables of raw (uncalculated) data.

1.3   Learning points

Summary

- The stages of the research process are:

  1. Choose topic
  2. Review literature
  3. Form hypothesis
  4. Design study
  5. Collect data
  6. Examine data
  7. Reach conclusion
  8. Report findings

- A hypothesis is a testable statement of what we think will happen in our research and gives us a clear starting point.

- There are different types of hypothesis: experimental, correlational, null, alternative, directional, and non-directional.

- Qualitative data is descriptive detail about an issue while quantitative data is a count or measurement of some kind.

- Measures of central tendency (mean, median and mode) inform us about central or 'typical' values for a set of data.

- Measures of dispersion (range and standard deviation) inform us about the spread of the values in a set of data.

1.4   End of topic test

End of Topic 1 test   Go online

Q14: Put the stages of the research process in order, starting with "Choose topic". *(7 marks)*

1	Choose topic
2	
3	
4	
5	
6	
7	
8	

Stages of the research process: Collect data, Examine data, Report findings, Reach conclusion, Form hypothesis, Design study, Review literature.

....

Q15: Describe the importance of conducting a literature review. *(3 marks)*

....

Q16: Which of these hypotheses is tested by the researcher? *(1 mark)*

a) Alternative
b) Correlational
c) Experimental
d) Null

....

Q17: Complete the diagram with the three types of experiment. *(3 marks)*

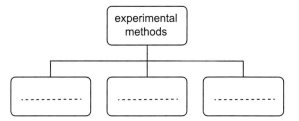

. . . .

Q18: Which of the following are included in the range of non-experimental research methods? *(1 mark)*

a) Field, Observation and Case Study
b) Observation, Case Study and Survey
c) Field, Case Study and Quasi
d) Case Study, Survey and Experiment

. . . .

Q19: Match the following descriptions to the correct statistical measures. *(5 marks)*

The most accurate measure of central tendency, which uses all of the values in a data set:	mode.
A measure of central tendency, calculated by ranking all values and finding the middle value:	range.
A measure of central tendency, determined by the most frequently occurring value:	standard deviation.
A measure of dispersion, calculated by ranking values and subtracting the lowest value from the highest:	mean.
A very accurate measure of dispersion, which uses all of the values in a data set:	median.

. . . .

Q20: Arrange the following sections in a report of a psychological investigation in the correct order. *(5 marks)*

1	
2	
3	
4	
5	
6	
7	
8	
9	
10	

Sections: Abstract, Appendices, Conclusions, Contents, Discussion, Introduction, Methods, References, Results, Title.

Unit 1 Topic 2

Experimental methods

Contents

Learning objective

By the end of this topic, you should be able to:

- explain the experimental method;

- explain and identify different types of variables that are used in experimental research, namely: independent, dependent, extraneous and confounding;

- explain and identify each of the following experimental designs: repeated measures, independent measures and matched pairs;

- explain and identify (from scenarios) the following sampling techniques: opportunity, random, stratified, systematic, self-selected and quota;

- explain the three main types of experimental research: laboratory, field and quasi;

- identify each of the three main types of experimental research from scenarios;

- evaluate each of the three main types of experimental research.

2.1   The experimental method

Learning objective

By the end of this section, you should be able to:

- explain the experimental method.

In Topic 1 you were advised to draw up hierarchies describing experimental and non-experimental methods. You will get the chance to add to these with the information you learn in this and the next topic.

The **experimental method** has an emphasis on strict procedures, which helps others replicate experiments to confirm, or otherwise, the original research findings. This is how scientific knowledge grows.

Consequently, the experimental method sets out to test a **null hypothesis** which, if rejected, allows the researcher to accept the experimental, or research, hypothesis. You may recall that you learned about this, also in Topic 1.

The experimental method is a controlled procedure that sees the manipulation of an **independent variable** (IV) in order to observe or measure its effect on a **dependent variable** (DV), e.g. age and performance on a memory test.

The essential features of the experimental method are the control, observation and measurement of variables.

Illustrating the hallmarks of a science, the use of the experimental method in psychological research makes us more confident about the **validity** of any cause-effect relationship established between an independent and dependent variable.

The experimental method also makes us more confident about the **generalisation** of our results to a wider **population**.

We will now consider the following features of the experimental method in more detail:

- independent and dependent variables;

- extraneous and confounding variables, including the experimenter effect and the Hawthorne effect;

- experimental designs, including repeated measures, matched pairs and independent measures;

- samples and populations;

- types of experiment;

- evaluation of the experiment.

2.2 Independent and dependent variables

Learning objective

By the end of this section, you should be able to:

- explain and identify different types of variables that are used in experimental research, namely: independent and dependent.

What is the effect of lack of sleep on weight gain by an individual?

Before we can perform an experiment designed to answer this question, we must determine the independent and dependent variable.

Independent variable

- The independent variable is the variable that you, as the experimenter, will vary to observe the effect.

- The independent variable is sometimes called the manipulated variable because it is the variable that the experimenter manipulates.

Dependent variable

- The dependent variable is the variable that you, as the experimenter, will measure and record - it is the data of the experiment.

- The dependent variable is sometimes called the "responding" variable because it is the variable that responds to the independent (or manipulated) variable.

Key point

There are usually various *conditions* of an independent variable in order to make comparisons. For example, in a study that wanted to find out if playing music to a foetus in the womb increased intelligence, there would be one condition where music was played to the foetus and another where it would not. The differences in the dependent variable would then be compared.

What is the effect of lack of sleep on weight gain by an individual?

To determine the independent and dependent variable, identify the two things that will (might) change:

1. lack of sleep;

2. weight of an individual.

Once you know the two things that are (or might be) changing, arrange them in a question like one of these.

- In this experiment, does the lack of sleep depend on weight gain?

- In this experiment, does weight gain depend on lack of sleep?

The variable that depends on the other is the dependent variable.

Weight gain depends on the lack of sleep so weight gain is the dependent variable.

It is important to understand that you don't yet have to know if weight gain depends on a lack of sleep - you just need to identify which variable you will be manipulating and which variable will respond to your manipulations.

In summary:

Independent variable	Dependent variable
• Intentionally manipulated	• Intentionally left alone
• Controlled	• Recorded
• Vary at known rate	• Vary at unknown rate
• Cause	• Effect

Key point

Cause and effect can only be established with experiments. No other method can do this.

Independent and dependent variables: Questions   Go online

Q1:   Do people that use mobile phones while driving have more accidents?

Identify the:

1. independent variable;
2. dependent variable.

....

Q2:   Smithers thinks that playing classical music in his factory will increase the productivity of workers. He creates two groups of 50 workers each and assigns each group the same task (in this case, they are supposed to staple a set of papers). Group A is placed in a room with classical music playing. Group B is in a room with no music playing. After an hour, Smithers counts how many stacks of papers each group has made. Group A made 1,587 stacks, Group B made 2,113 stacks.

Identify the:

1. independent variable;
2. dependent variable.

What should Smithers' conclusion be?

Independent and dependent variables: Poster exercise

Make a poster that shows three examples of how an independent variable can affect a dependent variable, e.g. "the smell of food from the canteen (IV - which would also have a condition where no smell from the canteen is available, for comparison purposes) can make you salivate (DV - which is the variable which would be measured, usually by taking and measuring saliva)".

There are some websites that can help you do this:

- https://www.thinglink.com/

- http://edu.glogster.com/

- http://www.posterini.com/

Your poster should include the following:

- a list of your three examples with an explanation that shows how you know which variable is independent and which variable is dependent;

- a table that graphically organises your three examples;

- a visual of each relationship obtained from a magazine, newspaper, the internet, etc.

Doing this will encourage your memory to retain and retrieve the relevant information at the relevant time. And you can have fun doing it!

Remember that:

- the independent variable is the one that the experimenter manipulates;

- the dependent variable is the one that the experimenter measures.

Key point

Independent and dependent variables are only used in experiments.

2.3   Extraneous and confounding variables

Learning objective

By the end of this section, you should be able to:

- explain and identify different types of variables that are used in experimental research, namely: confounding and extraneous.

The emphasis of the experimental method on strict procedures helps others replicate the experiment to confirm, or otherwise, the original research findings. This is how scientific knowledge grows.

Consequently, the experimental method sets out to test a null hypothesis (as you have already learned), which, if rejected, allows the researcher to accept the experimental, or research, hypothesis.

Confounding variables

Chance or random factors, which are often an alternative explanation for results in psychological research, are called **extraneous variables** and are of two kinds:

1. **random variables**, which just happen, making them impossible to control;

2. **confounding variables**, which can be anticipated and controlled

Examples of confounding variables would be:

- any **situational variable** found in the experimental setting;

- experimenter variables, such as experimenter and expectancy effect;

- participant variables, which are those participant peculiarities that can influence results.

Read on to find out more about each of these variable types.

Situational variables refer to the experimental situation itself. The environment, or where the experiment takes place, may influence our results. This is especially the case with laboratory experiments. Situational variables concern the physical environment of the experiment. In order to control situational variables, all of the participants taking part in our effects of age on memory experiment should experience the same environmental situation. Temperature, lighting, background noise, etc. would therefore be kept constant throughout our experimental procedure.

Experimenter variables unsurprisingly refer to the experimenter(s) themselves. You, the experimenter, can be a confounding variable. One experimenter variable known as the **experimenter effect** has suggested that experimenter characteristics such as age, sex and general behaviour may have subtle effects on participants' performance (Eagly & Carli, 1983).

Experimenter bias is a more common confounding variable in experimental research. Experimenter bias happens when the expectations of the experimenter influence the participants' behaviours. A classic example of experimenter bias is the expectancy effect discovered by Rosenthal & Fode (1963).
Find out more online at: https://sites.google.com/site/7arosenthal/

In order to control for experimenter variables, many experiments first do a pilot study or a rehearsal of the experiment. A pilot study, which can involve using the researchers as the 'participants', helps iron out confounding variables such as the experimenter and expectancy effect. Pilot studies give you an opportunity to develop an even more controlled experimental procedure, which we generally refer to as standardisation.

Remember that a confounding variable concerns other factors that could account for your result. A participant variable could then be the cause of any observed effect on your dependent variable, other than the manipulation of your independent variable.

Participant variables are confounding variables that come from the participants themselves. If you wanted to investigate the effects of alcohol on reaction time, and ran an experiment to do so, then participant variables could also include whether participants were male or female. This is because men and women have different metabolic rates and break down alcohol differently. Other participant variables that could interfere with our results are body fat, which influences the breakdown of alcohol, and drinking experience, or lack of it, etc.

These would include and demand characteristics and participant expectancy. Demand characteristics are any features of an experiment which help participants work out what is expected of them, and consequently lead them to behave in artificial ways (Orne, 1963). These features 'demand' a certain response. Participants search for cues in the experimental environment about how to behave and what (might) be expected of them.

Look at the following sections about the experimenter effect and the **Hawthorne effect** (also known as participant expectancy). The Hawthorne effect is a type of confounding variable associated with the participant, and was discovered in 1939 by Roethlisberger and Dickson.

We can control for such participant variables using a standardised experimental procedure called an experimental design. Experimental designs help control for confounding variables.

2.3.1 The experimenter effect

Rosenthal and Fode discovered a confounding variable called the experimenter effect in 1963.

They asked students to train rats to run through a maze. They told one group of students that they had been given particularly smart rats that would learn to run the maze quickly. The other group were told that they had dull rats that would be slow to learn to run the maze.

Rosenthal and Fode actually had no idea how clever, or otherwise, their rats were! The group who were told that they had smart rats later reported that they had learned to run through the maze quickly, while those who had been told that their rats were dull reported theirs to be slow.

The smart rat group produced data showing a better maze running performance in comparison to the dull rat group.

Rosenthal and Fode say that the students' (false) expectations about whether a rat was smart or dull had had an effect on the results. The group with the smart rats concluded the result that they did either because they put more effort into training their rats to run the maze or because their recording of the rats maze running abilities was affected by expectations.

The experimenter effect: Questions   Go online

Q3:   What was the aim of Rosenthal and Fode (1963)?

....

Q4:   What research method did they use?

....

Q5:   What were the two conditions of the independent variable?

....

Q6:   What was their dependent variable?

....

Q7:   What was their procedure?

....

Q8:   What were their results?

....

Q9:   What conclusion did they reach?

2.3.2   The Hawthorne effect

Participant expectancy is a confounding variable associated with participating in an experiment. Roethlisberger and Dickson first brought it to our attention in 1939 in their field experiment into 'the Hawthorne effect'.

Roethlisberger and Dickson were interested in the relationship between factory pollution and productivity levels at the Hawthorne electrical generating plant in America.

Their independent variables included changing the lighting conditions in the factory and the times that female workers could take their breaks.

They assessed the output of five female workers under differing working conditions for two years.

Much to their surprise, Roethlisberger and Dickson found that when they manipulated their independent variable of worsening working conditions, the women's productivity increased rather than decreased.

On investigation, they discovered that the women had worked harder because they wanted to please the psychologists. It was this 'wanting to please the psychologist' effect that produced their strange results.

Knowing that you are taking part in an experiment, and wanting to please, can create The Hawthorne Effect, which sees participants behave in an unnatural way.

The Hawthorne effect: Questions

Q10: What was the aim of Roethlisberger and Dickson (1939)?
....

Q11: What research method did they use?
....

Q12: What were the two conditions of the independent variable?
....

Q13: What was their dependent variable?
....

Q14: What was their procedure?
....

Q15: What were their results?
....

Q16: What conclusion did they reach?

2.4 Experimental designs

Learning objective

By the end of this section, you should be able to:

- explain and identify each of the following experimental designs: repeated measures, independent measures and matched pairs.

To control for extraneous variables, the experimental method uses different designs of which can be of three kinds:

1. repeated measures;

2. independent measures;

3. matched pairs.

Top tip

Experimental designs are not the same as experimental methods. Experimental designs are, as described here, ways of managing the participants of an experiment. Experimental methods are: laboratory, field and natural (which we will be looking at soon).

2.4.1   Repeated measures design

A **repeated measures** design (RMD) repeats the measure of performance, or dependent variable, under the differing conditions of the independent variable.

A repeated measure is a within-subjects design, because each participant takes part in each condition of the independent variable.

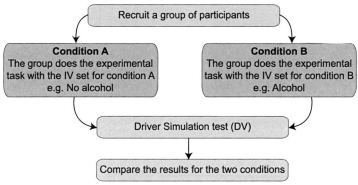

Repeated measures design

Advantages of RMD include:

- fewer participants are needed than for an independent groups design (as they all undergo all conditions rather than needing two or threedifferent groups for the various levels of the independent variable);

- there are fewer participant variables between groups than there are with an independent groups design.

Disadvantages of RMD include:

- order effects can occur in which what participants have done in one condition helps or hinder them in a subsequent one (e.g. learning, practice, boredom, fatigue, confusion) - counterbalancing, that is changing the order in which participants undertake the conditions, can help reduce order effects;

- researchers need to allow a gap between conditions which can means that participants drop out, or time of testing becomes a confound.

2.4.2   Matched pairs design

This design is characterised by matching participants on key characteristics.

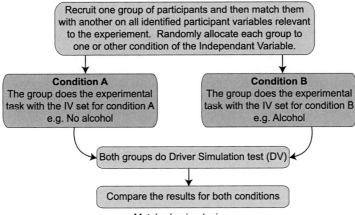

Matched pairs design

What this means is that participants would be matched on the basis of variables such as sex, age, socio-economic status, etc. depending on what the researcher is studying.

Once matched, participants are randomly allocated to the control and experimental group conditions. Applying a matched pairs design, participants would be matched on the basis of relevant confounding variables, then each matched participant would be randomly allocated to either the control condition A or the experimental condition B of the independent variable, and it would be ensured that each group mirrors the other as far as possible.

Advantages of the matched-pairs design include:

- avoiding order effects, which is the main advantage of the matched pairs design - participants, in whatever condition, are only asked to do one thing once;

- if you have matched participants properly on the basis of relevant confounding variables, it is a reasonably good procedure to control for participant variables.

Disadvantages of the matched-pairs design include:

- whether you have matched on the basis of relevant confounding participant variables, which is the main disadvantage of the matched pairs design - you can never be entirely sure that you have accounted for all of the important differences between people that may influence the results of your study and, as a result, it is difficult to control totally for all participant variables;

- the time and resources required to find out what individual differences are relevant to your study which, of course, you have to match;

- needing twice as many participants as in a repeated measures design (time is money, in research as in all other things).

2.4.3   Independent measures design

When more than one group of participants is used, and each group is exposed to a different condition of the IV. as an example, to create an independent groups design you could use two independent groups of participants, say the Kilmarnock History Club and Kilmarnock FC Supporters Club; you would then toss a coin and randomly allocate one group to the control condition (no alcohol), and the other to the experimental condition (alcohol).

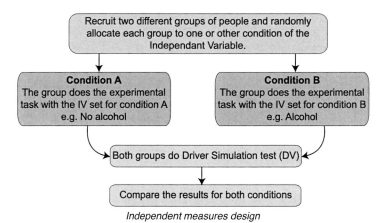

Independent measures design

Advantages of the independent measures design include:

- there are fewer order effects (learning, practice, boredom, fatigue, confusion) because different groups are undergoing different conditions and so are doing less than they would in a repeated measures design;

- there is no need to leave a gap between conditions because there are different participants for the different conditions.

Disadvantages of the independent measures design include:

- participant variables may act as confounds because people with certain characteristics may all end up in one group (e.g. dyslexia, sight problems, ADHD, high IQ);

- researchers need to recruit more participants than in a repeated measures design - twice as many if there are two levels of the IV, three times as many if there are three levels of the IV, etc.

Experimental designs: Questions   Go online

From the following descriptions of studies, state which design they are.

Q17: Loftus & Palmer (1974) took 45 students from a Californian university. They all watched a film clip of two cars colliding. Then they were split into five groups of nine participants. Each group was asked a question: "About how fast were the cars going when they hit/smashed/bumped/collided/contacted each other?" Estimates of speed were found to vary according to which verb had been used in the question.

a) Repeated measures
b) Matched pairs
c) Independent measures

. . . .

Q18: Dement and Kleitman (1957) studied five participants to see if REM was linked to dreaming. An electroencephalograph (EEG) was used to amplify and record the signals of electrodes which were attached to the participants' faces and scalps. Two or more electrodes were attached near to the participants' eyes to record electrical changes caused by eye movement. Two or three further electrodes were attached to the scalp to record brain activity, indicating participants' depth of sleep. The participants then went to bed in a quiet, dark room.

a) Repeated measures
b) Matched pairs
c) Independent measures

. . . .

Q19: Nisbett and Wilson divided students into two groups. They watched two different videos of the same lecturer. In one he gave advice to students in a warm and friendly manner; in the other video he said exactly the same words but in a cold and aloof way. Students were asked to score him on likeability. The ones who had seen the warm and friendly video scored the lecturer higher but they didn't know why!

a) Repeated measures
b) Matched pairs
c) Independent measures

. . . .

Q20: Stroop (1935) gave 70 college undergraduates a sheet of paper to read where the words matched the colour of the ink in which they were printed (e.g. 'pink' was printed in pink ink). The participants were asked to name the ink colour. They were also asked to read a sheet where the words did not match the ink colour (e.g. 'pink' would be printed in blue ink). Again, the participants were asked to name the ink colour. He found that responses were slower when ink colour and word did not match. Counterbalancing was used to eliminate order effects.

a) Repeated measures
b) Matched pairs
c) Independent measures

....

Q21: Researchers aimed to find a connection between the brain and being in love. Participants who rated themselves as being intensely in love viewed a photo of their beloved, did a distracter task, and then viewed a photo of a friend that they were not in love with while researchers took functional magnetic resonance imagery (fMRI). Each participant repeated the procedure six times. When participants looked at pictures of their beloved, the fMRI indicated activation of particular parts of the brain. Intense romantic love is connected with reward regions of the brain, as well as the motivation system needed to acquire rewards.

a) Repeated measures
b) Matched pairs
c) Independent measures

....

Q22: Bandura, Ross and Ross (1961) tested 74 nursery children. They were put into groups: a control group, single sex groups who saw a violent model of either the same sex or a different sex, and single-sex groups who saw a non-violent model of either the same sex or a different sex. Children who saw a model who was violent were more likely to commit violent acts, especially if the model was the same sex as them.

a) Repeated measures
b) Matched pairs
c) Independent measures

....

Q23: Yerkes and Dodson (1908) took 40 mice and trained them to use a maze by giving them electric shocks. They found that the performance of the mice in the maze increased with the stress of being given electric shocks, but only up to a point. When they reached a certain amount of stress, the performance of the mice declined.

a) Repeated measures
b) Matched pairs
c) Independent measures

....

Q24: Kiecolt-Glaser (1984) took blood samples from 75 first year medical students (a) one month before their final examinations (relatively low stress) and (b) during the examinations (high stress). She found that they had reduced immune systems during times of stress.

a) Repeated measures
b) Matched pairs
c) Independent measures

You may find it helpful to arrange the information above into a table, like this:

Design	Advantages	Disadvantages
Repeated measures		
Matched pairs		
Independent measures		

Experimental design refers to how participants are exposed to the IV, and to whether they undergo all conditions or levels of the IV, or just one.

Alternatively, you may create a poster about research designs, by hand, or by using an online poster creator, such as http://www.posterini.com/ or https://www.lucidpress.com/pages/examples/free-online-poster-maker.

Organising your information in this way helps you to file it away in memory, and makes it easier to recall when you need it.

Experimental designs: Notebook exercise

You will need your psychology notebook for this activity.

You can now add some detail to your hierarchies linked with experimental methods. Remember to add images to help make it more memorable.

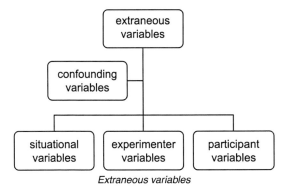

Extraneous variables

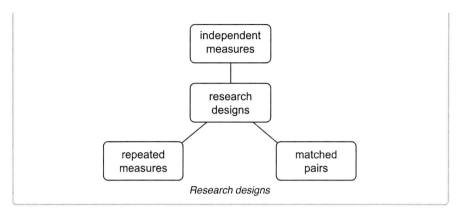

Research designs

We will move onto different types of experiment, all of which share the above key features.

2.5   Samples and populations

A **population** in psychological research (sometimes called a target population) is all of those people who you want your results to apply to, so if you wish to find out something about S6 students at British secondary schools, your population would be all S6 students at British secondary schools.

It would be a tall order to study all those in a population, so researchers study a sample, which they hope is representative of the target population.

There are a couple of concepts related to sampling that you need to understand:

1. **generalisability**: the extent to which results from a study can be related to a target population;

2. **representativeness**: the extent to which a sample is typical of a target population.

There are a variety of ways of choosing a sample, some of which are more generalisable and representative than others. We will begin with the one that you will use when conducting your research investigation, the opportunity sample.

Opportunity sample

This type of sample consists of whoever is willing and available to the researcher.

• Advantage: easy to gather.

• Disadvantage: high risk of bias (i.e. of not being representative).

Random sample

In this kind of sample, everyone in a target population has an equal chance of being chosen. To choose a random sample, you would need details of everyone in the target population (often problematic due to the Data Protection Act) from which to select your sample by using a random number table or a computer program.

- Advantage: usually the least biased, most representative (therefore generalisable) form of sampling.
- Disadvantage: can be time-consuming to select a random sample.

> **Top tip**
>
> The word 'random' can be misleading. Students often assume that it means the same as 'choosing anybody'. This is not the case. As you can surmise from the above definition, selecting a random sample is much more complex than this.

Stratified sample

In this kind of sample, important features (strata) in the research are identified in the target population, and these are then matched in the sample gathered.

- Advantage: tend to yield representative, generalisable findings.
- Disadvantage: the proportions may take time to select.

Systematic sample

This kind of sample selects participants at fixed intervals, e.g. every tenth person on a list or every sixth person through a door.

- Advantage/disadvantage: same as random sampling (systematic sampling is sometimes called quasi-random sampling.

Self-selected sample

This sample consists of those who have volunteered to participate, often by responding to an advertisement.

- Advantage: relatively easy to select.
- Disadvantage: the majority probably will not respond and those who do may by atypical of the target population in some way.

Quota sample

This type of sample is similar to a stratified sample but a pre-set number is drawn from each stratum and random sampling is not involved.

- Advantage: tends to yield representative findings.
- Disadvantage: the proportions may take time to select.

Samples and populations: Question   Go online

Q25: Match the following descriptions of samples on the left to the appropriate sampling techniques on the right.

A group of participants who responded to an advertisement in the student newsletter	systematic.
134 air force cadets comprising percentages reflecting all air cadets in Scotland in terms of ethnic origin, and selected randomly:	quota.
153 air force cadets comprising 20% from each ethnic origin known to represent all air cadets in Scotland:	self-selected.
210 air force cadets who have been selected from all air force cadets in Scotland by using a random number table:	stratified.
100 air force cadets who have been selected as their names appeared fifth or tenth on a troop roster:	random.

2.6   Types of experiment

Learning objective

By the end of this section, you should be able to:

- explain the three main types of experimental research: laboratory, field and quasi;
- identify each of the three main types of experimental research from scenarios.

The laboratory experiment involves the manipulation of an independent variable and the consequent observation/measurement of a dependent variable. Laboratory experiments take place in the closed, heavily controlled setting of a psychology laboratory, most often found in universities.

Like a laboratory experiment, the field experiment also sees the manipulation of an independent variable and the consequent observation/measurement of a dependent variable. The difference is that a field experiment takes place away from a laboratory, most often in the participants' natural environment, for example a school classroom, a playground, or the street.

Quasi experiments are those where one or both of the following conditions apply:

- the experimenter does not have control over the allocation of participants to the different levels of the IV;
- the researcher cannot control the IV.

This is because someone else controls the IV. The dependent variable is observed and measured nonetheless.

Types of experiment: Questions   Go online

A biopsychologist wants to know whether exposure to testosterone in adult female rats increases their aggressive behaviour. In order to test this, she injects ten adult female rats with a solution of testosterone . She then puts them in with other rats and observes them carefully, taking a measure of how many aggressive acts they show. Ten other female rats were also put in another cage with rats, and a measure of their aggressive acts was also taken.

Q26: Suggest a research hypothesis for this experiment.

. . . .

Q27: What is the independent variable?

. . . .

Q28: What is the dependent variable?

. . . .

Q29: What type of experiment is this? Give reasons for your answer.

2.7   Evaluation of the experiment

Learning objective

By the end of this section, you should be able to:

- evaluate each of the three main types of experimental research.

Criticisms of types of experiment are related to each other. The laboratory experiment often attracts criticism on the grounds of **ecological validity**.

They are sometimes 'not real'!

The further away from the laboratory a researcher goes, however, the more likely it becomes that random and **confounding variables** will interfere with the **validity** of the research (although ecological validity does increase).

Key point

Research validity is important. The more valid a piece of research is, the more it measures what it is supposed to measure. Take, for example, intelligence tests. Do they measure what they are supposed to (intelligence), or do they measure something else (practice, knowledge)? In other words, are intelligence tests valid measures?

Reliability is something else that decreases the further away from the laboratory research goes. A piece of research is reliable if different researchers in a different place and at a different time produce similar results when following the same procedures. The increase in confounding variables

---

that comes from non-laboratory (therefore less controlled) research interferes with this.

However, as a research method, the experimental method is assuredly the most rigorous of methodologies in psychology.

Try the following activities which consider the advantages and disadvantages of the three types of experiments to test your understanding of the experimental method.

Evaluation of the experiment: Questions   Go online

Q30: Complete the table with the experimental factors listed.

Advantages of the laboratory experiment	Disadvantages of the laboratory experiment

Experimental factors: Artificial situation, so lacks ecological validity; Cause and effect can be easily established; Control of extraneous variables; Demand characteristics can give away the aim of the experiment, affecting behaviour, results, conclusions; DV can be measured precisely; Experimenter bias can influence behaviours, results conclusions; Impossible to control for all extraneous variables; Procedures can be replicated easily, meaning it is high in reliability.

....

Q31: Complete the table with the experimental factors listed.

Advantages of the field experiment	Disadvantages of the field experiment

Experimental factors: Control of extraneous variables; Less stressful than being manipulated in a laboratory; Low reliability; Participants less influenced by demand characteristics; Participants less influenced by experimenter effects; Participants unaware they are being observed (ethics); Reduced validity; Situation true to life, so high ecological validity.

....

Q32: Complete the table with the experimental factors listed.

Advantages of the quasi experiment	Disadvantages of the quasi experiment

Experimental factors: Ecological validity; Establishing cause and effect; Little control over IV; Participants less influenced by demand characteristics; Participants less influenced by experimenter effects; Reliability.

2.8   Learning points

Summary

- The experimental method sets out to test a null hypothesis and places emphasis on strict procedures which helps others replicate experiments.

- Different types of variables are used in experimental research, namely: independent, dependent, extraneous and confounding.

- Experimental designs include: repeated measures, independent measures and matched pairs.

- Sampling techniques include: opportunity, random, stratified, systematic, self-selected and quota.

- The three main types of experimental research are: laboratory, field and quasi.

- The three main types of experimental research are identifiable from scenarios.

- The three main types of experimental research can be evaluated.

2.9   End of topic test

End of Topic 2 test   Go online

Q33: What does 'repeated measures' mean? *(1 mark)*

....

Q34: Give one advantage of repeated measures design. *(1 mark)*

....

Q35: Give one disadvantage of repeated measures design. *(1 mark)*

....

Q36: What does 'independent groups' mean? *(1 mark)*

....

Q37: Give one advantage of independent groups design. *(1 mark)*

....

Q38: Give one disadvantage of independent groups design. *(1 mark)*

....

Q39: What is meant by matched-pairs design? *(1 mark)*

....

Q40:

All types of experiment
IV manipulated and DV measured
Establish cause and effect
Experimental and null hypothesis

The above table highlights the similarities between different types of experimental methods. Complete the table below which highlights the differences using the experimental attributes listed, some of which will be used more than once. *(15 marks)*

Type of experiment	Laboratory	Field	Quasi
Setting			
Reliability			
Ecological validity			
Control			
Validity			

Attribute list: Artificial; Control only over IV; High; IV already occurring; Low; Real life.

....

Q41: The Hawthorne effect is an example of: *(1 mark)*

a) A participant variable.
b) A situational variable.
c) An experimental variable.

....

Q42: Demand characteristics are an example of: *(1 mark)*

a) A participant variable.
b) A situational variable.
c) An experimental variable.

....

Q43: Complete the following paragraph about opportunity sampling using the words from the list. *(6 marks)*

Opportunity sampling consists of taking the sample from people who are _____ at the time the study is carried out and who fit the criteria you are looking for. It is a popular sampling technique as it is relatively _____ and quick to do. For example, the researcher may use friends, family or colleagues. However, opportunity sampling can produce a _____ sample as it is easy for the researcher to choose people from their own social and _____ group. This sample would therefore not be _____ of your target _____ as your friends may have different qualities to people in general.

Word list: available, biased, cheap, cultural, population, representative.

....

Q44: Complete the following paragraph about random sampling using the words from the list. *(6 marks)*

Random sampling is a technique which is defined as a sample in which every _____ of the population has an _____ chance of being chosen. This involves identifying everyone in the target population and then selecting the number of participants that you need in a way which gives everyone in the population an equal chance of being picked. For example, you could get details of all students in your school or college and pick names using a random _____ table or a computer _____. This is the best technique for providing an _____ representative sample. However, this technique can be very time consuming and is often _____ to carry out, particularly when you have a large target population.

Word list: equal, impossible, member, number, program, unbiased.

....

Q45: Complete the following paragraph about stratified sampling using the words from the list. *(6 marks)*

Stratified sampling involves classifying the population into _____ and then choosing a sample which consists of participants from each one in the same _____ as they are in the population. A strength of this technique is that the sample should be representative of the population. However, stratified sampling can be very time consuming as the categories have to be identified and _____. As with _____ sampling, if you do not have details of all of the _____ in your target _____ you would struggle to conduct a stratified sample.

Word list: calculated, categories, people, population, proportions, random.

. . . .

Q46: Complete the following paragraph about self-selected sampling using the words from the list. *(6 marks)*

Self-selected sampling consists of participants becoming part of a study because they _____ when asked or they _____ to an advert. This technique is useful as it is _____ and relatively easy to do. It can also reach a _____ variety of participants. However, the _____ of participants who volunteer may not be representative of the _____ population for a number of reasons.

Word list: quick, respond, target, type, volunteer, wide.

Unit 1 Topic 3

Non-experimental methods

Contents

Learning objective

By the end of this topic, you should be able to:

- explain the non-experimental method;

- explain key features of, identify (from scenarios), and evaluate the following non-experimental methods: observational, survey and case study;

- explain, identify and evaluate the key features of each of five types of observational research: participant, non-participant, structured, unstructured and naturalistic;

- explain the following techniques used in surveys: interview, questioning, sampling;

- design a psychological survey.

3.1   The non-experimental method

The **non-experimental method** simply describes what is happening and are referred to as 'non-experimental' in design because there is *no independent variable involved*. As a result, no cause-effect conclusions can ever be drawn when using a non-experimental method of research.

For the purposes of this course, we should know about three of these methods:

- the **observational method**;

- the **survey method**;

- the **case study** method, within which the **interview method** is found.

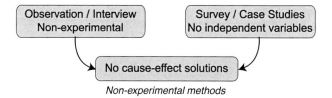

Non-experimental methods

The non-experimental method: Notebook exercise

You will need your psychology notebook for this activity.

Would the memories of S3 pupils improve by the time they reach S5?

Consider how you might get evidence either way for this.

What would your null hypothesis be? Would you use an experimental method?

Using the non-experimental methods diagram, explain your choice of research method.

This scenario is suggested only as a lead to help explain the sorts of research you may have to consider and to help differentiate between experimental and non-experimental methodologies.

Your psychology notebook should now have some information under the heading *Research problem*.

3.2   The observational method

Learning objective

By the end of this section, you should be able to:

- explain key features of, identify (from scenarios), and evaluate the observational non-experimental method;

- explain, identify and evaluate the key features of each of five types of observational research: participant, non-participant, structured, unstructured and naturalistic.

The observational method of research concerns the planned watching, recording, and analysis of observed behaviour as it occurs in a natural setting.

The observational method: Elements   Go online

Important elements used in the observational method include:

- video cameras;

- cameras;

- sound recorders;

- clipboards;

- and, of course, people to observe!

The observational method is a **non-experimental** design.

The absence of an **independent variable** does not allow any cause-effect conclusions to be drawn from observational research. Sound evidence is however important to the observational method.

Indeed, the observational method's key feature is a **standardised**, *planned, and systematic approach to objectively observe and record behaviour.* This is, of course, to generate all-important data upon which to base any conclusions.

3.2.1   Types of observation

Observations can be **overt** or **covert**, and are of five main types:

1. **participant observation**;

2. **non-participant observation**;

3. **structured observation**;

4. **unstructured observation**;

5. **naturalistic observation**.

Each of these involves the planned gathering, analysis and interpretation of mostly **empirical data** on observed behaviour.

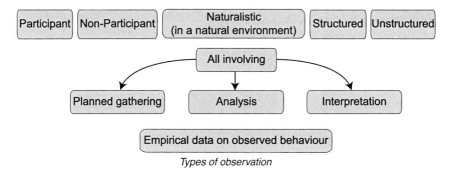

Types of observation

The observational method has both advantages and disadvantages as a research design in psychology.

Covert observations can be problematic regards **ethics** and disclosure.

Confounding variables also plague observations. These are infinite, and include **observer bias** and the **observer effect**.

If the researcher plans, structures, and conducts their observation appropriately, the observational method can be seen as a most **valid** and **reliable** form of non-experimental research in psychology mainly due to the observational method's high **ecological validity**.

Participant and non-participant observation

Participant observation, for example, sees the researcher *set up, and take part in* the observation of the behaviour under investigation.

Non-participant observation sees *no involvement* on the part of the researcher, with recordings of observed behaviours being taken from afar.

3.2.2 Observational techniques

Effective observation of behaviours always involves recording what happens *in a very structured way*. It is impossible to record everything that happens so very often a decision is taken regarding exactly what is to be observed, then a technique has to be developed to record the identified behaviour in some way. This allows for later analysis and is quick and easy. Sometimes behaviour is filmed so that researchers can watch it repeatedly and record behaviours very accurately. Behaviours may also be caught using photography and audio equipment.

Another technique used is an **observation schedule**. Observation schedules may be used in an open situation such as the one below, or when observing behaviour through a one-way mirror.

The following example could be used to record children's behaviour in a playgroup situation.

Checklist: Play behaviour: 15 minutes observation
Name of observer: _____
Date: _____

	Was behaviour observed? Yes or No
1	Child looked at books
2	Child played with sand
3	Child played with water
4	Child handled plastic cups
5	Child put together jigsaws
6	Child used construction set
7	Child used plasticine
8	Child did nothing for more than 2 minutes

Observation checklists are used to ensure both objectivity and accuracy of observation, especially when there is more than one observer involved in a research situation. This type of checklist is particularly useful for carrying out a thorough and systematic analysis of the behaviour of participants.

Observational techniques: Questions   Go online

Q1:   Complete the table using the list of factors provided.

Advantages of participant observation	Disadvantages of participant observation

List of factors: behaviours are less prone to misinterpretation because researcher was a participant; gives an 'insiders' view; observer effect; opportunity for researcher to become an 'accepted' part of the environment; possible lack of objectivity on the part of the observer.

....

Q2:   Complete the table using the list of factors provided.

Advantages of non-participant observation	Disadvantages of non-participant observation

List of factors: avoidance of observer effect; observer is detached from situation so relies on their perception which may be inaccurate.

....

Q3:   Complete the table using the list of factors provided.

Advantages of structured observation	Disadvantages of structured observation

List of factors: allows control of extraneous variables; lack of ecological validity; observer bias; observer effect; provides a safe environment to study contentious concepts; reliability of results can be tested by repeating the study; the implementation of controls may have an effect on behaviour.

....

Q4: Complete the table using the list of factors provided.

Advantages of unstructured observation	Disadvantages of unstructured observation

List of factors: gives a broad overview of a situation; only really appropriate as a "first step" to give an overview of a situation/concept/idea; useful where situation/subject matter to be studied is unclear.

. . . .

Q5: Complete the table using the list of factors provided.

Advantages of naturalistic observation	Disadvantages of naturalistic observation

List of factors: particularly good for observing specific subjects; provides ecologically valid recordings of natural behaviour; replication due to standardised procedures (designs/instructions); spontaneous behaviours are more likely to happen.

3.3 The survey method

Learning objective

By the end of this section, you should be able to:

- explain key features of, identify (from scenarios), and evaluate the survey non-experimental method;

- explain the following techniques used in surveys: interview, questioning, sampling;

- design a psychological survey.

The survey method of research asks a representative sample of people oral or written questions to find out about their attitudes, behaviours, beliefs, opinions, and values. The survey method gathers **quantitative data** on thoughts, feelings and behaviours we have in common or on which we differ.

Carrying out a survey

The term "survey" can be used as an umbrella term for a variety of methods that involve asking questions. A survey can thus consist of oral interviews or written questionnaires.

3.3.1   The Interview

The **interview method** is a conversation with a purpose.

Carrying out an interview

The interview method is non-experimental in design. The interviewer in one-to-one conversation collects detailed personal information from individuals using oral questions.

The interview is used widely in psychology to supplement and extend our knowledge about individual(s) thoughts, feelings and behaviours, or how they *think* they feel and behave.

Similar to a survey, interviews can give us both quantitative and qualitative data about participants' thoughts, feelings and behaviours. This is due to the **standardisation** and/or free ranging nature of questions asked.

The more structured or *standardised* interview questions are, the more able you are to get quantitative data. Quantitative data is reliable and easy to analyse.

The less structured and freer ranging the interview questions, the more qualitative your data becomes. Qualitative data is difficult to analyse and is not as reliable.

3.3.1.1 Interview types

	Structured	Unstructured
Interview type	Structured Semi-structured Clinical	Unstructured
Planning	Well planned and can be replicated	Unplanned to a large extent/more spontaneous
Modes	Face-to-face Telephone Videophone Internet	Participants more responsive
Generalisation	Assumptions can be generalised	Cannot generalise

A major feature, and difference, is the degree to which each type uses standardised and unplanned questions. Standardisation helps the reliability of your results and conclusions. The more use of unplanned questions, the less structured the interview becomes.

Interview types: Questions   Go online

Q6: Complete the table using the list of factors provided.

Advantages of a structured interview	Disadvantages of a structured interview

List of factors: allows generalisation of results/conclusions to the population from which the sample was drawn; data is more reliable as the issue is being investigated in a consistent way; insensitivity to participants' need to express themselves; restrictive questioning leads to restrictive answers; replication; standardisation of all questions can give quantifiable data; validity of questions asked - are they the right ones?.

....

Q7: Complete the table using the list of factors provided.

Advantages of a semi-structured interview	Disadvantages of a semi-structured interview

List of factors: ability to ask some spontaneous questions is sensitive to participants need to express themselves; data is reasonably reliable; its use of an occasional spontaneous question makes these answers difficult to quantify and analyse; replication; spontaneous questions asked of some and not others can be seen as unfair especially in personnel selection; standardisation of most questions gives quantifiable data.

....

Q8: Complete the table using the list of factors provided.

Advantages of a clinical interview	Disadvantages of a clinical interview

List of factors: as a result an inability to generalise your findings to a wider population; core questions and responses should be reliable and analysed easily; difficult to replicate; flexible, responsive and sensitive to participants; preparation of core questions should ensure validity; possible interview bias in their use of leading spontaneous questions.

....

Q9: Complete the table using the list of factors provided.

Advantages of an unstructured interview	Disadvantages of an unstructured interview

List of factors: as a result, an inability to generalise your findings to a wider population; difficult to replicate; flexible, responsive and sensitive to participants; highly detailed and ecologically valid qualitative data; possible interview bias in 'selective' use of leading and spontaneous questions; relaxed and natural for those taking part.

3.3.2 Sampling and surveys

Whether an interview or a survey is used, each asks a representative sample of people the same questions about particular attitudes, opinions, values and beliefs.

If the **sample** is truly representative, this allows the generalisation of results to the **population** from which the sample came.

Surveys can be used on their own or with other research methods such as **experimental**, **observational** and, of course, **interviews**.

The survey method shares an important feature with the more structured of interviews and observations. This is the gathering of data by self-report from a respondent or interviewee.

Survey modes see surveys conducted by post, face-to-face, by telephone, videophone and the Internet.

A good survey will be designed well, with standardised instructions and questions. A **pilot survey** is often conducted to allow this to occur.

3.3.3 Question types

Survey questions can be either *open* or *closed*.

Open questions give rise to open, descriptive answers, while **closed questions** restrict respondents' choice of answers.

Open questions can give you too much qualitative, descriptive information in answers, which makes working out our common or differing attitudes, opinions etc. difficult.

Closed questions, which give quantitative or numerical answers, are useful, especially if a **Likert scale** of measurement is used.

3.3.4 Advantages and disadvantages of the survey method

Advantages of the survey method of research are that surveys are cheap, easily administered, replicable, and a large amount of data can be collected from a lot of people in a fairly short time.

Most importantly, a well-designed survey, if given to a representative sample, allows the researcher to generalise their results to the population from which this sample came.

Disadvantages include poor design, **GIGO**, **reliability** and **validity**, **acquiescence response**, a tendency to give socially desirable answers, and response and sampling bias.

Advantages and disadvantages of the survey method: Question   Go online

For each question decide if the statement is an advantage or disadvantage of the survey method of research.

Q10: Cheap! If well designed it is a useful tool of research in its own right. Aids future research using other methods.

a) advantage
b) Disadvantage

....

Q11: Poorly designed instructions/questions see a survey suffer from the GIGO effect. 'Garbage in garbage out'.

a) Advantage
b) Disadvantage

....

Q12: Large amounts of standardised information can be obtained from a large number of people in a short period of time

a) Advantage
b) Disadvantage

....

Q13: Highly replicable: can be used on a longitudinal basis to constantly update questions of interest e.g. voting trends

a) Advantage
b) Disadvantage

....

Q14: Acquiescence response or social desirability bias is a tendency people have to agree or say 'yes'

a) Advantage
b) Disadvantage

....

Q15: Response set arises when respondents imagine patterns of desired answers to questions, and answer accordingly.

a) Advantage
b) Disadvantage

....

Q16: Easy to score, unless open-ended questions used. Obtain quantifiable data to help develop and support hypotheses.

a) Advantage
b) Disadvantage

....

Q17: Can generate empirical data giving a measurement of behaviours, attitudes, opinions, beliefs, values of population.

a) Advantage
b) Disadvantage

3.3.5   How to design a good psychological survey

Study the five principles behind survey design which ensure good practice.

1. Keep the language simple - Parten (1950) says that language used in a survey should be able to be understood by an 11 year old.

2. Keep the questions short and on one issue - the longer a survey the less likely folk will fill it in.

3. Avoid technical terms - as people will probably not know what you are talking about

4. Avoid leading questions - an example of a leading question is: "Have you stopped smoking cannabis? Yes/No". Whichever way the respondent answers this, they would be breaking the law. Think about it, and don't use leading questions in survey design.

5. Avoid emotive or moral questions - an example here would be: "Have you ever had an abortion? Yes/No". This type of emotive or moral questions asked of others is really none of our business!

3.3.6   Steps to a successful psychological survey

If you decide to use a survey as a method in psychological research, it's a good idea to adopt the following design model or research process:

• select an area of psychological interest;

• research the topic area to get ideas about what questions to ask - use the search engine http://www.sciencedirect.com/ as your starting point;

• write your questions down;

• use closed questions at the beginning of your survey to get good **quantitative data** about your sample;

• for better survey item analysis, use a Likert Scale to get quantitative data on answers to your survey item questions;

• mix up the sequencing of survey item questions in order to avoid response acquiescence set;

- write down your standardised instructions, which come at the beginning of your survey - yhey should also make reference to the general purpose of the survey, confirming that the respondent agrees to take part, has a right to withdraw etc. (see The http://www.bps.org.uk/s ystem/files/Public%20files/bps_code_of_ethics_2009.pdf);

- conduct a pilot survey with a small group of people - it is best if they are from the same group as those who will complete the final survey; their job is to tell you if they understand the standardised instructions and questions, if they can follow how to answer the questions etc;

- redraft and, if necessary, pilot it again - don't be lazy, remember GIGO;

- conduct your survey;

- debrief your respondents and give them an indication of how to find out the results;

- analyse your results.

That's it!

3.4   The case study method

> **Learning objective**
>
> By the end of this section, you should be able to:
>
> - explain key features of, identify (from scenarios), and evaluate the case study non-experimental method.

The case study method of research is a detailed in-depth investigation of a single case happening concerning a person, a family, an organisation, or an event.

The case study method of research is a detailed in-depth investigation into a single-case happening concerning an individual, organisation or animal.

Because of its interest in the *single* case, the case study is said to be **idiographic** in nature.

It is a method of enquiry that generates rich, mostly qualitative, descriptive detail about a unique individual, episode, situation etc.

The case study has been used in the psychoanalytic approach, examples being Freud's Anna O and Little Hans.

3.4.1 Advantages and disadvantages of the case study method

Developmental psychology has also used the case study as with **Koluchová** (1972, 1976, 1991), while the study of individual differences sees its use in single cases of interest concerning **intelligence, personality,** and **atypical behaviour**.

A case study can be **retrospective** or **longitudinal,** and can involve the use of **case histories, interviews, questionnaires, psychometric tests, diaries, observation** and **experiments**.

As a method of research, the case study's main advantage is its **ecological validity**. It is true-to-life. It collects detailed, in-depth information about a single-case concerning an individual, an organisation or an animal, in a humane manner.

Its disadvantages include an inability to generalise results, difficulties regarding **replication** and confirmation of earlier results, and the subjectivity and reliability of information got by self-report.

Interviewer bias and **observer bias** further disadvantages its usefulness as a scientifically credible method of research.

Explore the case study method further by trying the following activity.

Advantages and disadvantages of the case study method: Question Go online

Q18: Complete the table using the list of factors provided.

Advantages of the case study method	Disadvantages of the case study method

List of factors: cannot generalise results; detailed in-depth information got of a single case concerning a person, a family, an organisation or an event; high ecological validity; interviewer/observer bias; reliability of information collected by self-report; replication impossible, to confirm earlier results; sensitive to the individual, and sensitive issues concerning the individual.

3.5   Summary

You have met lots of new terminology in this topic, often not in any context. The following exercise may help you to clarify the new terms.

Summary: Notebook exercise

You will need your psychology notebook for this activity.

Consider the following hypothetical scenario: *"Who is the happiest person in your school?"*

Imagine that you had to design a study to find this happy person.

Here are a few issues you would have to consider.

- How do you measure "happiness"?
- What sort of study will you use and why? e.g. interview, survey, case study etc.
- Sampling - would you use everyone in the school? Pupils only? S5/S6 only? Or some pupils from each year group? Teachers? The Headteacher?

You may decide that you cannot even measure happiness!

Record you thoughts in your psychology notebook, which should have information under the heading of *happiness* as a result.

3.6   Learning points

Summary

- The non-experimental method describes what is happening and involves no independent variable.
- Non-experimental methods include: observational, survey and case study.
- The main types of observational research are: participant, non-participant, structured, unstructured and naturalistic.
- Techniques used in surveys include: interview, questioning, sampling.
- Psychological surveys can be designed using five key principles.

3.7 End of topic test

End of Topic 3 test   Go online

Q19: Why are the observational, interview, survey and case study methods of research said to be non-experimental in design?

a) Researchers don't wear a white coat when conducting them.
b) There is no dependent variable involved.
c) There is no independent variable involved.

....

Q20: What can be defined as the planned watching, recording and analysis of behaviour as it occurs in a natural setting?

a) Interview method
b) Observational method
c) Survey method

....

Q21: Ethics and disclosure are particularly problematic when conducting:

a) a structured interview.
b) an overt observation.
c) a covert observation.

....

Q22: Which method of research asks a representative sample of people oral or written questions about their attitudes, behaviours, beliefs, opinions and values?

a) Survey method
b) Experimental method
c) Observational method

....

Q23: Which non-experimental research method can be best described as a conversation with a purpose?

a) Survey method
b) Observational method
c) Interview method

....

Q24: GIGO refers to 'garbage in garbage out' and is a particular criticism of the:

a) survey method.
b) experimental method.
c) observational method.

....

Q25: What is a detailed, in-depth investigation into a single case concerning a person, a family, an organisation or an event?

a) An interview
b) A case study
c) A survey

....

Q26: A case study is said to have:

a) high ecological validity.
b) low ecological validity.
c) no ecological validity.

Unit 1 Topic 4

Calculating/presenting data using descriptive statistics

Contents

Learning objective

By the end of this topic, you should be able to evaluate the research process in psychology by:

- calculate and explain the key features of the following measures of central tendency: mean, median and mode;

- explain the key features of the following measures of dispersion: range and standard deviation;

- calculate the range;

- explain the kind of information that a correlation can give a researcher;

- identify a correlational technique used in a research method from a scenario;

- explain the key features of a correlation, including scattergrams.

4.1   Introduction

Statistical methods can help you by:

- allowing you to summarise large sets of numbers (data) quickly and efficiently;

- allowing you to make statements about a large group (a **population**) based on data from a smaller group (a **sample**);

- establishing causal relationships between and IV and DV.

Descriptive statistics are tools for describing and summarising the properties of an unwieldy amount of information from a sample.

4.2   Measures of central tendency

Learning objective

By the end of this section, you should be able to:

- calculate and explain the key features of the following measures of central tendency: mean, median and mode.

These measures tell us about **averages**. In Psychology, we measure, count or quantify data wherever possible.

There are three different types of measures of central tendency:

1. the **mean**;

2. the **median**;

3. the **mode**.

Mean

The mean is the arithmetical average of a set of numbers. To find the mean, add up the values and divide by the number of items. Be aware that the mean is susceptible to extreme values.

Example : Mean example 1

Find the mean of 34, 34, 452, 23, 35, 27, 40, 32

The mean is the sum of the values divided by the number of items which is $\frac{677}{8} = 84.625$

Hopefully you can see how the mean in the above example does not represent the other scores very well. The extreme score of 452 makes the mean an inaccurate average, in this instance.

Median

The median is the middle value in a data set.

To find the median, put the values in ascending order. If there is an odd number of values, the median is the middle value. If there is an even number of values, you take the mean of the two middle values. In either case, half of the values in the set will be above the median and half will be below it.

Examples

1. Median example 1

Find the median of 3, 5, 7, 9, 11, 13, 15

The median is the middle number, which is 9.

           . . . .

2. Median example 2

Find the median of 3, 5, 7, 9, 11, 13, 15, 17

The median is the mean of the two middle scores of 9 and 11, which is $\frac{20}{2} = 10$

Mode

The mode is the most frequently occurring value in a data set.

To work out the mode you quite simply count the number of times each value occurs.

Example : Mode example 1

Find the mode of 2, 5, 3, 5, 8, 2, 2, 5, 2, 6, 2, 2

The mode is the most commonly occurring value, which is 2 (occurring five times).

> **Top tip**
>
> The mean, median and mode are all averages, but only the mean is the arithmetical average.

We will now compare all three measures.

	Description	Advantages	Disadvantages
Mean	The mean is the sum of all the results included in the sample divided by the number of observations.	Quick and easy to calculate.	May not be representative of the whole sample.
Median	The median is the middle value of all the numbers in the sample. In other words, the median is the value that divides the set of data in half, 50% of the observations being above (or equal to) it and 50% being below (or equal to) it.	Takes all numbers into account equally.	More tedious to calculate than the other two Can be affected by a few very large (or very small) numbers.
Mode	The mode is the most frequently observed value of the measurements in the sample. There can be more than one mode or no mode.	Fairly easy to calculate.	Tedious to find for a large sample which is not in order.

Knowing the mean, median, or mode in a data set is often not enough in psychological research. We also need to know how spread out the scores are.

This is known as measures of dispersion.

The only measure of dispersion that we need to know about in this course is called the range.

4.3   Measures of dispersion

Learning objective

By the end of this section, you should be able to:

- explain the key features of the following measures of dispersion: range and standard deviation;

- calculate the range.

The range

The **range** is the difference between the highest and the lowest value in a data set.

Example : Range example 1

Find the range in the number of words recalled by the data set.

Participant	1	2	3	4	5	6	7	8	9	10
Words recalled	5	8	9	7	7	6	5	8	5	6

The range is the difference between the lowest value of 5 and the highest value of 9, which is
9 - 5 = 4

The main weakness with the statistical range is that, although it often gives a good indication of the spread of scores, its calculation depends on just two scores the highest and the lowest.

The range does not give an accurate reflection of a group of scores when it contains an odd score that is obviously higher or lower than the rest. One way to address this is to use the **standard deviation**, which refers to the average amount that all scores in a data set deviate from the mean.

Standard deviation

The standard deviation measures the spread of the data *about the mean*, in contrast with the range which illustrates the spread of scores.

On occasion, when comparing sets of data, the mean may be the same. However, the range may be different. For example:

• 15, 20, 17, 18, 15, 22

• 10, 30, 5, 35, 2, 25

Both of these data sets have the same mean ($\frac{107}{6} = 17.83$), but look again at the data - you will see that the range of the first (22) is less than the range of the second (33). You could now calculate a more precise measure of dispersion - the standard deviation (which you will not be required to calculate for Higher Psychology).

The steps you would take would be; firstly, calculate the **variance**:

• calculate the mean;

• subtract the mean from each raw score;

• square each result of the above (to cancel out negatives);

• add the squares.

Score X	Mean $\bar{X}$	$d\ (X - \bar{X})$	$d^2\ (X - \bar{X})^2$
600	394	206	42436
470	394	76	5776
170	394	-224	50176
430	394	36	1296
300	394	-94	8836

Sum $X = 1970$, Mean $= \frac{1970}{5} = 394$, Sum $d^2 = 108520$

Now you need to calculate the degrees of freedom (df). The reasons for doing this are highly technical. In this instance, it involves subtracting one from the sample size: $df = n - 1$

There are five items in our sample so by subtracting 1: $df = 4$

To find the standard deviation, all you need to do now is to:

• divide the sum of d^2 by df;

• take the square root of the result.

$$\sqrt{\frac{108520}{4}} = 164.7$$

The formula below is that for standard deviation (for a sample):

$$s = \sqrt{\frac{\sum (X - \bar{X})^2}{n - 1}}$$

where:

- s = standard deviation

- $\sqrt{}$ = square root

- $\sum$ = sum of

- X = score

- $\bar{X}$ = mean

Key point

Although the above calculation may help you understand measures of dispersion, including the variance and standard deviation, you will not have to calculate it in any part of Higher Psychology.

A small standard deviation shows that scores are spread narrowly around the mean, whereas a large standard deviation (like we have in the example above, 52.08) indicates that scores are widely spread around the mean. See this explained visually below:

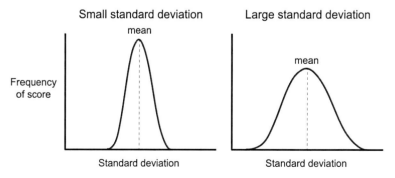

A small standard deviation (left) shows a narrow deviation from the mean while a large standard deviation (right) shows a wide deviation from the mean

4.4   Correlation

Learning objective

By the end of this section, you should be able to:

- explain the kind of information that a correlation can give a researcher;
- identify a correlational technique used in a research method from a scenario;
- explain the key features of a correlation, including scattergrams.

A correlation is not a research method as such, but a statistical technique used to indicate the degree of relationship between two co-variables.

Correlation refers to how strongly one variable is related to another and to the direction of the relationship - plus or minus, good or bad.

In this section, we will study:

- scattergrams;
- graphs and histograms;
- frequency distributions;
- pie charts;
- data curves.

4.4.1   Scattergrams

A **scattergram** is a graphical representation of a correlation.

The scattergram's trend line illustrates the strength, direction, and degree of positive or negative correlation. It may also indicate no correlation at all.

A correlation can be positive or negative. A positive correlation means that there is a positive relationship between the two independent co-variates, and that as one increases so does the other. Our scattergram here illustrates a positive correlation. Why do you think this is?

Scattergrams: Example   Go online

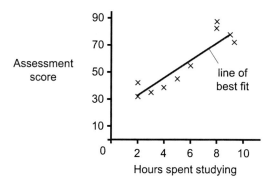

A scattergram illustrating the statistical relationship between hours spent studying and marks scored in an assessment shows a positive correlation between the two

Scattergrams: Notebook exercise

You will need your psychology notebook for this activity.

Q1:

1. Use the data below to draw a scattergram.
2. Use the scattergram to deduce if there is any relationship (a correlation) between 'hours spent socialising' and 'assessment score'.

Participant	1	2	3	4	5	6	7	8	9	10
Hours spent socialising (x)	1	2	3	4	5	6	7	8	9	10
Assessment score (y)	83	76	74	67	56	48	36	34	32	27

4.4.2   Graphs and histograms

When we change or manipulate an independent variable we often predict in our experimental hypothesis that there will be a difference in behaviour as a result.

A bar chart or bar graph is a way of showing information by the lengths of a set of bars. The bars are drawn horizontally or vertically. If the bars are drawn vertically, then the graph can be called a column graph or a block graph.

Here is what a column graph looks like.

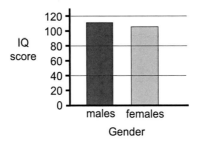

Column graph showing the relationship between gender and IQ scores

4.4.3   Frequency distributions

When you have a set of scores from participants, you can illustrate their frequency distribution using a histogram or frequency polygon. A common name for a frequency polygon is a line graph/curve.

Frequency distributions are important graphical representations in psychology. There are of two kinds of frequency distributions:

- histograms;

- frequency polygons.

A histogram is a bar graph that uses the width of the bars to represent the various classes and the height of the bars to represent their relative frequencies.

The frequency polygon or line curve is a graph that illustrates data by using lines to connect the points plotted for the frequencies of the data set.

In both instances, the variable under investigation is laid out along the horizontal *x* axis, while the dependent variable, or number of times the variable occurred, is laid out along the vertical *y* axis.

It is important that you label the axes of all of your graphs so that others can understand your work.

Compare these two ways to plot the frequency data from an example about IQ scores.

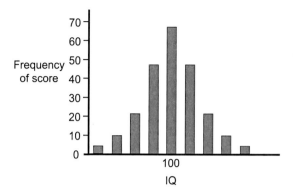

Bar chart or histogram showing the relationship between IQ and frequency of score

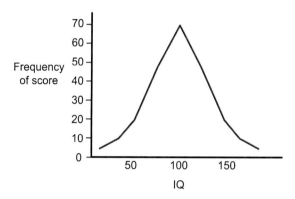

Frequency polygon showing the relationship between IQ and frequency of score

Where there are two conditions of a variable, it is a good idea to use a histogram to show the occurrence of each condition. Use a bar of one colour for one and a bar of another colour for the other. This helps you to make comparisons.

Here is an example of a frequency histogram to show the mean number of actual and expected days per year with snow cover over five different regions in the UK.

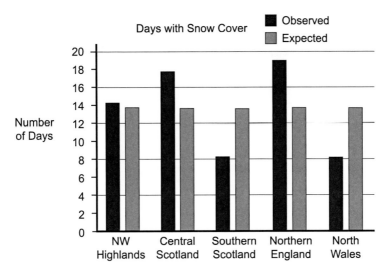

Frequency histogram showing the relationship between the mean number of actual and expected days per year with snow over five different regions in the UK

4.4.4   Pie charts

Another graphical representation is a pie chart, which is a circle with segments cut out of it.

Each segment of the pie chart represents a percentage of the whole. Pie charts give a clear visual representation of the different proportions of a variable that groups of participants share.

Based on official statistics we can use a pie chart to display what proportion of families in Britain live in different types of family structure, e.g. one parent families, two parent families, extended families etc.

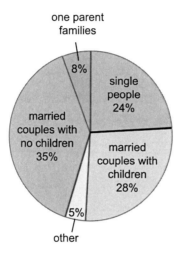

Pie chart showing the proportion of families in Britain living in different types of family structure

However, in order to construct a pie chart, it is always necessary to know the total occurrences of the variable under investigation and then how often it occurs for each group being studied.

4.4.5   Data curves

If you have to take measurements from the same participants at different times, this information can be graphically represented using a data curve.

Study this data curve which illustrates the effect of different amounts of practice on the number of errors made in a mirror drawing task.

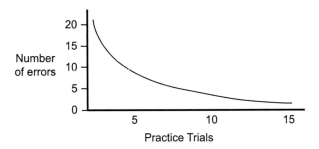

Data curve showing the relationship between practice trials and number of errors

4.4.6   Overlapping data curves

You can also have overlapping data curves on one graph to illustrate comparisons.

Our overlapping data curve allows us to illustrate two sets of results simultaneously.

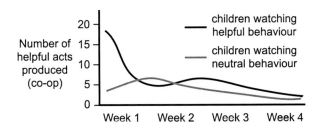

Overlapping data curve showing the relationship between time and the number of helpful acts produced by children who were either watching helpful or neutral behaviour

The *solid* line represents the number of altruistic or helpful acts observed in one group of children over a four week period after being shown a video that encouraged helping behaviour.

The *dashed* line represents the number of altruistic or helpful acts observed in another group of children over the same period who were shown a neutral video that did not show helpful or unhelpful behaviour to any real extent.

Overlapping data curves: Questions   Go online

Q2: Look at the overlapping data curve above, and suggest an experimental hypothesis for this investigation.

....

Q3: What were the two conditions of the independent variable?

....

Q4: What was the dependent variable?

With a data curve you can see at a glance the effect that the independent variable has had on the dependent variable over time.

In this case, helpful acts increased for the majority of children immediately after watching the helping behaviour video, but over the next month reduced to a level fairly close to that found in the group who watched the neutral behaviour video.

When using inferential statistics (where inferences or conclusions are drawn from the experimental data), these can be multidirectional.

In a one-tailed test we are judging the significance of our results away from the null hypothesis in one direction only. A change from the null hypothesis in either direction is known as a two-tailed test.

4.5 Learning points

Summary

- Measures of central tendency include the mean (the arithmetical average), median (the middle value) and mode (the most common value).

- Measures of dispersion include the range (the difference between extreme values) and standard deviation (the average amount that all value in a data set deviate from the mean).

- The range can be calculated as the difference between the highest and the lowest value in a data set.

- A correlation can indicate to a researcher if one variable is related to another and to the direction of the relationship.

- Correlational techniques used in a research method can be identified from the scenario.

- A correlation is a statistical technique used to indicate the degree of relationship between two co-variables; a scattergram illustrates the strength, direction, and degree of positive or negative correlation.

4.6 End of topic test

End of Topic 4 test   Go online

Q5: What term is used in psychology to describe the basic features of data we collect in our research? *(1 mark)*

a) Inferential statistics
b) Reverential statistics
c) Descriptive statistics

....

Q6: The mean, median and mode are measures of: *(1 mark)*

a) central tendency.
b) dispersion.
c) central dispersion.

....

Q7: If five participants recalled 12, 13, 12, 11 and 15 items in a memory experiment, the mean number of items recalled would be: *(1 mark)*

a) 12.4
b) 12.5
c) 12.6

....

Q8: If five participants recalled 12, 13, 12, 11 and 15 items in a memory experiment, the median number of items recalled would be: *(1 mark)*

a) 11
b) 12
c) 13

....

Q9: What statistical term describes the difference between the highest and lowest score in a data set? *(1 mark)*

a) Range
b) Scope
c) Variety

....

Q10: What research technique is used in psychology to indicate the degree of relationship between two co-variables? *(1 mark)*

a) An experiment
b) A survey
c) A correlation

....

....

Q11: What type of hypothesis predicts the direction a researcher expects their results to go? *(1 mark)*

a) One-tailed
b) Two-tailed
c) Three-tailed

....

Q12: What is used to illustrate a correlation? *(1 mark)*

a) Pie chart
b) Scattergram
c) Histogram

....

Q13: What term best describes data that has not been summarised in descriptive or graphical form? *(1 mark)*

a) Raw data
b) Rare data
c) Untreated data

Unit 1 Topic 5

Choice of method and ethical guidelines

Contents

Learning objective

By the end of this topic, you should be able to:

- apply and justify choice of method to research scenarios;

- explain ethical guidelines and their use in psychological research.

5.1   Applying and justifying choice of method to research scenarios

Psychological researchers need to know when and how different types of research approaches will be used to address the many research questions of interest to them. This question would most likely be addressed early in the stages of the research process, e.g. during the choice of topic or literature review.

Before tackling this section, remind yourselves below of experimental and non-experimental methods, and their strengths and their weaknesses. If you have constructed 'hierarchies', as suggested in the sections on experimental and non-experimental methods, it will be useful to have them available here.

5.1.1   Experimental methods

Experiments involve the manipulation of variables in order to discover cause and effect. They are examples of a research method which involves the deliberate manipulation of one variable and the measurement of another while attempting to eliminate as many extraneous variables as possible. The variable that is manipulated is the independent variable, and the one that is measured is the dependent variable.

There are three different types of experimental method: laboratory, field and quasi. Experiments produce quantitative data which can be analysed statistically.

Experimental methods: Questions   Go online

Q1: Complete the following paragraph about laboratory experiments using the words from the list.

The laboratory experiment is the one with the most _ _ _ _ _ _ _ over extraneous variables, so cause and effect are easier to establish. This also increases the _ _ _ _ _ _ _ (ability to measure what is intended to be measured) and _ _ _ _ _ _ _ (ability to repeat study and obtain very similar results). However, the close proximity of the researcher may result in experimenter _ _ _ _ _ _ _, and the procedures and apparatus used may result in _ _ _ _ _ _ _ characteristics. These may both interfere with the validity and reliability of results. The biggest issue with the laboratory experiment is its artificiality, which means it is low in _ _ _ _ _ _ _ validity.

Word list: bias, control, demand, ecological, reliability, validity.

. . . .

Q2: Complete the following paragraph about field experiments using the words from the list.

A field experiment is an experiment that is conducted in a natural setting. In field experiments, the participants are not usually _ _ _ _ _ _ _ that they are participating in an experiment. An independent variable is still _ _ _ _ _ _ _. Field experiments are usually _ _ _ _ _ _ _ in ecological validity and may avoid demand characteristics as the participants are unaware of being studied. However, in field experiments, it is much harder to control confounding variables and they are usually time consuming and _ _ _ _ _ _ _ to conduct. In field experiments, it is not usually possible to gain _ _ _ _ _ _ _ consent from the participants and it is difficult to _ _ _ _ _ _ _ the participants.

Word list: aware, debrief, expensive, high, informed, manipulated.

. . . .

Q3: Complete the following paragraph about quasi experiments using the words from the list.

A quasi experiment is where the independent variable is not manipulated by the researcher but occurs _____. These experiments are often called _____ experiments. In a quasi experiment, the researcher takes advantage of pre-existing conditions, for example an _____ that the researcher has no control over such as a participants' occupation. A strength of some quasi experiments is that participants are often unaware that they are taking part in an investigation and they may not be as _____ as laboratory experiments. However, it is argued that the use of quasi experiments means that it is harder to establish _____ relationships because the independent variable is not being directly manipulated by the researcher.

Word list: artificial, causal, event, natural, naturally.

5.1.2 Non-experimental methods

There are three different types of non-experimental method: observation, surveys and interviews, and case studies.

Non-experimental methods: Questions   Go online

Q4: Complete the following paragraph about observation using the words from the list.

These are investigations where the researcher observes a situation and _____ what happens but does _____ manipulate an independent variable. Observational studies therefore tend to be high in ecological validity as there is no intervention and if the observation is _____, the method avoids problems with demand characteristics. A main _____ of observational studies is that they get to see how participants actually behave rather than what they say they do. A further strength of observational studies is that they offer ways of studying behaviour when there are _____ problems with manipulating variables. On the other hand observational studies are difficult to _____, so are low on reliability. Cause and effect relationships _____ be established because of low control over extraneous variables. There is also the problem of observer _____ with observational studies. A number of ethical issues can arise with observational studies including problems with a lack of informed _____ and invasion of _____.

Word list: bias, cannot, consent, covert, ethical, not, privacy, records, replicate, strength.

. . . .

Q5:   Complete the following paragraphs about surveys and interviews using the words from the list.

Surveys use questionnaires, usually in a highly structured written form. Questionnaires can contain both open and _____ questions and participants record their own answers. Surveys allow a large _____ of people to be studied, and can obtain information about _____ and opinions.

Interviews are usually _____ and the interviewer records the responses. Interviews can be structured with a _____ set of questions or _____, whereby there is opportunity for more detailed information to be provided.

However, in both surveys and interviews, participants may not respond _____, either because they cannot remember or because they wish to present themselves in a _____ acceptable manner.   Social _____ bias happens when participants answer to portray themselves well.   Furthermore, questions must be unambiguous, clear and should not _____ respondents to answer in a particular way.

Closed questions are questions which provide a _____ choice. Such questions provide _____ data which is easy to analyse. However, these questions do not allow the participant to give such in-depth insights.   _____ questions are those questions which invite the respondent to provide more detail and provide _____ data.   Although these types of questions are more difficult to analyse they can produce more in-depth responses, provide the 'why' of behaviour.

Word list: attitudes, closed, desirability, lead, limited, one-to-one, open, qualitative, quantitative, predetermined, sample, socially, truthfully, unstructured.

. . . .

Q6:   Complete the following paragraph about case studies using the words from the list.

These are forms of qualitative, _____ research that is used to look at individuals or a small _____. Researchers collect data about participants using observations, interviews, protocols, tests, examinations of records, and collections of writing samples. This is called the compilation of a case _____. However, case studies cannot be _____ beyond the person or small group being studied, and they can be biased due to the close relationship that can build up between researcher and researched. They are often the only way to study very rare, or _____ cases, like multiple personality disorder, but _____ data can be unreliable.

Word list: descriptive, generalised, group, history, retrospective, unique.

5.1.3 Matching topic to method

Now use what you have revised in the previous sections about experimental and non-experimental methods to answer the following question about matching topics of research to appropriate methods.

Matching topic to method: Question	Go online

Q7: Your task below is to match each of the methods with one of the following research scenarios (by putting the appropriate letter next to the example). This will also help you to understand the early stages of the research process, where a researcher will be making decisions about which method, or methods, would be best to study his or her topic of interest.

a) Case study.

b) Naturalistic observation.

c) Survey.

d) Interview.

e) Experiment (field, quasi, laboratory).

1. Susan is interested in the relationship between the amount of rats kept in a cage and their levels of the stress hormone, cortisol. She puts one rat in one cage, five rats in onecage, and ten rats in one cage (all cages are of the same dimensions). After one week, she takes measurements of the levels of cortisol of each rat.

2. Tara has reported that she is hearing voices telling her that she is useless and that she should commit suicide. Dale is interviewing Tara about her experiences and, after each interview session, he writes a report describing Tara's behaviour, both verbal and non-verbal, and his interpretations of that behaviour.

3. Racquel is a psychology student in her final year at university who is studying gender differences in child care for her dissertation. This afternoon, she is sitting in a restaurant across from a cinema which is showing a children's movie. She is taking notes about the sex of those accompanying the children to the cinema.

4. David compiled a questionnaire about attitudes to drinking alcohol and underage drinking amongst a sample of 14 to 15 year-olds.

Now, write down your thoughts on the ethics of these research activities.

5.2   Ethical Guidelines

Before you look at this section, take a few minutes to think about, and take note of, some of the ways in which you expect to be treated; by individuals, by your teachers/lecturers, by shop assistants, organisations, etc. How do you expect them to behave towards you?

It is important that researchers behave in this way towards their participants also. They agree to abide by an ethical code of conduct created by the British Psychological Society (BPS). If they don't abide by these guidelines, there are consequences in terms of funding for their research, for their membership of the BPS, and even for their ability to call themselves psychologists.

Ethics are important because the aim of psychology is to help people by increasing our understanding of how best to do so. This aim is incompatible with causing people harm in research situations.

The British Psychological Society: Code of conduct (2009)

The British Psychological Society bases its code of conduct on four principles that we should all aspire to in our everyday life as well as in research situations:

- respect;

- competence;

- responsibility;

- integrity.

Psychologists must adhere to this code when practising their profession (e.g. in clinical, educational, organisational etc. settings), as well as when conducting research. Furthermore, you must adhere to these principles when conducting your Research Investigation. In order to do this, you must ensure that the following are considered carefully while planning and carrying out your research, in fact, they should be considered at every stage of the research process.

Risk

This relates to 'doing no harm', psychologically or physically. Eliminating physical risk is fairly straightforward, but how can you tell if people are being caused psychological distress? All other ethical principles relate to 'risk' and 'doing no harm'. Examples of research that would be deemed harmful would be that conducted with vulnerable groups, such as those under 16 years of age or people in abusive relationships.

Valid Consent

All research participants should be aware of what the research aims are (i.e. they should give informed consent), be aware of what will happen to their data, of what the research process will be, and how long it will take before they consent to take part. They should also be free to withdraw their data at any stage of the research process, up to and including publication. If the participant can be deemed 'vulnerable' (e.g. under 16 years-of-age), consent from a parent or guardian should be sought.

Confidentiality

Subject to the requirements of legislation, including the Data Protection Act, information obtained from and about a participant during an investigation is confidential. This means that any identifying information should not be kept, and definitely not published.

Giving Advice

You are not psychologists! If in the course of conducting your research someone asks for your advice on a personal and/or psychological matter, it is your duty to tell them this and to advise them to speak with someone who is qualified to deal with their concerns. If in doubt, see your teacher/lecturer.

Deception

If you have studied psychology before, you may have come across some instances where participants were deceived to quite a shocking degree (e.g. Milgram). This, I'm sure you can see, relates directly to the issue of 'risk' above, in that there is the potential to cause psychological distress and harm (e.g. by setting up a situation where participants are left feeling stupid). Research should always be designed to maintain the dignity and autonomy of participants as far as is possible.

Debriefing

When the research procedure has finished, it is important for participants to be given the chance to discuss the research process. This is done in the debriefing process. Sometimes, this may be simply a reminder of the research aims, and that participants have the right to withdraw, to confidentiality etc. The main point is that participants should leave the research situation in the same state in which they entered it.

Ethical Guidelines and Code of Conduct: Questions	Go online

Read the following brief descriptions of studies. Which ethical principles have been violated from the following list.

1. Risk

2. Valid consent

3. Confidentiality

4. Giving advice

5. Deception

6. Debriefing

Q8: In a tube station, someone collapses. The person is acting, he is part of the research team, and the event is staged. Bystanders are observed covertly to see if they help and how long they take to help.
....

Q9: An experimenter in a pick-up truck, with a rifle visible in the back, and a sticker on the bumper saying "VENGEANCE" stops at the red lights. The experimenter does not move when the lights turn green thus blocking the traffic.

....

Q10: A researcher is conducting a survey into eating habits. She reads each participant a brief, stating the aims of the research and assuring them of the confidentiality of all data collected. She also reminds them of this at the end of the research. One participant says that she is worried about her friend who has lost a lot of weight recently. She worries that she has developed an eating disorder. The researcher tells her not to worry, that this often happens in young girls - she'll grow out of it.

....

Q11: An experiment was conducted to test a new drug for depression. For the experimental group, a psychiatrist wrote a new prescription for depression without discussing it with the patients. For the control group, she prescribed their normal prescription.

....

Q12: An observer hides (covert observation) in public toilets for men and records the time taken before participants begin to urinate and the time they take to urinate. A confederate of the researcher either stands in the next urinal to the participant or one urinal 'away'.

You will encounter ethics again when you undertake your assignment.

5.3   Learning points

Summary

- Choice of method can be applied and justified to different research scenarios.

- Ethical guidelines have an important use in psychological research.

5.4   End of topic test

End of Topic 5 test   Go online

> Researchable idea: will people be more likely to help a person that they think is drunk
> than a person that they think is disabled?

Q13: Which general type of research method would most likely be used to explore and
investigate the idea?

a) Experimental
b) Non-experimental

....

Q14: What specific type of research method would be best?

....

Q15: Which is the primary type of data that should be recorded?

a) Qualitative
b) Quantitative

....

Q16: What actual data should be collected?

....

Q17: Give a reason for your choice of method and what, if any, issues may be encountered
with regards reliability and validity?

Researchable idea: do phonics-based reading programmes in primary schools produce reading gains?

Q18: Which general type of research method would most likely be used to explore and investigate the idea?

a) Experimental
b) Non-experimental

....

Q19: What specific type of research method would be best?

....

Q20: Which is the primary type of data that should be recorded?

a) Qualitative
b) Quantitative

....

Q21: What actual data should be collected?

....

Q22: Give a reason for your choice of method and what, if any, issues may be encountered with regards reliability and validity?

> Researchable idea: what are the opinions of teaching professionals on the use of social media in education?

Q23: Which general type of research method would most likely be used to explore and investigate the idea?

a) Experimental
b) Non-experimental

....

Q24: What specific type of research method would be best?

....

Q25: Which is the primary type of data that should be recorded?

a) Qualitative
b) Quantitative

....

Q26: What actual data should be collected?

....

Q27: Give a reason for your choice of method and what, if any, issues may be encountered with regards reliability and validity?

Researchable idea: does short-term memory decline after age 70?

Q28: Which general type of research method would most likely be used to explore and investigate the idea?

a) Experimental
b) Non-experimental

. . . .

Q29: What specific type of research method would be best?

. . . .

Q30: Which is the primary type of data that should be recorded?

a) Qualitative
b) Quantitative

. . . .

Q31: What actual data should be collected?

. . . .

Q32: Give a reason for your choice of method and what, if any, issues may be encountered with regards reliability and validity?

Researchable idea: does sleeping fewer than 7 hours per night result in declines in cognitive ability?

Q33: Which general type of research method would most likely be used to explore and investigate the idea?

a) Experimental
b) Non-experimental

....

Q34: What specific type of research method would be best?

....

Q35: Which is the primary type of data that should be recorded?

a) Qualitative
b) Quantitative

....

Q36: What actual data should be collected?

....

Q37: Give a reason for your choice of method and what, if any, issues may be encountered with regards reliability and validity?

Researchable idea: is a man's Type 1 schizophrenia a result of genes or family interactions?

Q38: Which general type of research method would most likely be used to explore and investigate the idea?

a) Experimental
b) Non-experimental

....

Q39: What specific type of research method would be best?

....

Q40: Which is the primary type of data that should be recorded?

a) Qualitative
b) Quantitative

....

Q41: What actual data should be collected?

....

Q42: Give a reason for your choice of method and what, if any, issues may be encountered with regards reliability and validity?

> Researchable idea: are children more aggressive after playing the game Minecraft in school?

Q43: Which general type of research method would most likely be used to explore and investigate the idea?

a) Experimental
b) Non-experimental

....

Q44: What specific type of research method would be best?

....

Q45: Which is the primary type of data that should be recorded?

a) Qualitative
b) Quantitative

....

Q46: What actual data should be collected?

....

Q47: Give a reason for your choice of method and what, if any, issues may be encountered with regards reliability and validity?

Read the following brief descriptions of real studies and indicate which ethical principles have been violated from the following list:

- risk;

- valid consent;

- confidentiality;

- giving advice;

- deception;

- debriefing.

Q48: The Monster Study (1939) was a stuttering experiment on 22 orphan children. After placing the children in control and experimental groups, the researcher gave positive speech therapy to half of the children, praising the fluency of their speech, and negative speech therapy to the other half, belittling the children for every speech imperfection and telling them they were stutterers.

....

Q49: In the infamous Stanford Prison Experiment, volunteer students playing the role of prisoners were put into a situation that was purposely meant to cause disorientation, degradation and depersonalisation. Guards (also students who were randomly assigned to their role) were not given any specific directions or training about how to carry out their roles. Though at first the students were unsure of how to carry out their roles, eventually they had no problem. The second day of the experiment invited a rebellion by the prisoners, which brought a severe response from the guards. Things only went downhill from there.

....

Q50: In the 1970s and 1980s, psychiatrists in the South African army selected members of the armed forces who were suspected of being homosexual. Those who did not respond to methods such as electric shock, drug or hormone treatments, to 'cure' their homosexuality, were chemically castrated or given sex-change operations. These were white males, mostly aged 16 - 24.

Unit 1 Topic 6

Research investigation

Contents

Learning objective

By the end of this topic, you should be able to:

- evaluate the research process in psychology by using research skills to generate, select, organise, interpret, analyse and evaluate information;

- use communication skills to present information, including a report on psychological research.

6.1   Introduction

The assignment is worth 40 marks of the total 100 marks for the Higher (CfE) Psychology Group Award. The marks for the assignment and exam question paper are added together to give a grade for Higher Psychology (A - D). This assignment is one component of the course assessment, and the exam question paper is the other.

This section needs attention from both you as a pupil/student and your teacher/lecturer. There is important information from the SQA for both pupils and teachers. This information is about the assignment that you have to carry out.

The sections immediately following this will provide you with an overview of the requirements of the assignment for Higher Psychology. More detailed guidelines on how to construct the report of the assignment (on which you will be marked by SQA examiners), follow on from the overview.

Ethical guidelines

It is **essential** that you are familiar with the ethical guidelines as established by the British Psychological Society. You learned about these in the previous sections of this area of study, and they can also be found at http://www.bps.org.uk/. Ethical issues should be addressed before conducting the research - always check these with your lecturer/teacher.

6.2   Stages of the assignment

You will carry out a piece of research which must be based on a brief selected from a bank of SQA briefs relating to different topics in the Higher (CfE) Psychology course. Conducting this research will allow you to apply the skills, knowledge and understanding you have gained by studying Higher (CfE) Psychology.

The assignment has five stages.

1. Review the topics and related research you have learned as part of the course.

2. Choose a topic for your won primary research

3. Carry out background research on the topic outlined in the brief.

4. Plan primary research according to the topic brief and following ethical guidelines.

5. Carry out primary research according to the research plan and following ethical guidelines.

6. Produce a report that conforms to the style and format of a psychology research report.

Your teacher/lecturer will decide when you should begin this assignment - it will be when you are reasonably familiar with research methods, processes and the topic of your research. You will also be familiar with how to compile a report of your investigation, which you will find in the following sections, as well as the ethical guidelines referred to previously.

Although your teacher/lecturer will be available to give you advice (e.g. on resources, materials, clarification regarding the wording of the research brief), you will be working independently throughout this assignment.

Review the topics and related research you have learned as part of the course

Think about topics you are interested in and related research that you could use as the key research to base your assignment on.

Choose a topic for your won primary research

With the help of your teacher or lecturer, choose a suitable research topic. Remember to consider the potential ethical issues related to the choice of topic, as well as the resources available to help you to complete the assignment.

Carry out background research on the topic outlined in the brief

The next stage is to carry out background research. Background research are those studies that have informed the topic of your research - there will be a selection of these provided in your brief. You will explain these studies, and how they relate to your own, in the Introduction section of the report of your investigation. Remember to keep a note of the full references of these studies - you will need these for your in-text citations and References page (marks will be deducted if this is not done comprehensively).

Plan your research according to the brief and following ethical guidelines

When you have identified an aim and hypothesis for your research, you will decide the design of your study and specify whether you will use independent measures, repeated measures, matched pairs or correlational design. You will need to define the variables involved, i.e. the independent variable (IV), dependent variable (DV) or covariables (if the study is correlational). Remember - these should be stated precisely - they should be operationally defined. You will need to consider any potential extraneous and/or confounding variables and how you could control them. Also, you will need to identify the sampling method you will use (likely to be opportunity sampling), and the sample you will choose from your target population. You will gather or create materials required for the research, and devise clear, step-by-step instructions for the research procedure to be followed when conducting the research.

You will also need to consider if you need some help carrying out the research task, e.g. someone to hold materials, keep note of timings, etc. If you do require help, your helper must also be working under the supervision of your teacher/lecturer. Remember, once you have constructed a research plan, give it to your research supervisor to ensure that any ethical considerations are being addressed.

Carry out primary research according to the research plan and following ethical guidelines

You will then conduct the research itself, according to the procedures you have planned previously and ethical guidelines, and collect results. You will choose appropriate descriptive statistics (mean, median, mode, range) with which to analyse your results (you won't need to calculate a standard deviation or correlation). These results will suggest whether or not you can refute your null hypothesis.

Reasonable assistance may be provided by your teacher/lecturer, e.g.

- advice on available resources;

- what to consider when making decisions about the method or sample.

Reasonable assistance does *not* include:

- directing you to specific resources;

- providing model answers;

- providing any feedback on drafts.

Produce a report that conforms to the style and format of a psychology research report

This report is the assessment evidence that will be sent to SQA for marking.

It will be in the style and format of a psychological report which follows a conventional style, i.e.

1. Title

2. Contents

3. Introduction

4. Method

5. Results

6. Discussion

7. Conclusion

8. References

9. Appendices

Note that a psychological report usually also contains an Abstract between the Contents and Introduction, but this is not required for this assignment.

The report should be hand-written or word-processed, and it should be between 2,000 and 2,500 words long, excluding references and appendices. **Markers will be instructed to stop marking when the word count exceeds the maximum by 10%.** You must include a statement of the word length of the completed report, excluding appendices and references.

6.3   Referencing

This is where you state, in the globally accepted format known as the Harvard Referencing System (HRS), the primary source of any psychologist, psychological theory, or study that is DIRECTLY referred to in the text.

Examples

1.

Coolican, H. (1999) *Research Methods and Statistics in Psychology*, Hodder and Stoughton

. . . .

2.

Eysenck, M W. (1999) *Principles of Cognitive Psychology*, Psychology Press

. . . .

3.

Gleitman, H. (1991) *Psychology*, W.W. Norton and Company

Note the style/format of the References. This is important with author, year of research, title, and publisher. If particular information from a text book has been used to inform the research, then the page number of the book must also be provided.

6.4 Detailed marking instructions for the assignment

What follows are the marking instructions used by the assignment markers to assign marks for each section of your report. Use them to guide you towards constructing a report that gains the most marks possible.

6.4.1 Introduction

The first section includes the marking instructions for the Introduction section of the report.

Overview of marking	Mark range	Marking instructions
Accurate and relevant descriptions You are expected to carry out background research to select and interpret relevant psychological theories, concepts, and research studies in order to set your research topic in a psychological context.	0-10	Up to 8 marks can be awarded in a variety of ways for using background research to describe the psychological context for your own research study. A maximum of two of these marks can be awarded for each description of a relevant psychological theory, concept or research study. 1 mark can be awarded for each accurate and relevant description. *Up to 2 marks* are specifically awarded for the aim and hypothesis. Each of the two marks must be awarded in the following way: • *1 mark* for describing the aim of your own study - this should have a clear link to background research; • *1 mark* for accurately stating the experimental or alternative hypothesis, including clear expression of variables.

The opening paragraph should contain:

- the general area of the research (e.g. psychopathology, memory, stress, etc.);

- the specific topic of your research (e.g. phobias, encoding in short-term memory, conformity, etc.).

Introduction: Question   Go online

Q1:   Read the following example Introduction, then use the marking guidelines to allocate marks.

This investigation deals with the area of the biological approach[1], the topic is psychopathology[2] and the specific topic is phobia[3]. The biological approach explains behaviour and mental processes, such as thinking, in terms of physiology and genetics (Keegan, 2002). Psychopathology, known also as abnormal psychology, studies behaviours and mental processes which differ from what is considered as normal (Gleitman, Fridlund and Reisberg, 1999). These are called mental disorders (Colman, 2009). They include phobias. A phobia is an irrational fear that obstructs an individual's life (Atkinson, Atkinson, Smith, Bem and Nolen-Hoeksema, 2000). The DSM-IV-TR categorised phobias into social phobia, agoraphobia and specific phobias (including fear of animals). The latter are the most frequent (Gross, 2005)[4].

Seligman (1971 cited in Cardwell, Clark and Meldrum, 2000) explained phobias in terms of 'biological preparedness'. He argued that humans and animals are genetically preprogramed to stay away from stimuli that might be dangerous. These would be a real danger in the evolutionary past (Gross, 2005). His claim was supported by Garcia and Koelling (1966 cited in Cardwell et al, 2000) who carried out a study into phobias on rats. They found that it is easy to condition fear in rats for certain stimuli and difficult for others. Thus, their research provided evidence that phobias aid survival in animals (Psychology Concepts, 2013).[5]

A number of researchers carried out an investigation of phobias towards snakes and flowers. Ohman (1986 cited in Atkinson et al, 2000) found that in rhesus monkeys it is easier to condition fear of snakes than fear of flowers. Additionally, he found that the fear of the former takes longer to extinguish than the fear of the latter. Cook and Mineka (1990 cited in Atkinson et al, 2000) also conducted a study into phobias on infant rhesus monkeys. They showed the animals videos with adult monkeys displaying fear of snakes and fear of flowers. Afterwards, the monkeys demonstrated a fear of snakes but not a fear of flowers. Furthermore, Hugdal and Ohman (1977 cited in Gross, 2005) found that it is easier to condition people without phobias to a fear of snakes than to a fear of flowers in laboratory settings.

This investigation aims to replicate a study conducted by Bennett-Levy and Marteau (1984)[6]. They examined whether humans are prepared to fear certain animals. Two groups of participants took part in that research and each of them filled in a different questionnaire. One group assessed 29 animals in terms of how afraid of them they were and how near to the animal they would go (nearness). The second group evaluated the same animals on a three point scale in terms of their ugliness, sliminess, speed and sudden movements. The researchers found a strong positive correlation (0.82) between the ugliness and fear. Furthermore, they found a strong positive correlation (0.87) between the ugliness and nearness.

The aim of this research is to find out the basis of people's fear of animals. The correlational hypothesis is there will be a relationship between the animals' appearance and participants' fear (two tailed). The null hypothesis is that there will be no relationship between animals' appearance and participants' fear. Any relationship between the variables will be down to chance alone.

Possible marks	Included in example	Actual marks
Research set in its theoretical context. Background studies. *Up to 8 marks*		
Aim and hypothesis *Up to 2 marks*		

Total marks for Introduction section: /10

6.4.2 Method

This section of the report has four subsections, under the following subheadings.

1. Design: include the method (experimental lab, field or natural; non-experimental), along with reasons why this method was chosen; the design (if experimental method used) along with a reason for this design being used; the IV and DV, or covariables.

2. Sample: population from which sample chosen, sampling technique used, total number of participants, number of males, number of females, age range.

3. Materials: all materials used, e.g. stop watch, pencils, questionnaires, etc. (all of the materials listed here should appear in the Appendices. Marks may be deducted if they are not.)

4. Procedure: step-by-step, what participants had to do from when they entered the research situation to when they left it. This section should be written so that it can be replicated by someone else - check this section over to make sure that you have gone into sufficient detail once it is written. This section must include any ethical guidelines that were adhered to, e.g. participants briefed, debriefed, gave informed consent, etc.

Find marking guidelines for this section below.

Overview of marking	Mark range	Marking instructions
All relevant information for the method used in your primary research must be included in this section of the report; however you may refer to appropriate supplementary information contained in the appendices. Your descriptions must be sufficient to enable the research to be replicated.	0 - 10	A **maximum of 6** marks can be awarded in the following way: • *1 mark* for identifying your method and justifying why you have chosen this method, including identification of design (where appropriate); • *1 mark* for describing research variables ; • *1 mark* for describing extraneous / confounding / controlled variables; • *1 mark* ffor identifying the sampling method you have chosen, with a justification for your choice; and a description of your participants; • *1 mark* for identifying the materials you used, as well as where these can be found in appendices (to allow for replication); • *1 mark*for fully describing your procedure; A **maximum of 4** marks can be awarded for an explanation of how you have implemented BPS ethical guidelines and avoided ethical breaches, for example, deception and breach of confidentiality. You will be awarded **0 marks** if: • you only make general comments about ethics; • your research is unethical; • you use participants under the age of 16.

Method: Question   Go online

Q2: Read the following example Method, then use the marking guidelines to allocate marks.

The study was conducted using surveys; this is a non-experimental method of investigation. This method was chosen because it enables quick and cheap collection of large amount of information. Then, correlation was used to analyse the data. It was chosen because it allows the examination of relationships between variables.[1]

The researchers used a repeated measures design in which all participants took part in the conditions of both co-variables. This type of a design was chosen because it made possible for the researchers not to use as many participants and because the individual differences of participants do not have such an effect on the results.

The two co-variables were ratings of animals' appearance and participants' fear. Animals' appearance was assessed by participants on the questionnaire no 1 (Appendix 4), on a three point rating scale, from "not ugly" to "very ugly" via "quite ugly". The participants' fear was assessed on the questionnaire no 2 (Appendix 5), on a three point rating scale, from "not harmful" to "very harmful" via "quite harmful".

All participants were given the same standardised instructions (Appendix 1), which enabled the researchers to treat them in the same way and to avoid the participants being influenced by the researcher's behaviour (Eysenck, 2002). However, the investigation was conducted in two different rooms, which meant that there were two different conditions. The researchers controlled extraneous variables such as room size, light and temperature. The possible confounding variables were participants' mood and their stress level, as well as the noise level of the room.[2]

Materials

Several materials were used for the investigation. These included:

- the standardised instructions (Appendix 1);
- the brief (Appendix 2);
- the consent form (Appendix 3);
- the questionnaire no 1 (Appendix 4);
- the questionnaire no 2 (Appendix 5);
- the debrief (Appendix 6) and pens.

Sample

25 participants took part in the research. All of them were at least 16 years old. There were 11 females and 14 males. 14 participants (11 females and 3 males) were Access to Social Sciences students. These participants might not be naive to the research. The remaining participants were naive to the research. The participants were selected through opportunity sampling from the target population of North East Scotland College students in Fraserburgh Campus. This method of sampling was chosen because it is a quick and convenient method of obtaining participants.

Procedure

There were two groups of participants. The first of them consisted of 11 females and 3 males, the second of 11 males. Each of these groups was tested in a different small room during the afternoon. The researchers followed the standardised instructions (Appendix 1)[3] in their investigation. All participants were welcomed by the researchers and asked to sit down.

Then the brief (Appendix 2) was read aloud to them. It explained the aim of the research, the confidentiality of responses and the participants' right to withdraw at any time. The researchers explained the difference between a phobia and a fear, and then asked if the participants had phobias. No one stated that they had. Then, the consent forms (Appendix 3) were distributed to all participants. The form was read aloud by the researcher, who asked the participants to sign it, if they agree to take part in the investigation.

Next, the participants were given the questionnaire no 1 (Appendix 4) face down. Then, they were asked to turn it over and start filling it in. When the researcher saw that all participants had completed the questionnaire no 1, the questionnaire no 2 (Appendix 5) was handed over. Then, the participants were asked to fill it. Once all of the participants had filled in that questionnaire, both questionnaires were collected. Next, the debrief (Appendix 6) was read aloud and handed out to all participants. It summarised the purpose of the investigation, reminded the participants that their responses were confidential and that they had the right to withdraw. Finally, the participants were asked if they had any questions and thanked for participating in the research.

Possible marks	Included in example	Actual marks
1 mark for identifying your method and justifying why you have chosen this method, including identification of design (where appropriate).		
1 mark for describing research variables.		
1 mark for describing extraneous / confounding / controlled variables.		
1 mark for identifying the sampling method you have chosen, with a justification for your choice; and a description of your participants.		
1 mark for identifying the materials you used, as well as where these can be found in appendices (to allow for replication).		
1 mark for fully describing your procedure .		

Total marks for Method section: /6

6.4.3   Results

Firstly, explain how you have analysed your raw (unanalysed) data. You will have used measures of central tendency (mean, median, mode - all three, or just those that are best for the data you have collected). State which measures you have used, and why you have used them.

Secondly, include a summary table that contains the measures you have described above. Always have a sentence or two explaining what the reader of the report should notice about the measures in the table.

Then, include any graphs or charts that you have used to describe your data, e.g. bar chart, pie chart, line graph, scattergraph, etc. Again, this graph or chart should never stand alone: it must be accompanied by a sentence or two explaining to the reader what is noticeable about the data contained within. Charts must have a title, the x and y axes labelled, and a legend, if required, in order to gain full credit.

Finally, provide the main results again, and say whether or not they suggest that you can reject the null hypothesis, or not.

Find marking guidelines for this section below.

Overview of marking	Mark range	Marking instructions
Interpreting and presenting data/results in an appropriate format	0-6	The **6 marks** are awarded in the following way. • *2 mark* for justifying your choice of statistical procedure(s); • *1 mark* for accurately carrying out appropriate statistical procedures, as demonstrated in your calculations (which must be included in appendices); • *2mark*marks for presenting your data in an appropriate format(s). To gain full marks, a table and graph must be included, with appropriate title and accurate labels and legend (if appropriate). These must provide enough information to enable interpretation; • *1 mark* for an accurate statement on whether the results support or refute your hypothesis.

Results: Question   Go online

Q3: Read the following example Results, then use the marking guidelines to allocate marks.

Descriptive statistics were used to analyse results. Measures of central tendency such as mean, median, and mode, were calculated. The mean was used as the most accurate measure of central tendency because it takes into account all the values of the data. However, it is easily affected by extreme scores. For that reason the median was used as it is less affected by extreme scores. Additionally, the mode was used because it shows what the most occurring values were.

Summary table

As can be seen from the table below, the lowest mean score was for acoustic encoding, although the medians were the same for each condition.

	Iconic	Acoustic	Semantic
Mean	2.2	1.5	2.1
Median	2	2	2
Mode	1 and 4	0 and 3	0 and 3

Measures of central tendency

Graph

The bar chart below displays visually the results.

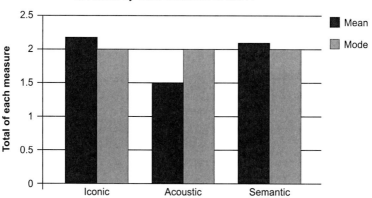

Measures of central tendency and standard deviation by each condition of the IV

Conditions of the IV

The results do not support the experimental hypothesis that the participants will remember more words which are semantically processed (mean = 2.1) than those processed visually (mean = 2.2) and acoustically (mean = 1.5). The results show that more words were remembered in the iconic condition than in the other two conditions. Therefore, the null hypothesis for this study, *the level of processing will have no effect on recall and any difference in results is due to chance alone*, could not be rejected.

Possible marks	Included in example	Actual marks
2 marks for justifying your choice of statistical procedure(s).		
1 mark for accurately carrying out appropriate statistical procedures, as demonstrated in your calculations (which must be included in appendices).		
2 marks for presenting your data in an appropriate format(s). To gain full marks, a table and graph must be included, with appropriate title and accurate labels and legend (if appropriate). These must provide enough information to enable interpretation.		
1 mark for an accurate statement on whether the results support or refute your hypothesis.		

Total marks for Results section: /6

6.4.4 Discussion

Firstly, give your statistical results again, and what they infer for the null hypothesis. This may seem a bit repetitive, but research reports are not meant to be read from beginning to end. They tend to be read in sections, hence the repetition.

The next paragraph will analyse your results in relation to those that you described in the Introduction section of your report. Don't bring in any new research here. Do your results concur with your background studies? Are there differences? Why might this be? Is your sample different, your procedures, etc?

Then, you evaluate your own procedures, giving the strengths and weaknesses. This is so that researchers who come after you can learn from what went well, and what didn't - this way, science progresses. For each weakness, provide suggestions as to how they may be overcome.

You will gain credit for providing generic weaknesses (e.g. opportunity sampling is biased and cannot be generalised from, field experiments have ecological validity, etc.) but more marks will be gained for also including strengths and weaknesses specific to your own procedures. What went wrong (if anything)? What could be improved on? What went particularly well, that should be used again if the study were to be repeated?

Now, you suggest real world applications of your research: can it be used to improve study techniques, can it be used to help relieve stress, improve memory, etc. And/or an idea may have occurred to you about further research that could be conducted in a similar area.

The Discussion section should end with a conclusion, which restates your statistical results, their implications for the null hypothesis, and a brief statement stating what can be concluded from this about behaviour.

Find marking guidelines for this section below.

Overview of marking	Mark range	Marking instructions
Relevant points of analysis You are expected to provide an analysis of your results in relation to relevant psychological theories and/or concepts and previous research referred to in the introduction to your report. Analysis requires you to identify parts, the relationship between them, and their relationships with the whole. Analysis can involve drawing out and relating implications and drawing conclusions.	0-8	*Up to 8 marks* can be awarded in a variety of ways for the analysis of results. One mark can be awarded for each relevant analytical point made anywhere within the discussion section of the report. A point of analysis could be made by identifying features of the results and: • *1 mark* for explaining the ways in which they confirm or refute the research hypothesis, or are inconclusive; • *1 mark* for explaining relationships between research variables; • *1 mark* for explaining the possible effect of variables other than the research variables; • *1 mark* for explaining the ways in which your results are the same or different from other research results; • *1 mark* for explaining the relationship between your own research results and the results of previous research; • *1 mark* for drawing out and relating the implications of your own research findings in terms of further research or real world applications; • *1 mark* for drawing conclusions about points of analysis; • *1 mark* for giving any other acceptable response.

(the above table continues on the next page)

Overview of marking	Mark range	Marking instructions
Relevant points of evaluation You are expected to evaluate your chosen research method. To evaluate, you must make a judgement based on criteria or determine the value of something. This could involve making a judgement about the research method and design used, or sampling method and participant group chosen.	0-4	*Up to 4 marks* can be awarded in a variety of ways for evaluation of the method used for your own research. One mark can be awarded for each relevant point of evaluation that includes evidence of a reason for the judgement. Evaluation must be specific to your own research study and supporting reasons must be given for evaluative points made, e.g. "this is unreliable because...", or "this is a strength because...". A point of evaluation could include making a judgement about: • *1 mark* for the method, design and ethics of the research; • *1 mark* for extraneous variables that should have been controlled; • *1 mark* for ecological validity; • *1 mark* for participant bias; • *1 mark* for similarities/differences to methodologies used in background research; • *1 mark* for the data collected; • *1 mark* for any other relevant information.

Discussion: Question   Go online

Q4: Read the following example Discussion, then use the marking guidelines to allocate marks.

The mean results were 2.1 for the semantic condition, 2.2 for the iconic condition and 1.5 for the acoustic condition, which showed that more words were remembered in the iconic condition than in the other two conditions. This indicated that the null hypothesis for this study, *the level of processing will have no effect on recall and any difference in results are due to chance alone*, could not be rejected. Therefore, the findings did not support the Levels of Processing theory proposed by Craig and Lockhart, who suggested that information is remembered best when it is processed semantically.

The advantage of the research was that ethical issues were addressed properly. The participants were given an informed consent, which clarified their right to withdraw from the experiment at any time and ensured them that the information they provided would be treated confidentially. Moreover, the participants were briefed prior the experiment and debriefed afterwards. They were explained that the experiment was not an intelligence test and that it should not affect them in any way. Finally, they were given the phone number that would enable them to contact X in case they wished to discuss the experiment.

The limitation of the study was the sample that was used. The participants were selected by means of opportunity sampling, which is an unrepresentative method. As a result, the sample used was not representative of the target population of the members of Y. A way of improving this would be selecting participants by means of random sampling, which gives all members of the population the opportunity to take part in the research (Keegan, 2008). However, due to the 1998 Data Protection Act, it would be impossible to access the data of the members of the college and to use random sampling. Additionally, the sample was small, which is a problem because the results could be affected by individual differences such as good memory strategies developed by some people. The way of improving that could be to use a larger sample which would be more representative and that would enable to control for individual differences. Moreover, some participants were psychology students and they might have insight into the aims of the research, which might have resulted in demand characteristics. This could be improved by not having psychology students in the future.

Another advantage of the study was that it was a laboratory experiment, which is easy to replicate due to the use of standardised instructions. However, the disadvantage of a laboratory experiment is low ecological validity because it does not show how we memory is used in everyday life. A way of improving that would be using another method that has high ecological validity in the future, such as an observational study or field experiment.

The researchers used repeated measures design, in which the same participant took part in all experimental conditions. The advantage of the design was that participants' individual differences did not affect results for different conditions of the IV. However, the results could be affected by order effects, such as fatigue or boredom. The way to overcome the order effect would be to use matched pairs design in the future (Hill, 2009).

The weakness of the research was the room in which the experiment took place. There were dots on the walls, which might have a negative impact on the participants' ability to concentrate and might have affected the results of the experiment. Additionally, the high level of noise in the room might have led to the participants' difficulties with concentrating on the experimental tasks. A way of improving that in the future would be conducting the experiment in a room with thick walls and without dots on them.

Another weakness of the experiment was the very short time that was given to the participants to carry out the tasks. It might be argued that the participants might have recalled more words if they were given more time. This might be improved in future by allocating at least two minutes instead of only one minute for the test and tor the recall part of the experiment.

The implications of this study could be applied to real life situations such as strategies for revising. For example, it might be suggested that using colour and capital letters in revision notes might help to enhance attention and, as a result, aid the memorisation of key words and phrases.

A future experiment that might be conducted, in order to further explore the results of the experiment, could investigate whether the age of the participants is a determining factor in the recall of the information. This might have enable the researcher to verify the common sense belief that the older you are the more difficult it is to learn new things.

Conclusion

The mean results were 2.1 for the semantic condition, 2.2 for the iconic condition and 1.5 for the acoustic condition, which did not support the experimental hypothesis that *the participants will remember more words which are semantically processed than those processed visually and acoustically*. On the contrary, the results showed that more words were remembered in the iconic condition than in the other two conditions. This indicated that the null hypothesis for this study, *the level of processing will have no effect on recall and any difference in results is due to chance alone*, could not be rejected.

Note: this section is a bit trickier to mark, as you have to make value judgements as to whether the criteria have been met, or not. Have a go, anyway.

Possible marks	Included in example	Actual marks
1 mark for explaining the ways in which they confirm or refute the research hypothesis, or are inconclusive.		
1 mark for explaining relationships between research variables.		
1 mark for explaining the possible effect of variables other than the research variables.		
1 mark for explaining the ways in which your results are the same or different from other research results.		
1 mark for explaining the relationship between your own research results and the results of previous research.		
1 mark for drawing out and relating the implications of your own research findings in terms of further research or real world applications.		
1 mark for drawing conclusions about points of analysis.		
1 mark for giving any other acceptable response.		
1 mark can be awarded for each relevant point of evaluation that includes evidence of a reason for the judgement. Evaluate must be specific to your own research study and supporting reasons must be given for evaluative points made, e.g. "this is unreliable because...", or "this is a strength because...".		

Total marks for Discussion section: /12

6.4.5   References, presentation and style

Marks are also allocated for having used a standard referencing style (e.g. Harvard), the presentation of your report (sections under correct headings, title page, contents page, etc, all appropriate information under headings present and accurate, etc.) and style (always writing in 3rd person - no "we", "I", "our", no "prove", "significant results" etc.). Also for having appendices that include all materials.

Find below the marking instructions for presentation, style and references. There may be only two marks up for grabs, but this may make the way in which marks are allocated. There may be only four marks up for grabs, but this may make a difference between and A and B grade, or a pass or fail.

Overview of marking	Mark range	Marking instructions
Appropriate presentation and style	0-4	The **2 marks** are awarded in the following way • You must present your research in the style and format of a psychological research report. • The whole report must be organised correctly, include a title, and all sections must be in the correct order, with all appropriate information in the correct section. You must also use appropriate terminology and the correct tense throughout. • Your references must be organised in such a way as to enable a third party to locate the information.

Marking guidelines can also be found at http://www.sqa.org.uk/

Many thanks to Malgorzata Kasprzyk for allowing us to use her Research Investigation.

6.5   Learning points

┌ Summary ┐

• The research process in psychology can be evaluated by using research skills to generate, select, organise, interpret, analyse and evaluate information.

• Communication skills can be used to present information, including a report on psychological research.

Unit 1 Topic 7

Research test

The following is a reminder of what you need to know to be able to complete the assessment for this area of study:

- explain the stages in the research process in psychology;

- evaluate one experimental and one non-experimental method;

- evaluate one sampling method;

- calculate the mean, median and mode;

- apply a relevant research method to a scenario;

- explain an ethical issue relevant to a piece of research.

Research test   Go online

Q1:   Explain the stages in the research process in psychology. *(16 marks)*
In order to get maximum credit for this answer, do the following:

- name each stage;
- give a brief explanation of each stage;
- explain how each stage informs the next.

. . . .

Read the following research scenario and answer the questions that follow.

Researchers thought that students would work best when given some choice over the methods employed by their teachers. Students were selected based on who was available in the social area of the school at the time of the study and were allocated to one of two conditions. One was teacher-centred: in this condition, student participants had no choice over which topics were taught or how they were taught. The other condition was student-centred: in this condition, students could decide which topics to cover, choose who they wanted to work with and devise their own homework schedules. End-of-term results were collected to see if there was a difference between the two conditions. Each participant sat the same exam, scored out of 100.

Condition 1 Teacher-centred methods (/100)	Condition 2 Student-centred methods (/100)
78	65
32	65
42	78
53	86
32	87
78	97
98	67
67	75
87	57
67	88

Q2: Explain and evaluate the research method used in the above scenario. *(6 marks)*

To maximise your marks, include the following:

- name the research method;
- explain each of the key features of the method;
- provide strengths and weaknesses of the method.

....

Q3: Name and evaluate the sampling method used in the scenario. *(3 marks)*

....

Q4: Name and explain an ethical issue that can be found in the BPS Code of Conduct (2009). *(2 marks)*

....

Q5: Calculate the mean, median and mode for the two sets of data given. Remember to show your workings. *(6 marks)*

The researchers also wanted to find out the opinions of students on the different approaches to teaching/learning so they carried out a survey using a questionnaire.

Q6: Evaluate the survey method of research. *(5 marks)*

Unit 2: Individual Behaviour

Unit 2 Topic 1

Sleep and dreams (mandatory topic)

Contents

Learning objective

By the end of this area of study, you should be able to describe, explain, evaluate, apply and analyse:

- biological processes relating to sleep and dreams, which must include:
    - the role of the brain in sleep
    - circadian rhythms
    - non-REM and REM sleep and dreaming
    - Oswald's (1966) Restoration theory of sleep
    - the aims, methods, results and conclusions of Dement & Kleitman's (1957) study of the relation of eye movements during sleep to dream activity.

- cognitive processes relating to sleep and dreams, which must include:
    - sleep to facilitate information processing
    - Crick and Mitchison's (1986) reorganisational theory of dreaming
    - The aim, methods, results and conclusions of Czeisler et al's (1990) study of exposure to bright light and darkness for shift work.

- psychodynamic processes relating to sleep and dreams, which must include:
    - conscious and unconscious processes
    - manifest and latent content of dreams
    - defence mechanisms

- factors affecting sleep, which must include:
    - impact of drugs
    - impact of light

1.1 Introduction

The Individual Behaviour area of study contains the mandatory content:

* "Sleep and dreams"

... and the three other topics from which you and your lecturer will choose one to study:

* Depression

* Memory

* Stress

You are advised to discuss your choice of topic with your teacher or lecturer to make sure that the combination is complementary.

You will find a timeline below of the significant events in the development of psychology as a field of study, followed by an overview of some of the debates within the subject. Please note that the history of psychology is not examinable, but is presented for the sake of putting the contents of the subsequent topics into context.

Applications

One way in which students can help explain and analyse human behaviour is to try to apply knowledge gained from psychology to our behaviour.

For example, in regard to stress (one of the optional topics of study for this area of study), many psychologists have informed us why we become stressed (work, redundancy, not passing your Higher Psychology exam, etc.). If they can inform us why we become stressed and the effect(s) this might have on our mind and body, they can sometimes tell us how to help reduce or eliminate these effects.

Cognitive psychology suggests that a person who is stressed may suffer from disorganised thoughts, lack of self-esteem or disruptive speech patterns. They may recommend various therapies, such as cognitive behavioural therapy (CBT). This moderates our thinking to become more positive.

In this way, no matter the variety of psychologist or the area looked at, psychology and its various areas of study can identify problems and suggest solutions which are normally based on some kind of evidence.

Students are therefore **strongly** recommended to research several applications of each theory.

1.2 Psychology time-line

The list below is a small 'snap-shot' of the beginnings of psychology. It demonstrates that a lot has happened in a relatively short time. This progress has aided psychology in the understanding of human beings in many ways, but it is dependent on many disciplines other than psychology, including the advancement of medicine (drugs, DNA), engineering (PET scans), society (AIDS) and many more examples.

Year	Event
1878	*G. Stanley Hall* becomes the first American to earn a Ph.D. in psychology. Hall eventually founds the American Psychological Association.
1879	*Wilhelm Wundt* founds the first experimental psychology lab in Leipzig, Germany. The event is considered the starting point of psychology as a separate science.
1881	*Wundt* forms the professional journal Philosophische Studien (Philosophical Studies).
1883	*G. Stanley Hall* opens the first experimental psychology lab in the United States at John Hopkins University.
1885	*Herman Ebbinghaus* published his famous Über das Gedächtnis ("On Memory"), which was later translated to English as "Memory. A Contribution to Experimental Psychology". In the work, he describes his learning and memory experiments that he conducted on himself.
1886	*Sigmund Freud* begins providing therapy to patients in Vienna, Austria. *Joseph Jastrow*, a student of G. Stanley Hall at Johns Hopkins University, receives the first doctorate in psychology. He later becomes professor of psychology at the University of Wisconsin and serves as president of the American Psychological Association in 1900.
1888	*James McKeen Cattell* becomes the first professor of psychology at the University of Pennsylvania.
1890	*James McKeen Cattell* publishes "Mental Tests and Measurements", marking the beginning of the practice of psychological assessment. *William James* publishes "Principles of Psychology". *Sir Francis Galton* creates correlation technique to better understand relationships between variable in intelligence studies.
1892	*G. Stanley Hall* forms the American Psychological Association (APA), which initially has just 42 members. *Wundt's* student Edward B. Titchener moves to America.
1894	*Margaret Floy Washburn* completes her training under Tichener.

1895	Edward Thorndike develops the Law of Effect.
1896	Functionalism, an early school of psychology, focuses on the acts and functions of the mind rather than its internal contents. Its most prominent American advocates are William James and John Dewey, whose 1896 article "The Reflex Arc Concept in Psychology" promotes Functionalism. The founder of psychoanalysis, Sigmund Freud, introduces the term in a scholarly paper. Freud's psychoanalytic theory asserts that people are motivated by powerful, unconscious drives and conflicts. He develops an influential therapy based on this assertion, using free association and dream analysis. Edward B. Titchener, a leading proponent of structuralism, publishes his Outline of Psychology. Structuralism is the view that all mental experience can be understood as a combination of simple elements or events. This approach focuses on the contents of the mind, contrasting with functionalism. After heading a laboratory at University of Pennsylvania, Lightner Witmer opens the world's first psychological clinic to patients, shifting his focus from experimental work to practical application of his findings.
1900	Sigmund Freud publishes "Interpretation of Dreams".
1901	The British Psychological Society is formed. With publication of the Manual of Experimental Psychology, Edward Bradford Titchener introduces structuralism to the United States. Structuralism, an approach which seeks to identify the basic elements of consciousness, fades after Titchener's death in 1927.
1904	Mary Calkins is elected as the first female president of the APA. Calkins, a professor and researcher at Wellesley College, studied with William James at Harvard University, but Harvard denied her a Ph.D. because of her gender.
1905	Alfred Binet publishes the intelligence test "New Methods for the Diagnosis of the Intellectual Level of Subnormals". Alfred Binet and Theodore Simon develop a scale of general intelligenceon the basis of mental age. Later researchers refine this work into the concept of intelligence quotient (IQ); mental age over physical age. From their beginning, the accuracy and fairness of such tests are challenged.
1906	Ivan Pavlov publishes his findings on classical conditioning. Morton Prince founds the Journal of Abnormal Psychology.
1907	Carl Jung publishes "The Psychology of Dementia Praecox".
1908	Clifford Beers publishes "A Mind That Found Itself", detailing his experiences as a patient in 19th-century mental asylums. Calling for more humane treatment of patients and better education about mental illness for the general population, the book inspires the mental hygiene movement in the United States.
1909	Calkins publishes "A First Book in Psychology". Sigmund Freud and Carl Jung visit the United States for a Psychoanalysis Symposium at Clark University organised by G. Stanley Hall. At the symposium, Freud gives his only speech in the United States.

1912	*Edward Thorndike* publishes "Animal Intelligence". The article leads to the development of the theory of operant conditioning. *Max Wertheimer* publishes "Experimental Studies of the Perception of Movement", leading to the development of Gestalt Psychology.
1913	*Carl Jung* begins to depart from Freudian views and develops his own theories, which are eventually known as analytical psychology. *John B. Watson* publishes "Psychology as the Behaviourist Views It". The work helps establish behaviourism, which views human behaviour arising from conditioned responses. In contrast to psychoanalysis, behaviourism focuses on observable and measurable behaviour.
1915	*Sigmund Freud* publishes work on repression.
1917	Then president of the APA, *Robert Yerkes*, writes the Alpha and Beta Tests for the Army to test intelligence. Standardised intelligence and aptitude tests are administered to two million U. S. soldiers during WWI. Soon after, such tests are used in all U.S. armed forces branches and in many areas of civilian life, including academic and work settings.
1919	*John B. Watson* publishes Psychology, From the Standpoint of a Behaviourist.
1920	*Watson and Rosalie Rayner* publish research the classical conditioning of fear with their subject, Little Albert. Swiss psychologist *Jean Piaget* publishes "The Child's Conception of the World", prompting the study of cognition in the developing child. *Francis Cecil Sumner* is the first African American to earn a Ph.D. in psychology under G. Stanley Hall at Clark University. Sumner later serves as chair of the Howard University psychology department.
1921	Swiss psychiatrist *Hermann Rorschach* devises a personality test based on patients' interpretations of inkblots.
1925	Gestalt Psychology is brought to America with the publication of *Wolfgang Kohler's* "Perception: An Introduction to the Gestalt Theory."
1929	Psychiatrist *Hans Berger* invents the electroencephalogram and tests it on his son. The device graphs the electrical activity of the brain by means of electrodes attached to the head.
1932	*Jean Piaget* becomes the foremost cognitive theorist with the publication of his work "The Moral Judgment of Children".
1933	After the Nazi party gains control of the government in Germany, scholars and researchers in psychology and psychiatry are persecuted. Many, including Freud, whose books are banned and burned in public rallies, move to Britain or the United States.
1935	*Henry Murray* publishes the Thematic Appreception Test (TAT). Alcoholics Anonymous (AA) is founded by *Bob Smith* of Akron, Ohio. AA's group meetings format and 12-step programme has become the model for many other mutual-support therapeutic groups. *Kurt Koffka*, a founder of the Gestalt movement, publishes "Principles of Gestalt Psychology". Gestalt (German for "whole" or "essence") psychology asserts that psychological phenomena must be viewed not as individual elements but as a coherent whole.

1936	*Walter Freeman* performs the first frontal lobotomy in the United States at George Washington University in Washington, D.C. By 1951, more than 18,000 such operations have been performed. The procedure, intended to relieve severe and debilitating psychosis, is controversial.
1937	Psychologist *Karen Horney* publishes "The Neurotic Personality of Our Time". Horney goes on to challenge many of Freud's theories, as have many later psychologists and scholars. Specifically, she questions Freud's theories on the Oedipal Complex and castration anxiety.
1938	*B.F. Skinner* publishes "The Behaviour of Organisms", introducing the concept of operant conditioning. The work draws widespread attention to behaviourism and inspires laboratory research on conditioning. Italian psychiatrist and neuro-pathologist *Ugo Cerletti* and his associates treat human patients with electrical shocks to alleviate schizophrenia and psychosis. Electroconvulsive therapy (ECT), while controversial, is proven effective in some cases and was still in use in 2001.
1942	*Carl Rogers* developed client-cantered therapy and publishes "Counselling and Psychotherapy". His approach encourages respect and positive regard for patients.
1946	*Anna Freud* publishes "The Psychoanalytic Treatment of Children", introducing basic concepts in the theory and practice of child psychoanalysis.
1951	Studies are published, reporting that the drug imipramine may be able to lessen depression. Eight years later, the FDA approves its use in the United States under the name Tofranil.
1952	"The Diagnostic and Statistical Manual of Mental Disorders" is published. The anti-psychotic drug chlorpromazine (known as *Thorazine*) is tested on a patient in a Paris military hospital. Approved for use in the United States in 1954, it becomes widely prescribed.
1954	*Abraham Maslow* publishes "Motivation and Personality", describing his theory of a hierarchy of needs. He also helps found humanistic psychology. In "Epilepsy and the Functional Anatomy of the Human Brain", neurosurgeon *Wilder G. Penfield* publishes results from his study of the neurology of epilepsy. His mapping of the brain's cortex sets a precedent for the brain-imaging techniques that become critical to biopsychology and cognitive neuroscience. Social Psychologist *Gordon Allport* publishes "The Nature of Prejudice", which draws on various approaches in psychology to examine prejudice through different lenses. It is widely read by the general public and influential in establishing psychology's usefulness in understanding social issues.
1956	Inspired by work in mathematics and other disciplines, psychologists begin to focus on cognitive states and processes. *George A. Miller's* article "The Magical Number Seven, Plus or Minus Two" on information processing is an early application of the cognitive approach.
1957	*Noam Chomsky* publishes "Syntactic Structures", marking a major advancement in the study of linguistics. The book helps spawn the field of psycholinguistics, the psychology of language.

1958	*Harry Harlow* publishes "The Nature of Love", which describe his experiments with rhesus monkeys on the importance of attachment and love.
1961	*Albert Bandura* conducts his now famous Bobo doll experiment.
1963	*Albert Bandura* first describes the concept of observational learning to explain personality development.
1973	After intense debate, the American Psychiatric Association removes homosexuality from the Diagnostic and Statistical Manual of Mental Disorders (DSM). The widely used reference manual is revised to state that sexual orientation "does not necessarily constitute a psychiatric disorder."
1974	*Stanley Milgram* publishes "Obedience to Authority", which presented the findings of his famous obedience experiments. A new brain scanning technique, Positron Emission Tomography (PET), is tested. By tracing chemical markers, PET maps brain function in more detail than earlier techniques.
1976	*Richard Dawkins* publishes "The Selfish Gene", which begins to popularise the idea of evolutionary psychology in which knowledge and principles from evolutionary biology are applied to research on the structure and function of the human brain. It offers new ways of looking at social phenomena such as aggression and sexual behaviour.
1980	The DSM-III is published.
1981	The epidemic of acquired immunodeficiency syndrome (AIDS) and human immunodeficiency virus (HIV) infection presents mental health professionals with challenges ranging from at-risk patients' anxiety and depression to AIDS-related dementia.
1990	*Noam Chomsky* publishes "On Nature, Use and Acquisition of Language". In "Acts of Meaning, Four Lectures on Mind and Culture", *Jerome Bruner* helps formulate cultural psychology, an approach drawing on philosophy, linguistics, and anthropology. Refined and expanded by Hazel Markus and other researchers, cultural psychology focuses on the influences and relationship among mind, cultural community and behaviour.
1991	*Steven Pinker* publishes an article in Science introducing his theory of how children acquire language, which he later details further in his book "The Language Instinct".
1994	The DSM-IV is published.
2000	Genetic researchers finish mapping human genes. Scientists hope to one day, isolate the individual genes responsible for different diseases. Sixteen public research institutions around the world complete a "working draft" mapping of the human genetic code, providing a research basis for a new understanding of human development and disease. A similar, privately funded, project is currently underway. The latest revision of the Diagnostic Statistical Manual of Mental Disorders (DSM) is published in a version for personal digital assistants (PDAs). The manual, first published in 1954, outlines prevalence, diagnosis, and treatment of mental disorders. Only 132 pages on first printing, by 2000 it was 980.
2002	*Steven Pinker* publishes "The Blank Slate", arguing against the concept of tabula rasa.

1.3   Biological processes relating to sleep and dreams

This section provides an introduction to sleep in terms of the nightly sleep cycle, the functions and theories of sleep, including dreams, and sleep disorders such as insomnia.

Stages in the sleep cycle

Stage 1

The sleep cycle begins and is relatively light. The brain produces alpha waves (slow). This is the first 5 - 10 minutes of sleep where the sleeper will usually report not being asleep if awoken.

Alpha waves

Stage 2

Approximately 20 minutes into sleep, the brain begins producing rapid, rhythmic bursts of brain waves (sleep spindles). This stage also involves light sleep, during which the brain produces theta waves. Generally, there is a decrease in body temperature and a decrease in heart rate.

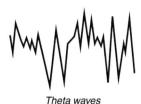

Theta waves

Stage 3

Approximately 30 minutes into sleep, deep, slow brain waves (delta waves) emerge. These are much slower than beta and alpha waves, hence this stage is referred to as slow wave sleep (SWS). The person would be very difficult to wake.

Delta waves

Stage 4

A period of very deep sleep which lasts 30 minutes. Bed-wetting and sleepwalking can occur at the end of this stage.

Stage 5

This stage is known as 'paradoxical' sleep because the brain is very much active and accompanied by rapid eye movement (REM). However, the body is paralysed. EEGs show a mixture of brain waves.

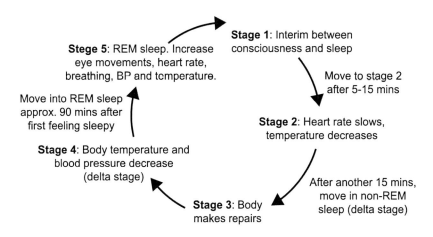

Stege 5: REM sleep. Increase eye movements, heart rate, breathing, BP and tcmperature.

Stage 1: Interim between consciousness and sleep

Move into REM sleep approx. 90 mins after first feeling sleepy

Move to stage 2 after 5-15 mins

Stage 2: Heart rate slows, temperature decreases

Stage 4: Body temperature and blood pressure decrease (delta stage)

After another 15 mins, move in non-REM sleep (delta stage)

Stage 3: Body makes repairs

Stages in the sleep cycle

A typical night's sleep takes you from stage 1 to 5, then back to 2, and finally into REM. This whole cycle (ultradian rhythm) then repeats itself three or four more times during the night, each cycle lasting about 90 minutes, which means we typically get 7.5 hours or more sleep per night (all being well). With each subsequent cycle, more and more time is spent in REM sleep and less time in SWS.

Top tip

This sleep cycle could be made very nicely into a mindmap of your own, with added pictures to give you more chances to store and retrieve information when you need it (e.g., at exam time).

The nightly sleep cycle is illustrated as follows.

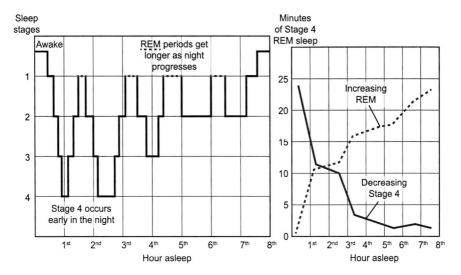

Graphs of the nightly sleep cycle

1.4   REM and non-REM sleep and dreaming

This section provides an introduction to REM and non-REM sleep.

1.4.1   REM sleep

The brain is very active at night. This is the period when most dreams occur. Eyes dart around; breathing rate and blood pressure vary widely. Limbs are paralysed, because a control region in the brain stem sends signals to shut off neurons in the spinal cord, preventing us from acting out our dreams.

The first researchers to investigate the different stages of sleep and demonstrate a link between REM sleep and dreaming were Dement and Kleitman in 1957 in their study *The relation of eye movements in sleep to dream activity*.

In order to prepare yourselves for learning this study, which is compulsory for this topic, you may wish to access some online videos of people sleeping, noting the times and frequency of REM throughout a short section of the sleep cycle.

Exam questions on key studies can ask you about the aims, hypotheses, method, results, conclusion and evaluation so the presentation of research studies are structures in the same way in this course.

Research by Dement and Kleitman

Aim
The aim of the research was to find out if there was any kind of relationship between REM sleep and dreaming. REM is a stage in the cycle of sleep where the eyeballs can be seen to move rapidly over the eyelids. The research aimed to be able to objectively measure the stage of sleep where dreaming was taking place by matching it up with a physiological response (REM) during sleep.

Hypotheses
There were a number of different hypotheses:

- that there would be a relationship (correlation) between REM and reports of dreaming;
- the dream itself would link to a particular pattern of eye movement;
- that the duration of the eye movement would match up with the reported duration of the dream.

Method

- Laboratory experiment.
- 9 adult participants.
- Observed sleeping over a number of nights.
- Repeatedly wakened during sleep.
- EEG measurements recorded brain activity and activity round the eyes.
- Participants asked to report if they had been dreaming, and if so, what it was about.

Results

- REM sleep was linked to dreaming in most cases (but not all).
- The patterns of eye movements showed a link with the type of dream which the participant recalled.
- The duration of REM also showed a relationship with the reported duration of the dreams.

Conclusion
The report concludes that "It seems reasonable to conclude that an objective measurement of dreaming may be accomplished by recording REM during sleep. ... It thus became possible to objectively study the effect on dreaming of environmental changes, psychological stress, drug administration, and a variety of other factors and influences." (Dement and Kleitman, 1957, p. 346, in Higher Psychology Course Support Notes, SQA).

Evaluation

However, although there does appear to be a relationship between REM sleep and dreaming, this was not found in all cases, but Dement and Kleitman do not say why this may be. Also, there is the problem of ecological validity. How often do you go to sleep in a laboratory with EEG electrodes attached to your skull? Do you think you would get a good night's sleep?

Other research conducted in more natural settings do seem to confirm Dement and Kleitman's finding that dreaming is linked with REM sleep. Furthermore, research such as Dement and Kleitman's has allowed other psychologists to study the link between sleep and dreams, and what the purpose of them may be (e.g. Oswald's 1980 study into the restorative purpose of sleep).

1.4.2 Non-REM sleep

Non-REM sleep is any sleep that is not REM sleep, and consists of three separate stages:

1. *Light sleep* —half awake, half asleep. Eyes are closed but the person can be easily wakened. Some experience muscle contractions (hynagogic jerks).

2. *True sleep* —breathing becomes regular. Body temperature and heart rate decrease as the body prepares to enter deep sleep. This stage covers about half of adult sleep.

3. *Deep sleep* —the sleeper is unresponsive to the outside environment and is unaware of any sounds or other stimuli. Temperature, breathing, heart rate and blood pressure are all at their lowest during stage 3 sleep. Parasomnias (e.g. night terrors, sleep-walking and bed-wetting) take place during this period. If awakened during this stage, a person will feel very groggy and may take up to 30 minutes to 'get going'. Children and young adults tend to have more stage 3 sleep than adults, and the elderly may experience little or no stage 3 sleep at all.

1.5 The role of the brain in sleep

All animals sleep or have periods of sleep-like inactivity, but the exact reasons as to why we sleep still remain mysterious. However, as well as investigating the role of the brain in sleep, we will also look at one biological theory of sleep: Oswald's (1966) Restoration theory, which you must know well.

1.5.1 Circadian rhythms

A circadian rhythm is like a biological clock, genetically programmed to help you attune to night and day. The name circadian comes from the Latin for "around the day". Amongst other things, it is responsible for regulating the inner sleep-wake cycle. Have you experienced jet lag? Did it interfere with your sleep-wake cycle? If you have, it is because of your circadian rhythm being out of whack!

Resetting the clock in spring and autumn, and accidents can also upset our circadian rhythm. This is due to the hormone, melatonin, which is secreted by the pineal gland (increases in darkness, decreases with light), and is part of the circadian rhythm process.

The circadian cycle is controlled by both internal and external factors:

- internal (biological) factor: endogenous pacemakers (biological clock, the sleep-wake cycle);
- external/environmental cues: exogenous zeitgeber.

1.5.2   Endogenous zeitgebers

The circadian rhythm is the degree to which your body aligns to the cycle of light and darkness that defines a day.

The suprachiasmic nucleus (SCN) is mostly responsible for keeping the circadian rhythms in sync. with nature's rhythm. The circadian rhythm is relatively set at 24 hours by changing light and dark exposure. The SCN cooperates with the pineal gland which releases melatonin, and the hypothalamus, which governs most motivational behaviour.

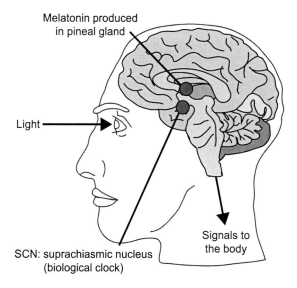

1.5.3   Exogenous pacemakers

Think about the changes that occur in the environment across the different seasons. How do we make adjustments for this?

Our biological clock is reset on a daily basis using cues from the environment, e.g. sunset and sunrise (both being light cues, see below). This process is called entrainment. There are three main zeitgebers:

1. light —which can reset the SCN —Campbell and Murphy (1998) found that if light was shone on the back of participants' knees, their circadian rhythms altered;

2. social cues —such as mealtimes of going to bed at the same time each night;

3. temperature —this is what triggers hibernation in animals.

Can you think of ways in which our changing society can affect the above zeitgebers?

* Light pollution (more artificial light)

* Less set family mealtimes

* Global warming affecting hibernation cues in animals

A study that was conducted into the effect of exogenous zeitgebers (in this instance, light and dark) on circadian rhythms was conducted by Czeisler et al. in 1990. They describe how, when the sleep-wake cycle falls out of alignment due to shift work, people operate at a far lower level of performance, saying that these effects can be similar to those that occur after drinking too much. This is another mandatory study that you will need to know well.

The biology of sleep and dreams: Research by Czeisler *et al.* (1990)

This study is also compulsory for this mandatory topic.

Aim
To find out whether disturbances in the sleep-wake cycle created by working at night could be prevented by a treatment program of exposure to bright light during the night, and darkness during the day.

Hypothesis
Exposing night workers to treatment involving bright light at night and almost complete darkness during the day will prevent disturbances to circadian rhythms involving the sleep-wake cycle.

Method

* Czeisler and his colleagues applied this treatment to eight young men who worked at night.

* There were five control and five treatment studies conducted in all.

* In the control conditions, participants undertook sedentary (seated) work at night and in ordinary daylight.

* In the experimental condition, participants were exposed to bright light at night and nearly complete darkness during the day.

* The core body temperature of participants (which falls during sleep) was recorded continuously over the course of the research.

* Participants asked to report if they had been dreaming, and if so, what it was about.

Results

- The mean temperatures of the control group fell during the night, which would normally happen during sleep.

- The mean temperatures of the treatment group, who had received the bright light/darkness treatment, fell (after four days of treatment) at midday.

In short, the treatment group had successfully adapted their circadian rhythms to the nighttime work schedule, whereas the control group had not. They continued to experience the sleep part of the circadian rhythm at night, when working. Furthermore, the treatment group's circadian adaptation also included shifts in concentration, urinary excretion rate, alertness and cognitive performance.

Conclusion
Czeisler and his team concluded that disturbances in the sleep-wake cycle, including associated declines in alertness, performance and quality of daytime sleep, can be treated effectively with scheduled exposure to bright light at night and darkness during the day.

Evaluation
It used to be believed that humans were relatively insensitive to the effects of light: studies like this have shown that they are, in fact, highly sensitive. Light is the primary synchroniser of the body to the 24 hour day. This study, and others like it, have led to the design of light treatments for night workers, jet travellers and those who experience circadian sleep disorders.

However, although this study illustrates the effect of disturbances to circadian rhythms on behaviour and cognitions, it doesn't tell us how this effect occurs. We still don't understand the exact mechanisms by which light and dark affect us.

Studies like this are expensive and time consuming to run, plus participants may have been adversely affected by having their temperatures taken constantly, which may have affected the validity of the results.

1.5.4   Evidence for the role of the SCN in the sleep-wake cycle

Research, such as that conducted by DeCoursey et al (2000) has found that if the SCN is damaged or removed, sleep-wake cycles are affected.

Folkard (1996) found that if 'mutant' hamsters are bred so they have a circadian rhythm of 20 instead of 24 hours and their SCNs are transplanted into normal hamsters, they will display the 20 hour rhythm.

However, the SCN appears to be the main endogenous pacemaker, but body temperature continues to fluctuate when the SCN is removed, which suggests the existence of another pacemaker.

1.5.5 Activities

Circadian rhythms Go online

Complete the following paragraphs about circadian rhythms using the words listed.

Q1: _____ rhythms have a cycle of about 24 hours, such as the _____. There are five stages of sleep, one of which is _____ sleep. _____ rhythms are those located within the body. The main human exogenous pacemaker is the_____ nucleus. External factors, such as light, _____, clocks, etc., are known as exogenous _____.

Word list: circadian, endogenous, REM, suprachiasmic, zeitgebers.

Suprachismic nucleus Go online

Q2: Complete the following paragraphs about circadian rhythms using the words listed.

_____ rhythms have a cycle of about 24 hours. Rhythms which have a cycle of longer than 24 hours are called _____ rhythms, e.g. the menstrual cycle. Cycles of less than 24 hours are controlled by _____ rhythms, e.g. the 90 minute sleep cycle. There are five stages of sleep, one of which is _____ sleep. Research into ultradian rhythms include the REM and dreaming study by Dement and _____ in 1957.

_____ rhythms are those located within the body. The main human endogenous pacemaker is the _____ nucleus. External factors, such as light, _____, clocks etc., are known as exogenous _____. _____ and sleep deprivation are both examples of sleep disorders associated with disruption of biological rhythms. Effects include deficits in health, task performance and _____.

Word list: circadian, endogenous, infradian, insomnia, Kleitman, memory, REM, suprachiasmic, ultradian, zeitgebers.

....

Q3: Complete the following paragraphs about the suprachiasmic nucleus using the words from the list.

The SCN obtains information about _____ from the optic nerve in the eye: in the morning, there is more light; in the evening, there is less light. The SCN then sends a _____ to the pineal gland.

When there is lots of light, the pineal gland _____ the production of _____ ('sleepy hormone'). When a decrease in light is detected, the pineal gland _____the production of melatonin (usually at night). Melatonin induces sleep by inhibiting brain mechanisms responsible for _____.

The SCN therefore controls the _____ cycle by inhibiting the production of melatonin during the day.

Word list: inhibits, light, melatonin, signal, sleep-wake, stimulates, wakefulness.

Test your knowledge on the biology of sleep and dreams   Go online

Q4:   An example of an endogenous pacemaker is: *(1 mark)*

a) the infradian rhythm.
b) an exogenous zeitgeber.
c) the suprachiasmic nucleus.
d) REM sleep.

. . . .

Q5:   Evidence that contradicts the notion that the SCN is the only pacemaker includes: *(1 mark)*

a) rats die when it is removed.
b) people don't go into REM sleep when it is removed.
c) body temperature continues to fluctuate when it is removed.
d) All of the above.

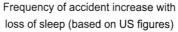

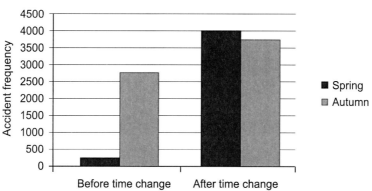

Frequency of accident increase with loss of sleep (based on US figures)

Q6:   Does the frequency of accidents increase or decrease after the clocks change in spring?

a) Increase
b) Decrease

. . . .

Q7:   Does the frequency of accidents increase or decrease after the clocks change in autumn?

a) Increase
b) Decrease

....

Q8: Why might this be?

a) People have reduced sleep quantity after the spring time change, and increased sleep quantity after the autumn time change.
b) People have increased sleep quantity after the spring time change, and decreased sleep quantity after the autumn time change.
c) People suffer more hay fever in spring.
d) People have a reduced need for sleep in spring and an increased need for sleep in autumn.

Q9: Match the terms with their definitions. *(8 marks)*

Sleep efficiency:	types of exogenous zeitgebers.
Ultradian rhythms:	a hormone, derived from serotonin, which plays a role in sleep.
Light and temperature:	a sleep disorder that results in feeling sleepy at all times of the day.
Suprachiasmic nucleus:	a pea-sized organ in the brain that secretes the hormone melatonin.
Melatonin:	daily cycle of biological activity influenced by environmental variation.
Pineal gland:	occur more than once in a 24 hour cycle, including sleep-wake cycle.
Circadian rhythms:	ratio of total sleep time in bed compared with amount of actual sleep.
Insomnia:	part of the brain responsible for our biological clock.

Introduction to sleep and dreams: Dement and Kleitman questions   Go online

Q10: Decide whether each of the following is a strength or a weakness of Dement and Kleitman's study.

Strengths	Weaknesses

Strengths and weaknesses: Ecologically valid studies have confirmed Dement and Kleitman's findings; Has led to the development of other research into the purpose of sleeping and dreaming; Low ecological validity; Some participants dreamt in NREM sleep.

Czeisler *et al* notebook exercise

You will need your psychology notebook for this activity.

Read over the key features of this study again, then complete the table below.

Names of Researchers	Czeisler, C.A., Johnson, M. P., Duffy, J. F., Brown, E. N., Ronda, J. M. and Kronauer, R. E
Aim	
Hypothesis(es)	
Procedure (what they did)	
Results (what they found)	
Conclusion (what do the results imply about human behaviour)	
Evaluation	

Check your understanding of Czeisler *et al* by showing your notebook entry to your teacher or tutor.

1.5.6   The restoration theory (Oswald, 1966)

This theory answers the question, "why do we sleep?" by stating that we sleep because it restores a worn-out body and replenishes vital substances. More specifically, REM sleep is for the restoration of brain substances (e.g. neurotransmitters), and non-REM sleep is for the restoration of body functions.

A study which supports this theory was conducted at the Northwestern University in 2010. This study of elderly patients suffering from insomnia (the inability to maintain "normal" sleep cycles), found that regular aerobic exercise led to faster sleep onset and more time spent asleep, presumably because sleep was required to restore the functions depleted during this exercise.

Another study by Shapiro et al. (1981), which compared marathon and non-marathon runners, found that running long distances increased slow-wave sleep (SWS, or non-REM sleep) and decreased REM sleep on the first two nights after the marathon, which supports Oswald's proposal that this is when the body is repaired.

A study of complete sleep deprivation in rats found that they died within 3 weeks, suggesting that sleep serves a biological purpose and the fact that every animal sleeps for at least two hours suggests some restorative function.

However, the restoration theory is insufficient because mass and metabolism does not correlate as well as the grazing and meat eating distinctions evident in other studies.

Furthermore, Horne and Harley (1988) suggested that the longer sleep associated with exercise is due to the heating of the brain that happens during periods of extended activity, not the wear and tear of the body that it creates. They tested this theory by heating the heads and faces of participants with hairdryers, and 4 out of their 6 participants were found to then have longer periods of slow-wave sleep. This may be because sleep is required to protect the brain from potential damage caused by an overheated brain. Horne also suggests that sleep is not required for the restoration of the body —that can happen during periods of wakeful rest. However, he does suggest that REM sleep is required for the restoration of the brain.

1.6 Cognitive processes relating to sleep and dreams

Sleep to facilitate information processing

Essentially, information processing is what a computer does. In fact, the information processing that we perform in our minds is sometimes compared to the way in which a computer works —this is called a computer analogy. Cognitive psychologists, including those interested in the study of sleep and dreams, will sometimes use a computer analogy to explain sleep as information processing.

There are three main steps involved in information processing in a computer, as follows:

Information processing

All of the above are examples of information processing, which is what a computer does. In fact, the information processing that we perform in our minds is sometimes compared to the way in which a computer works - this is called a computer analogy. There is a branch of computing science devoted entirely to this idea which is called **artificial intelligence**. There are three main steps involved in information processing in a computer as follows.

Input (from the senses in humans)

Information processing:

* perception;
* attention;
* language;
* memory;
* thinking.

Output

One theory of the function of sleep and dreams from an information processing perspective is the information consolidation theory of sleep, which is based on cognitive research. You may have heard of this theory, which suggests that the function of sleep is to process information that has been acquired during the day, so we are better prepared for the day to come.

There is also compelling evidence (e.g. Born and Wilhelm, 2011) that a function of sleep may be to support the formation of long-term memory (one of the cognitive functions identified on the previous page). The idea is that memories are temporarily stored in short-term memory (in a part of the brain called the hippocampus), then gradually get transferred to a long-term memory store, situated in the neocortex, or are forgotten. It is during sleep that this transfer from short-term to long-term memory happens, specifically deep sleep. The implications of this are that without good quality sleep, we would be unable to function properly during the day. If you think about it, we are our memories - they form our consciousness. Without the memory consolidation function that sleep provides, we would not form long-term memories, which would affect our sense of self. Support for this idea stems from a number of sleep deprivation studies demonstrating that a lack of sleep has a serious impact on the ability to recall and remember information.

You will find some examples of sleep deprivation studies here:
http://www.world-of-lucid-dreaming.com/sleep-deprivation.html

1.6.1   Schemas, sleep and dreams

One way in which information may be organised in sleep could be through the development of schemata. A schema is pre-existing mental structure, acquired on the basis of experience. Originally proposed by Bartlett, Piaget suggested that schema is the mechanism by which children develop their understanding of the experiences they learn about and encounter. Once developed, the schema then functions to guide our behaviour in the future. For example, we develop a schema for eating behaviour at a young age, which likely runs a bit like this.

1. You hear someone (mum, dad, brother, sister) shout "dinner time";

2. You (reluctantly?) leave your computer game and go downstairs;

3. You sit at a table, which is laid with plates, cutlery, sauces, etc.

4. Food is brought to the table.

5. You eat the food with a fork, knife, spoon, etc.

6. You fight with your brother/sister/dog.

You may have developed a different schema, which involves plates being on laps and eating in front of the TV. Whichever schema you have developed for eating, it will help you to know what to do, until it becomes automatic.

So far, so good, but now your parents take you to a restaurant. The eating schema you have developed, and which has served you very well up to now, will simply not do in this situation. You need to develop another schema; in the meanwhile, however, you feel insecure, being afraid you will use the wrong fork and/or knife, or spill things over yourself, which wasn't such a big deal at home, but there are stranger here who will judge you!

What schema may you now develop for eating in restaurants? Once this schema has developed, it will guide your behaviour the next time you go to a restaurant. You will expect menus, being greeted by waiting staff, etc.

There is much research evidence (e.g. Durrant et al, 2011) that sleep helps the assimilation of newly formed information, if it is compatible with an existing schema. This would mean that, in the restaurant scenario, you would learn the new information more quickly because you already have a similar schema for eating at home: although there are differences, there are many similarities, too. Durrant et al have found that sleep facilitates the assimilation of new information, probably because neurons associated with the new information triggers the firings of neurons in the related schema.

This happens over and over again, in a loop, during sleep, so the new memory is both strengthened and incorporated into the schema. It happens even faster if there are many layers of overlap between the two (or more) schemas. Of course, this process happens during wakefulness, too, but Durrant's and others' research has shown that it happens more efficiently and quickly during sleep. Short naps of 90 minutes (nREM) after learning something new has the same effect. A good reason for daytime napping!

The evidence for the link between sleep and its function to aid cognitive processes is vast. It also supports the notion, mentioned earlier, that the hippocampus is highly implicated in the processing of memories, particularly long-term memories. It also confirms the importance of slow-wave sleep (deep sleep) to our wellbeing. Case study evidence, like Tripp and Gardner, also confirm the importance of sleep, so supporting evidence can be found in real life as well as in laboratories.

Much of the early research in this area used rats as subjects, which is unethical, and there is the problem of whether we can generalise the findings from rats to humans, whose cognitions are much more complex. The laboratory findings are undermined by the artificiality of the sleep which is likely to be produced in sleep laboratories, which usually involve having equipment attached to the body, often the head.

Try it out for yourself: after re-read the "Information consolidation theory of sleep", explained previously in this section, and then read over other theories on the function of sleep explained previously in the introduction to this topic (the restoration theory, the ecological theory and the reorganisation theory). Then sleep on it. You should find that as you have begun to develop a schema for explanations of sleep, these new theories will be relatively easy to pick up. Once you have done this, re-read the section on the "Information consolidation theory of sleep" to remind yourself of why this happened.

Faulty cognition and irrational thoughts

It is known that sleep disorders can be caused by faulty thinking (cognitive biases) about sleep. For the estimated one third of adults who experience insomnia, cognitive behavioural therapy (CBT) may offer some relief.

> CBT is an application of the cognitive explanation of sleep and dream, so can be used in a response to a question asking you to analyse in the exam.

Research shows that CBT reduces false beliefs about sleep (the cognitive part) and also addresses the behavioural aspect, such as what to do when you are lying in bed and can't fall asleep. A 2002 study by Dr. Morin highlighting people's misconceptions about sleep found those that who received CBT reduced their false beliefs, which resulted in increases in the amount of time they spend in bed actually sleeping.

Some of the main cognitive biases associated with sleep are:

- arbitrary inference —an inference drawn in the absence of little or any supporting evidence, e.g. "I haven't slept for a week: it's completely caused by a chemical imbalance in my brain, so I can't do anything about it except take sleeping pills";

- selective abstraction: a conclusion based on only one element of many, e.g. "I can't get a night's sleep. My whole life is a mess!";

- overgeneralisation: a sweeping generalisation made on the basis of a single, probably trivial, event, e.g. "I can't sleep. I can't do anything right!";

- magnification and minimisation: sometimes called catastrophising, or making a mountain out of a molehill, e.g. "If I don't get a fully 8 hours of sleep tonight a catastrophe will happen."

Studies have shown that CBT for insomnia (e.g. Edinger et al, 2001) worked better than either relaxation programmes or a placebo treatment for people with insomnia. Also in 2001, a German study by Backhaus et al found that the benefits of short-term CBT had long-term effects. After therapy, the participants improved their total sleep time and sleep efficiency and reduced the time before falling asleep and negative sleep-related thoughts, and those improvements were sustained over at least 6 years.

Look up some of the strengths and limitations of CBT, such as
http://www.nhs.uk/Conditions/Cognitive-behavioural-therapy/Pages/Advantages.aspx.

The reorganizational theory of sleep and dreams (Crick and Mitchison, 1983)

According to this theory, the purpose of dreaming (particularly in REM sleep), is to help us to 'unlearn' I'), items that would otherwise clutter our thought processes. We dream to forget, in other words.

Crick and Mitchison developed their theory after investigating work done with computer programs that had been developed to simulate neural connections in the brain. It was discovered that these programs could become overloaded by unnecessary and undesirable bits of information (called 'parasitic connections'), to the extent that an 'unlearning' system had to be created to delete them.

Crick and Mitchison hypothesised that the same thing may happen in the brain. They took a evidence for these 'parasitic connections' occurring in the brain:

- 'spikes' which are recorded by EEGs during REM sleep (see the 'spikes' in the different waves of the stages of the sleep process described at the beginning of this section)

- the bizarreness of dreams.

These EEG spikes were an unlearning mechanism which served to knock out these parasitic connections. If we didn't have dreaming, more and more bizarre connections would be made, creating brain overload, and our memories would become more and more disorganised and confused.

However, if this theory was correct, people who take some drug therapies which reduce REM sleep (e.g. Monoamineoxidase inhibitors —MAOIs —for depression) would experience memory dysfunction, but people taking these drugs report improvement in, not a reduction of, memory function. Furthermore, most dreams are not bizarre —they are mostly fairly banal and straightforward. It is just that we are more likely to remember the strange ones! Another important criticism of the reorganisation theory of sleep and dreams is that there is no evidence that human brains make parasitic connections — they only appear to occur in artificial intelligence programs.

Summary

Like all explanations and theories in psychology, the information processing explanation has strengths and limitations.

Strengths	Limitations
Cognitive explanations, like information processing, use mostly the laboratory experiment as a research method, which makes such explanations *highly scientific*	*Reductionist*: it could be argued that cognitive explanations are reductionist as they ignore influences other than cognition on behaviour, such as hormonal influences (e.g. melatonin).
Many useful applications: cognitive explanations of sleep and dreams have given us many useful treatments for sleep disorders like insomnia, such as CBT-I (Cognitive Behavioural Therapy for Insomnia).	*Low ecological validity*: although cognitive explanations are scientific, laboratories are not where we usually sleep, or use our memories. This makes the results of studies difficult to generalise to the real world.

1.6.2 Activities

Cognitive approach to sleep and dreams: Double entry journal

Complete the following table, to help you to:

- summarise the cognitive approach to sleep dreams;

- organise the information you have learned in this section;

- make connections with what you have learned.

The first two parts have been completed for you. After this, summary headings only are included - it is your job to add a summary, in your own words, under each heading, and the connections you make. Do your memory even more of a favour by adding images.

Topic summary	Connections that I made
Cognitive psychology is the study of internal mental processes, such as: • perception; • attention; • language; • memory; • thinking.	I can see a pattern in these mental processes. The initial letters make the word PALM with a 'T' on the end.
The way in which we think is often likened to how a computer processing information - information processing. It works like: stimulus > PALMT > behaviour	This is like the COD game I play. The input (stimulus) is made by me using the controller, the console uses processes equivalent to PALMT to process my input, and this converts to actions that can be viewed on the monitor (behaviour).
Information consolidation theory of sleep	
Schemas, sleep and dreams	
Faulty cognitions and irrational thoughts	

Double entry journal

Cognitive approach to sleep and dreams: Information processing Go online
question

Q11: Match the following terms with their descriptions. *(5 marks)*

Perception:	the ability to take in and store information, as well as to retrieve it when required.
Attention:	the process of using knowledge and information to make plans, interpret, and constructively interact with and make predictions about the world in general.
Language:	the internal process by which an organism becomes aware of and interprets external stimuli.
Memory:	the ability to 'tune out' irrelevant information, and focus only on the relevant.
Thinking:	a formal system of communication which uses a combination of words and/or symbols, whether written or spoken.

Cognitive approach to sleep and dreams: Information consolidation
theory of sleep notebook exercise

You will need your psychology notebook for this activity.

Using the weblink http://www.world-of-lucid-dreaming.com/sleep-deprivation.html, have a look at the cases of Peter Tripp and Randy Gardner. Take a note of how the sleep deprivation they experienced affected their cognitions (problem-solving, memory, attention, perception, language).

How does sleep enhance information processing?

1.7   Psychodynamic processes relating to sleep and dreams

Dreaming is nothing new, but it is safe to assume our dreams differ substantially from those of our ancestors. For example, our waking distractions and concerns or anxieties are quite different from our forebears (i.e. we generally do not concern ourselves with being mauled by various creatures). Experiences that are key to being human, however, do not change, such as pleasure/pain, communicating, loving, fighting, giving birth, being chased, falling, feeling surprise, excitement, disappointment, etc. These same experiences have occurred in humankind for thousands of years.

All the way back to ancient Jewish tradition and to earlier civilisations and cultures, the life circumstances of the dreamer were thought just as important to the interpretation of the dream as the dream content itself; this view is still largely held by contemporary psychologists, too. Ancient Egyptian dream symbol analysis is equivalent to modern-day dream dictionaries. Dreams were believed to carry messages in the ancient world, and those messages were either indications of

---

what's to come in the future, or instructions handed down from the deities. The ancient Greek philosopher Plato (c. 428 - 347 B.C.) connected dreams to the "lawless wild beast that peers out in sleep", which was a precursor to what Freud termed "leakages from the unconscious" some 2,000 years later.

Dreams as wish-fulfilment

Freud, the founder of the psychoanalytic theory, insisted that dreams are a form of fulfilling suppressed wishes. If a wish (likely to be sexual in origin) goes unsatisfied during the dreamer's normal day, the mind reacts to this 'internal stimuli' by transforming it into a visual fantasy —allowing the dreamer to satisfy his or her desire. The result of which is a peaceful night's sleep.

Freud suggested that dreams provide a psychic safety valve to discharge unacceptable feelings. The dream's manifest (apparent) content may also have symbolic meanings (latent content) that signify our unacceptable feelings.

- Manifest content: the story of the dream as the dreamer dreams it - the story they tell.

- Latent content: the hidden content of the dream: its real meaning.

The latent content hides behind the manifest content, e.g. Lynn dreamt that she was walking down a street trying to hold onto a huge, slippery fish. Her therapist said she was experiencing anxiety over being able to do her new job effectively. In this example, the latent content (as described by the therapist) is that she was experiencing anxiety over being able to do her new job effectively, while the manifest content (as described by Lynn) is that she was walking down a street trying to hold onto a huge, slippery fish.

Dreamwork

Freud believed that the function of dreaming was to act as the guardian of sleep. This is the essence of dreamwork —keeping unconscious thoughts hidden. If a person is to sleep undisturbed, unconscious desires must be disguised or else the dreamer would become distressed and wake up. This is why Freud called dreams "the royal road to the unconscious": if a dream can be understood, then contents of the unconscious mind can also be understood.

Dreamwork also involves transforming latent into manifest content. The process by which this process can disguise and distort the latent content includes the following four ways.

1. **Condensation**: two or more latent thoughts are combined to make up one manifest dream image. For example, a place in a dream may include features of many places we have been.

2. **Displacement**: instead of focussing on the intended object, a meaningless object is focussed on. For example, one of Freud's patients, known as 'The Butcher's Wife', dreamt about giving a supper party, but she only had smoked salmon in the house. She found that she couldn't buy anything else because the shops were shut, and she couldn't phone the caterer because the phone was out of order. She had to abandon her idea of the supper-party. Freud interpreted this dream as the Butcher's wife displacing her fear of her husband's infidelities (he wanted to lose weight so wished she would not have supper parties) with thin women.

3. **Symbolism**: this is what people often think about when they think of Freud's theory - 'when you dream about a banana it is really a penis' and so on. In fact, the popular view in some ways is quite correct - Freud maintains that "the very great majority of symbols in dreams are sexual symbols", and he lists numerous symbols which can be used to represent sexual processes and the genital organs of both sexes. However, tracking down a symbol's meaning had to be backed up by other evidence from the dream.

For example, Freud suggested that objects such as towers, ties, weapons, sticks, rockets and the like were all symbols for the male organ/an erection. Boxes, cases, flowers, cupboards, ovens, caves and other hollow objects represented the female genitalia. Dreams of walking up a staircase, horse-riding or dancing could signify a sexual act.

This could therefore explain the reason why the causes of 'wet dreams' are usually never the result of dreaming about an actual sexual act.

Before reading the following table, it is important to note that Freud did not believe that symbols in dreams had fixed meanings, but he did believe that some symbols were fairly universal.

Common dream symbols	Some potential meanings
Vermin	Brothers and sisters
House	The human body
Kings and queens	Parents
Water	Birth
A journey	Death
Clothes and uniforms	Nakedness

4. **Secondary elaboration**: this is where all of the jumbled up symbols and behaviours are made into a (kind of) coherent story.

Analysing dreams

Dream analysis involves the translation of the manifest content into latent meaning, by analysing each of the above four processes:

- by unpicking the process of condensation to see how two or more ideas are condensed into one, e.g. a dream about a man may be a dream about both one's father and one's lover, a dream about a house might be the condensation of worries about security as well as worries about one's health;

- by identifying potential displacement, e.g. one of Freud's patients who was extremely resentful of his sister-in-law, referring to her as a dog, dreamed of strangling a small white dog - Freud interpreted this as representing his wish to kill his sister-in-law, but if the patient would have really dreamed of killing his sister-in-law, he would have felt guilty - the unconscious mind transformed her into a dog to protect him;

- by interpreting the symbols in dreams;

- by unravelling the secondary elaboration to obtain the latent content of a dream.

Dora: A case study involving dream analysis (1905)

Dora: A case study involving dream analysis (1905)

Dora (real name Ida Bauer) was a patient of Freud's, who was diagnosed with hysteria. Hysteria was a relatively common diagnosis until the mid-20th century for extreme emotional excess. It resulted in a range of physical symptoms (e.g. dumbness, paralysis of a limb) which had no physical cause. They were psychosomatic, i.e. a physical symptom with a psychological cause.

Freud's approach to treatment was through the talking cure and dream analysis: psychodynamic therapy. A trained psychoanalyst could interpret symbols in dreams, and themes in the 'stream of consciousness' which resulted from psychoanalysis, to identify the unconscious problem, bring it to the conscious mind, resolve it and thereby alleviate the symptoms.

As always with case studies, Freud begins with a very detailed case-history of Dora, and her family and social relationships, which he found to be typical of the **Oedipus complex**.

Herr and Frau K. were friends of Dora's family. When Dora was 14, she was assaulted by Herr K. who pressed his genital region on her, which caused her to feel disgust and run away. Dora associated an act which should be pleasurable with disgust and experienced displacement: the traumatic experience in one part of her body was later transferred to another.

In the meantime, Frau K. began an intimate relationship with Dora's father while nursing him through an illness. According to Freud, Dora had repressed homosexual feelings for Frau K.

Freud interpreted two of Dora's dreams. In one, her home had been set on fire and her father tries to rescue her. Dora's mother, however, wants to rescue her jewels. Freud claimed that the jewel-case (manifest content) represented Dora's genitals (latent content), which are under threat from Herr K. (represented in the dream by her father).

The second dream involved Dora receiving a letter from her mother in which she requires Dora to return home for her father's funeral. She finds herself looking for a train station in a strange town, constantly asking people how far away the station was and always learning that it is five minutes away. Finally, she comes to a forest where a man tells her that the station is two and half hours away. Although she is eventually able to see the station, she cannot reach it. Suddenly, she finds herself at home and cannot remember how she got there. Freud determines that the dream was conceived as a fantasy of revenge against her father and Frau K., a kind of wish fulfilment which she could not, in real life, enact. Freud also connects the letter that Dora receives from her mother in the dream to a letter that she actually received from Herr K., arguing that this displacement indicates how traumatic her experiences with Herr K. had actually been.

Freud's case study of Dora was lauded as one of the most important of the 20th century. However, Freud's locating of all symptoms in sexual urges was, and still is, strongly criticised. Other factors involved at the time, other than sexual ones, are likely to be implicated in Dora's symptoms, such as the fact that she was Jewish at a time when there was significant anti-Semitic prejudice in Germany and Austria. Freud was also Jewish, and this may also have affected the dynamic between him and Dora, which would make retaining objectivity difficult on his part.

However, Freud did identify how traumatic unwanted sexual experiences were to adolescents; he was ahead of his time in this respect.

Incidentally, Dora rejected Freud's interpretation of her dreams and left the therapy before it was due to end. Freud, of course, claimed that this was because she had transferred her disgust with Herr K. onto him.

1.7.1   Activity

Psychodynamic approach to sleep and dreams: Dream analysis

Use dreams of your own and your friends (if they are OK with this of course!) to analyse, using the following table. There is a completed example below.

Title:	Date:
Category:	Lucidity:
Keywords:	Description:
Manifest content	Latent content

Title: Frankie and Benny's	**Date:** 27/09/2014
Category: nightmare?	**Lucidity:** mildly lucid.
Keywords: Michael Car Car park Tall man Laundry Mum	**Description:** I was at Frankie and Benny's with my mum eating dinner and when we left the restaurant we saw Michael and his coworkers leaving the mall. My mum and I walked to the car; she was holding laundry and she threw it in the back seat. Then we walked back to the restaurant to get more. I told my mum I would drive the car closer so she wouldn't have to walk as far. I walked back to my car and got in. I was scrolling though my Twitter while my car warmed up and I heard a noise. It sounded like my bumper had fallen off. I looked in my rear view mirror but I didn't see anything. I went to start my car but, before I did, Michael walked around the side of my car and tipped it on its side. Michael walked around and opened the car door that is now in the air and says "come out". I climbed out of the car and the tallest man in there grabs me and throws me onto the pavement. Then, all of Michael's friends gather round and start kicking me. They are all wearing uniforms from McDonald's. I know they go on beating me up for a while, but I kind of fall asleep while it's happening so I don't remember how long it actually was.
Manifest content Mum throws laundry in back seat. The dreamer helps by driving closer . Michael tips the car over and beats up the driver with the help of his friends . They are wearing uniforms. The uniforms are from McDonald's. A tall man comes out and throws the dreamer onto the ground. The dreamer falls asleep while being beaten up.	**Latent content** Mum has 'dirty laundry' that she wants to hide. The dreamer also wants to keep mum's 'dirty laundry' hidden. Michael has something to do with the secret and wants to stop the dreamer from helping to hide it. He tells him 'come out'. They are seen to be authority figures. They are associated with unhealthy food. Maybe this is associated with unhealthy sex and so is the secret. Does the tall man represent the dreamer's father? Does he punish the dreamer for allowing the dirty laundry to be seen? A defence against feelings of guilt for letting the secret out.

1.8   Factors affecting sleep

There are factors that can affect the functioning of the brain, which therefore also affect our sleep and dreams. These factors can be biological or environmental. Here, we will examine how the following can interfere with the optimal functioning of the nervous system:

* drugs;
* light.

Impact of drugs

Neurotransmitters are chemical messengers in the nervous system. Some psychoactive drugs (where mood or behaviour is altered) mimic our neurotransmitters and some actually use our own neurotransmitters. Either way, this causes all kinds of abnormalities and problems.

Caffeine and alcohol are probably the most popular drugs in the world. Each day, people consume caffeine in their tea, coffee, cocoa, cola, chocolate, and some drugs. Many people take coffee in the morning as it is a stimulant, so helps increase alertness for the day ahead, but if we take it nearer bedtime it may keep us awake as it increases adrenaline production. Adrenaline is a hormone released from the adrenal glands and its function is to prepare us for fight or flight —it a key hormone in the stress response which causes feelings of irritability, anxiety, sleep disturbance, rapid heartbeat and excessive urination. It also blocks other sleep-inducing hormones, such as melatonin. You can see why it can keep you awake at night! In moderate doses, (between one and three 8oz cups per day), you can still feel these symptoms.

Caffeine can have a stimulating effect as soon as 15 minutes after it is consumed, and will persist for several hours: it takes about 6 hours for half of the caffeine to be eliminated. S, if you have that cup of coffee or bottle of cola at 4 o'clock in the afternoon, the effects of the caffeine will still impact on your sleep if you go to be at 10pm, and beyond.

Impact of light

You learned about the profound effect that the exogenous zeitgeber of light has on sleep in the section on biological explanations of sleep. Exposure to light early in the day stimulates the production of serotonin which encourages feelings of wakefulness, alertness, and energy. Light exposure at night also stimulates alertness, which has an obvious effect on our ability to sleep! Light exposure during the evening can make it harder to fall asleep. Insufficient darkness throughout the night can lead to frequent and prolonged awakenings (see the Czeisler et al study)

The absence of light (darkness) sends a critical signal to the body that it is time to rest by increasing the production of melatonin (the darkness hormone), produced in the pineal gland. Increases in melatonin cause the muscles to relax, produces feelings of drowsiness and drops in body temperature. Melatonin levels naturally rise during the early evening as darkness falls, peaking at around 3am, when levels decline and levels of serotonin (the sunshine hormone) begin to increase. Light exposure at the wrong times alters the circadian rhythm (the biological mechanism that regulates sleep-wake cycles) in ways that interfere with both the quantity and quality of sleep. Evening light exposure inhibits this naturally timed rise of melatonin, which delays the onset of the body's transition to sleep and sleep itself.

Light as a factor that impacts sleep has become more of a problem since the invention of electricity, as we can now have artificial light at whatever time of day we wish. Artificial light does impact our ability to sleep, particularly the blue light associated with digital devices, such as tablets, mobile phones and TVs.

1.9 End of topic test

End of topic 1 test   Go online

Introduction to sleep and dreams

Q12: The stages of the sleep cycle last for approximately:

a) 60 minutes.
b) 70 minutes.
c) 80 minutes.
d) 90 minutes.

....

Q13: If the stages of the sleep cycle are normal, a night's sleep will last for around:

a) 4.5 hours.
b) 6 hours.
c) 7.5 hours.
d) 9 hours.

....

Q14: What does REM stand for?

....

Q15: Name two symptoms that a person might experience as a result of being deprived of REM sleep over a period of two weeks. *(2 marks)*

....

Q16: What were the findings of research carried out by Gregory *et al*? *(1 mark)*

a) Rats died when deprived of sleep for two weeks.
b) There is a link between family conflict in childhood and insomnia in adulthood.
c) Dreams are associated with REM sleep.
d) That when living in a cave, the sleep-wake cycle shortens to 20 hours.

....

Q17: Some evidence for the effects of sleep deprivation on our ability to process information has come from data concerning the frequency of accidents. What were the findings? *(1 mark)*

a) More accidents happen after the clocks go forward in spring because people have had one hour less sleep.
b) Fewer accidents happen after the clocks go back in autumn because people have had one hour more sleep.
c) Both of the above.
d) There was no effect.

....

Q18: Complete the paragraph. *(3 marks)*

Secondary insomnia is associated with stress, age or _____ conditions. Primary insomnia has no obvious _____ so appears to be an illness in its own right. It is by far the most _____ form of insomnia.

....

Q19: Match the treatments for insomnia with their descriptions. *(3 marks)*

Cognitive behavioural therapy:	can help regulate the sleep-wake cycle (no restorative sleep).
Medicine:	creates positive associations with sleep cues and other advice.
Stimulus control therapy:	tries to restore restorative sleep by changing faulty cognitions.

Cognitive approach to sleep and dreams

Q20: The way we think, according to the computer analogy, goes like: *(1 mark)*

a) information processing > output > input
b) input > information processing > output
c) output > input > information processing
d) information processing > input > output

....

Q21: In the computer analogy, the above process relates to: *(1 mark)*

a) senses > perception, attention, language, memory, thinking > behaviour
b) behaviour > perception, attention, language, memory, thinking > senses
c) perception, attention, language, memory, thinking > senses > behaviour
d) senses > behaviour > perception, attention, language, memory, thinking

....

Q22: A schema may be defined as: *(1 mark)*

a) a computer analogy.
b) CBT for insomnia.
c) a pre-existing mental structure acquired on the basis of experience.
d) a sleep disorder that results in early morning wakening.

....

Q23: The information consolidation theory of sleep suggests that: *(1 mark)*

a) schemas act to restore the mind's cognitive resources.
b) the function of sleep is to process information acquired during the day.
c) sleep functions to restore the body's resources, like neurotransmitters, that had been depleted during the day.
d) someone who does not sleep for more than one month will die.

....

Q24: The restoration theory of sleep and dreams states that:

a) we 'dream to forget'.
b) we need to get rid of parasitic connections in the brain, so do so in sleep.
c) 'spikes' found in EEGs of sleeping people are evidence of 'unlearning'.
d) All of the above

Psychodynamic approach to sleep and dreams

Q25: Dreamwork is: *(1 mark)*

a) analysing dreams for latent content.
b) where information is pushed into the unconscious.
c) what the mind is doing while we sleep.
d) a case study.

....

Q26: When two or more latent thoughts are combined to make up one manifest dream image, this is called:

a) symbolism.
b) condensation.
c) displacement.
d) secondary elaboration.

....

Q27: Why has Freud's case study of 'Dora' been criticised?

a) Sexism
b) Lack of compassion for the patient.
c) Lack of objectivity.
d) All of the above.

....

Q28: Freud said that most of our mind is conscious.

a) True
b) False

....

Q29: The latent content of dreams is:

a) the actual content of the dream.
b) the manifest content of the dream.
c) the unconscious content of the dream.
d) elaboration.

....

Q30: The manifest content of dreams is:

a) the actual content of the dream.
b) the manifest content of the dream.
c) the unconscious content of the dream.
d) elaboration.

....

Q31: When all of the jumbled up symbols and behaviours are made into a (kind of) coherent story, this is called:

a) condensation.
b) symbolism.
c) displacement.
d) secondary elaboration.

....

Q32: Freud believed that dreams such as being naked in public meant different things to different people.

a) True
b) False

....

Q33: A strength of Freud's dream theory is that:

a) it can be generalised widely.
b) in-depth data is gained over a period of time - the data is valid.
c) dream analysis is a successful treatment for anxiety.
d) he always hypnotised his patients.

....

Q34: Repression is:

a) where information is pushed into the unconscious mind.
b) the manifest content of a dream.
c) taking out frustrations on a safe, rather than unsafe, object.
d) at the top of the iceberg model.

....

Q35: Caffeine is:

a) a stimulant drug
b) a depressant drug
c) a restricted drug
d) is not a drug

....

Q36: Caffeine stays in your system for at least:

a) 2 hours after consumption
b) 4 hours after consumption
c) 6 hours after consumption
d) 8 hours after consumption

....

Q37: Caffeine inhibits the production of:

a) adrenaline
b) noradrenaline
c) serotonin
d) melatonin

....

Q38: Caffeine stimulates the production of:

a) adrenaline
b) noradrenaline
c) serotonin
d) melatonin

....

Q39: Light enters the eye and is detected by the:

a) adrenal glands
b) suprachiasmic nucleus
c) frontal lobes
d) hypothalamus

....

Q40: Tablets, mobile phones and PCs emit:

a) white light
b) ultraviolet light
c) blue light
d) pink light

....

Q41: Light inhibits the production of:

a) adrenaline
b) serotonin
c) melatonin
d) the daylight hormone

Unit 2 Topic 2

Memory (optional topic)

Contents

Learning objective

By the end of this topic, you should be able to:

- provide a definition of memory with examples;
- describe, explain, evaluate, apply and analyse the multi-store model of memory;
- describe, explain, evaluate, apply and analyse the working memory model;
- describe, explain, evaluate, apply and analyse explanations of forgetting.

By the end of this section, you should be able to describe, explain, evaluate, apply and analyse:

2.1 Introduction to memory

The Oxford Dictionary defines **memory** as:

> "The faculty by which the mind stores and remembers information".

You will learn about different memory stores and processes, in particular:

- encoding,
- storage, and
- retrieval

Memory is our ability to store, use and retrieve information from our experiences in the environment. It is one of the information processors, alongside perception, attention, language and thinking. Memory involves receiving information from the five senses and giving it a code (encoding), retaining that information (storage), and bringing it back to mind at a later point (retrieval).

There are two theories of memory that you need to know about:

- The Multi-store model of memory (MSM)
- Working Memory (WM)

. . . before you go on to find out about why we forget.

Introduction to memory: Notebook exercise

You will need your psychology notebook for this activity.

Answer each of the following questions using an introductory statement and an example from your life. To write a good introductory statement, rephrase the question. Doing this exercise will help you to understand some of the theories and explanations of memory.

1. Overall, what kind of memory would you say that you have: excellent, good, average or poor? Why?

2. What kind of information do you remember best: faces, shapes, colours, smells, names, dates, facts, etc.? Why?

3. What kinds of information do you have the greatest difficulty remembering? Why do you think that this type of information is hard for you to remember?

4. Is there any kind of information of which you remember a great deal, e.g. football scores or movie trivia? Why do you remember this information so readily?

5. Think about some of the information from your early school years that you can still easily recall. What factors contributed to this information becoming firmly embedded in your memory?

6. What kinds of memory techniques do you use? Have you ever tried any in the past that don't work?

---

7. Do you ever find yourself recognising someone's face, but be unable to recall the name that goes with it? When you are introduced to new people, do you do anything special to remember their names? If so, what?

8. Do you ever feel that you have the information that you need, but you just can't seem to retrieve it? Have you ever recalled the information you were seeking just a few minutes too late? What do you do if this happens?

2.2   The Multi-store model of memory (MSM)

The founder researchers for the multi store model were Atkinson and Shiffrin (1968). They proposed that, in order for information to become lodged in memory, it must pass through three stores. The following diagram summarises their ideas.

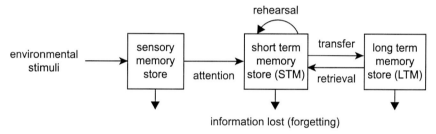

This diagram is very much a basic representation of the model. A fuller representation will develop as we go deeper into the model, clarifying both the discrete parts and the various functions.

Sensory memory

No matter which model of memory is being discussed, it is agreed that the first part of our memory process starts with stimuli from our environment which stimulate the sensory nerve cells responsible for sight, touch, taste, etc.

In the multi store model, the sensory memory store initially deals with incoming signals. The information passes into the sensory memory for a very short time —probably less than second. This is comparable with a reflex and, therefore, some would argue that storage is not involved and thus it is referred to as the Dual Store Model. The time in sensory memory is so short that it is difficult to imagine how much processing occurs. Certain psychologists suggest that the sensory store acts as a filter of the sensory stimuli, directing the resultant nerve signals from the various sensors into the short-term memory.

Imagine being in a completely dark room and asking someone to trace out a number using a torch so that can recognise the number, which is known as the 'light dot' technique. Think about what would be happening in the sensory memory store. You would have to remember the position of the light dot at different times and combine them to produce an image of the number. Imagine if the trace was so slow that you had forgot the position of the dot towards the start by the time it reached its final point. You may not then recognise the number. If the number being traced was 3 then, using the light dot technique, the positions could be interpreted as an 8 instead. You may have seen this effect when using some types of digital calculators.

Light dot activity

Try the light dot tracing task in a dark room with someone tracing the shapes of numbers using a torch, varying the speed of the traces from 1/10 second up to around 5 seconds.

What did you find? At which speed were the numbers easiest to identify?

The important aspect of this task is to give you an idea of the functioning speed of sensory memory. For visual sensations, this type of memory is known as iconic memory. For auditory sensations it is known as echoic memory.

2.2.1   Short-term memory

Research suggests that short-term memory (STM) is more complex than sensory memory.

Information stays longer in the STM and there is also a bigger capacity for information. When you look up a new telephone number and immediately punch it into the phone, you are probably using short-term memory —note that modern telephone numbers have 11 digits. That is a lot to remember.

Encoding, capacity and duration in STM feat.

Encoding —Conrad (1964) suggests that all information that ends up in memory is coded acoustically, using sound. Any visual information is transferred into acoustic codes —the coding process may be *you see a house, you say to yourself "house"* and that implants the house in your memory.

Conrad showed participants strings of letters and asked them to recall them immediately. Mistakes tended to involve replacing the correct letter, e.g. "C", with one that sounded similar, e.g. "P", "D" or "T". The mistakes occurred even when the letters were presented visually, without vocalising them.

Shulman (1970) thought that STM encoded information using visual and semantic (meaning) codes. Heyer and Barrett (1974) suggested that visual images that are difficult to code acoustically can be stored in STM. It is now accepted that encoding in STM involves all three types of codes - acoustic, visual and semantic. Possibly, acoustic coding is the most important, especially when we consider rehearsal strategies.

Capacity —what is the capacity of short-term memory? Howard (1983) coined the phrase the immediate memory span for capacity —this was the maximum number of items that could be recalled after one presentation.

A classic study was carried out by George Miller (1956) into memory capacity. Miller pointed out that there was a

magical number 7, plus or minus 2 items of information that could be processed through STM

Miller was referring to **chunks** of information rather than discrete items.

Let's try and clarify this.

Example: Consider the following two strings of digits:
6192738 —this is seven discrete digits
9876 321 —these are the same digits but arranged/organised differently into two chunks 9876 and 321

The first series will be more difficult to remember than the second organised series. This is an example of organising information into categories or chunks to improve the capacity of STM.

Millers' '7 chunks' could be discrete digits, grouped digits, discrete letters, grouped letters etc. The important issue here is that it does not matter which form the information comes in —digits, letter, etc. —the key is that the capacity is always about seven items.

The Multi-store Model of Memory —capacity in STM

The idea of capacity is illustrated below. Your immediate memory span is the number of numbers, letters, 'words' etc. that you can remember without making a mistake.

Activity 1: Ask your partner to prepare a list of numbers. The list should be as follows: start with a three digit number, then a four digit number, then a five digit number and so on up to ten digits. Your partner should not let you see the list. Your partner should then write down the first number on a blank sheet of paper and allow you to see it for 1 second only. You have to repeat the number you have seen. Note the number of digits you reach before making a mistake.

Activity 2: Try the same task, but using random letters (starting with a group of three letters up to ten letters). Ensure that the letters do not make up a recognisable 'word' (even if it is nonsensical).

Activity 3: Now try this task again but using nonsensical 'words', e.g. "SCRALE" (again starting with a three letter word up to a ten letter word).
Consider a variation on this: do the results change if instead of seeing the numbers, letters or 'words', your partner reads them out to you?

2.2.2   Duration

Duration —short-term memory is believed to hold information for about 15 to 30 seconds (Brown and Peterson, 1959).

A procedure by Brown (1958) and Peterson (1959) was used to measure how long unrehearsed information remained in STM. (An example of rehearsed information would be if you were asked to remember and recall a series of words in a memory task and you were to repeat them to yourself after seeing them until such point that you are asked to recall them. This is known as a rehearsal loop.) Participants were presented with a group of letters, e.g. 'YFM', and asked immediately to count backwards e.g. 754, 751, 748 etc., until a given signal, then the participants were asked to recall the letters 'YFM'. The recall interval (time spent counting backwards) is varied from about 3 seconds to 25 seconds.

The diagram below provides an indication of the results (note that the data is adapted from Peterson and Peterson). Duration in STM appears to be about 18 seconds.

A graph of time against number of syllables recalled

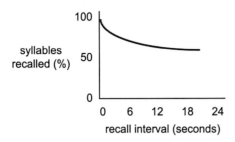

Activity to illustrate the existence of two main stores (STM and LTM)

Ask someone to call out to you and others, if in a class situation, the following list of words —past experience has shown that calling out and showing the words at the same time helps.

This a free recall task —as soon as the last word is read out you will be asked to write down as many of the list words as you can recall.

tag	table	pen
cup	note	coin
hat	pipe	test
clip	bulb	grass
foot	hole	blue
salt	work	

The order of the words when being read out is important, but you may write them down, when recalling, in any order you wish.

Consider the results.

In order to illustrate the Primacy/Recency effects best then a large sample of subjects would be useful —this may not be practicable therefore consider the set of results shown by the graph below. This is a smooth graph but it is more than likely your graph would be spiked, especially if the sample is small. Some words near the middle of the list can have special associations for particular people and therefore remembered better —this can cause spiking.

The larger the sample, the smoother the graph should be.

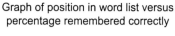

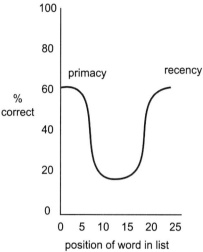

Graph of position in word list versus percentage remembered correctly

primacy   recency

% correct

position of word in list

What do the hypothetical results in the graph tell us? The two high points are labelled as Primacy and **Recency**.

Primacy —the first few words in the list "bag, table, pen, ... " are recalled well. This probably happens as subjects rehearse these first words by repeating them to themselves as —"bag, bag, bag, table, table, bag, table, pen, pen, bag, table, pen... ". This rehearsal strategy incorporates these words into LTMry for later retrieval. Hence, 60% remembered the first words, dropping to 20% by the tenth word.

Recency —the words called out last during the activity were, in reverse order, "work, bed, tape... ". These were the most recent into your memory and are probably being recalled from your STM —they are freshest in the STM and therefore are more likely to be recalled.

Note that the middle group of words from the list, from about "coin" to "blue" are normally least.

2.2.3   Long-term memory

Can you remember the following:

- What was on TV last night?
- What you had for breakfast yesterday?
- What you did last Friday?
- What you did at your last birthday party?
- What you did on your first day of school?

You will probably remember some details from most, or even all, of the above. You are using long-term memory (LTM) to do this. Information that remains in the brain for more than a few minutes probably ends up in LTM or is lost. We will see later that the retrieval process for LTM is very important, especially when we consider that a lifetime of information is stored there.

What are the features of long- term memory in the multi store model?
As with STM, let us consider encoding, capacity, and duration with respect to long-term memory and then we will look at retrieval.

Encoding —as with much of the research in memory, there is not a definitive picture for LTM. Debatably, the same three processing codes feature in LTM as in STM, but to different extents - the codes are visual, acoustic and semantic. There is extensive research which suggests that semantic coding is by far the most important in LTM. Acoustic coding is important in STM and in transferring information from STM into the LTM by means of rehearsal strategies. Baddeley (1966) suggested that coding in LTM was either procedural or declarative.

- **Procedural coding** deals with those skills and procedures that we do almost automatically —driving a car, riding a bike, walking, swimming etc. Internalising by means of repetitive practice is important in procedural memory. The more we practice using a calculator, for example, the easier it becomes to key in numbers or functions without consciously thinking about it. The process becomes automatic.

- **Declarative coding** is where we encode facts about our world to LTM using semantic and episodic memory. Consider the following examples:

    o My car is a Mazda 623 Atlantis
    o My previous house, which I left 4 years ago, is in Fraserburgh
    o I know that the word philosophy is spelt PHILOSOPHY

Episodic coding is thus used to encode information about events to LTM —what the event was, when it happened and what happened etc., e.g. I arranged to meet at my friend's house at noon yesterday or I remember going to John's party last Tuesday. These are further examples of encoding, storing and retrieving LTM using episodic memory.

Remember: semantics is about facts / words, episodic is about events.

We mainly encode to LTM on the basis of semantic memory.

Capacity —there appears to be no limit to the capacity of LTM, in which all of the memories of a lifetime can be stored. There are recent suggestions that some memories may be passed on through our genes. Human memory outstrips the memory system of the biggest, most efficient computer.

Duration —long term memory is relatively permanent or infinite.

Retrieval —often, the issue with memories in LTM is accessibility.

Imagine trying to retrieve items of information that have been coded and stored for many years without use. As mentioned previously ,an important feature of LTM is the retrieval process. Try to imagine the awesome amount of information in LTM and yet we can retrieve items almost instantly. This is an amazing feat which we take completely for granted.

2.2.4 How does retrieval occur?

Retrieval essentially involves recall or recognition of stored information in LTM. Recognition tasks are easier than recall because they contain more cues. Consider the following two questions:

1. Which of the following has the shortest duration?

  - a) Long-term memory
  - b) Shot-term memory
  - c) Sensory memory
  - d) Declarative memory

2. What is the capacity of STM?

Question 1 could have been asked as 'Which type of memory has the shortest duration?' By listing the types, all we are being asked to do is *recognise* the type.

Question 1 is therefore about *recognising* an answer from the cues provided.

Question 2, in comparison, is about recall.

Tulving (1973), as part of his Encoding Specificity Hypothesis, stated the following: "Only that can be retrieved that has been stored, and how it can be retrieved depends on how it was stored".

Let us pursue this line of thinking further. Remember the Library Model? The ease of finding a specific book about chemistry in a library is very dependent on how the book was stored —if it is stored alphabetically under the subject area then you would first check the subject list and look under "C" for chemistry and go to the corresponding section of the library. You would then scan the books alphabetical until you find the one that you are looking for. However, it is not as simple as that, as you will have experienced if you have gone into a massive library where chemistry has many shelves of books. You would need further clues to find your specific book, e.g. a sub-category of chemistry such as "organic chemistry", the author, the Dewey code, even a piece of knowledge as simple as "is the book a large tome or a paper back?". All the information would help you in your retrieval search.

Several factors can affect the retrieval process.

The difficulty in accessing a memory from LTM may involve the following:

- The **distinctiveness** of the memory relative to other LTM stored information.

- How interconnected the memory is to other information and the quality of this interconnectivity.

- The current state of the memory and the condition that existed when the memory was first stored.

- The frequency of access of that particular memory —the more a memory is recalled the easier it becomes to recall again.

Remembering an incident, such as car crash, involves recalling facts, images and events. It also involves the brain assimilating this information, other partial information, and logically organising all of this into a memory of the incident. This process of memory reconstruction can be fraught with difficulties.

This section has been focusing on the multi store model of memory, essentially based around the work of Atkinson and Shiffrin (1968). We have digressed at times to help explain the functioning of the various stores in the model. How robust is the model?

In the world of psychology, there has been lots of support, with much empirical evidence, for the model.

2.2.5 Glanzer and Cunitz (1966)

Their research was similar in methodology to Atkinson, using a free recall task but with an interference prevention task given immediately after the last item on the word list. Under these conditions the recency effect disappeared —the reason given suggested that the interference task dislodged the last words from short term memory —the last words were no longer the most recent bits of information entering the STM.

The hypothetical graph below illustrates results from such an experiment, showing quite clearly the tailing off of the recency effect after about the 10th word.

Graph of position of word to probability of recall

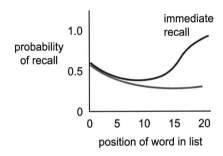

position of word in list

2.2.6 Korsakoff's syndrome

Korsakoff's syndrome gives interesting physiological support for Atkinson and Shiffrin's multi-store model of memory. Korsakoff's syndrome occurs with some chronic alcoholics when they decide to give up drink. The sudden alcohol withdrawal can trigger Korsakoff's syndrome, where they exhibit effective STM functioning, but impaired LTM. This suggests evidence for two separate memory stores, such as STM and LTM. Korsakoff's syndrome can be avoided easily by taking vitamin supplements during detoxification.

2.2.7 Evaluation of the Multi-store Memory Model

Strengths of the Model.

1. At first sight, the model seems a plausible explanation as to how memory moves through a series of stores.

2. There is evidence to support the model (e.g. Glanzer and Cunitz, 1966, Peterson and Peterson, 1959).

3. Data from patients who have suffered brain damage is another source of evidence for the validity of the multi store model. The most famous amnesia cases here are HM (Milner, 1966) and Clive Wearing. Both patients had severe damage to the areas of their brains that contain the hippocampi; HM's brain was damaged during surgery to reduce epileptic fits, and Clive Wearing had a severe form of herpes that caused brain damage. After suffering their brain damage, both HM and Clive Wearing lost the ability to form new long term memories. Both had normally functioning short term memories, but as STM only has a duration of up to 30 seconds anything that happened to them was completely forgotten. They could remember things from their pasts prior to their brain damage. This finding provides strong evidence that short term and long term memory are completely separate entities in the human brain.

Limitations of the Model.

1. Many psychologists suggest that the model is too simple. For example, STM seems to be able to do far more than Atkinson and Shiffrin's model suggests. This is one of the reasons why Baddeley and Hitch developed the Working Memory model, which is the next model of memory you will be learning about, and which focuses only on the functioning and structures of short-term memory.

2. Studies have shown that rehearsal strategies between STM and LTM do not always lead to storage.

3. De Groot (1966) —this was a study of expert chess players whose capacity for recalling stress positions, as long as they fitted with the known rules, were exceptional, suggesting very efficient STMs. However, when the chess pieces were randomly arranged, recall was no better than for non-chess players. De Groot implies that expert chess players use chunking and *gestalten* to aid STM, and that STM and LTM may not be so separate and distinct as the multi-store model suggests.

2.3   Working memory model

The working memory model was developed by Baddeley and Hitch (1974) who believed there was more to STM than Atkinson and Shiffrin's MSM suggested. They conceived of STM as having more than one component (see diagram below). It breaks STM down into subsystems (slave systems), a central control system (Central Executive) and an integration system (episodic buffer).

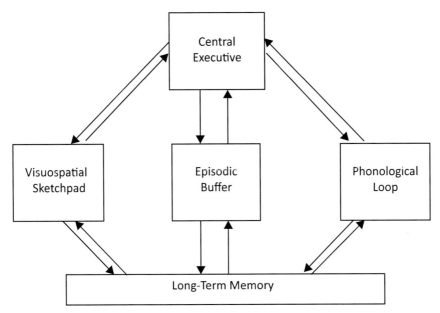

Many researchers refer to short-term memory as **working memory**. "Working" is meant in terms of storing and processing information. Working memory is important in our everyday mental work such as:

- remembering the names of people and where they work;
- remembering telephone numbers;
- booking and catching a train or bus;
- playing a piano;
- checking your change at the supermarket.

2.3.1 Central Executive

The most important component is the central executive; it is a control system which is involved in problem solving/decision-making, setting task goals, monitoring and correcting errors, starting the rehearsal process, switching attention between tasks, inhibiting irrelevant information, and its major role is to direct information to the slave system that is most suited to processing it. It also controls attention and plays a major role in planning and integrating information, not only from the slave systems but also from LTM. It is flexible and can process information from any modality (sound, vision, touch), although it does have a limited storage capacity and so can attend to a limited number of things at one time.

- Coding: any sensory code
- Capacity: limited

The Central Executive picks and chooses the information from the Phonological Loop and the Visuo-spatial sketchpad that go into the Episodic Buffer to form an episode of memory. The Episodic Buffer also seems to "download" episodes from LTM, sending them on to the Central Executive to be analysed and maybe recalled to conscious memory.

The two slave systems described below have separate responsibilities and work independently of one another.

2.3.2   The phonological loop

This is a subsystem of the WM which deals with **verbal material** (the 'inner voice'). The working of the phonological loop is shown when we say a phone number over and over in our heads (subvocally) in order to maintain it while we search for our phone. It is an important system as it helps us to maintain information over short periods of time for cognitive activities, such as reading, and mental arithmetic (where we use words in our heads to help us calculate). Research has shown that in tests of serial recall, when participants are prevented from engaging in subvocal rehearsal during a delay period that is inserted between stimulus presentation and recall, overall performance suffers (Baddeley, Thomson, & Buchanan, 1975). This suggested that the ability to keep verbal information in working memory depends on subvocal, articulatory rehearsal.

Further evidence for the phonological loop comes from Baddeley et al. (1975). They presented their participants with visual presentations of word lists for a brief time, then asked them to write them down in serial order. In condition 1 the lists contained 5 familiar, one-syllable English words, e.g. harm, wit, twice. In condition 2, the 5 words were polysyllabic e.g. organisation, university, association. Baddeley and his colleagues found that more short words were recalled, which they called 'the word length effect'. They concluded that the capacity of the loop is determined by the length of time it takes to say a word rather than by the number of items. The estimated time was 1.5 seconds. Also, Gathercole and Baddeley (1990) found that children with hearing problems had impaired memory and had difficulties saying whether words rhymed, perhaps suggesting that there is a phonological loop deficit being illustrated in their studies, which further supports its existence.

Word length activity

This activity is about testing word-length effects in short term memory. Use it to find out about memorising short and longer words under different circumstances. Your results are worth noting, but they are only meant for you to reflect on for now so just try the two tests 'for fun'!

Take 20 seconds to memorise the first table of words. Cover them up and write down as many as you can.

cat	boy	post	map
pin	mill	bit	sun
farm	top	city	back
walk	year	eye	bag
road	shoe	car	face

Now try the same with the next table (only 20- seconds again):

colour	table	fashion	paper
timer	wrestle	object	truthful
stapler	rocket	printer	nation
model	cottage	embark	fearless
glitter	hunter	ladder	marble

Compare your results. You should find that you are able to remember a greater number of words in the first table.

Explanation

In a word-length effect task with immediate recall it is expected that participants would remember more of the short words than the long words. There is evidence in such an experiment for suggesting that the word length effects depend on access to an articulation process.

- Coding: verbal in speech based form (acoustic)

- Capacity: limited (1.5 seconds, see Baddeley et al. study, above)

2.3.3 The visuo-spatial sketchpad

As the phonological loop is dedicated to the storage and maintenance of verbal material, the visuo-spatial sketchpad is dedicated to the storage and maintenance of visual (the 'inner eye') and spatial material (a spatial task would be when you navigate from home to college/school —you have a mental, spatial representation of the route).

The visuo-spatial store also has limited capacity. Shepard and Feng (1972) asked participants to imagine folding flat shapes in order to make a cube. They had to decide whether the arrows would meet head on.

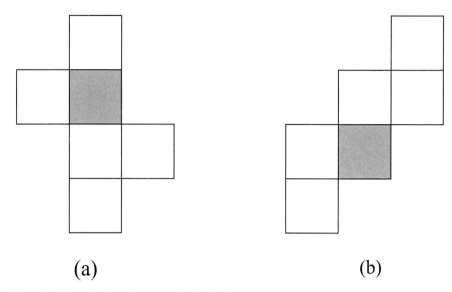

(a)   (b)

They found that the time taken to make the decision was related to the number of folds they would have had to make if they had actually been doing the task. Therefore, people are likely to find it difficult to do two tasks simultaneously if they both use the visuo-spatial sketchpad.

- Coding: visual and spatial

- Capacity: limited

2.3.4   The episodic buffer

This is a component of the Working Memory model that was added by Baddeley in 2000, in order to explain how information from the slave systems of the phonological loop and the visuo-spatial sketchpad was integrated, and how information from long-term memory was retrieved into the system. It stores information in a code that is multi-dimensional (it can cope with information from all of the senses in one code). It also has a sense of time, so we experience events as happening in a logical sequence.

- Coding: all modalities in one code

- Capacity: limited

2.3.5 Working memory activity

Working memory activity

Try the following calculations in your head:

a) 321 x 3

b) 274 x 3

c) 241 x 2

d) 362 x 14

Ask someone else to do the sums as well and then discuss the results.

You could also try asking someone to provide some similar sums for you. Sum (a) should be easier to do than (b), because (b) involves 'carrying': 3 x 4 is 12, therefore carry one 10 into the tens column.

Sums (a) and (c) should both be easy —no carrying is involved.

However, sum (d) requires holding lots of information in your mind while attending to other information and, therefore, sum (d) will normally be the most difficult.

So what do these sums tell us? By working out these calculations you will be involved in remembering the numbers and in using the rules of arithmetic. Remembering the numbers in the sums is a short term memory task. Remembering the arithmetic rules is a long term memory task.

This example possibly provides you with some insight into how the concept of working memory is different from the concept of short-term memory. Working memory has an added dimension which allows 'working with' or using information.

2.3.6 Key study into the Working Memory Model by Baddeley and Hitch (1973)

Aim: to test if doing two tasks, each using the same slave system, would increase the difficulty of the task.

Method: Participants were given a tracking task (following a spot of light with a pointer around a circular path while imagining block capitals such as H, T, F and E. They were asked to start at the bottom left-hand corner, to respond to each angle with a 'Yes' if it include the bottom or top line of the letter and a 'No' if it did not. Another group of participants were asked to carry out the tracking task while performing a verbal task (which uses a different slave system —the phonological loop).

Results: Participants had great difficulty in tracking the spot of light and accurately classifying the corners. The two tasks were competing for the same limited resources of the visuo-spatial sketchpad. This is supported by the finding that participants could carry out the tracking task easily while performing the verbal task.

Conclusions: doing two tasks which require the use of the same slave system increases the difficulty of the task, which suggests that there are separate slave systems for different types of information.

Evaluation: This is an innovative way of testing the functioning of the phonological loop, however, it does not reflect how we use our memories in real life. It therefore lacks mundane realism. Also, as it was carried out in a laboratory, it does not reflect behaviour in the real world. It therefore lacks ecological validity.

2.3.7   Evaluation of the Working Memory Model

Strengths of the Model:

1. The WM model is more plausible than the MSM because it explains STM in terms of active processes rather than passive.

2. Verbal rehearsal is accepted as one optional process within the phonological loop, rather than the only way to transfer information to LTM, as the MSM suggests.

3. The working memory model is supported by empirical evidence, in particular by Baddeley's own research which suggests that the STM is complex and easier to accommodate in the working memory model than in the multi store model. The working memory model can explain how we can do two tasks at once if they involve different subsystems and why it is we have trouble with some tasks that involve the same subsystem (see key study above).

4. The working memory model has practical applications in supporting children's reading. There are suggestions that reading difficulties are linked to limitations in the Phonological Loop. "Baddeley and Lewis (1981) found that articulatory suppression led to difficulties in reading and understanding texts." —from Revise Psychology for AS Level by Brody and Dwyer.

5. Brain scans show different areas of the brain are used for visual and verbal tasks, which supports the WM model.

However, the model has also been criticised for the following reasons.

Limitations of the Working Memory Model:

1. The role of the Central Executive is not fully understood, and is not well researched. Furthermore, no-one knows about the limitations of its capacity. Because the concept of the Central Executive is so vague, it is difficult to test, so is unfalsifiable: this makes it unscientific. It is likely to be comprised of more than one store.

2. It fails to account for musical memory as we are able to listen to instrumental music without impairing performance on other acoustic tasks.

2.4   Forgetting

In a class situation the teacher should read out the passage provided and also let you see the passage to read for yourself. If you are working on your own, read the passage once through and continue with your work.

The dawn broke with an extravaganza of colour. Yellow, lime green, gold and several varieties of red hues, shone bright and clear. I was still working on the Pickering case and getting nowhere fast, so I hardly noticed this beauty of the day. I decided to go and see Ann Pickering to see if she could shed any light on the disappearance of her notorious, drug-baron, husband. My silver Ford Cougar was parked outside. I'll need to have the scratches and the wing mirror seen to, after the bump with the milk float in Mandela Place on Saturday.

The recall of the reading passage came some time after the reading, so it is expected that much of the passage will be forgotten by the time you are asked to write down your thoughts. The passage is quite lengthy so it is to be expected that there will be very low accuracy in remembering the passage —forgetting will be high normally. Psychologists study the recall results of such exercises to learn about forgetting.

There are four key theories of forgetting that we are going to look at:

- trace decay
- interference
- forgetting due to the absence of cues
- forgetting due to brain damage

2.4.1 Trace decay (forgetting in STM)

One theory of forgetting is trace decay (or sometimes just decay). It is a theory of forgetting from STM, and is related to its limited duration (30 seconds or less). This theory emphasises the problems of availability that arise if memories decay or simply fade away. This may result from lack of effective rehearsal or inefficient processing of information.

As long ago as the nineteenth century, psychologists were looking at the idea of trace decay. Ebbinghaus (1850-1909) conducted experiments to prove that we do forget things. He was the only participant in the studies though and you already know how invalid and unreliable the results of his work could be through using such a small sample group! However, his methodology was excellent and his results have been replicated today.

The methodology Ebbinghaus used was to learn lists of nonsense syllables and test how many he could remember at various time intervals.

A nonsense syllable is a consonant-vowel-consonant combination, where the consonant does not repeat, and the syllable does not have any other meaning. BOL (which sounds quite like 'Ball') and DOT (already a word) would then not be allowed, but syllables such as DAX, BOK, and YAT would all be acceptable.

Ebbinghaus came up with 2,300 nonsense syllables. He would write the nonsense syllables on slips of paper, put them in a box and then pull out a number of random syllables and then write them down in a notebook. The next stage would be to use a metronome (a mechanical device, often used by pianists to make a regular clicking sound) and with the same voice (tone and pitch) he would read out the syllables and attempt to remember them at the end of the procedure.

Over a relatively short period of time, his recall was good, but it decreased as the retention interval got longer. He found that there was a large increase in forgetting the nonsense syllables over the first hour after learning and then forgetting increased more slowly.

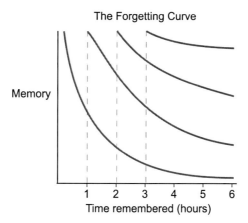

The Forgetting Curve

Memory

Time remembered (hours)

When he tried to re-learn forgotten lists, he found that he needed less practice, which suggested that each time you learn something, some sort of trace is left in your memory which is not enough for total recall, but does make subsequent learning quicker.

2.4.2   Research which supports trace decay

Peterson and Peterson (1959) conducted a study on the Duration of STM. Their study, and conclusions are outlined below.

Aim

They wanted to test their hypothesis that information was held in the STM for approximately 20 seconds, after that it disappears if rehearsal is prevented. The aim was to prove that the duration of STM is approximately 20 seconds. Another aim was to investigate if information was lost from STM as a result of decay.

Method

Participants were presented with sets of nonsense syllables in sets of three (as Ebbinghaus had done) which they were then asked to recall in order after a delay of 3, 6, 9, 12, 15 and 18 seconds. The independent variable (IV) was therefore the time delay. The dependent variable (DV) was the number of nonsense syllables recalled.

Participants were given an interference task where they had to count backwards in threes from a random three-digit number to prevent rehearsal (known as the Brown-Peterson technique). Recall of the nonsense syllables had to be 100% accurate and in the correct order in order for it to count as correctly recalled.

Results

The percentage recall was:

* After 3 seconds —80%

* After 6 seconds —50%

* After 18 seconds —less than 10%

Conclusion

The participants' recall decreased steadily between 3 and 18 seconds which suggested that the duration of the STM is not much more than 18 seconds.

Evaluation

One of the main problems with decay theory is that it is more or less impossible to test it and so it is purely theoretical. In lab situations, it is not possible to create a situation in which there is a blank period of time between presentation of material and recall. Once you have presented information participants will rehearse it. If you prevent rehearsal by introducing a distracter task, it results in interference with the memory so it is not purely looking at decay

Decay theory also has difficulty explaining the observation that older people sometimes have incredible memories of events that happened many decades before. If memories are 'fading' with time because the synaptic links aren't being used, then how does this explain how older people can sometimes remember events from their youth with great clarity?

2.4.3 Interference (LTM)

Another theory of forgetting, this time in LTM, is that of interference. Interference theory suggests that, over a period of time, more material will be stored and that this will become confused with what is already there. This is often due to similarities in the ways in which information is encoded.

Looking into the causes of forgetting in LTM is more complex than it has been for STM (trace decay). Two types of interference are defined:

- Proactive interference —where material learnt first interferes with material learnt later.

- Retroactive interference —where material learnt later interferes with material learnt earlier.

An experiment into the influence of proactive and retroactive interference might go as follows:

Proactive Interference

Group	1st time	2nd time	3rd time
Experimental	Learn list A	Learn list B	Recall list B
Conrol	-	Learn list B	Recall list B

The result of this experiment would be that the experimental group will find that they have proactive interference so it will be the control group who will be able to recall more of List B.

Retroactive Interference

Group	1st time	2nd time	3rd time
Experimental	Learn list A	Learn list B	Recall list A
Conrol	Learn list A	-	Recall list A

The result of this experiment would be that the experimental group will find that they have retroactive interference so it will be the control group who recall more of List A.

Interference activity

How does interference affect your life? Think of the studying that you have done. Imagine that you were starting to learn a new language each term —how would your previous learning affect the learning you were doing now? Select proactive or retroactive interference to decide your answer to A and B.

Last term	This term	
Studying German vocab.	Studying French vocab.	Difficult to remember the German words because of A
Studying French vocab.	Studying Italian vocab.	Difficult to remember Italian next term because of B.

1. A should be:

   - a) proactive interference
   - b) retroactive interference

2. B should be:

   - a) proactive interference
   - b) retroactive interference

Interference theory of forgetting: notebook exercise

You will need your psychology notebook for this activity.

Think about how you handle information when you are studying. If you are learning some new facts do you work hour after hour? Note the suggestion from interference earlier. New information will interfere with existing information. Best to study for a short time then take a break —you probably know this already, but now note that there is a psychological basis to this.

Does listening to music interfere with your learning or does it help? Can you watch television and learn? Note down how these interferences may affect your learning. What type of interference will influence your learning/memory most?

Write down your conclusions in your psychology notebook.

2.4.4   Evaluation of interference theory

Again, interference is an attractive, neat theory which could explain how we forget things. It has fallen out of popularity in some ways because many of the tests conducted to show that interference occurred were performed under artificial laboratory conditions so can't fully be related to the real world of memory and forgetting. It also tells us very little about the cognitive processes involved in forgetting.

2.4.5 Theories of forgetting: Cue-dependent (LTM)

Cue-dependent theory (or sometimes 'cue-dependent retrieval failure') is our final theory about how we forget and, like interference, it relates to LTM.

This theory suggests that we forget because information may actually be available in our brains, but it is temporarily inaccessible. Have you ever said "it's on the tip of my tongue" when someone asks you to recall something? This is an example of cue-dependent retrieval failure -you definitely know something, it feels so close that it is on the tip of your tongue, but it is slightly out of reach in your memory as if the retrieval cues needed are not present.

Example :

Cue-dependency

Have you ever seen any of the 'X-men' films which feature Hugh Jackman in the role of Wolverine? Throughout the first film of the series, the character tries to remember his origins and how he was created as a mutant. It is not until the third film that he fully remembers how he was created when he finds himself in the actual laboratory in which it took place.

Wolverine finds that the memories that are just out of reach are cue-dependent. When he finally finds the place where he was created, this is enough of a cue to help aid his memory into remembering the actual event.

Tulving (1974) argued that information would be more easily retrieved if the cues present when the information was stored were also present when its retrieval was required. The retrieval cues could be:

- external (or contextual) dependent cues —what the environment was like when the memory was stored, e.g. the colour of the room, pictures on the wall)

- internal (or state) dependent cues —what feelings were experienced when the memory was stored, e.g. happy, sad, etc.

Godden and Baddeley conducted a study that illustrates context-dependency in 1975. Their aim was to investigate the effects of context cues on recall. To see whether words learned in the same environment they are recalled in are recalled better than in a different environment to learning. To see if this applies in a natural setting, words learned and recalled either on land or under water.

18 members of a diving club took part in a repeated measures design consisting of 4 conditions —learning words on land and recalling on land, learning words on land, recalling under water; learning under water recalling under water, learning under water, recall on land. In the underwater condition this was at 20ft below surface. They had to learn 38 unrelated words which they heard twice during the learning stage. This was played through a diving communication device and the words were presented in blocks, with a 4 second interval in between to ensure the noise of the breathing apparatus did not affect hearing. As a distraction they then had to listen to and write down 15 numbers. There were 24 hours between conditions and the study conducted over 4 days. PP's were tested in pairs.

Godden and Baddeley found that around 50% better recall when learning and recall take place in the same environment, 40% more words were forgotten when the condition changed. Recall for learning on land and recall on land was 13.5 compared to 8.6 when they learned the words on land and had to recall under water. This supports the notion that environmental cues do improve recall and supports cue dependent theory.

A study that supports the effect of emotional state on recall was conducted by Goodwin et al. in 1969. They asked male volunteers to perform memory tasks that involved learning and remembering words while either sober or under the influence of alcohol. They found that, as would be expected, good retention of the words if the volunteers had been sober at learning and sober at recall. Perhaps unsurprisingly, if volunteers were sober at learning but drunk at recall, their memory was relatively impaired. And, volunteers who were drunk at learning and sober at recall were also amnesic.

To explain these phenomena, Tulving proposed the **Encoding Specificity Principle,** which is that human memories are more easily retrieved if the state (emotional cues) at the time of retrieval are similar to those in existence at the time the memory was stored.

2.4.6   Evaluation of cue dependent theory

The difference in environmental contexts has to be significant to affect memory and it is almost impossible to replicate in a laboratory situation. However, imaginative contextual recreation of cues has been found to help eye-witnesses remember details of an event they were witness to.

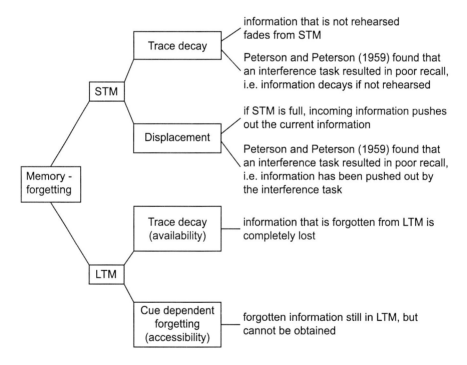

2.4.7   Forgetting due to brain damage

Brain damage can take place due to a number of reasons, including physical injury, neurological disease or the use of certain drugs, and can result in amnesia (disturbance or loss of memory). The two types of amnesia are anterograde (as explained above, where the ability to store new memories is impaired) and retrograde (where a person's pre-existing memories cannot be recalled). Anterograde amnesia occurs most commonly as a result of brain damage. Sometime they both exist together, which is called global amnesia.

Many kinds of amnesia are associated with damage to the hippocampus, which is used in the encoding, storage and retrieval of memories. If there is a blockage in the pathways along which information travels during the processes of encoding or retrieval, or the hippocampus is missing or damaged, then the brain may not be able to form new memories or retrieve some old ones.

In most cases, amnesia is a temporary condition, lasting from a few seconds to a few hours, but the duration can be longer depending on the severity of the damage, up to a few weeks or even months. Although it is very rare for anyone to experience total (permanent) amnesia, one well-known case of long-lasting and acute total (retrograde and anterograde) amnesia, perhaps the worst case of amnesia ever recorded, is that of the British musician Clive Wearing, who suffered damage to his brain as a result of an encephalitis virus in 1985. Because the damage was to an area of his brain required to transfer memories from working memory to long-term memory, he is completely unable to form lasting new long-term memories, and his memory is therefore limited to a short-term memory of between 7 and 30 seconds, to the extent that he will greet his wife like a long-lost friend even if she only left to go into the kitchen 30 seconds ago. However, Wearing still recalls how to play the piano and conduct a choir, despite having no recollection of having received a musical education, because his procedural memory was not damaged by the virus.

In general, memories of habits (procedural memory) are usually better preserved than memories of facts and events (declarative memory), and the most distant long-term memories, such as those of childhood, are more likely to be preserved. When memories return, older memories are usually recalled first, and then more recent memories, until almost all memory is recovered.

Forgetting notebook activity

You will need your psychology notebook for this activity.

Write down word for word as best you can the passage that you read or that was read to you in the sub-section about 'forgetting'.

Discuss the results of the recall.

- How accurate was the recall?

- What parts of the passage were forgotten or remembered best?

- Did names come easily?

- Were you able to remember details?

- How did you do with lists —such as the colours of the dawn?

- Did you invent words, ideas, etc. that were not part of the original passage?

- If there were a number of you doing the recall task, did any patterns emerge? Were there any differences in remembering according to gender or age group, for example?

- How many made up their own list of colours? For instance, how many included orange as one of the passage colours?

Add your comments and conclusions to your psychology notebook.

2.5   End of topic test

End of Topic 2 test   Go online

Memory

Q1:   Memory is our _____ processing ability to store, use and retrieve information we receive from the environment.

a) information
b) mnemonic
c) inference
d) reconstructive

....

Q2:   The process of putting information into the brain is known as:

a) encoding.
b) retrieval.
c) storage.

....

Q3:   The process of extracting information from the brain is known as:

a) encoding.
b) retrieval.
c) storage.

....

Q4:   The process of keeping information in the brain is known as:

a) encoding.
b) retrieval.
c) storage.

Q5:   Iconic memory lasts for around:

a) 1 day
b) 1 hour
c) 1 minute
d) 1 second

....

Q6:   What is the Miller magic number for bits of information memorised?

a) 3
b) 5
c) 7
d) 10

....

Q7: Who were the researchers behind the working memory model?

a) Glanzer and Cunitz
b) Baddeley and Hitch
c) Miller and Miller
d) Peterson and Peterson

. . . .

Q8: Conrad (1964) suggested that the type of environmental stimuli which affects memory the most is:

a) sight
b) smell
c) sound
d) touch

. . . .

Q9: If you could remember the first question that you answered in a maths test yesterday, what type of memory store would you be using?

a) long-term
b) semantic
c) sensory
d) short-term

Forgetting

Q10: Lack of effective rehearsal or insufficient processing of information is called:

a) trace decay
b) interference
c) cue-dependent
d) state-dependent

. . . .

Q11: When information is stored, but is difficult to retrieve, this is called:

. . . .

Q12: Confusion is called:

a) trace decay
b) interference
c) cue-dependent
d) state-dependent

. . . .

Q13: When you do well in an exam because it took place in the same room where you learnt the subject of the exam, this is called:

a) trace decay
b) interference
c) context-dependent
d) state-dependent

Unit 2 Topic 3

Stress (optional topic)

Contents

Learning objective

By the end of this section, you should be able to describe, explain, evaluate, apply and analyse:

- the physiology of stress which must include:
  - the general adaptation syndrome
  - the sympathetic medullary system
  - the hypothalamic pituitary-adrenal system
  - the role of cortisol
  - the role of immunosuppression on physical health
  - the aims, methods, results, evaluation and conclusions of one study into the physiology of stress

- sources of stress, which must include:
  - life changes and daily hassles
  - the effects of workload and control on workplace stress

- individual differences in the stress response, which must include:
  - Type A and Type B personality types
  - hardiness
  - the aims, methods, results, evaluation and conclusions of one study into individual differences in the stress response

- types of coping strategies, which must include:
  - drug therapy
  - stress inoculation therapy
  - social support, including instrumental and emotional

Before we go on to look at some explanations for stress, we need to define it.

The Oxford Dictionary defines **stress** as

"A state of mental or emotional strain or tension resulting from adverse or demanding circumstances".

We have all heard the term 'stress' before (particularly exam stress!), but what exactly is it and what effect does it have on us?

Stress can be defined as a feeling we experience when

"demands exceed the personal and social resources the individual is able to mobilise"

(Lazarus, 1984).

For Lazarus, stress is a state of anxiety produced when events and responsibilities exceed an individual's ability to cope.

When you are stressed, you may feel:

- anxious;
- frustrated;
- tricked.

Your body may react with:

- sweaty palms;
- furrowed brows;
- tensed muscles.

Alternatively, stress is

"the nonspecific response of the body to any demand made upon it"

(Selye, 1956).

These demands can be a threat, a challenge or any kind of change that requires our body to adapt. Our body's response is automatic and immediate.

3.1   Biological approach to stress

The physiological model of stress is of importance to psychology because it understands stress in terms of our emotional response to whatever has caused it.

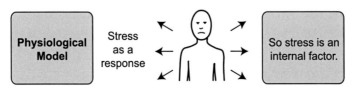

Our emotional response to environmental stressors is governed by our physiology, in particular our hypothalamus and autonomic nervous system. Both operate individually and together to allow us to cope better in stressful situations.

General adaptation syndrome

To understand the short and long-term effects of stress better, Hans Selye, the Austrian-born physician, identified the general adaptation syndrome (GAS). GAS is a descriptive term.

He called this syndrome *general* because it is produced by agents, which have a general effect upon large portions of the body, and *adaptive* because it stimulates defence. He considered it to be a *syndrome* because its individual manifestations are coordinated and even partly dependent upon each other.

Following his experiments with rats, where he measured their physiological responses to external stressors such as heat and cold, prolonged restraint, and surgical procedures, Selye (1956) extrapolated from these studies to human beings.

He was able to tell us that the general adaptation syndrome (GAS) is our body's defence mechanism against both the short- and long-term effects of stress.

"Stress is the non-specific response of the body to any demand made upon it." (Selye, 1956)

Stress is one cause of the general adaptation syndrome.

The consequences of results of unrelieved stress include tiredness, irritability, lack of concentration and difficulty in sleeping. We may also experience hair loss.

Over and above stress itself, the general adaptation syndrome is further influenced by our general health and bodily well being, gender, age, ethnic or racial background, level of education, socio-economic status (SES), and genetic makeup etc.

Some of these variables are biological in origin and are difficult, or impossible, to change.

Taylor *et al* (2000) indicates that men and women respond somewhat differently to stress, with women in stressful situations being more likely to use what is called the 'tend and befriend' response rather than the classical 'fight or flight' pattern.

These researchers also note that most of the early studies of the effects of stress on the body were conducted with only male subjects.

Notwithstanding, Selye thought that the general adaptation syndrome involved two major systems of the body: our nervous system and our endocrine (or hormonal) system.

He then went on to outline three distinctive stages in the evolution of the general adaptation syndrome.

Stage 1: Alarm Reaction (AR)

- Presence of stressor registered.

- Stress response systems activated.

- ACTH secrected.

- Glucocoticoids secreted.

- Adrenaline and noradrenaline secreted.

This stage has our body prepare to expand energy. When the stressful situation happens, our body is thrown into a state of shock. Physiological changes occur, and our body temperature and blood pressure are initially lowered. Physiological arousal to 'fight or flight' takes over.

As suggested above the first stage of the general adaptation syndrome is called alarm reaction. Alarm reaction is our immediate reaction to a stressor. In the initial phase of stress, we demonstrate a 'fight or flight' response, which prepares our body for physical activity.

However, our initial alarm reaction response to stress can also decrease the effectiveness of our immune system, particularly if prolonged. We can thus be more susceptible to illness during this phase.

Stage 2: Resistance (SR)

- Body's stress response is fully activated trying to cope with the stressor.

- 'Fight or Flight' response less effective.

If stress is prolonged, the body still tries to maintain 'normal' functioning; however, we remain in a state of arousal in order to cope with the stressor. Continued exposure to the stressor (or additional stressors) eventually drains the body of its resources and leads to the third stage.

Stage 2 of the GAS could be renamed the stage of adaptation, instead of the stage of resistance.

This is because during prolonged periods of stress our body adapts to the continual stress placed upon it. Our body will physiologically adapt to allow us to survive better for longer.

If for example the stressor is starvation, possibly due to anorexia, during SR the person could experience a reduced desire for physical activity in order to conserve energy. The body would also adapt to maximise the absorption of nutrients from any food that is ingested.

Stage 3: Exhaustion (SE)

- Energy reserves depleted.

- Hormone levels depleted.

- Immune system collapses.

- Stress related illnesses become more likely.

During this stage, our bodily resources become so depleted that exhaustion occurs and our susceptibility to illness increases.

At this third and final stage stress may have continued for some time. Consequently our body's resistance to the stressor may gradually reduce, or collapse altogether.

Generally, this means our immune system, and our body's ability to resist disease, may be almost totally destroyed.

This sounds dramatic but patients who experience long-term stress may succumb to heart attacks or severe infection due to such reduced immunity.

This makes sense, in that a person with a stressful job may experience long-term stress that might lead to high blood pressure, and an eventual heart attack.

Stress isn't all bad!

Selye did not regard stress in a purely negative light. He frequently pointed out that stress is an inevitable part of life, which can result in pleasure, as well as fear or anxiety.

As he says

"Stress is not even necessarily bad for you; it is also the spice of life, for any emotion, any activity, causes stress"

(Selye, 1956)

Later researchers coined the term *eustress*, or pleasant stress, to reflect that positive experiences such as a promotion, completing a degree or training programme, marriage, travel, etc. which, while stressful, can also be joyful.

Selye also tells us that our perception of stress, and our response to it, is highly individualised. A job or sport that one person finds anxiety provoking or exhausting may, on the other hand, be appealing and enjoyable to someone else. As said earlier, what is distress for one is eustress for another.

In *The Stress of Life* (1956), Selye recommends an approach to stress that he describes as

"living wisely in accordance with natural laws."

3.1.1   Research

Key study into the biology of stress: Selye (1956)

Hans Selye performed the following research into stress in 1956.

Aim

To find the link between long-term stress and illness.

Method

A laboratory experiment was conducted whereby rats were exposed to several severe but non-lethal stressors, for example, exercise, mutilation, poison and injury. The rats were then observed over a period of time to see how they responded.

Results

Selye found that the response to these stressors could be categorised into three, distinct, stages.

1. Alarm —the rats' first reaction was the activation of the hypothalamo-pituitary-adrenal cortex (HPA) axis, the nervous system (sympathetic nervous system) and the adrenal glands. Cortisol, adrenaline, and noradrenaline were released - these provide the body with instant energy: this is known as the 'fight-or-flight' syndrome. The rats were now immediately equipped with enough energy to handle the stressor, however, if this energy is repeatedly not used by physical activity, it can become harmful.

2. Resistance —in this stage of resistance, the rats' bodies tried to cope with the stressor. The parasympathetic nervous system attempted to preserve the resources that have been depleted during the alarm stage, and hormones were released to restore the body's balance (homeostasis). This stage in itself did no harm to the rats: however, if this recovery process was impeded, say by another stressor coming along, then real damage can occurred.

3. Exhaustion —at this phase, the stress had continued for some time. The rats' ability to resist was lost because all coping resources were gone. The adaptation process was over and not surprisingly; this stage of the general adaptation syndrome was the most hazardous to the health of the rats. Chronic stress damaged nerve cells in tissues and organs. Particularly vulnerable was the hippocampus section of the brain (in humans, this can lead to impaired memory, and to depression). The autonomic nervous system was also affected, which contributed to chronic illnesses occurring in rats, like heart disease and stomach ulcers.

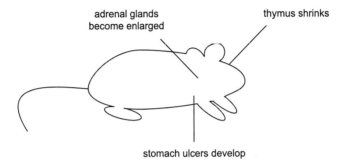

adrenal glands become enlarged

thymus shrinks

stomach ulcers develop

Conclusion

Selye determined that there is a limited supply of adaptive energy to deal with stress. That amount declines with continuous exposure.

Evaluating Selye

As psychologists, we should be constantly evaluating any theory that we are offered to see if it 'fits' with our original ideas on the subject.

Strengths of the GAS

1. Selye's work alerted the world of medicine to the link between stress and illness, which helped to create therapies for stress-related illnesses.

2. It was the first systematic attempt to describe the body's response to stress.

3. It does help to explain how physical stressors can cause illnesses.

Weaknesses of the GAS

1. The model does not work for all stress. For example, Mason (1995) says that stressors vary in the amount of adrenaline and cortisol they produce, depending on the level of anger or fear. This challenges the model.

2. It ignores psychological factors, such as personality and gender.

3. Much of the research supporting the model comes from studies carried out on animals. This is unethical as the animals are caused distress and pain, and there is a problem with generalising findings from studies conducted on non-human animals to humans —there are key differences.

4. We also apply our higher-level cognitive processes of perception, attention, language, memory, and thinking to our analysis and response to stressors - these are ignored in Selye's model.

3.1.2   Activities

GAS notebook exercise

You will need your psychology notebook for this activity.

The general adaptation syndrome (GAS) is an important explanation of the stress response. Summarise your own thoughts in your psychology notebook under the heading GAS, either in a diagram or text using the three headings:

1. Alarm

2. Resistance

3. Exhaustion

You should now have information in your notebook under the heading of *general adaptation syndrome (GAS)*.

Biological approach to stress: GAS questions   Go online

Q1:   Hans Selye identified the General Adaptation Syndrome in 1956.

a) True
b) False

. . . .

Q2:   Selye discovered the GAS after his experiments on cats.

a) True
b) False

. . . .

Q3:   The GAS involves our nervous system.

a) True
b) False

. . . .

Q4: There are three stages regards the GAS.

a) True
b) False

....

Q5: The alarm reaction prepares our body to expend energy.

a) True
b) False

....

Q6: Flight-or-fight firstly occurs at the SE stage.

a) True
b) False

....

Q7: The resistance stage could be renamed the adaptation stage.

a) True
b) False

....

Q8: Prolonged stress can seriously affect our immune system.

a) True
b) False

Seyle's work was important in flagging up the medical aspect of stress. You may wish to include the questions and answers on GAS in your psychology notebook.

3.2 Short-term response to stress

How our body responds to stress is understood in terms of two physiological pathways that are regulated by our hypothalamus in our brain. These two pathways, routes or axes produce biochemical hormones that influence how our body feels and behaves towards whatever is stressing us in the first place.

Study the following diagram which shows how the release of hormones helps us to respond to stress in both the short and in the long term. The next few sections will study it in more depth.

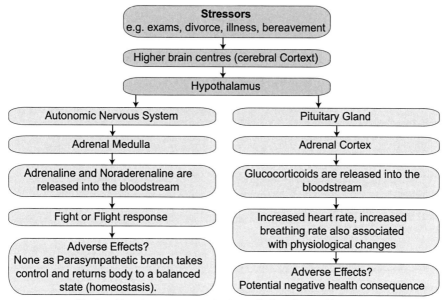

Short and long term responses to stress via the release of hormones

The adrenal glands

The two physiological pathways or axes that govern how we respond to stress are linked in our body by way of our adrenal glands, which are to be found just above each of our kidneys.

Our adrenal glands are part of our endocrine system and, like it, are controlled by our hypothalamus. Our adrenal glands have two parts: the adrenal cortex and the adrenal medulla. The adrenal cortex, which is the outer part of our adrenal gland, releases a series of hormones called glucocorticoids into our bloodstream.

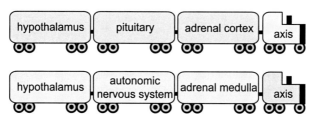

The adrenal medulla releases hormones such as adrenaline and noradrenaline into our bloodstream. Both help us deal with stress in the short and long term.

The hypothalamus is found at the base of the brain, and has a small structure sitting above it called the pituitary gland. They control the endocrine system in our body.

The endocrine system secretes hormones in to our bloodstream, which act as chemical 'messengers' instructing our body what to do. . Hormones can have dramatic effects on our behaviour and emotions.

In a stressful situation our pituitary gland or 'master gland' secretes certain hormones into our bloodstream. These travel via our bloodstream to various parts of our body e.g. the kidneys, where they initiate the release of further hormones, which have us behave in particular ways.

Short-term response to stress

Our immediate and short-term response to an environmental stressor involves the hypothalamic-ANS-adrenal medulla axis or pathway.

Our immediate response shocks the sympathetic branch of the autonomic nervous system into action.

Consequently five things happen.

1. The sympathetic branch stimulates the adrenal medulla in our adrenal glands.

2. The adrenal medulla then secretes two hormones: adrenaline and noradrenaline.

3. These hormones arouse activity in our sympathetic nervous system and reduce activity in the parasympathetic nervous system.

4. Arousal of the sympathetic nervous system leads to the 'fight or flight' response (Cannon, 1914) which prepares the body for action, either by fighting or fleeing the threat or danger.

5. Once the 'threat' is over, the parasympathetic branch takes control and brings the body back into a balanced state. This is called homeostasis.

No adverse effects are experienced by us in our short-term response to stress. Indeed this innate ability has survival value for us.

Short-term response to stress notebook exercise

You will need your psychology notebook for this activity.

Imagine the scenario that you are walking through a wood near your home. Suddenly a large ferocious snarling dog appears yards in front of you.

Explain your body's short-term response to this situation from a physiological point of view.

Structure your answer as follows:

- Identify the stressor in the above situation;

- Briefly explain the elements that go to make up the hypothalamic-pituitary-adrenal pathway;

- Describe the body's short-term reaction on this basis.

Write down your answers in your psychology notebook.

You should now have information in your notebook under the heading of *short-term response to stress.*

3.3   Long-term response to stress

Long-term response to stress —the hypothalamic pituitary-adrenal system (HPPA)

Prolonged exposure to a stressful situation demands that our body expends vast amounts of energy.

Our body's counter-shock response helps minimise any damage that might be done to it due to prolonged exposure to stress. This involves the pituitary gland controlling hormonal release to provide high energy compounds and the specific hormone cortisol, which affects glucose (sugar) metabolism.

The physiological effects of our body's long-term response to stress are similar to those of the short-term.

The long-term maintenance of increased heart and breathing rates, and associated physiological changes in our body, do however have negative health consequences for us.

The role of cortisol

Scientists have known for years that elevated cortisol levels interfere with learning and memory, lower immune function and bone density, weight gain, increased blood pressure and cholesterol levels, and heart disease.

Chronic stress and elevated cortisol levels also lead to a lower life expectancy. Recent studies have also linked elevated cortisol levels as a potential trigger for mental illness and decreased resilience —especially in adolescence.

Cortisol is released in response to fear of stress by the adrenal glands as part of the fight-or-flight mechanism. The fight-or-flight mechanism, as you have seen, is part of the general adaptation syndrome defined by Hans Selye in 1936. He defined two types of 'stress': eustress (good stress) and distress (bad stress).

Both eustress and distress release cortisol as part of the general adaptation syndrome. Once the alarm to release cortisol has sounded, your body becomes mobilised and ready for action —but there has to be a physical release (by fighting or fleeing). Otherwise, cortisol levels build up in the blood, which wreaks havoc on your mind and body.

Eustress creates a heightened state of arousal, which is invigorating and often linked with a tangible goal (e.g. finish revising the role of cortisol for the exam). Cortisol levels return to normal upon completion of the task. Distress doesn't provide an outlet for the cortisol and causes the fight-or-flight mechanism to backfire. Ironically, our own biology —which was designed to ensure our survival as hunters and gatherers —is sabotaging our bodies and minds in a sedentary digital age.

HPPA and SAM

You could create a board game for yourselves and/or your classmates based on the HPPA and SAM processes.

3.4 The role of immunosuppression on physical health

The role of stress on immunosuppression notebook exercise

You will need your psychology notebook for this activity.

- On the internet, look up the role of NK cells in providing natural immunity.

- Also, look up the role of lymphocytes (T cells and B cells) on specific immunity.

Write what you find in your notebook. This will provide an introduction and foundation for your study of the role of stress on immunosuppression.

You should now have information in your notebook under the heading of *The role of stress on immunosuppression.*

The immune system is a protection mechanism design do defend us against the millions olf bacteria, microbes, viruses, toxins and parasites that would like to invade our body. Cells of the immune system include lymphocytes, T-cells, killer T-cells, macrophages and cytokines. If the immune system stops functioning, we are prone to all sorts of infections and illnesses that could seriously affect our health, or worse.

Some research, such as that by Segerstrom and Miller (2004) found that stress can strengthen natural immunity. This is as a result of acute (short-term) stress. However, much of the research focuses on the effect of chronic (long-term) stress, which tend to illustrate that this type of stress leads to immunosuppression.

When a person experiences chronic (or long term) stress, the effect may be to produce an under or over vigilant immune system, with the result that the person becomes unwell. People who are, for example, studying for exams, have suffered a bereavement, are moving home etc. may notice they suffer coughs and colds more often than when they are not going through a stressful time.

As you have learned, when stress extends beyond the acute stage (i.e. it becomes chronic), the HPPA is triggered, and signals the pituitary gland to release adrenocorticotrophic hormone (ACTH) which in turn triggers adrenal cortex to release of cortisol the output of cortisol.

The adrenal cortex increases in size after ACTH continues to be released (presumably to cope with a greater need for cortisol production), but it shrinks when levels of ACTH have been lowered for a period of time.

The function of cortisol is to activate the "fight-or-flight" response in order to tackle a stressor. It does this by releasing glucose into the bloodstream to feed the muscles and organs required to flee or fight. One of the body's systems that is sacrificed (as it is not needed to flee or fight) is the immune system. This is fine if the stressor is acute —the immune system is soon up and running again, but become problematic if the stress is prolonged.

One of the key pieces of research that illustrates this was carried out by Janet Kiecolt-Glaser in 1995.

Kiecolt-Glaser's aim was to demonstrate the direct effects of stress on the immune system by looking at how quickly wounds heal. In a field experiment, Kiecolt-Glaser obtained a group of 13 female participants using volunteer sampling who were caring for relatives suffering from senile dementia. There were two groups of participants, matched on the basis of age and income, but not marital status. All participants were given a would, which was a cut of 3.5mm just below the elbow. The wounds were dressed and treated by a nurse in the same way for each participant. Another measure of immune functioning was taken. The researchers assessed levels of cytokines (a biochemical substance involved in regulating the body's immune response). Participants were also given a 10 item perceived stress scale to check how stressed they actually felt. Kiecolt-Glaser found that complete wound healing took much longer in the carers than in the control group. It was also found that cytokine levels were lower in the carers than in the control group and on the perceived stress scale, the carers also did actually indicate that they were feeling more stressed. This shows that chronic stress suppresses the functioning of the immune system (immunosuppression), which in turn increases vulnerability to illness.

Evaluation of Kiecolt-Glaser

Strengths

1. This study was a field study which is conducted in a real life setting, which means that it was real-life stress that was being investigated, so the findings can be generalised beyond the research setting.

2. Kiecolt-Glaser's findings are supported by other findings, such as Marucha who found that wounds heal more quickly in students during their summer holidays compared to 3 days before an exam.

Weaknesses

1. Kiecolt-Glaser studied only females. The results, therefore, may not relate to men —they may respond differently to stress.

2. A volunteer sample was used, which means that the research will be populated with similar people (e.g. Type A personalities are more likely to volunteer). This means that the findings are not able to be generalised to the general population.

Activity on immunosuppression   Go online

Q9:
The HPA axis is the body's "stress system" which controls levels of cortisol and other important stress related hormones, as well as the _____. Any stress lasting longer than a few minutes results in increased levels of _____ being released from the adrenal cortex. This happens as a result of activation of the pituitary gland which causes the release adrenocorticotrophic hormone (ACTH), which in turn causes the adrenal cortex to release cortisol.

Prolonged release of ACTH causes the _____ to increase in size (presumably to cope with a greater need for cortisol production), whereas long-term ACTH deficiency causes it to shrink.

This system is referred to as the hypothalamic-pituitary-adrenal axis (or HPA axis). The ultimate result of the HPA axis activation is to increase levels of cortisol in the blood during times of stress. Cortisol's main role is in releasing glucose into the bloodstream in order to facilitate the _____ response. It also suppresses and modulates the immune system, digestive system and reproductive system.

Stress causes an increased overall cortisol output. During _____ stress, changes occur to areas in the brain resulting in increased sustained activation of the HPA axis. Long-term stress, however, can result in negative feedback to the HPA axis, resulting in _____. Whether or not chronic stress results in high or low cortisol output depends on the nature of the threat, the time since onset, and the person's response to the situation.

Long-term stress can lead to exhaustion, due to the _____ of the HPA axis in the brain.

Word list: cortisol, suppression, immune system, "fight-or-flight", chronic, adrenal cortex

Biological explanations of stress practical

Try the following process (it may be best to get someone to talk you through it). It will take about 10 minutes.

> Warning: do not attempt this exercise if you have an injury of any kind, if you have drunk alcohol or taken any other depressant drug.

Follow the steps in order:

1. Select a comfortable chair, preferably a reclining one.

2. Find a quiet room.

3. Close both eyes, take two deep breaths, and feel yourself 'let go'.

4. Extend both arms straight out and clench your fist. Gradually increase the tension level until all of the muscles in your fingers and hands are fully tight. Now relax. Let your arms drop naturally. Be aware of the difference between feeling 'tense' and 'relaxed'.

5. Extend both arms again, straight out, and tense the muscles of your lower arm and elbow. Hold the position and become aware of the feeling. Now relax. Let your arms drop naturally to your side.

6. Tense the muscles in your forehead by frowning. Hold this expression and become aware of the feeling. Now relax. Let all the muscles in your forehead become smoother and smoother.

7. Tense the muscles in your neck. Hold the position and become aware of the feeling. Now relax.

8. Tense the muscles in your neck. Hold the position and become aware of the feeling. Now relax.

9. Tense the muscles in your shoulder. Hold the position and become aware of the feeling. Now relax.

10. Tense the muscles in your back, first the upper back then the lower back. Hold the position and become aware of the feeling. Now relax.

11. Tense the muscles of your chest. Hold the position and become aware of the feeling. Now relax.

12. Tense the muscles in your stomach. Hold the position and become aware of the feeling. Now relax.

13. Tense the muscles in your abdomen. Hold the position and become aware of the feeling. Now relax.

14. Tense the muscles in your upper leg including all of the muscles of the thigh. Hold the position and become aware of the feeling. Now relax.

15. Tense the muscles in your lower leg including all of the muscles of the knee and calf. Hold the position and become aware of the feeling. Now relax.

16. Tense the muscles in your feet and toes. Hold the position and become aware of the feeling. Now relax.

17. Now concentrate on relaxing all of the muscles of your body. Become aware of any areas that might still be tense in any way and relax them, Maintain this state of total muscle relaxation for at least two to three minutes.

18. Open your eyes, stretch, and feel refreshed (assuming that you haven't fallen asleep by this point).

You could test the effectiveness of this relaxation therapy for yourself.

1. Take your pulse and record your heart rate as a 'before relaxation' measure. You can take your pulse by placing the index and second finger on your wrist, one inch below the base of you thumb, and counting the pulse for 10 seconds. Multiply the number of beats by six to give your heartbeat per minute.

2. Practice the above 18 steps.

3. Immediately after, take your pulse again (or have someone else do it if you are too relaxed). Record the heartrate as 'after relaxation'.

4. Record your results (or draw up a table like the below, of doing this in a group).

Participant	Heart rate before relaxation	Heart rate after relaxation
1		
2		
3		
4		
5		
Mean/mode		

Biological explanations of stress: Exercise practical

On a piece of paper, draw a line (continuum) with the labels 'very relaxed' at one end and 'very stressed' at the other, and place a mark on the line to indicate how stressed/relaxed you feel —label this mark BE.

Jog on the spot for one minute (unless there is any reason why you can't, (e.g. injury or heart condition).

Finally, place another mark on the line according to how stressed/relaxed you feel now —label this mark AE.

If you are doing this in a group, you could draw up a table like the below. Before doing this, you will need to assign a score ranging from 0 (exceedingly laid back — practically asleep) to 60 (completely frazzled).

Participant	Stressed/relaxed before exercise (BE)	Stressed/relaxed after exercise (AE)	Difference +/-
1			
2			
3			
4			
5			
Mean/mode			

Points to consider:

- Is your BE (the group's mean BE) rating greater than the mean of the 'after exercise' rating?

- Does this suggest that people are more relaxed after exercise?

- If you did this activity in a group, were there any notable individual differences?

- Apart from the exercise, what else may have affected the relaxed/stressed rating?

3.5 Sources of stress

We've now finished looking at the physiology of stress and will go on to find out about sources of stress, including:

- life changes and daily hassles

- the effects of workload and control on workplace stress

Life changes

Life changes are those changes in our lives which disrupt our normal routines. They include both positive and negative events such as marriage, divorce a new job, moving house, etc. A number of researchers argue that life changes are a major source of stress, whether positive or negative.

Research into life changes was conducted in 1964 by Holmes and Rahe, who were the first to record the effects of life events. From their work in hospitals, Holmes and Rahe noticed that certain life events in their patients seemed to be associated with stress and poor health (e.g. heart disease). Each event, called a Life Change Unit (LCU), had a different "weight" for stress. The more events the patient added up, the higher the score. The higher the score, and the larger the weight of each event, the more likely the patient was to become ill.

The scale they created was called The Social Readjustment Rating Scale or SRRS. You can have a go at the youth and adult version of the scale, here https://www.mindtools.com/pages/article/new TCS_82.htm

The scoring for the SRRS is as follows:

0-149: low stress level

150-199: mild life changes

200-299: moderate stress level

300 +: high stress level

Holmes and Rahe's SRRS notebook exercise

You will need your psychology notebook for this activity.

What were your thoughts when carrying out the SRRS, and when you found out your score? Take a note of them.

Now, look up the following studies that evaluate the reliability and validity of Holmes and Rahe's SRRS

- Michael & Ben-Zur 2007, not all life events correlate with ill health —which looks at how coping strategies can make a difference between experiencing distress or eustress.

- Complete the Life Experiences Survey which you will find below this box, and take note of what is different about this survey from that of Holmes and Rahe.

Write what you find in your notebook. This will provide the basis of an evaluation of the SRRS.

You should now have information in your notebook under the heading of *Sources of stress: Life Changes*.

Evaluation of Life Events as sources of stress

Strengths

- This was the first attempt to try to quantify stressors to find a way of relating these to the increasing findings that highly stressed people did experience more ill-health.

- There is evidence to suggest that a relationship exists between the number of life events experienced recently and the chance of catching colds.

Weaknesses

- Not everyone experiences the same stressor in the same way —some will find the same life event much more or much less stressful than someone else. For example, divorce may be a relief for some, while being devastating to others.

- Holmes and Rahe conducted their research on men. This means that the study was androcentric, and the findings cannot generalise to women.

- The SRRS is now outdated (you may have noticed this when you completed it!), and cannot apply to people in today's society.

- The connection that Holmes and Rahe found between stress and life events is correlational, which means that they are associated, but not necessarily that life events cause stress-related illnesses.

3.6 The Life Experiences Survey (Sarason, I., Johnson, J., and Siegel J. 1978)

Listed below are a number of events which sometimes bring about change in the lives of those who experience them and which necessitates social readjustment. Please check those events that you have experienced in the recent past and indicate the time period during which you have experienced each event.

For each item you check, please indicate the extent to which you viewed the event as having either a positive or negative impact on your life at the time the event occurred. That is, indicate the type and extent of impact that the event had. A rating of -3 would indicate an extremely negative impact. A rating of 0 indicates neither positive nor negative. A rating of +3 would indicate an extremely positive impact.

http://www4.ncsu.edu/~kklein/html/sarason.htm by Sarason et al.

Daily hassles

Daily hassles are relatively minor events arising out of day-to-day living such as losing your house keys and missing the college bus. Some researchers, such as Delongis et al. (1982) claim that these daily hassles are better predictors of stress than life events.

References

Kohn, P. & Macdonald, J.E. (1992). The Survey of Life Experiences: A decontaminated hassles

3.6.1 Research into daily hassles: Delongis et al. (1988)

Aim: To see whether the SRRS or their own daily hassles scale was a better predictor of later health problems.

Method: 100 participants from around San Francisco aged between 45- 64 well educated with high income asked to complete 4 questionnaires once a month for a year. They were given a 'hassles' scale which included 117 hassles, e.g. concern about weight, crime. They also gave them an 'uplifts' scale, which included 135 uplifts, e.g. promotion, relations with friends. For comparison, participants also completed a Life Events questionnaire, which include 34 major events. Finally, they also completed a health questionnaire, which asked them about their overall health, any symptoms of ill-health they had, and their energy levels.

Results: Both the frequency and intensity of daily hassles had a significant impact on health. Uplifts had little effect on health.

They concluded that daily hassles is a better predictor of illness than life events (as measured by the SRRS).

Lazarus (1999) suggests the accumulation effect is at work in creating ill-health. An accumulation of minor daily stressors creates persistent irritations, frustrations, and overloads which then result in more serious stress reactions such as anxiety and depression. There is also the amplification effect —chronic stress caused by major life changes may make people more vulnerable to daily hassles.

Accumulation
Minor hassles build up and multiply leading to a severe stress reaction (Ill-health).

Amplification
Already experiencing chronic stress makes people less able to deal with hassles.

Evaluation of daily hassles as sources of stress

Strengths

- There is some research support for the notion that daily hassles are good predictors of ill-health. For example, Flett et al. (1995) studied a total of 320 students (160 per gender) who read a scenario describing a male or female individual who had experienced either a major life event or daily hassles and then rated the amount of support (both emotional and practical) that the person would receive and seek from others. Individuals who had suffered major life events were rated higher in both seeking and receiving support from significant others. The findings suggest that compared to major life events, the greater negative influence of daily hassles on psychological adjustment may be due, in part to the reduced social and emotional support received from others. This presumably means that one reason why daily hassles are such a negative influence on later health is that we don't receive adequate social support to deal with them.

- Bouteyre et al. (2007) investigated the relationship between daily hassles and the mental health of students during the transition from college to university. Results showed that 41% of the participants suffered from depressive symptoms and there was a relationship between scores on the hassles scales and the incidence of depressive symptoms. Therefore Bouteyre et al.s research supports the idea that there is a link between daily hassles and the development of health problems.

- Gulian et al (1990) found that participants reporting a difficult day at work subsequently reported higher levels of stress on their commute home. when unresolved hassles from work are carried forward into the driving situation: events e.g. the actions of other road users, are more likely to be interpreted as stressful by the driver.

Weaknesses

- There are individual differences in how daily hassles are perceived, which is not accounted for in Delongis' theory. For example, Miller et al (1992) studied 250 people over 50 years of age and their relationship with their pets. For females, pets were commonly associated with uplifts, but for males, pets were more likely to be associated with hassles. This shows that there are individual differences in the way that both males and females perceive stressors in their lives. What is relaxing to one might be stressful to another.

- Again, the study was correlational, so a cause and effect relationship between daily hassles and ill-health cannot be made. We can only say that there is a relationship between them.

Sources of stress questions   Go online ❄

Q10: What is the difference between a daily hassle and a life event?

....

Q11: Give three examples of daily hassles.

....

Q12: Describe the SRRS.

....

Q13: Explain one weakness of this scale.

....

Q14: Name a study that investigates life events.

....

Q15: What conclusions did Delongis make about daily hassles and life events?

....

Q16: Explain **one** strength and **one** weakness of Delongis' study.

....

Q17: Explain how *Bouteyre et al's study supports Delongis'* findings.

3.6.2 Research

The effects of workload and control on workplace stress

Marmot et al (1997) aimed to investigate the association between workplace stress and stress-related illness in male and female civil servants. The researchers used the 'Job-Strain Model' which proposes the workplace leads to stress and illness in 2 ways:

- high workload —creating greater job demands

- low job control —e.g.: over deadlines, procedures, etc.

Marmot et al reasoned that, in the Civil Service, higher-grade employees would experience stress from high workload whereas low grade employees would experience stress from low job control.

Procedure:

A sample of 10,308 civil servants aged 35-55 (6895 men (67%) and 3413 women (33%)) were investigated in a longitudinal study over 3 years. Research methods included questionnaires and observation. Job control (an aspect of workplace stress) was measured through both a survey and by independent assessments of the work environment by personnel managers, using job specifications and role responsibilities. Job control was assessed on 2 occasions, 3 years apart. The survey also covered workload and social support. Records were kept of stress-related illness and the participants were checked for signs of cardiovascular disease —e.g. chest pains. A correlational analysis was carried out to test the association between job control and stress-related illness.

Results:

Participants with low job control were 4 times more likely to die of a heart attack than those with high job control. They were also more likely to suffer from other stress-related disorders such as cancers, strokes and gastrointestinal disorders. These findings were significant after other factors, such as employment grade, negative attitude to employment, job demands, social support, physical inactivity and other risk factors for chronic heart disease had been accounted for.

Conclusions: Control over workload and social support helps reduce stress and stress-related illnesses (e.g. chronic heart disease).

Evaluation of Marmot et al

Strengths

- A large sample was used, which means that the results are less likely to be affected by individual differences (e.g. genetic susceptibility to CHD)

- This was a longitudinal study, which means that events were investigated as they happened, not retrospectively, which relies on people's memories of events. Human memory is notoriously unreliable, so findings from longitudinal studies are more likely to be accurate.

Weaknesses

- Marmot and his colleagues used a self-report method of research, which means that the results may have been affected by the *social desirability bias* —i.e. participants may have responded in ways that make them appear in a positive light. This affects the validity of the findings.

- There may also have been demand characteristics, i.e. participants may have guessed that an association between job control and stress-related illness was being looked for, and so reported low job control if suffering from illness and high job control if not.

- This was yet another correlational study, which means that there was no control over the variable (job control), which makes interpretations difficult as cause and effect cannot be established (causation can only be established when an IV is directly manipulated). Therefore, it cannot be said that low job control causes stress-related illness; only that an association can be established. This lack of control also means that other factors such as personality and coping skills may be involved in the association.

- The jobs performed by those high and low in control differed in several ways other than simply control, i.e. those having high levels of job control generally earn more money, have more interesting jobs, have more opportunity for interpersonal, than those having low levels of job control. We do not know which of these factors is most closely associated with heart disease.

3.7 Individual differences and the stress response

Type A and Type B personality types

Friedman and Rosenman are two American cardiologists who in 1974 discovered a link between personality type, stress and coronary heart disease.

While coronary heart problems are associated with smoking, obesity, diabetes, lack of physical activity and old age, Friedman and Rosenman felt these variables did not account for all its occurrences.

Friedman and Rosenman went on to study their own patients, discovering that certain behaviours were more likely to exist in people with heart disease than in others. They called this combination of behaviours the Type A behaviour pattern, and the absence of them Type B.

Key study — Research by Friedman and Rosenman (1974)

Aim:
To test the hypothesis that Type A individuals are more likely to develop coronary heart disease than Type B individuals.

Method:
Medical case histories, interview and observation were used. 3200 healthy young men aged 39-59 from the San Francisco area were assessed for their personality type. All were found to be free from coronary heart disease at the start of the research. Any change in this situation was recorded for the next eight and a half years. Assessing Type A/B behaviour patterns was done by means of a structured interview using two kinds of information.

   a) answers given to pre-set interview questions such as how participants reacted to queueing, driving in slow traffic, deadlines at work, and problems at home
   b) Observation of participants' behaviour during the interview such as their way of speaking e.g. loudness, speed of talking, and their tendency to show impatience and hostility calculated by their reaction to the interviewer deliberately interrupting them from time to time

On the basis of these measures the participants were classed as A1 (Type A), A2 (not fully type A), X (equal amounts of Type A and B) and B (fully Type B) personalities.

Results:
70 percent of the 257 who developed coronary heart disease during the study had been assessed as Type A individuals at the beginning of the study. This association remained significant even when risk factors known to be associated with heart disease such as smoking and obesity were taken into account.

Conclusion:
The Type A personality is an independent risk factor regards heart disease. Men characterised as Type A personalities are roughly twice as likely to develop coronary heart disease as their Type B counterparts.

Evaluation:
Although aspects of lifestyle were controlled for, there may have been other variables that could have affected vulnerability to heart disease, such as elements of hardiness.

This was not an experimental study, so cause and effect cannot be assumed; other studies have failed to show a relationship between Type A behaviour and heart disease.

The study was conducted on American males only, as well as those aged between 39-59 so the findings cannot be generalised to non-American females outwith that age range.

Friedman and Rosenman reported that as many as 50 percent of the (US) population can be classified as Type A personalities.

- Impatience
- Competitiveness
- Easily irritated
- Quick to anger
- Suspicious
- Hostile
- Driven to achieve
- Aggressive

- Highly successful but dissatisfied
- Try to do more than one thing at a time
- Preoccupied with deadlines
- Rapid, loud speech
- Often interrupt others

The Type A Personality Type

Type A Health Problems
Type A personalities are two and a half times more likely to develop coronary heart disease than type B personalities. Type A personalities are prone to high blood pressure and high cholesterol levels.

Type B Personality Type

Type B personalities are usually relaxed, not excessively competitive, emotionally stable and psychologically secure.

Type B Health Problems
In a stressful situation the Type B personality is likely to be less hostile than their Type A counterpart and consequently suffer fewer heart related health problems.

Type C Personality Type

Type C, D and ER personalities have now also been identified. Temoshok (1987) proposed a Type C personality who has problems expressing emotions, particularly negative ones like anger.

Type C Health Problems
The Type C personality is more prone to cancer but there is no evidence to suggest the Type C personality causes cancer.

Type D Personality Type

The Type D personality is anxious, gloomy and socially inept.

Type D Health Problems
Burne (1999) reports the Type D personality is four times more likely to have recurring heart attacks

Type ER Personality Type

The Type ER personality is the emotional responder. These individuals demonstrate wild mood swings from great elation to deep despair.

Type ER Health Problems

These mood swings reduce blood flow to the heart and they are four times more likely to suffer a heart attack as a result (Burne, 1999).

You can test yourself for Type A/Type B personality here: http://www.psych.uncc.edu/pagoolka/TypeAB.html

---

Friedman and Rosenman notebook exercise

You will need your notebook for this activity.

Critically evaluate Friedman and Rosenman's research. Do you think anything could have been improved on?

Your answer should include the following points:

- all of the participants were male

- all of the participants were from the same area

You should now have an entry in your journal — *Type A behaviour and stress.*

Evaluation of the Type A/Type B theory of individual differences in stress

Strengths

- Many other researchers have researched the link between CHD and Type A personality. For example, Glass et al. (1980) who tested men whilst they were playing a video game that was rigged so no-one could win. On the basis of an interview, the participants were categorised as being either Type A or Type B and put into groups depending on this categorisation. A confederate was with each group while the video game was being played. In half of each group, the confederate was silent, and harassed the other half. Blood pressure and heart rate were measured, and there was no difference found between the groups when the confederate was silent. But the Type A group reacted much more strongly than the Type B group when they were being harassed.

Weaknesses

- There are also studies which do not support a relationship between Type A behaviour and CHD, such as Ragland and Brown. They carried out a follow-up study of Freidman and Rosenman's participants 22 years after the original study. They found no relationship between personality type and death from CHD, which challenges the claim that personality type is a major risk factor.

- Also, Myrtek conducted a meta-analysis of 35 studies of the relationship between personality type and CHD. They found an association between CHD and only one component of the Type A personality —hostility. There was no evidence of an association between CHD and other components of the Type A personality. This challenged Friedman and Rosenman's conclusion that Type A behaviour was a significant risk factor for death by CHD.

Hardiness

Psychological hardiness refers to the coping strategies, attitudes and beliefs that help people work through the stressors of life. These traits tend to fall into three major categories: challenge, control and commitment.

- **Commitment:** Sometimes described as "stickability", this describes the ability for an individual to carry out tasks successfully despite any problems or obstacles that arise. It has two elements. One is the extent to which a person is goal orientated. This is about the extent to which they will make promises, to themselves and to others. The other element is the extent to which they do what it takes to keep that promise. One implication is that a mentally tough person will often be naturally hard working. They are also likely to persevere with difficult tasks. Someone with a low commitment score would avoid making promises and shy away from anything that carries a sense of measurement.

- **Challenge:** This describes the extent to which individuals see problems, setbacks, and challenges as opportunities. Those who see them as opportunities will actively seek them out and will identify problems as ways for self-development. Those at the other end of the scale see problems as threats. It determines to some extent how people deal with change and with new situations.

- **Control:** This describes the extent to which people feel they are in control of their lives and their work. If you ask someone who scores highly on this scale to do something which may be out of their comfort zone then their default response would typically be "Give it to me. I can do it". They are more likely to volunteer and more likely to be prepared to handle several things at once.

  People at the other end of the scale are likely to hold back, to prefer to do one thing at a time and are likely to show (e.g., dismay and discomfort) what they feel to others.

You can test yourself for hardiness, here: https://testyourself.psychtests.com/testid/2099

3.7.1 Kobasa (1979) — research into the hardy personality

Aim:
To investigate whether a 'hardy' personality impacts on an individual's ability to defend against the negative effects of stress.

Procedure:
Kobasa studied 800 American business executives using the SRRS — 150 of whom were identified as having high stress levels, some with a low illness record and others with a high illness record. Kobasa have these 150 participants a hardiness questionnaire.

Results:
High stress/low illness participants scored highly on all 3 characteristics of hardiness. High stress/high illness participants scored much lower, suggesting that hardiness defends against the negative effects of stress.

Conclusion:
the 'hardy' personality encourages resilience and helps an individual to cope with stress.

Evaluation:
Further evidence supports Kobasa's findings, for example, Lifton et al (2006) found that low hardiness was disproportionately represented amongst those who had dropped out of university.

However, Kobasa's research relied on self-report measures, which means that some participants might provide false information in order to appear more stressed or more relaxed because of social desirability. This will affect the validity of Kobasa's results.

Furthermore, Kobasa's results might be affected by a third variable — 'hardy' people might exercise the control element of their personality to ensure they spend time relaxing, which will itself reduce stress. This is a weakness because the relationship between hardiness and someone's ability to cope with stress might not be as direct as Kobasa assumed.

3.7.2 Activities

What you now know about stress

You may find it useful to now build mind map of "what I know so far" about the biology, individual differences and sources of stress.

Stress management notebook exercise

You will need your psychology notebook for this exercise.

Once you have completed your mind map, think about and note down what you think these explanations suggest about how stress might be managed.

You should now have an entry in your notebook titled Stress Management.

3.8   Coping strategies

Coping strategies

Coping strategies are the ways in which we attempt to reduce the negative effects of stress. Some of these strategies are psychological (stress inoculation therapy and social support), or physiological (drug therapy), and there are benefits and drawbacks of each.

Drug therapy

Drugs help manage stress by altering the body's response to a stressor and making it easier to deal with.

Different drugs act on the body in different ways:

Benzodiazepines are anti-anxiety drugs that act on the brain. They are the most widely prescribed drug treatment for clinical disorders.
They work by increasing a natural brain chemical (neurotransmitter) called GABA, which has the effect of slowing activity in neurons and therefore overall brain activity.

Benzodiazepines react with the GABA sites on the outside of the receiving neuron. This opens a channel allowing Cl- ions to enter the neuron. Cl- ions make the neuron less responsive to other neurotransmitters that would usually excite the neuron. This will result in an individual feeling calmer and much less anxious about things that would otherwise cause stress.

Betablockers are another drug treatment for stress which acts on the sympathetic nervous system. and work by reducing by the activity of adrenaline and noradrenaline, which are key agents in the *sympathomedullary* response to stress.

Essentially, these hormones are blocked by the drug, which attaches itself to beta-adrenergic receptors on the heart and blood vessels. The receptor is therefore not stimulated and adrenaline and noradrenaline have no effect in increasing heart rate and blood pressure. This reduces a key part of the body's response to stress.

Evaluation of drug therapy for stress

Strengths

- Medication is a useful option for managing stress, especially in the short term. It can be used to help individuals deal with a stressful or anxiety provoking event such as redundancy or bereavement. Once an individual has stabilised their emotional response to stress they can begin to tackle the source of the stress.

- Drugs have been shown to be effective in treating stress . Drugs are tested in clinical trials with placebo conditions. A wide range of studies have shown that drugs can be highly effective and also safe for the short term treatment of major stress events and anxiety.

- Drug treatment can help an individual deal with the emotional side of a problem while they are coming to terms with a major stress event. This allows the individual to stabilise and begin to tackle the cause of the problem or to adjust their psychological response. They can be used alongside more long-term psychological treatments (e.g. cognitive behavioural therapy (CBT)).

- Drugs are extremely convenient. They are easy to administer and they work very quickly. These drugs are prescribed by a doctor so they are used in a supervised and safe way.

- Drugs are relatively cheap compared to psychological treatments, such as CBT.

Weaknesses

- Drugs only tackle the symptoms of stress, but they don't tackle cause. In the longer term, they are unhelpful.

- Stress drugs can have side effects such as drowsiness and fatigue, which makes it dangerous to undertake some activities such as driving while taking them.

- Increased use of drugs increases tolerance. This means that you need a higher dosage in order to achieve the same effect. This is because the body starts to adapt to the presence of the drug and adjusts its response. If an individual stops taking the drugs they will experience side effects, such as increased anxiety.

Overall drugs are not a good long-term solution to managing stress.

Stress Inoculation Therapy (SIT)

Stress inoculation training (SIT) is a cognitive stress reduction technique that is based on the principles of cognitive-behavioural therapy (CBT). It is called 'cognitive' because it concentrates on people's perceptions of stress and the way that they think about the stressful situation and their ability to cope. The aim of SIT is to prepare people to cope with stress in a similar way to which an injection prevents a disease. Training people to deal with stress before it becomes a problem involves three stages.

1. Conceptualisation: patients identify and express their feelings and fears - they are encouraged to imagine stressful situations, analyse what is stressful about them and how they might deal with them.

2. Skill acquisition and rehearsal: patients practise how to relax and how to express their emotions. Specific skills may be taught, such as positive thinking, communication skills, study skills and time management.

3. Application and follow through: patients are supported through progressively more threatening real-life situations while applying the newly acquired skills - this practise enables the person to use these skills to cope with future stressful situations.

In this therapy, Meichenbaum (1985) harnesses the power of positive thinking. In the table below, you will find some coping and reinforcing self-statements used in SIT.

Preparing for the stressful situation	Handling a stressful situation
• What is it I have to do? • I can develop a plan to deal with it. • Don't worry. Worry won't help anything. • No negative thoughts, just think rationally.	• One step at a time, you can deal with it. • Relax, you're in control, you can deal with it.
Coping with the feeling of being overwhelmed	**Reinforcing self-statements**
• It will be over shortly • It's not the worst thing that can happen. • Label your fear from 0 to 10 and watch it change. • Just keep the fear manageable.	• It worked, you did it! • You can be pleased with the progress you're making. • It wasn't as bad as you expected. • I was able to do it because I was well prepared.

There is some research support for the effectiveness of SIT, e.g. Sheehy and Horan (2004) reported the case of law students who received four weekly sessions of SIT each lasting 90 minutes. They recorded lowered levels of anxiety and an improvement in the grades of weaker students.

SIT: Turning negatives into positives activity

Q18:

Match the positive responses listed in the examples of negative thoughts.

Focusing on the problems — we dwell on the problem, instead of the situation.	
Expecting the worst — we always expect the worst, which only promotes anxiety.	
Thinking in absolutes — we often exaggerate reality.	

Positive thoughts:

a) Replace the exaggerations with more accurate and positive words. 'I often expect the worst to happen, but I can change that.'

b) Always assume that most problems have a solution, and ask 'How could I make this situation better?'

c) Always give yourself a more positive thinking outcome. 'What can I do to prevent myself from thinking the worst?'

There is some research support for the effectiveness of SIT, e.g. Sheehy and Horan (2004) reported the case of law students who received four weekly sessions of SIT each lasting 90 minutes. They recorded lowered levels of anxiety and an improvement in the grades of weaker students.

3.8.1 Research

Research into SIT by Meichenbaum

Meichenbaum performed research into cognitive stress reduction techniques in 1972 which led to his development of stress inoculation training.

Aim
To find how successful SIT would be in treating stress.

Method
This was a field experiment using a matched pairs design (matched on gender and anxiety levels), where student volunteers were assessed before and after treatment using self-report and grade averages. Participants were randomly allocated to one of the three groups: SIT; waiting list (control) and systematic desensitisation.

Results
Meichenbaum found that performance on the tests improved in the SIT group when compared with the other two, and that both the SIT and systematic desensitisation groups performed significantly better than the control group. Self-reports indicated that those in the SIT group reported more reductions in their anxiety levels, although both therapy groups showed overall improvements compared to the control group.

Conclusion
We can conclude from this that SIT is better for students experiencing exam stress than either systematic desensitisation or no treatment at all.

Evaluation
The results and conclusions show that SIT is a usual application, being a more effective way of treating students for exam-stress than some other methods.

As a matched pairs design was used, both order effects and individual differences have been controlled for, thus improving ecological validity.

However, it is difficult to generalise to a wider population which asks the question of whether the study is reliable based on the small sample size.

Another problem that would affect the study's reliability and generalisability is that the sample consisted only of students (who have characteristics that are not typical of the general population), creating problems of ethnocentricity.

Evaluation of SIT

Advantages	Disadvantages
SIT focuses on the cause of stress (unlike drug treatments) and ways of coping with it.	Only successful with patients who are already determined to give the time and make the effort to help themselves.
Effective for both short- and long-term stressors and can be combined with other treatments.	Most research into SIT is based on narrow samples (mainly white, middle-class, well-educated people) so may not generalise to other populations.
Increased feelings of being 'in control', and improved communication and time-management skills lead to increased confidence and self-efficacy.	Some stressful situation are completely out of the control of the individual, for example, a repetitive job or having to travel to work or traffic jams, etc.
There are no physiological side-effects.	

Social support, including instrumental and emotional

We, as human beings, are social animals, so it makes sense that we need social support to maintain psychological and physical health. Social support is thought to provide a buffer, or shield, to protect someone from the negative effects of stress (the **buffering hypothesis**). Social support systems may lengthen a person's life and improve their health and wellbeing.

There is research support for this; studies have shown that there is a relationship between a strong social support system and the ability to fight cancer, avoid Alzheimer's disease and cardiovascular illness. Also, a strong social support system can help avoid psychological illnesses, such as depression, anxiety, and post-traumatic stress disorder.

Research that supports the idea that social support acts as a buffer against stress was conducted in 2014 by Wang *et al.* 632 undergraduates completed questionnaires on perceived stress, perceived social support and depression. Wang et al. found that social support did provide a buffer against depression. The impact of high stress on those who also had a high level of social support was not as great as those with high stress and a low level of social support.

Social support works by decreasing stress levels in the body, by reducing the production of cortisol. As you have learned, cortisol can suppress the digestive, reproductive, and immune systems. When the immune system is suppressed, there is an increased risk for becoming ill.

There are three ways in which social support acts as a buffer:

1. Social support lessens the impact of a stressor

   For example, planning a wedding can be stressful, but the social support received from family and friends reduces the negative effects. On the other hand, someone without this social support would feel exhausted and overwhelmed.

2. Social support reduces the intensity of the negative symptoms of stress

   Being able to release tensions and frustrations and ask questions of family and friends decreases feelings of stress. Someone without social support will not be able to release these negative feelings, so will be more likely to feel the full force of them.

3. Social support can give you healthier ways of coping

When stressing about exams, say, has a family member or friend ever advised you to take a walk in the sunshine, or take a break from revision and have a cup of coffee? This is an example of social support providing you with alternative, healthy ways of coping that you may not have thought of yourself. Without social support, you would not have the benefit of this extra knowledge and alternative ways of dealing with things.

You can find out more about the remarkable effect of social support in this story about a town in America called Roseta: https://www.huffingtonpost.com/dr-rock-positano/the-mystery-of-the-roseta_b_73260.html

Emotional and Instrumental social support

Emotional support involves acting as a confidante for someone, being a 'shoulder to cry on'. For example, you might offer emotional support to someone by listening and offering sympathy after they've had bad news.

Instrumental support is offering help or assistance in a tangible and/or physical way, such as providing money to someone who's lost their job or helping someone who's bedridden by preparing dinner. Both emotional and instrumental support are important.

While there's a lot of research on the effects of social support on stress, there is some disagreement on whether people need social support all the time or just during times of stress.

Emotional and instrumental social support

Sheila has just been diagnosed with rheumatoid arthritis, which affects her mobility and flexibility, as well as her mood. Sheila's friends will come round with prepared meals, her sister will help with the housework, and all of her friends and family make sure that they visit her and take her out for trips to the shops, etc. They also make sure they spend time with her and listen when she is brought low by the condition.

After reading the above scenario, identify which acts provide instrumental support and which acts provide emotional support to Sheila.

3.9   End of topic test

End of Topic 3 test   Go online

Q19: Stress is the body's reaction to a change that requires a physical, mental or _____ adjustment or response. *(1 mark)*

a) balanced
b) emotional
c) psychic
d) social

....

Q20: Stress can come from any situation or thought that makes you feel frustrated, _____, nervous or anxious. *(1 mark)*

a) angry
b) bored
c) happy
d) pensive

....

Q21: Eustress is the name: *(1 mark)*

a) of a researcher into the effects of stress on mice.
b) given to the negative effects of stress.
c) given to the positive effects of stress.
d) given to what causes the stress response.

....

Q22: Distress can result in: *(1 mark)*

a) physical and psychological illness.
b) physical illness only.
c) psychological illness only.
d) neither physical nor psychological illness.

....

Q23: Racism is an example of a: *(1 mark)*

a) short-term stressor.
b) chronic stressor.
c) frequent stressor.
d) non-stressor.

Q24: Distress and eustress are both potentially harmful. *(1 mark)*

a) Yes
b) No

....

Q25: List four health risks that result from chronic stress. *(4 marks)*

Q26: The cognitive approach works on the assumption that it is necessary to refer to _____ mental processes such as thought, perception and language in order to understand and explain behaviour. *(1 mark)*

a) explicit
b) external
c) general
d) internal

. . . .

Q27: The cognitive approach views stress as the result of: *(1 mark)*

a) faulty thinking and maladaptive behaviour.
b) dysfunctional behaviour and poor perceptions.
c) faulty thinking and poor perceptions.
d) dysfunctional and maladaptive behaviour.

. . . .

Q28: What does CBT stand for? *(1 mark)*

. . . .

Q29: One form of CBT which is targeted at coping with stress is known as stress inoculation therapy (SIT). Who developed it in the 1970s? *(1 mark)*

a) Lazarus and Folkman
b) Meichenbaum
c) Parkes
d) Travis and Shear

. . . .

Q30: The three stages of SIT aim to help clients to replace 'self-defeating thoughts' with more positive ones. Which of the following lists the stages in the correct order? *(1 mark)*

a) Conceptualisation, application and skill acquisition.
b) Conceptualisation, skill acquisition and application.
c) Skill acquisition, conceptualisation, application.
d) Skill acquisition, application, conceptualisation.

End of Topic 3 activity

Watch the movie, Black Swan. Analyse it in relation to:

- The General Adaptation Syndrome (GAS)
- The Hypothalamic Pituitary-Adrenal axis
- The Sympathetic Medullary axis
- Individual differences (Type A/Type B and Hardiness)
- Types of social support (emotional and instrumental)
- Social isolation

If working in a group, you could create a poster based on your findings and present it to the class.

Unit 2 Topic 4

Depression (optional topic)

Contents

Learning objective

By the end of this topic, you should be able to explain, evaluate, apply and analyse:

- Major Depressive Disorder and Persistent Depressive Disorder (DSM-V —2012 revision).

- Biological causes of depression, which must include:

  ○ the role of neurochemistry
  ○ the role of hormones
  ○ the role of diathesis-stress

- Biological treatments for depression, which must include:

  ○ SSRIs (Selective Serotonin Reuptake Inhibitors), tricyclics, SNRIs (Serotonin Norepinephrine Reuptake Inhibitors), MAOIs (Monoamine Oxidase Inhibitors), ECT (Electroconvulsive Therapy)

- The aims, methods, results, evaluation, and conclusions of one study into the biology of depression.

- Beck's cognitive theory, which must include:

  ○ the cognitive triad
  ○ negative self-schema
  ○ faulty information processing

- The aims, methods, results, evaluation, and conclusions of one study into cognitive causes or treatment of depression.

4.1   Introduction

Do you think that society sees mental illness in the same way they see physical illness? Why or why not and what implications does this have for people suffering from mental illness?

Depression —notebook activity

You'll need your psychology notebook for this activity.

Respond to the following quote by the psychologist Dorothy Rowe:

Depression is a prison where you are both the suffering prisoner and the cruel jailer.

What does she mean and what implications does this have for the treatment of depression?

Depression is more than simply feeling unhappy or fed up for a few days. Most people go through periods of feeling down, but when you're depressed you feel persistently sad for weeks or months, rather than just a few days. This is an important area of study in psychology as it is predicted that depression will be the second most important health condition (after heart disease) in the world. You will be learning about two depressive disorders:

- Major Depressive Disorder, and
- Persistent Depressive Disorder

Diagnosing disorders using the DSM

The DSM (Diagnostic and Statistical Manual of Mental Disorders) is one of the most important books in the world of psychopathology. It attempts to categorise and describe every problem that can occur in the mind, from schizophrenia to borderline personality disorder to something called mathematics disorder, which is essentially being so bad at mathematics that it amounts to a mental problem.

Mental health professionals all over the world use the DSM for assessment and diagnosis of mental disorders, but it does not include information or guidelines for treatment of any disorder. However, deciding on an accurate diagnosis is the first step toward beginning to be able to appropriately treat mental disorders such as depression.

The DSM classification system was developed in the USA in 1952. The current version is DSM-V (the fifth revision).

Major Depressive Disorder

This is known as the 'common cold' of psychological disorders (this term reflects the extent of the disorder, but not its severity. It is the number 1 reasons why people seek mental help). It tends to run in families and can be triggered by stressful events (as you will find when we look at the diathesis-stress model). Women are twice to three times as likely as men to become depressed. An episode of depression serious enough to require treatment occurs in about 1 in 4 women and 1 in 10 men at some point in their lives. Some people have two or more episodes of depression at various times in their life. The prevalence of major depression is between 5% and 10%.

Diagnosing Major Depressive Disorder

The Diagnostic and Statistical Manual fifth revision (DSM-V) uses criteria (A —C are given below) to help doctors, clinical psychologists and psychiatrists diagnose Major Depressive Disorder (MDD):

A. Five (or more) of the following symptoms have been present during the same 2-week period and represent a change from previous functioning; at least one of the symptoms is either (1) depressed mood or (2) loss of interest or pleasure.

 Do not include symptoms that are clearly attributable to another medical condition.

1. *Depressed mood most of the day, nearly every day, as indicted by either subjective report (e.g. feels sad, empty, hopeless) or observation made by others (e.g. appears tearful). (**Note:** in children and adolescents, may be irritable mood.)*

2. *Markedly diminished interest or pleasure in all, or almost all, activities most of the day, nearly every day (as indicated by either subjective account or observation by others.)*

3. *Significant weight loss when not dieting or weight gain (e.g. a change of more than 5% of body weight in a month) or an increase in appetite nearly every day (**Note:** in children, consider failure to make expected weight gain.)*

4. *Insomnia or hypersomnia nearly every day.*

5. *Feelings of worthlessness or excessive or inappropriate guilt (which may be delusional) nearly every day (not merely self-reproach of guilt about being unwell.)*

6. *Diminished ability to concentrate, or indecisiveness, nearly every day (either by subjective account or observation by others.)*

7. *Recurrent thoughts of death (not just fear of dying), recurrent suicidal ideation without a specific plan, or a suicide attempt or a specific plan for committing suicide.*

B. The symptoms cause clinically significant distress or impairment in social, occupational, or other important areas of functioning.

C. The episode is not attributable to the physiological effects of a substance or to another medical condition.

These diagnostic criteria are explained well in this video 'I had a black dog: his name was depression': https://youtu.be/XiCrniLQGYc

The DSM-V is meant to be used by trained medical professionals, such as psychiatrists. It is very unwise to self-diagnose using these DSM-V symptoms —always see your GP if you are concerned.

Major Depressive Disorder   Go online

Q1:   Read the following case study of Leanne, who has Major Depressive Disorder. Then:

- identify those symptoms of MDD that she does show, and
- those symptoms of MDD that she does not.

Jessica is a 28 year-old married female. She has a very demanding, high stress job as a second year medical resident in a large hospital. Jessica has always been a high achiever. She graduated with first class honours in both university and medical school. She has very high standards for herself and can be very self-critical when she fails to meet them. Lately, she has struggled with significant feelings of worthlessness and shame due to her inability to perform as well as she always has In the past.

For the past few weeks, Jessica has felt unusually fatigued and found it increasingly difficult to concentrate at work. Her coworkers have noticed that she is often irritable and withdrawn, which is quite different from her typically upbeat and friendly disposition. She has called in sick on several occasions, which is completely unlike her. On those days, she stays in bed all day, watching TV or sleeping.

At home, Jessica's husband has noticed changes as well. She's shown little interest in sex and has had difficulties falling asleep at night. Her insomnia has been keeping him awake as she tosses and turns for an hour or two after they go to bed. He's overheard her having frequent tearful phone conversations with her closest friend, which have him worried. When he tries to get her to open up about what's bothering her, she pushes him away with an abrupt "everything's fine".

Although she hasn't ever considered suicide, Jessica has found herself increasingly dissatisfied with her life. She's been having frequent thoughts of wishing she was dead. She gets frustrated with herself because she feels like she has every reason to be happy, yet can't seem to shake the sense of doom and gloom that has been clouding each day as of late.

Ref: http://www.psyweb.com/Casestudies/CaseStudies.html

It is important to note that doing this exercise is to help you with understanding the diagnostic criteria for MDD. It does NOT enable you to diagnose anything!

Major Depressive Disorder

In pairs or small groups, create a poster or presentation aimed at increasing understanding of the symptoms of Major Depressive Disorder —and also what to do in order to get help.

Persistent Depressive Disorder

Persistent depressive disorder (PDD), (formerly known as *dysthymia*), is a chronic depression that is present for most days over a period of two years. The symptoms are milder than major depressive disorder but have additional symptoms. When PDD occurs along with MDD in the same person, this is known as a double depression. About 30% of depressions are classified as chronic.

A diagnosis of persistent depressive disorder must meet all of the following criteria:

The individual must be in a depressed mood for most of the day for the majority of days over at least a two year period, indicated either by subjective account or the observation of others. In children and adolescents, the duration must be at least one year, and the mood can be irritable.

> A **manic episode** is characterised by period of at least one week where an elevated, or unusually irritable mood exists. A person experiencing a manic episode is usually engaged in significant activity beyond their normal activities. People describe a manic mood as feeling very euphoric, "on top of the world," and being able to do or accomplish anything. The feeling is like extreme optimism —but on steroids.

While depressed, two or more of the following must be present:

- Poor appetite or overeating;

- Insomnia or hypersomnia;

- Low energy or fatigue;

- Low self-esteem;

- Poor concentration;

- Feelings of hopelessness;

- During the two year period, the symptoms have not been absent for less than two months at a time;

- The criteria for a major depressive order may be continuously present for the two years;

- The individual has never experienced a manic or hypomania episode;

- The criteria for cyclothymic disorder has never been met;

- The criteria for schizoaffective disorder, schizophrenia, delusional disorder or other psychotic disorder does not better explain the disorder;

- Drug abuse or another medical disorder do not explain the symptoms.

> **Cyclothymic disorder** causes mood changes —from feeling low to emotional highs. It is a milder form of bipolar disorder

---

Persistent Depressive Disorder

Go online

Read the following case study of John, who has Persistent Depressive Disorder. Then:

- identify those symptoms of PDD that he does show, and

- those symptoms of PDD that he does not;

- why a diagnosis of PDD is likely —not MDD.

Q2:

John Smith is a 30-year-old married male who feels down most of the time. He experiences frequent, intrusive thoughts that he is not good enough, despite personal and professional successes. He tries to overcompensate for his thoughts by taking on more than he can handle, which leads to failure and furthers his feelings of inadequacy. His wife suggests that he seek help after finding him crying. The following is an excerpt from his intake interview with his psychiatrist.

"I feel pretty worthless and have felt that way for a long time - for over ten years. It feels normal to be down. Sometimes I start to feel better, but it never lasts - I feel bad about my life most of the time. I don't think that I'll amount to anything and I might never be successful at work. I feel exhausted all of the time. I have trouble sleeping. I've been waking up in the middle of the night and can't stop thinking about all of my failures. I've lost weight in the past few months. Food just doesn't taste as good as it used to. I feel hopeless and often have trouble concentrating when I'm with my family and friends. Maybe I'm just pessimistic."

John's psychiatrist tells him that his experience isn't normal and diagnoses him with persistent depressive disorder. He prescribes an antidepressant and begins to conduct therapy with John. John begins to feel better after therapy sessions and a month on the medication.

John has never experienced a manic or hypermanic episode, cyclothymia or schizoafffective episode. His symptoms cannot be explained by drug abuse or other medical disorder.

MDD and PDD compare and contrast activity

Q3:

Create a table and put those symptoms that are only relevant to MDD in one column, those that are only relevant to PDD in another, and those that are common to both in the third.

Evaluation of DSM-V

Strengths

- Once a diagnosis has been made using the DSM-V, an appropriate treatment can begin.

- Using the DSM-V standardises the diagnosis of mental disorders, such as Major Depression and Persistent Depressive Disorder. This should make it unlikely for there to be bias in terms of diagnosis.

- Attempts have been made over the 5 iterations of the DSM to reduce cultural, sexual and gender bias.

Weaknesses

- Treating mental health conditions is the highest area of spending within the NHS. This means there are financial implications when a diagnosis appears in a diagnostic manual or is removed from it. "Official diagnoses" create a demand for medicines and funded research. A 2011 article in the Psychiatric Times points out that 67% of the DSM-5 task force had direct links to the pharmaceutical industry that makes medical drugs. The fact that the task force met in secret to compile DSM-V led to the criticism that the process was corrupt.

- The DSM-5 has been criticised for 'medicalising' normal behaviour and mood.

- A particular criticism is over grief. It's normal and healthy to grieve when a loved one dies. DSM-IV contains a "bereavement exclusion criterion" for Major Depressive Disorder. This meant that you couldn't be diagnosed as depressed if you had been bereaved (lost a loved one). DSM-5 removes this exclusion, allowing for a grieving person to be diagnosed with a mental disorder.

You will now move on from the symptoms of depression, to some explanations of the causes, beginning with some biological explanations.

Nature or nurture?

You will need your psychology notebook for this activity.

In a group, or on your own, discuss whether you think that nature or nurture are most influential in whether or not people experience depression. Why/why not?

Take a note of the points you make in your discussion in your psychology notebook. You should now have notes under the title 'Depression —nature or nurture'.

4.2 Biological explanations of depression

Biological explanations look for causes of depression in our biology, i.e. in our genetic make-up or physiology.

The role of neurochemistry in depression

This explanation sees depression as resulting from a fault in how the **neurotransmitter, serotonin,** is taken up by synapses in the brain.

A neuron is structured as below:

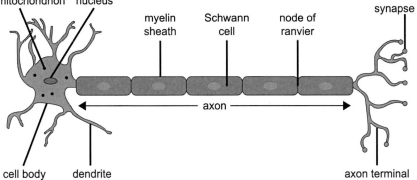

To understand about the role of serotonin in depression, you only need to know about the synapse, the axon terminal, the synaptic cleft, and the dendrites.

Neurotransmitter notebook activity

You will need your psychology notebook for this activity.

Look up what each of these parts of a neurotransmitter does, then take a note of these in your notebook.

- Synapse

- Axon terminal

- Dendrites

- Synaptic cleft

Show what you have written to your teacher/lecturer for checking.

This video explains the role of serotonin in depression: https://youtu.be/KispXWwDaOc

Depression may result from:

- low production levels of serotonin
- lack of receptor sites for serotonin

- inability of serotonin to reach the receptor sites

- shortage of tryptophan (the chemical from which serotonin is made)

Many researchers believe that if any of these neurochemical problems occur, depression can be the result.

Evaluation of the role of neurochemistry in depression   Go online

Q4:

Decide whether each of the following is a strength or a weakness.

- There is no way to measure serotonin levels in the living brain. Therefore, there have not been any studies supporting the serotonin explanation of depression.

- Blood levels of serotonin are measurable —and have been shown to be lower in people who suffer from depression —but researchers don't know if blood levels reflect the brain's level of serotonin.

- SSRIs, which are medication given for depression and target serotonin, are successful in treating the symptoms of depression, supporting the idea that there is a link between serotonin and depression.

- It is not known whether the dip in serotonin causes the depression, or the depression causes serotonin levels to drop.

- Medications that work on serotonin levels —SSRIs (selective serotonin reuptake inhibitors) and SNRIs (serotonin and norepinephrine reuptake inhibitors) —reduce symptoms of depression, but exactly how they work is not fully understood.

The role of hormones in depression

Noradrenaline is one of the few chemicals in the body that works as both a neurotransmitter and a hormone. It is better known as a stress hormone and its role is to prepare your body for action (fight or flight) in response to a stressor. It makes sense, then, that low levels of noradrenaline can result in feeling the opposite of energised —i.e. tired, unfocused and losing interest in life —depression, in other words. Some researchers believe that low levels of noradrenaline result in depression, whilst others suggest that it is caused by a dysfunction in the brain area responsible for dealing with norepinephrine

Noradrenaline is a naturally occurring catecholamine found in the nervous system. The **catecholamine hypothesis** is based on the fact that low levels of norepinephrine have been found in people who suffer from depression. The deficiency of norepinephrine in certain brain circuits is associated with depression. Norepinephrine goes through the limbic system, which is a part of the brain which is important in regulating emotions. Some studies suggest that low levels of serotonin can lead to a drop in norepinephrine levels, which then leads to depression.

Evaluation of role of noradrenaline in depression Go online

Q5:

Decide whether each of the following is a strength or a weakness.

- People who take medication for anxiety (e.g. reserpine), which lower levels of noradrenaline, sometimes develop depression.
- Drugs which treat levels of noradrenaline increase these levels very quickly, but the symptoms of depression can take two to three weeks to decrease.

The role of diathesis-stress in depression

In contrast to biological explanations, which sees the causes of depression as being located in the body, the diathesis-stress explanation sees depression as being caused by an interaction between having a genetic pre-disposition to develop the disease (diatheses), and the stress caused by life experiences. This interaction will lead to some people being more vulnerable to developing depression than others. For example, some people may have more diatheses (genetic pre-disposition and/or imbalances in neurotransmitters and hormones), and will develop depression without having to experience many stressors, and those with a lesser degree of diatheses may not develop depression at all if they have a relatively easy life.

Some stressors include loss, unemployment, relationship difficulties, puberty, marriage, retirement, alcoholism or drug abuse. People will react differently to each type of stressor: depression may be triggered by divorce in some, but may be a release for others, which will increase immunity from depression.

According to the diathesis-stress model, therefore, depression is caused by a complex interaction between psychological, social and biological factors. This implies that no one treatment on its own will be effective in treating depression.

Diathesis-stress explanations of depression activity

On your own or in a group, create a game where diathesis —stress is a race, with one competitor having a high diathesis (who will be near the finishing line), and one with a low diathesis, and a diagnosis of depression as the finishing line. Try to fit in as many stressors as you can between the start and finishing line of each competitor.

4.3   Biological treatments for depression

These include:

- SSRIs (Selective Serotonin Reuptake Inhibitors)

- Tricyclics

- SNRIs (Serotonin Norepinephrine Reuptake Inhibitors)

- MAOIs (Monoamine Oxidase Inhibitors), and

- ECT (Electroconvulsive Therapy)

Chemotherapies (drug treatments) are available for a range of psychological disorders, including depression. One of the major strengths of biological explanations has been the development of effective drugs with which to treat mental illness. As you will see, they act on the neurotransmitter(s) associated with each illness.

Selective Serotonin Reuptake Inhibitors (SRRIs)

These are the most common medical treatment for depression, and are effective in 80-90% of cases. SSRIs work by improving the function of nerve cells in the brain that regulate emotion. When these brain cells (called neurons) send signals to one another, they release a little bit of the neurotransmitter, serotonin so that the message can be delivered. They then have to take back the serotonin they released so they can send the next message. This process of replacing the neurotransmitter is called "reuptake."

For those with depression, the areas of the brain that regulate mood and send messages using serotonin might not function properly. SSRIs help make more serotonin available by blocking the reuptake process. This allows serotonin to build up between neurons so messages can be sent correctly. SSRIs are called "selective" serotonin reuptake inhibitors because they specifically target serotonin. The following SSRIs are approved in the UK to treat depression:

- Citalopram (Cipramil)

- Escitalopram (Cipralex)

- Fluoxetine (Prozac)

- Fluvoxamine (Faverin)

- Paroxetine (Seroxat)

- Sertraline (Lustral)

Evaluation of SSRIs   Go online

Q6:
Decide whether each of the following is a strength or a weakness.

- Treats the symptoms, not the causes of depression.
- Have fewer side effects than other medications for depression.
- Are effective in 80-90% of cases.
- Are unsuccessful in 10-20% of cases.
- They can have side effects, such as:
    - Insomnia
    - Headaches
    - Rash
    - Blurred vision
    - Drowsiness
    - Dry mouth
    - Agitation or nervousness
    - Feeling dizzy
    - Pains in the muscles or joints
    - Upset stomach, nausea or diarrhoea
    - Reduced sexual desire
    - Problems with erection or ejaculation
- Some people (especially children or young adults) can have increased thoughts of suicide
- Some people experience no side effects and others find they disappear after a few weeks.
- The SSRI, Paroxetine, is associated with withdrawal effects, such as nausea, insomnia, agitation and dizziness.
- Treat the symptoms of depression, not the cause.
- Not dangerous if overdose is taken.
- The majority of SSRIs are not physically addictive (see exception for Paroxetine).

Selective Noradrenaline Reuptake Inhibitors (SNRIs)

SRRIs target only one neurotransmitter (serotonin) whereas, SNRIs block the reuptake of two (it is known as a dual reuptake inhibitor), serotonin and noradrenaline. SNRIs is a newer type of anti-depressant.

The following SNRIs are approved in the UK to treat depression:

- Desvenlafaxine (Newven)
- Duloxetine (Cymbalta)
- Levomilnacipran (Fetzima)
- Venlafaxine (Effexor)

Evaluation of SNRIs   Go online

Q7:

Decide whether each of the following is a strength or a weakness.

- Have fewer side effects than other medications for depression
- Are unsuccessful in 10-20% of cases
- They can have side effects, such as:
  - Insomnia
  - Headaches
  - Rash
  - Blurred vision
  - Drowsiness
  - Dry mouth
  - Agitation or nervousness
  - Feeling dizzy
  - Pains in the muscles or joints
  - Upset stomach, nausea or diarrhoea
  - Reduced sexual desire
  - Problems with erection or ejaculation
  - Excessive sweating
- Some people experience no side effects and others find they disappear after a few weeks.
- More effective in cases where both serotonin and noradrenaline are affected.
- Treat the symptoms of depression, not the cause
- Are effective in 80-90% of cases
- SNRIs are not physically addictive
- Not dangerous if overdose is taken.

All of the strengths and weaknesses of SSRIs apply here, but side effects are less powerful. Additional side effects include:

- Excessive sweating

SNRIs are more effective than SSRIs if both neurotransmitters are effected.

The next two types of anti-depressants (tricyclics and MAOIs) have been around for a long -time and are associated with more debilitating side-effects and can be dangerous if an overdose is taken (which is not an issue with SSIRs and SNRIs).

Tricyclics

Like reuptake inhibitors, tricyclics seem to block the reabsorption of serotonin and adrenaline back into nerve cells after these chemicals are released into a synapse, making more available, thereby alleviating the symptoms of depression. Like MAOIs, they would not be the first treatment given to someone with depression because of the severity of the side effects, but can be useful when other anti-depressants have not worked.

The following tricyclics are approved in the UK to treat depression:

- Amitriptyline
- Desipramine
- Imipramine
- Nortriptyline

Evaluation of tricyclics Go online

Q8:

Decide whether each of the following is a strength or a weakness.

- Useful in cases where other anti-depressants have failed.
- Cause side effects, which although similar to those found with SRRIs and SNRIs, are more severe and more likely, such as:
    ○ Blurred vision
    ○ Dry mouth
    ○ Constipation
    ○ Weight gain or loss
    ○ Low blood pressure on standing
    ○ Rash
    ○ Hives
    ○ Increased heart rate
    ○ Reduced sex drive
    ○ Difficulty with urinating
- Associated with withdrawal symptoms, such as nausea, headache and dizziness
- Interacts with blood pressure medication
- Helps 65% of patients
- Is not effective with 35% of patients
- Associated with heart problems in some

Monoamine Oxidase Inhibitors (MAOIs)

MAOIs were among the first type of antidepressant developed, but have largely been replaced by SSRIs which are safer and have fewer side effects. They can be used as a last resort medication when other antidepressants have failed.

Like tricyclics, SSRIs and SNRIs, MAOIs relieve the symptoms of depression by acting on brain chemistry.

Monoamine oxidase is an enzyme which is involved in the removal of the neurotransmitters serotonin, noradrenaline and dopamine. MAOIs prevent this removal, which makes more of these neurotransmitters available, thereby easing the symptoms of depression.

The following MAOIs are approved in the UK to treat depression:

- Isocarboxazid (Marplan)

- Phenelzine (Nardil)

- Selegiline (Selgil)

- Tranylcypromine (Parnate)

Evaluation of MAOIs   Go online

Q9:

Decide whether each of the following is a strength or a weakness.

- MAOIs also affect other neurotransmitters in the brain and digestive system, causing side effects, which include:
    ◦ Dry mouth
    ◦ Nausea, diarrhoea or constipation
    ◦ Headache
    ◦ Drowsiness
    ◦ Insomnia
    ◦ Dizziness or lightheadedness
    ◦ Involuntary muscle jerks
    ◦ Low blood pressure
    ◦ Reduced sexual desire or difficulty reaching orgasm
    ◦ Weight gain
    ◦ Difficulty starting a urine flow
    ◦ Muscle cramps
    ◦ Prickling or tingling sensation in the skin (paresthesia)
- As well as side effects, there are safety concerns associated with MAOIs, which need careful monitoring by the person taking them and their GP, for example:
    ◦ Dangerous interactions with certain food and drinks containing high levels of tyramine (an amino acid that regulates blood pressure, found in cheese, sauerkraut, cured meats, draft beer and soy products. The interaction of tyramine with MAOIs can cause dangerously high blood pressure, which means that those taking them should exclude these products from their diets.
    ◦ Can cause serious reactions when taken with other medication, such as other antidepressants, pain-killers, cold and flu treatments, allergy medication and some herbal treatments.
- Can be useful in cases where other anti-depressants have not worked.
- Takes two to three weeks for it to affect the symptoms of depression.
- Treats the symptoms, not the causes of depression.

Biological treatments for depression activity

On your own or in a group, create an information leaflet or video explaining each treatment, including benefits and drawbacks.

Biological treatments for depression activity

In the table below, in one column put those features that belong only to SSRIs in one circle of the Venn, those that belong only to SNRIs in another, to tricyclics in another, and to MAOIs in another. In the intersection between two circles, put those features that pertain to both relevant anti-depressants. In the intersection between all circles, put those features of anti-depressants that are common to all.

You'll probably need to draw the Venn on a larger piece of paper.

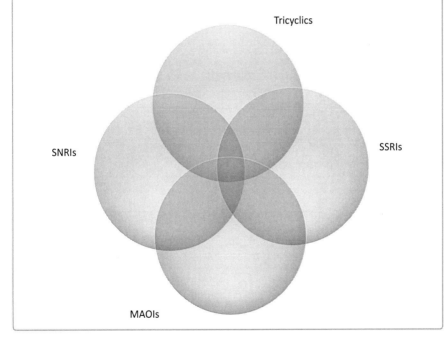

Electroconvulsive therapy (ECT)

Electroconvulsive therapy (ECT) is the best treatment for those with hard-to-treat depression. It is a painless medical procedure performed under general anesthesia that is considered one of the most effective treatments for severe depression. It can be lifesaving.

Sometimes, waiting the two or more weeks for anti-depressants to work is dangerous for patients with suicidal thoughts. ECT is particularly useful, here, as it works very quickly. However, the drawback is that the effects of ECT usually don't last, and further treatments will likely be necessary.

ECT involves delivering an electrical stimulation to the brain through electrodes which are applied to the scalp, which causes a seizure. This seizure helps relieve the symptoms of depression, for reasons which are not fully understood.

During the procedure, the person receiving the ECT will be under general anaesthesia, so will not feel anything. A muscle relaxant is also given so that the body does not move during the seizure.

The number of required sessions varies. Many people have six to 12 sessions administered 2-3 times per week over a period of several weeks.

Evaluation of ECT as a treatment for depression   Go online

Q10:

Decide whether each of the following is a strength or a weakness.

- Studies have shown that ECT works for many people who have treatment-resistant depression. One study of 39 people with treatment-resistant depression compared the effects of an antidepressant with ECT. After two to three weeks, 71% of people who received ECT had a positive response to treatment. But only 28% who received the antidepressant had a positive response after four weeks of treatment (Acta Psychiatrica Scandinavia 1997).

- ECT is associated with side effects, the most common of which is short-term memory loss. However, some people report that they have long-term memory loss, as well. ECT also causes a brief rise in heart rate and blood pressure during the procedure, so it may not be recommended in people with unstable heart problems.

- ECT can often work quickly, which can be lifesaving.

- 50% or more of the people who receive this treatment will relapse within several months if there is no subsequent treatment (for example, antidepressants) to prevent relapse

---

Study into the biology of depression — Caron (2013)

Aim: To see if stress induced depression in mice with low levels of serotonin.

Method: Caron *et* al used mice that had been bred to have low levels of serotonin (20-40%), and a control group of mice who had normal levels of serotonin. The team exposed the mice to stress by briefly housing them with an aggressive stranger mouse every day for 7-10 days. To test for depression-like behaviours, the researchers then examined whether the test mice would avoid interacting with the stranger mouse.

Results: The control mice did not exhibit these depression symptoms after a week of social stress, but the serotonin-deficient mice did. However, both groups eventually displayed depression-like symptoms following longer periods of stress exposure.

Conclusion: Mice with low serotonin levels are more susceptible to social stressors than mice with normal levels of serotonin.

Evaluation: It is unethical to cause distress to animals, such as lowering their levels of serotonin. However, this is an objective way to measure the effects of stressors on serotonin, and thereby symptoms of depression. This means that the study could improve the wellbeing of people with depression by suggesting better ways of treating it. It is also questionable whether the results from mice samples will generalise to humans —we have very different brain structure and functions. Also, a 'tail-suspension test' was used to measure symptoms of depression in the mice —humans can't be tested in this way, which reduces the mundane realism of the study (its ability to relate to real-life behaviours). However, the symptoms the reduced serotonin mice exhibited did mimic the symptoms of humans with Major Depressive Disorder.

You'll now move on from biological explanations and treatments for depression to look at cognitive explanations.

Reference: *Kafui Dzirasa, Sunil Kumar, Benjamin D. Sachs, Marc G. Caron and Miguel A. L. Nicolelis Cortical-Amygdalar Circuit Dysfunction in a Genetic Mouse Model of Serotonin Deficiency. The Journal of Neuroscience. 6 March 2013, 33 (10) 4505-4513*

4.4   Cognitive explanations of depression

The main assumption of cognitive explanations of depression is it arises because of the way we think. You will be learning about:

Beck's cognitive theory, which must include:

- the cognitive triad
- negative self-schema
- faulty information processing

Albert Ellis identified the following types of faulty and irrational thinking:

Faulty thinking strategy	Explanation
Polarised thinking	Seeing everything as black or white, e.g. "I score 19/20 on that test, but I got one question wrong so I'm a failure."
Overgeneralisation	We come to a general conclusion based on one, single event, e.g. "I failed my driving test —I will definitely fail it again."
Catastrophising	Making a mountain out of a molehill, e.g. "I lied about the grade that I scored in my psychology exam —that makes me the worst person in the world." Or "that interview went badly —I will never get a job"
Magnification	Blowing small but negative things out of proportion, making them much more than they need to be, e.g. "my teacher said that I was really good at psychology, that I work hard and do the homework set. She also said that I can be a bit chatty sometimes. I'm terrible in the psychology class!"
Minimisation	Minimising your strengths as if they were worthless, e.g. when someone praises you for a job well done, you thank them, but think to yourself that they are just being polite, or they feel sorry for you.
Personalisation	Relating something that happened to someone else to yourself, e.g. blaming yourself for something you didn't do, such as your parents divorcing.

Cognitive biases —name that bias!   Go online

Match each of the thoughts below to one of Ellis's faulty thinking strategies.

Q11: "Mrs Johnstone is mean to me all the time!"

a) Polarised thinking
b) Overgeneralisation
c) Catastrophising
d) Magnification
e) Minimisation
f) Personalisation

....

Q12: "I passed my practical driving test, but only because the examiner wanted to get away early."

a) Polarised thinking
b) Overgeneralisation
c) Catastrophising
d) Magnification
e) Minimisation
f) Personalisation

. . . .

Q13: "I just know that he moved seats as he doesn't want to sit next to me."

a) Polarised thinking
b) Overgeneralisation
c) Catastrophising
d) Magnification
e) Minimisation
f) Personalisation

. . . .

Q14: "I can't believe that she won't go out with me! My life is over."

a) Polarised thinking
b) Overgeneralisation
c) Catastrophising
d) Magnification
e) Minimisation
f) Personalisation

. . . .

Q15: "Everyone says that I gave a good speech at my colleague's leaving do, but I know I hesitated a couple of times. I feel like I ruined it."

a) Polarised thinking
b) Overgeneralisation
c) Catastrophising
d) Magnification
e) Minimisation
f) Personalisation

. . . .

Q16: "I cheated on my psychology exam. I am a bad person."

a) Polarised thinking
b) Overgeneralisation
c) Catastrophising
d) Magnification
e) Minimisation
f) Personalisation

Change the negative to a positive activity

Q17:

Change the following negative thoughts into rational, positive thoughts. The first one is done for you.

Negative thought	Bias involved	Rational, Positive Thought
"I got into trouble at school today. I just know they are going to exclude me tomorrow."	Catastrophising	I did something at school today that I'm not proud of, but everyone makes mistakes and it's not the end of the world! I'll try harder tomorrow not to make the same mistake again.
"My friend looked at her watch when I was talking today. She must think I'm boring."		
"I got an award at assembly yesterday, but that's no big deal. I'm not really that good a student."		
"I only got a B in my psychology test. I always fail. I shouldn't even have tried."		
"I can't believe I ate that Mars bar! I'm so fat and ugly."		
"Another student called ma a name once today. People are always making fun of me."		

Your turn!

List any dysfunctional, negative thoughts you often have. Then try to think of more rational, positive alternatives. Create a table as seen below:

Negative thought	Bias involved	Rational, Positive Thought

4.5   Beck's cognitive theory of depression

According to Dr Aaron Beck, negative thoughts, generated by dysfunctional beliefs are the major cause of depressive symptoms. The more negative thoughts someone has, the more severe the depressive symptoms will be.

The cognitive triad

Beck also believes that there are three main dysfunctional beliefs that dominate depressed people's thinking:

1. Negative beliefs about the self (I am defective or inadequate),

2. Negative beliefs about the world (all of my experiences result in defeats or failures), and

3. Negative beliefs about the future (the future is hopeless).

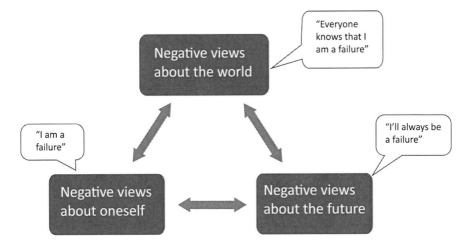

Together, these three themes are described as the Negative Cognitive Triad. We can all think in this way sometimes, but If someone thinks in this way all of the time, depression is very likely to occur (if it has not already occurred).

For example:

Imagine that you have just been laid off from your job. Thinking rationally, you may be upset by this, but explain it in terms of the company you work for doing badly financially, not that there was anything wrong with you or the work you do. After a short while, you pick yourself up and start looking for another job.

If you are thinking irrationally, however, you would put the redundancy down to a failure in yourself, (I just wasn't good enough) and you are unlikely to get another job anyway (interviewers will see that I am just not good enough), so there's not point applying for any (the fact that I'm a failure, and that this is obvious to everyone, won't change).

You can see how his style of thinking will likely result in depression.

Other types of negative thinking that people with depression typically show are what Beck called silent assumptions. These **silent assumptions** are believing "I should", "I ought" and "I must", e.g. "I must earn a salary of over £30,000 per year" or "I should have more friends." According to Beck, people who suffer from anxiety hold silent assumptions such as:

- 'it is absolutely necessary for everyone worthwhile to be loved by everyone they know.'

- 'when things don't work out the way I want them to, it's a catastrophe'

- 'I must constantly be on the lookout for danger'

- 'a person of worth must be capable and competent in all areas of their life'

Negative self-schema

A schema is a 'package' of knowledge, which stores information and ideas about our self and the world around us. These schemas are developed during childhood and according to Beck, depressed people possess negative self-schemas, which may come from negative experiences, for example criticism, from parents, peers or even teachers.

A self-schema can be about what you look like:

"I am pretty." "I am ugly."

. . . or about your interests:

"I like music." "I like football."

. . . your personality:

"I am shy." "I am sensitive."

. . . your behaviours:

"I can lead effectively." "I am unassertive."

Find out about your self-schema

You can find out about your own self-schema by answering the question "Who am I?"

Write down 15 things about yourself. Think about those things that would help someone you don't know find out about 'the real you'.

Of course, your self-concept will be far more complex than your responses to the 15 questions, "Who Am I?". As we go through life and gain new knowledge and experiences, we are constantly adding to and changing our existing self-schemas. This is good news, as if you find that your self-concept (your self-schema) is negative in any way, you can change this by changing the way you think about yourself (perhaps by doing activities like the 'Change the negative to a positive" activity given earlier).

A person with a negative self-schema is likely to interpret information about themselves in a negative way, which could lead to cognitive biases, such as those outlined above. Thinking about yourself in this negative way can lead to depression.

Faulty information processing

As well as dysfunctional beliefs, Beck said that depressed people pay **selective attention** to those things that reinforce these negative beliefs about themselves, the world and the future, and ignore evidence to the contrary that is right in front of their noses! For example, when being praised by the boss for their performance, depressed people will find and focus on the one negative comment made (they magnify its importance, and minimise the importance of the many positive comments made). This failure to pay proper attention is known as **faulty information processing**.

The aims, methods, results, evaluation, and conclusions of one study into cognitive causes or treatment of depression.

Alloy et al (1999)

Aim: To investigate the thinking style associated with depression.

Method: American 20 year olds were tested for their thinking style and placed into groups of either: positive or negative thinking styles. They then retested them 6 years later.

Results: They found that only 1% of those in the positive thinking styles group developed depression, while 17% developed it in the negative thinking styles group.

Conclusion: The results show that there does appear to be a link between depression and thinking styles.

Evaluation: The study was longitudinal (it took place over a long period of time). This makes the results more valid as the thinking styles were measured at the time —there was no need to rely on the memory of the participants (memory is notoriously unreliable). Because the participants were chosen on the basis of thinking styles alone, there is no way of knowing if it is the thinking style that influenced having depression 6 years later, or some other factor. Furthermore, the sample chosen may not be representative of the target population (they were all in their early 20s), which makes the sample biased. Also, the study does not make clear if it is the depressive thinking style is the cause or the consequence of having depression.

Reference: *Alloy, L. B. & Abramson, L. Y. (1999) The Temple-Wisconsin Cognitive Vulnerability to Depression (CVD) Project: Conceptual background, design and methods. Journal of Cognitive Psychotherapy: An International Quarterly, 13, 227-262.*

Evaluation of Beck's cognitive theory of depression   Go online

Q18:

Decide whether each of the following is a strength or a weakness.

- Results of study by Alloy et al support Beck's theory that depression is caused by faulty thinking styles.

- There is much other research evidence supporting Beck's theory. For example, Brown et al (1995) found that their sample of university students who received poor exam scores were having negative thought about themselves (they felt they did not deserve to be at university), their future (they may not pass the course), and the world (they no longer enjoyed the course).

- It is difficult to establish a cause and effect relationship between negative thinking and depression. This is because it is not known if the negative thinking is the cause of depression, or as a result.

- Beck's theory has been criticised as reductionist, as it does not account for other, non-cognitive factors which may be responsible for depression, such as biological ones.

- The effectiveness of Cognitive Behavioural Therapy (CBT) supports Beck's theory. CBT is just as effective at treating depression as anti-depressants, which supports Beck's assertion that depression is a cognitive disorder.

4.6   End of topic test

End of Topic 4 test   Go online

Q19: Depression is a(n):

a) emotional disorder
b) mood disorder
c) personality disorder
d) psychotic disorder

....

Q20: What are signs and symptoms of depression?

a) loss of interest or pleasure in hobbies and activities
b) thoughts of death or suicide or suicide attempts
c) body aches, low energy, and fatigue
d) all of the above

....

Q21: What causes depression?

a) environmental factors
b) genetics
c) cognitive factors
d) all of the above

....

Q22: By the year _____, depression will be the second most important health condition after heart disease in the world:

a) 2020
b) 2025
c) 2030
d) 2035

....

Q23: The difference between MDD and PDD is:

a) with PDD, the symptoms have lasted for over 2 years
b) MDD involves fatigues, whereas PDD does not
c) MDD involves also having an episode of mania
d) PDD involves also having cyclothymia

....

Q24: A criticism of the DSM-V is that:

a) it could be accused of having medicalised normal behaviour
b) it could be creating a demand for medicines which benefit the (already rich) pharmaceutical industry
c) both of the above
d) none of the above

....

Q25: The chemical that moves from the axon of one neuron across a gap to the dendrite of another is a(n):

a) gray matter
b) myelin
c) glial cell
d) neurotransmitter

....

Q26: The role of serotonin in depression involves:

a) lack of receptor sites for serotonin
b) not enough serotonin
c) too much reuptake of serotonin
d) all of the above

. . . .

Q27: Noradrenaline is:

a) a neurotransmitter
b) a hormone
c) a catecholamine
d) all of the above

. . . .

Q28:

Complete the following diagram of a neuron by identifying the missing labels.

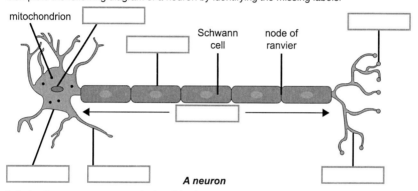

A neuron

Label options: axon; axon terminal; cell body; dendrite; myelin sheath; nucleus; synapse

. . . .

Q29: Diatheses include:

a) unemployment and relationship difficulties
b) genetic predispositions
c) puberty and the menopause
d) alcoholism and drug abuse

. . . .

Q30: SSRIs work by:

a) making more serotonin available by blocking reuptake
b) blocking the reuptake of serotonin and noradrenaline
c) stopping the enzyme monoamine oxidase from removing serotonin, noradrenaline and dopamine
d) creating a brain seizure to relieve the symptoms of depression

. . . .

Q31: SNRIs work by:

a) making more serotonin available by blocking reuptake
b) blocking the reuptake of serotonin and noradrenaline
c) stopping the enzyme monoamine oxidase from removing serotonin, noradrenaline and dopamine
d) creating a brain seizure to relieve the symptoms of depression

....

Q32: MAOIs work by:

a) making more serotonin available by blocking reuptake
b) blocking the reuptake of serotonin and noradrenaline
c) stopping the enzyme monoamine oxidase from removing serotonin, noradrenaline and dopamine
d) creating a brain seizure to relieve the symptoms of depression

....

Q33: ECT works by:

a) making more serotonin available by blocking reuptake
b) blocking the reuptake of serotonin and noradrenaline
c) stopping the enzyme monoamine oxidase from removing serotonin, noradrenaline and dopamine
d) creating a brain seizure to relieve the symptoms of depression

....

Q34: According to Beck, depression is caused by:

a) a negative self-schema
b) faulty information processing
c) both a & b
d) none of the above

....

Q35: The cognitive triad includes:

a) a negative self-schema
b) a myelin sheath
c) negative views about the future
d) silent assumptions

....

Q36: Thoughts such as 'I should' and 'I must' are collectively called:

a) a negative self-schema
b) a myelin sheath
c) negative views about the future
d) silent assumptions

. . . .

Q37: Paying selective attention to those things that reinforce negative beliefs about yourself, and not enough to positive things is known as:

a) negative views about the future
b) faulty information processing
c) silent assumptions
d) a negative self-schema

. . . .

Q38: A study conducted into faulty information processing was carried out by:

a) Caron (2013)
b) Milgram (1961)
c) Alloy et al (1999)
d) Dement & Kleitman (1957)

Unit 3: Social Behaviour

Unit 3 Topic 1

Conformity and obedience (mandatory topic)

Contents

Learning objective

By the end of this area of study, you should be able to describe, explain, evaluate, apply and analyse:

- types of conformity, which must include:
  - identification
  - compliance, and
  - internalisation
- factors (explanations) of conformity, which must include:
  - normative influence
  - informational influence
  - individual factors: gender, self-esteem
  - situational factors: group size, group unanimity, task difficulty
  - cultural factors: collectivist and individualistic cultures
- the aims, methods, results, evaluation and conclusions of Mori and Arai (2010) reproduction of the Asch experiment without confederates
- factors (explanations) affecting obedience, which must include:
  - perceived legitimate authority
  - socialisation
  - authoritarian parenting
  - autonomous and agentic levels of behaviour
  - situational factors: proximity, location, wearing a uniform
- • the aims, methods, results, evaluation and conclusions of Milgram's (1963) Behavioural study of obedience , and relevant knowledge from Milgram's subsequent related studies.

1.1 Introduction

The Social Behaviour area of study contains the mandatory content:

- Conformity and obedience

...and the three other topics from which you and your lecturer will choose one to study:

- Prejudice
- Social relationships
- Aggression

You are advised to discuss your choice of topic with your teacher.

1.2 What is conformity?

Conformity happens all the time: in school, after school, with friends and even with family. If you and two of your friends are trying to decide what to do at the weekend, you may have three separate opinions, e.g. a football match, a school disco or the cinema. Rather than not doing anything at all, you are likely to conform to a group decision following a discussion and then go along with that. It may not be your first choice though — or even your second!

Hayes (2000) tells us that **conformity** is: "The process of going along with other people ... acting in the same way they do".

Kelman (1958) suggested that we yield to group pressure to conform to new norms of behaviour because of one of three types of conformity: **compliance**, **identification** and **internalisation**.

Compliance	Identification	Internalisation
Compliance is a change in our behaviour but not our opinion as a consequence of a request from someone.	Identification occurs when we change our behaviour and/or opinion when we want to identify with a particular group.	Private change or internalisation is a change in our behaviour and in our opinion (Kelman, 1958).
It often relies on rewards or coercion by someone in power.	We desire a relationship with members of that group.	Internalisation of others' views or opinions, are more likely to affect how we think, feel and behave.
		It often stems from knowledge and credibility.
Public conformity, but not a private change in opinion.	Public confirmity, but not necessarily a private change in opinion.	Public and private conformity.

Kelman's three types of conformity

Of the three, compliance is the least effective form of social pressure because only the outward behaviour is affected. External influences on behaviour in the form of rewards and sanctions must be constantly in place in order to have a lasting change in a person's behaviour. Identification as a means of social pressure is valuable if we perceive the agent of influence as attractive.

Of the three, internalisation of another person's or group's, attitude or opinion is the most effective method of social pressure. We appear to have an innate need to be correct. Internalisation gives us support and confirms our 'rightness' (*Turner, 1991*). Nevertheless, there are individuals with confidence in themselves to buck the norm and have opinions and attitudes that are generally not accepted. However, these individuals are few and far between.

Introduction: Questions   Go online

In each of the following questions there is a statement of behaviour. Decide which type of conformity is demonstrated: compliance, identification or internalisation.

Q1:   Deciding to do the Duke of Edinburgh Award because your friends are doing it.

a) compliance
b) identification
c) internalisation

....

Q2:   Converting to Christianity.

a) compliance
b) identification
c) internalisation

....

Q3:   Voting for a political party after hearing their views and deciding you've changed your opinion.

a) compliance
b) identification
c) internalisation

....

Q4:   Deciding to go to see a film you don't wish to see.

a) compliance
b) identification
c) internalisation

....

Q5:   Going along with the gang to decide to break into a shop.

a) compliance
b) identification

---

c) internalisation

. . . .

Q6:   Joining the Girl Guides/Scouts as your friends are all members.

a) compliance
b) identification
c) internalisation

Introduction: Notebook exercise

You will need your psychology notebook for this activity.

Sum up Kelman's three types of conformity and also briefly evaluate the three types.

Check your understanding of *Kelman's three types of conformity* by showing your notebook entry to your teacher or tutor.

1.3   Factors affecting conformity

When deciding whether we want to conform, we can use external (informational influence) and internal (normative influence) cues to make our decision. There are also other factors such as cultural, individual, situational and social factors which also have a bearing on our conformity rates.

Informational influence refers to changing behaviour based on the assumption that the others in the group know more than us, especially in situations where we are unsure of the correct thing to do (see the Jenness study and the Sherif study). It is based on a person's need for certainty (the desire 'to be right'). When we are not sure how to behave, we copy others. They act as informational resources for how to behave because we presume they know what they are doing. Copying them reduces the likelihood of criticism; this is important as we care about what people think about us. This leads to such effects as people taking no notice when a person is mugged in public (bystander effect).

A useful example of the informational influence of conformity is a study by Sherif which was carried out in 1936 and relates to the autokinetic effect.

Sherif (1936): Research

Aim
Sherif investigated how group norms were created using what is known as the **autokinetic effect** which is a perceptual illusion in which the observer imagines movement of a stationary spot of light.

Participants
All the subjects in the autokinetic experiments were male undergraduate and graduate students with ages in the range of 19-30. Participants were *not* suitable if they wore glasses

---

or if they majored in psychology (i.e. if they knew anything about the autokinetic effect there was no point in using them).

Method

Sherif put participants on their own in a dark room and focussed a spot of light onto a screen in front of them. He asked each participant how far, and in what direction, they thought the light had moved. The spot of light was stationary, but participants thought it had moved as a consequence of Sherif's leading question. Estimates of the apparent movement of the light were recorded.

The autokinetic effect experimental set-up

Results

The procedure was carried out again in groups of three (triads). In the group situation, all answers were found to be close to the estimates given by the first person. All of the participants ignored their previous estimates. Moreover, when put into new triads, participants reported the perceived movement of the light in terms of the previous triad's group norm rather than their first estimates.

Evaluation

There are a few problems with this study.

1. Sherif did not control for eyesight or age. This is important because these variables could have influenced the outcome of the study. Wren (1999) identifies these variables as influential in the autokinetic effect.

2. Sherif used an imprecise measure. It is ambiguous because it is not obvious what the correct answer is.

3. Sherif only used three people in his group situation - can three members really constitute a group?

Conclusion

Regardless of the criticisms, Sherif does show us how opinions can be influenced by the group norm.

Sherif (1936): Questions

Go online

Q7: What are the features of a good sample of participants?

. . . .

Q8: Were the participants used in "Sherif (1936) and the autokinetic effect" a representative sample? Explain your reasoning.

. . . .

Q9: Explain two strengths of the experimental method of study.

. . . .

Q10: Explain one weakness of the experimental method of study.

Sherif (1936): Notebook exercise

You will need your psychology notebook for this activity.

Make notes about Sherif's study under the following headings.

- Aim

- Participants

- Method

- Results

- Conclusion

- Critique

Check your understanding of *Sherif's autokinetic effect* by showing your notebook entry to your teacher or tutor.

Sherif (1936): On the Internet

Go online

For more details about this study have a look at:
http://www.brocku.ca/MeadProject/Sherif/Sherif_1935a/Sherif_1935a_2.html

Normative influence is the ability that others have to influence an individual to conform to the social norms. People want to be accepted and they have a need for social approval (the need to 'fit in'). In order to live together in relative harmony, we need to agree on a set of beliefs, values, attitudes and behaviours. However, normative influence need not be internalised —we do not have to agree with the norms to be accepted, just abide by them (compliance). Social norms can be clear or explicit. An example of an explicit social norm, or declared rule of behaviour, would be the no smoking signs found in all enclosed public places in Scotland.

In collectivist cultures, group decision making is highly valued, but in individualistic cultures people are more concerned with their independent success than the well-being of their community.

1.3.1   Cultural factors in conformity

Does our cultural background have an effect on our levels of conformity? It would seem that it does. In some societies, the willingness to conform is valued, while in others it is not. For example, in the West we value men and women who can think independently and sometimes do things that are against the wishes of general society. In some cultures, this type of action is very much frowned upon, and group consensus is valued over individuality. For example, in some parts of Africa being gay is illegal and seen as immoral. This can lead to marriages of convenience —a sham marriage. In this way it 'protects' the man from being viewed as immoral and allows the couple to be a couple —obediently. In the UK it was thought desirable that children should be "seen and not heard". In other words, children were encouraged to be quiet (obey) and speak when spoken to. Most obeyed this rule because failure to do so may have had dire consequences - ask your grandparents! Many experiments on obedience and conformity have been carried out, some of which are included later in this section, but researchers will normally use white, middle-class men.

Smith, Bond and Kagitcibasi (2006) used the Asch research, but this time on various cultures. They found that obedience rates ranged from 14% (Belgian students) to 58% (Indian teachers). They found that rates were lowest in individualistic societies (America and North Europe) at 25.3% than collectivist (Africa, Asia) at 37.1%.

For information on another study please see The Bulletin of the Psychonomic Society, 1978, Vol 11 (4), 267 - 269. "A Cross-Cultural Study of Obedience" by M. Shanab and K. Yahya

Individualism vs Collectivism —Smith and Bond (1998) wished to ascertain if culture and obedience are linked. They found that people who belong to individualistic cultures, such as American and British cultures, were more likely to behave independently than those from collectivist cultures such as China, some parts of Africa and Japan.

1.3.2   Individual factors in conformity

Self-esteem —research has shown that those with a low need for approval, i.e. those with high self-esteem, are less likely to conform than those with lower self-esteem. This is likely because those with higher self-esteem have more confidence in their own judgements, and less fear of potential rejection or ridicule from those who do not agree with their judgement (compliance due to normative influence). An example might be that you have just started a new job and feel that you are good at it, so will not feel a strong need to conform to your co-workers. However, you may feel that you lack the experience of another colleague who has been doing the job for a lot longer than you have. In this case, you are likely to conform to what they do, or what they ask (or may you copy what they do - informational influence, which will help increase your self-esteem as you get better at the task). As you get better at the task, your original compliance will become identification and may lead eventually to internalisation.

Gender —many studies (e.g. Mori and Arai, see page) have found gender differences in conformity, generally showing that women conform more than men. Maslach et al. (1987) found that women are likely to conform when discussing male-oriented subjects, like football, and men when discussing more female-oriented subjects, like child-rearing.

Note that the study by Ash as well as Mor and Arai study are mandatory and you should know them very well.

A useful example of the normative social influence of conformity is the study by Asch in 1952.

Asch (1952): Research

Aim
The Asch conformity experiments, published in 1952, were a series of studies that starkly demonstrated the power of conformity in groups. These are also known as the **Asch Paradigm**. Solomon Asch addressed the ambiguity of Sherif's study by using a very clear measure in his conformity study. There was only one right answer, which was very obvious.

Participants
The laboratory experiments used groups of male college students. Each group consisted of one naive participant and seven Asch **confederates**.

Method
Participants identified the line on their diagram that matched a given line. When the task was completed Asch asked the group to identify the correct answer one by one. The naive participant was always seated near the end and last or second last to give his answer. Asch was interested in how the naive participant would answer in these circumstances.

In the experiment proper, Asch's confederates were primed to give the wrong answer in 12 of his 18 presentations. For example, when asked which line matched X (see following diagram), the confederates who came before the naive participant would answer B, when really the answer was C.

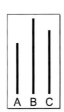

One of the pairs of cards used in the Asch conformity experiments - the card on the left has the reference line and the one on the right shows three different comparison lines

Results
In a control group, with no pressure to conform to an erroneous view, only one subject out of 35 ever gave an incorrect answer. However, when surrounded by individuals, all voicing an incorrect answer, participants provided incorrect responses on a high proportion of the questions (37%). 75% of the participants gave an incorrect answer to at least one question.

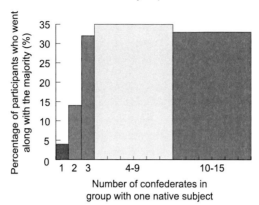

Size of unanimous majority in the Asch conformity experiments

Size of group
Asch's later studies discovered that as group size increased to a maximum of three others, conformity increased.

Harmony of group opinion:
When the group results were not harmonious, i.e. when one confederate gave a different answer (not necessarily correct), conformity rates dropped.

Ambiguity:
When the task was ambiguous (comparison lines were similar in length to each other), group conformity increased. The more ambiguous the task, the greater the likelihood that an individual would conform to the group opinion.

Evaluation
The Asch experiments are important when looking at conformity, but bear in mind these criticisms.

1. Asch reports the average rate of conformity to be 37%, yet many participants did not conform at all (26%).

2. Methodology - Asch can also be criticised on methodological grounds. He used a biased sample in that it consisted entirely of male undergraduates from an American University. His sample did not reflect society at large. Therefore, generalising the results of his conformity experiment to society is rather presumptuous.

3. His experiments took place in a laboratory, which lacks ecological validity.

4. Perrin and Spencer (1980, 1981) tell us that the Asch effect was a "child of its time". In the 1950s, the USA was very conservative and anti-communist. Showing any hint of being different from the norm held grave consequences for current and future employment.

Conclusion

Asch's experiment reinforced the conclusions of Sherif's experiment and went further in the investigation of conformity.

Asch (1952): Questions   Go online

Q11: One of the criticisms levelled at Asch was that the sample was biased. How would you redesign the sample to make it far less biased?

. . . .

Q12: Name the type of graph used to show Asch's results.

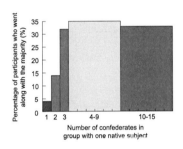

. . . .

Q13: What type of experiment is this piece of research by Asch an example of?

a) Field
b) Natural
c) Laboratory

In 2010, Kazuo Mori and Miho Arai, from Tokyo University, decided to try to update the study by Asch (1952).

Mori and Arai (2010): Research

Aim

- To find out if similar results to Asch could be obtained without using confederates.

- To find out if gender or culture made any difference to the overall results.

Participants

104 Japanese Undergraduates participants, who knew each-other, took part - 40 men and 64 women.

Method

The fMORI technique was used —participants wore filter glasses that allowed them to watch the same video but see different things. All participants had normal eyesight. There were several groups of four, with one participant in each group having been given a different type of filter in the glasses. This filter made them perceive a different line length to the others in their group. Each participant stated their answer out loud. By using the fMORI technique, it meant that everyone was a true participant, unlike the Asch study which used confederates. At the end of the experiment, Mori and Arai used a questionnaire to ascertain if participants noticed anything odd or if they were confident in their judgements of the length of the lines.

Results

Female participants conformed to the majority in about a quarter of cases while male participants did not conform to the majority view.

Conclusion

This experiment showed similar conformity patterns to Asch in 1952, but was very different in one respect; there was no conformity among minority men.

Mori and Arai (2010): Notebook exercise

You will need your psychology notebook for this activity.

Complete the table below, evaluating strengths and weaknesses of the study carried out by Mori and Arai (2010).

Strengths	Weaknesses
Example - large number of participants used, which may mean that this study is more representative than that by Asch.	Example - although a large number of participants were used, they were all undergraduates.
. . .	. . .

Check your understanding of *Mori and Arai (2010)* by showing your notebook entry to your teacher or tutor.

Mori and Arai (2010): Reading

For more information see the International Journal of Psychology, 45:5, 390-397. Mori and Arai (2010): no need to fake it —reproduction of the Asch experiment without confederates.

1.4   Situational factors in conformity

Following Asch's original research, numerous variations of his line judgement task were carried out. These variations include the following situational factors in conformity: group size, unanimity and task difficulty.

Group size: Asch carried out a variation of his original research to find out how the size of the group affects rates of conformity. These variations ranged from one confederate to 15 confederates, and the rate of conformity varied dramatically. When there was just one confederate, the real participant conformed on 3% of the trials. When the group size increased to two confederates, the real participant conformed on 12.8% of the critical trials. When there were three confederates, the real participant conformed on 32% of the trials, which was the same percentage as Asch's original experiment, in which there were seven to nine confederates.

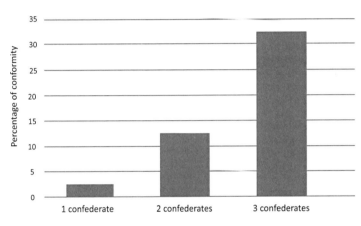

The conclusion of this finding is, therefore, that conformity reaches its highest level with just three confederates. Asch found that the rate of conformity did not increase as he added confederates beyond this number.

Unanimity — In Asch's original experiment, the confederates all gave the same wrong answer. In one variation of Asch's experiment, one of the confederates was told to give the correct answer throughout. In this variation, the rate of conformity dropped to 5%. This shows that if the real participants has support for their belief, then they are more likely to resist the pressure to conform. Furthermore, in another variation, one of the confederates gave a different incorrect answer to the majority. In this variation, conformity still dropped significantly, this time to 9%.

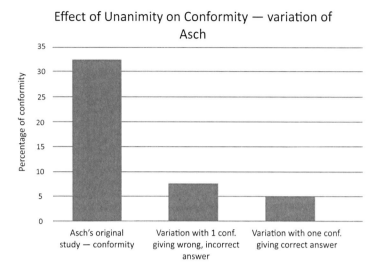

This shows that if you break the group's unanimous position, then conformity is reduced, even if the answer provided by the supporter is incorrect. A study conducted by Melanie Spreadbury (2014) at the Laurentian University in Canada, found that this applied to virtual groups, too.

Task difficulty —in Asch's original experiment, the correct answer was always obvious. In one of his variations, however, he made the task more difficult by making the difference between the line lengths significantly smaller. In this variation, Asch found that the rate of conformity increased. This is likely to be the result of informational influence, as individuals look to another for guidance when competing the task, as the correct answer is unclear.

Informational and normative social influence: Notebook exercise

You will need your psychology notebook for this activity.

Make brief notes about your understanding of:

- the informational influence —in making you conform;
- the normative influence —in making you conform;
- individual, situational and cultural factors.

Check your understanding of *informational and normative influence* by showing your notebook entry to your teacher or tutor.

Factors which affect our willingness to conform: Discussion

Think through each of the following scenarios and:

1. Decide whether you would conform or not.

2. Give a reason for your decision.

3. Say if it was a situational or individual factor, or both.

A) You are out with your friends on a Saturday night. Your curfew is midnight, but your friends want to go on to a party.

B) Your group of friends all opt into doing Duke of Edinburgh after school. It clashes with your job, which you like.

C) You are in a sports team and your opponents have a 'star' player. Would you foul their star player, if encouraged by your teammates, to help with the match?

D) Your registration teacher has asked you all to 'buddy' a new first year pupil —none of your friends has volunteered, but a person that you fancy has.

Factors which affect our willingness to conform: Notebook exercise

You will need your psychology notebook for this activity.

Make some notes about the reasons that people conform.

Divide your answers into normative influence, informational influence, individual factors, situational factors and cultural factors

Check your understanding of factors which affect our willingness to conform by showing your notebook entry to your teacher or lecturer.

1.5 Conformity summary

We are more likely to conform when:

- task difficulty —the task asked of us is difficult or unclear;

- unanimity —when all other members of your group are in agreement;

- normative influence —the desire to be liked;

- informational influence —the desire to be right;

- gender —conflicting evidence, but some evidence that females conform more readily than males;

- group size —conformity increases to a group size of 3, then stabilises;

- self-esteem —people who have a high need for approval (low self-esteem) show more conformity that those with a lower need for approval (higher self-esteem);

- cultural factors —collectivist cultures, where the group is valued more than the individual, show higher levels of conformity than individualistic cultures, where the individual is valued over the group.

The following exercise could be used as part of your revision. It contains some of the key points that have been covered on the subject of conformity.

Conformity mindmap: Notebook exercise

You will need your psychology notebook for this activity.

A mindmap is not meant to replace revision; it is merely an aid to help it. You should personalise your mindmap with pictures, bullet points (of important words or studies) and colour to help you revise the subject of conformity. Try to add links to the mindmap between types, factors and studies, then show this to your teacher or lecturer for checking.

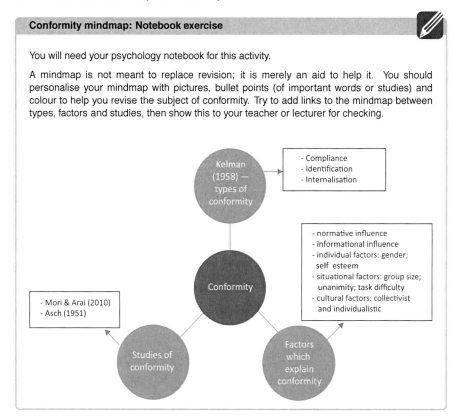

1.6 What is obedience?

We often hear the word **obedience**, especially in school, but what is it and how does it differ from conformity? Read the following, disturbing example of US soldiers' actions during the Vietnam war.

> Captain Medina told his soldiers to destroy all crops, kill all livestock, burn all houses, and to pollute the water wells of a village presumed to harbour the enemy. He is alleged to have told them to kill non-combatants.
>
> On entering the village, there was no resistance. Yet, during the next three hours, houses were burned to the ground, livestock was slaughtered and women were raped. Groups of villagers were gathered together and shot. Approximately five hundred non-combatants died.
>
> During this period, captain Medina remained outside the village. He gave an order to conserve ammunition. This resulted in his men bayoneting their victims, including babies.
>
> The atrocity ended when officer Thompson and his men noticed, from their helicopter, that civilians, including very young children, were being slaughtered. They saved the remaining villagers who were holed up in a bunker, including a wounded child, who was rushed to hospital.

When asked why they had committed such an atrocity, the soldiers blamed their superior officer and claimed they were just obeying orders.

Definition of Obedience — our willingness to follow the orders of someone in a position of authority over us.

In the example above, the soldiers willingly (we might say *blindly*) obeyed Captain Medina's orders. It was only when people watching outside the situation intervened that the atrocity stopped.

1.6.1 Obedience and conformity — the differences

Obedience and conformity are both forms of social influence. Although at first they seem quite similar, they are distinctly different from one another.

	Obedience	Conformity
Who is involved?	Occurs within a hierarchical structure	Can occur between people of equal status as well as within a hierarchy
Emphasis on	Power	Acceptance
Behaviour adopted	Differs from the behaviour of the authority figure	Is similar to that of the whole group
Explicit/implicit action	The prescription for action is explicit	The requirement to yield to group pressure is often, though not always, implicit
Participants	Embrace obedience to explain behaviour	Deny conformity

Key differences between obedience and conformity

Obedience and conformity - the differences: Notebook exercise

You will need your psychology notebook for this activity.

Make notes under the following headings.

- Conformity

- Obedience

- The differences between obedience and conformity

Check your understanding of *obedience and conformity* by showing your notebook entry to your teacher or tutor.

1.7   Factors affecting obedience

We have all obeyed commands at one time or another from an authority figure - a teacher, a cadet sergeant, a guide or scout leader, a parent, the police etc.

There are several factors which affect our obedience and they are:

- perceived legitimate authority;

- socialisation;

- authoritarian parenting;

- autonomous and agentic levels of behaviour;

- situational factors: proximity, location, wearing a uniform.

Perceived legitimate authority —if we think that someone has the right to tell us what to do, then generally we will obey. An example might be a police officer. They have legitimate authority over us and failure to obey may result in some sort of legitimate punishment. This is called coercive power and it should also be noted that this type of authority responds very well to the use of a uniform. This helps us realise that this is a real policeman with real, legitimate power over us. A piece of research to help back this up is offered from Zimbardo - some of the participants took the role of prisoners whilst others took the role of guards. Both adopted the uniform for that role and the consequences were dire. See YouTube. The experimenter in Milgram's research was also a perceived legitimate authority figure, as shown by his wearing of a lab coat.

Hofling's (1966) study also shows the power of perceived legitimate authority, as nurses obeyed an order of a doctor (doctors are perceived to have legitimate authority), even although this was against the rules (see below).

Socialisation —the reason for differences in obedience levels may be due to the socialisation process. This process occurs from birth and continues throughout our lives. It teaches us the 'rules of life' in a formal and informal manner; in other words, what is the correct behaviour for every given situation. This has a link to the way we are parented, schooled, our social class and many other aspects. For example, if our parents are authoritative, this may lead us to internalise the need to obey —we will normally do as we are told. Binding factors keep us in an agentic state; we fear disruption to our social situation and may not question authority.

Authoritarian parenting —this is a theory which stems from around the end of WW2 and is associated with Theodore Adorno. Adorno wished to find out if blind obedience was associated with being German and he used case studies, interviews and psychometric testing. He also devised and his 'f-scale' questionnaire with the 'f' standing for fascist. He found that people who scored high on the 'f-scale' were normally brought up by very strict parents who demanded obedience at all times. This resulted in the children, as adults, being rigid in their beliefs, conventional and viewed their own group as being superior. This means that if someone outside their group tells them to do something they are unlikely to do so. If someone from their own group tells them to do something and they view this person as being high in authority, they will obey - no matter the costs.

Autonomous vs Agentic state —an agentic state is when an individual carries out the orders of an authority figure and acts as their agent, with little personal responsibility. In Milgram's original experiment, the participants were told that the experimenter had full responsibility and therefore they could act as his agent, carrying out the experimenter's orders. If the participants were told that they were responsible, it is possible that Milgram's participants would have been much less likely to obey.

Milgram argued that we operate in one of two ways when faced with social situations. Individuals can act autonomously and take responsibility for their own behaviour, or they can enter an agentic state, where they do not feel responsibility for their actions as they are carrying out the orders of an authority figure. When a person changes from autonomous to agentic state, they have undergone an agentic shift.

Situational factors: Proximity —there will be times when you feel at ease in dealing with a decision and this comes under autonomous. Sometimes we may feel that we do not have the confidence or expertise to deal with the problem and so are happy to leave this to someone else. An example might be that you have just started a new job and feel that you are good at it. However, you may feel that you lack the experience of another colleague who has been doing the job for a lot longer than you have. In this case, you are happy to them deal with it.

Effect of Proximity on Rates of Obedience

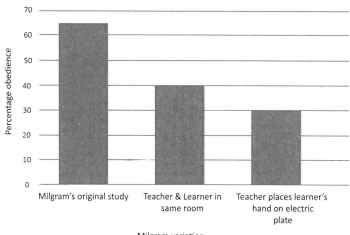

Milgram variation

The proximity of the authority figure also affects the level of obedience. In another variation, after the experimenter had given the initial instructions, they left the room. All subsequent instructions were provided over the phone. In this variation, participants were more likely to defy the experimenter and only 21% of participants administered the full 450 volts.

Situational factors: Location —Milgram conducted his original research in a laboratory of Yale University, which is a prestigious, Ivy League university in Boston, USA. In order to test the influence that location had on obedience, Milgram conducted a variation in a run down office building in Bridgeport, Connecticut. The experiment was no longer associated with Yale University and was carried out by the Research Association of Bridgeport. In this variation, the percentage of participants who administered the full 450 volts dropped from 65% to 47.5%. This highlights the impact of location on obedience, with less prestigious locations resulting in a reduction in obedience.

Situational factors: Wearing a uniform —in most of Milgram's variations the experimenter wore a lab coat. Milgram examined the power of the uniform in a variation where the experimenter was called away and replaced by another 'participant' in ordinary clothes, who was in fact another confederate. In this variation, the man in ordinary clothes came up with the idea of increasing the voltage every time the learner made a mistake. The percentage of participants who administered the full 450 volts in this situation dropped from 65% to 20%, demonstrating the dramatic power of a uniform.

Bickman (1974) also investigated the power of uniform in a field experiment conducted in New York. Bickman used three male actors: one dressed as a milkman; one as a security guard; and one in ordinary clothes. The actors asked members of the public to follow one of three instructions: pick up a bag; give someone money for a parking meter; and stand on the other side of a bus stop sign which said 'no standing'. On average, the guard was obeyed on 76% of occasions, the milkman on 47% and the pedestrian on 30%.

Effect on wearing a Uniform on Obedience

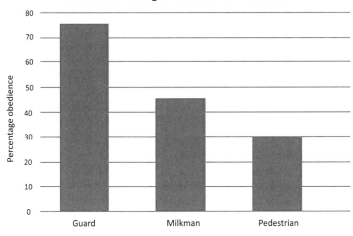

Uniform type worn

Hofling *et al* (1966): Research

It was not just Milgram who looked into studying obedience. Hofling *et al* also looked at this issue, but they conducted a more real-life experiment.

Like Milgram, Hofling looked at the *agentic state* and *perceived legitimate authority* as being explanations for obedience.

Aim
The researchers were interested in whether nurses would always obey a doctor's orders, even when doing this would endanger the lives of the patient.

Participants
22 wards in various American hospitals were used. The participants were the nurses in that ward. The nurses did not realise they were participating in a study.

Method
Experimental medicine was placed in each of the 22 wards in the dispensary where other medicines were located. It was labelled "Astroten", but was actually just glucose which would be harmless to the majority of the population. The label on the Astroten box said that the safe maximum daily dose was only 10mg.

A researcher, posing as a doctor, would phone the ward and say that he was from the psychiatric department. He would instruct the nurse to give Mr. X a dosage of "Astroten" of 20mg, which is double the maximum dose stated on the box. In all of the wards, written authority was needed before drugs would be administered. However, the doctor said to the nurse that he was "running late and would sign the authorisation when he arrived".

Another group was also used which consisted of 22 nurses who were interviewed and explained the scenario above (of an unknown doctor phoning and doubling the dosage) and asked what they would do.

Results

The results were very interesting to Hofling *et al*, in part because of the difference between the two groups of nurses:

- 21 of the 22 nurses interviewed said they would disobey the doctor;

- 21 of the 22 nurses in the phone situation obeyed the doctor and gave a dangerous dosage.

When the phone nurses were debriefed and questioned later, the following statements were made:

- 11 said that they had not noticed the discrepancy in the dosage that they had been ordered to administer;

- 10 did notice the discrepancy, but thought that it would be safe if the doctor had ordered it.

Conclusion

The nurses believed that they would not obey a doctor unquestioningly, yet, in reality, it was a very different story.

1.7.1   Milgram (1963)

A great study to look at to see how obedience works is one conducted by Milgram. As you read this study, you will become aware of the following explanations for obedience:

- perceived legitimate authority;

- graduated commitment;

- agentic state.

The Milgram experiment was very famous in America in the 1960s. Milgram's study wanted to research the question: *will people inflict great harm on others simply because they are told to do so?* The results of the study were made public and caused an outcry - read on and find out why.

Milgram (1963): Research

Aim

In 1963, social psychologist Stanley Milgram began a series of experiments in America. He investigated the belief that the Nazi Holocaust of World War II identified the German national character flaw. He intended to run the study first in America and then in Germany, but he didn't ever run it in Germany because the results indicated a human flaw, not a German one.

Participants

Milgram placed an advertisement in a newspaper to recruit 40 male participants to take part in the experiment. Participants included professionals, white collar and unskilled workers aged between 20 and 50. All were paid $4.50 for taking part.

Method

On arrival, the participant was taken to a room with another 'volunteer' (actually a confederate). A psychologist told the duo that the purpose of the experiment was to assess the effect of punishment on the learning process. The teacher's role (the participant was always assigned this role) was to assist the learner to remember a set of learned words by giving him an electric shock whenever an error was made. The learner was then taken into a nearby room and strapped into a chair. Electrodes were attached to the confederate's arm.

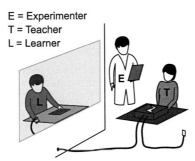

E = Experimenter
T = Teacher
L = Learner

The Milgram experimental set-up

In front of the teacher was a shock generator with thirty switches. On the left was a switch marked *15 volts*. The switches were clearly identified with increasing voltages, ending with one marked 450 volts. In order that the participant was clear about the intensity of the voltage, there was also a series of labels on the switches reading *slight shock, moderate shock, very strong shock, danger - severe shock*, concluding with two labelled *XXX* (indicating death).

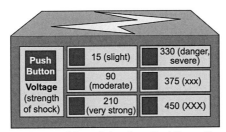

Examples of some of the switches from the Milgram Experiment

Pairs of words were identified. During the experiment, the first words of the pairs were read out by the teacher. The learner's task was to state the other word from each pair. When the learner made a mistake, as they would do deliberately, the teacher was then required to shock them with 15 volts. Each time the learner made a mistake, the shock was to be increased.

However, at 75 volts, the learner would be heard to moan. At 105 volts, the learner would cry out in pain. At 150 volts, they would raise their voice and beg the teacher to stop. The experimenter would have a list of prompts to encourage the teacher to continue. At 180 volts, the learner would be screaming and banging on the wall and complaining of a heart condition. If a participant teacher protested about administering electric shocks at any stage, the experimenter would use sequential standardised commands or 'prods':

1. "Please continue" or "Please go on";

2. "The experiment requires that you continue";

3. "It is absolutely essential that you continue";

4. "You have no other choice, you must go on".

The experiment ended when the 450-volt shock had been reached and administered, or when the participant teacher withdrew from the experiment by walking out.

Results

The results of Milgram's study were surprising:

- every one of the 40 teacher participants kept administering electric shocks to the 300-volt mark;

- at 300 volts, only five (or 12.5%) defiant participants stopped;

- 26 (or 65%) of obedient participants went on to inflict the maximum 450-volt shock to the learner-confederate, even though they were aware that to do so meant the learner's death.

The participants showed various signs of extreme distress as Milgram recorded: "In a large number of cases the degree of tension reached extremes that are rarely seen in laboratory studies. Subjects were observed to sweat, tremble, stutter, bite their lips, groan and dig their fingers into their flesh. One sign of tension was the regular occurrence of nervous laughing fits. Full-blown, uncontrollable seizures were observed for three subjects." (*Milgram, 1963*)

After the experiment, the participants were debriefed. Milgram gave participants a number of psychometric tests to measure psychological distress.

Evaluation

As with any psychology experiment an evaluation needs to be done. For Milgram's experiment the following comments were levelled at the study:

- laboratory experiments lack ecological validity;

- Milgram used all male participants therefore cannot generalise to the whole population;

- ethically suspect - participants were not given the right to informed consent or the right to withdraw (the 'prods' ensured continued engagement);

- Baumrind (1964) criticised Milgram for causing psychological distress to his participants;

- Milgram explained the Nazi-driven atrocity as a consequence of **blind obedience** to authority but this is a very simplistic conclusion. He ignored the benefits that may have tempted German citizens, e.g. plundering individuals of their material possessions, including their gold fillings etc. (*Mandel, 1998*)

Milgram (1964) defended his research saying that:

- he believed that his research was not **unethical** because his results could not have been predicted;

- he gave a full debrief and his participants did not come to any psychological harm;

- he did not physically stop his participants from leaving;

- he had his participants undergo a psychiatric assessment one year later. No signs of psychological harm were found.

Conclusion
Milgram concluded that obedience, or our compliance with an explicit request from an authority figure, is a very powerful reason behind why we often behave as we do.

The following explanations for obedience can be observed and deduced from Milgram's experiment:

- perceived legitimate authority;

- graduated commitment (having agreed to give a 15 volt shock, it was hard to refuse to give a 45 volt one);

- agentic state (the participants argued afterwards that they thought the university had sanctioned the study).

Milgram's agency theory

Milgram thought that when we obey orders from others, we give up personal responsibility for our actions. We see ourselves as the authority figure's agent, acting on their bequest.

Milgram's participants went from an autonomous state, where they had personal control of their situation, to an agentic state, where they felt themselves to be the instrument for carrying out another person's actions (Milgram, 1974). Milgram thinks that our ability to submit to the authority of others allows us all to achieve collective goals. If we all did what we wanted, thus acting autonomously, anarchy would result.

Milgram (1963): Questions	Go online

Q14: Who were the participants in this study?

....

Q15: Were they a representative sample?

....

Q16: How must the subjects have felt after they found out that the experiment was not about learning but was actually about obedience to authority?

. . . .

Q17: What ethical issues do you feel Milgram should have considered in his experiment?

. . . .

Q18: Explain one strength of the experimental method in psychology.

Milgram (1963): Notebook exercise

You will need your psychology notebook for this activity.

Milgram's is a long and complex study, but a very important one. If you are asked a question about obedience in your Higher exam it is highly likely that you will have to mention it.

You should make notes on this study under the following headings.

- Milgram's research question

- Background

- Participants

- Method

- Results

- Conclusions

- Evaluation

- Milgram's defence

Check your understanding of *Milgram's obedience study* by showing your notebook entry to your teacher or tutor.

1.7.2   Variations on Milgram's study

Milgram's original study in 1963 showed high levels of obedience from the participants used (65%). Since 1963, Milgram and others have carried out variations on this study to see if obedience is still likely to take place.

Variations on Milgram's study: Questions Go online

Read the condition shown in each question and decide if you think there would be more or less obedience to authority than Milgram's original 65%..

Q19: Proximity of learner. The teacher (real participant) had to press the hand of the learner (confederate) onto the shock plate

....

Q20: Proximity of experimenter. The actual instructions were given over the phone to the teacher.

....

Q21: Perceived authority. The experiment was not conducted in a esteemed university setting but rather a run down building.

....

Q22: Individual differences. Rather than just look at the same type of participants as Milgram had, the participants were varied. Would the following be more or less likely to be obedient than Milgram's participants?

- More educated
- Military personnel

1.8 Obedience summary

- Occurs as a result of a direct order from an authority figure.
- Emphasis is on the acceptance of power.
- Behaviour adopted differs from the behaviour of the authority figure.
- The action is explicit.
- Factors which affect obedience include:
  - perceived legitimate authority;
  - socialisation;
  - authoritarian parenting;
  - autonomous and agentic levels of behaviour;
  - situational factors: proximity, location, wearing a uniform (variations of Milgram).
- Studies include Milgram (mandatory study), Bickman and Hofling.

The following exercise could be used as part of your revision. It contains some of the key points that have been covered on the subject of obedience.

Obedience mindmap: Notebook exercise

You will need your psychology notebook for this activity.

A mindmap is not meant to replace revision. It is merely an aid to help it. You should personalise your mindmap with pictures, bullet points (of important words or studies) and colour to help you revise the subject of obedience.

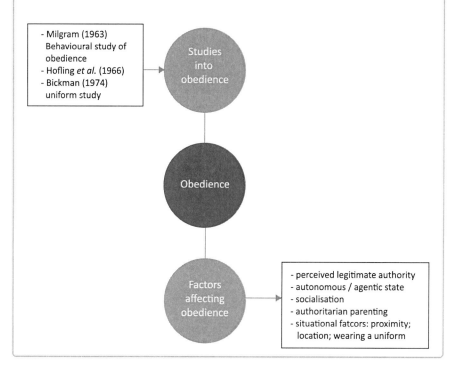

1.9 Learning points

Summary

- Compliance, identification and internalisation are types of conformity.

- Factors affecting conformity include: normative and informational influence, cultural factors, individual factors and situational factors.

- Studies into conformity include Asch's line judgement study, and Mori & Arai's adaptation of Asch's study. Other relevant studies include the autokinetic effect study by Sherif .

- Obedience and conformity are different.

- People obey due to: perceived legitimate authority, proximity, wearing of a uniform, authoritarian parenting, agentic or autonomous levels of behaviour, and location.

- Studies into obedience include: Milgram's Behavioural study, Bickman's uniform study and Hofling et al's nurses study.

1.10   End of topic test

End of topic 1 test   Go online

Q23: Normative influence is defined as the need to: *(1 mark)*

a) be accepted by others.
b) stand out from the crowd.
c) conform.
d) belong to a group.
e) internalise our feelings.

....

Q24: Which of the flowing four factors can affect our levels of conformity? You may choose more than one answer. *(1 mark)*

- The difficulty of the task
- Gender
- Group size
- If you have low self-esteem
- The setting

....

Q25: Complete the paragraphs using the words listed. *(10 marks)*

Mori and Arai carried out a study about _____ in 2010. They decided to try to update the study by Asch. Their aims were to find out if similar results could be obtained without the use of confederates, and whether or not _____ or _____ made any difference to the overall results.

The _____ used was as follows: 104 undergraduate participants, who knew each other, took part (40 men and 64 women). They used the fMORI technique so participants wore filter glasses. All participants had normal _____. Groups of four were tested - one participant in each group was given a different type of filter in the glasses without knowing. This filter made them perceive lines of a different _____ to the others in their group. Each participant stated which lines matched out loud. By using this technique it meant that everyone was a true _____, unlike the Asch study.

Mori and Arai used a _____ to ascertain if participants noticed anything odd or if they were confident in their judgements of the length of the lines. _____ participants conformed to the majority in about a quarter of cases while _____ participants did not conform to the majority.

Word list: conformity, culture, eyesight, female, gender, length, male, method, participant, questionnaire.

. . . .

Q26: Complete the paragraph using the words listed. *(10 marks)*

_____ influence is when we _____ our behaviour as a _____ of information from people we regard as _____. To us, their views are valid and _____. This demonstrates a need for _____. When we are not sure how to behave in a certain situation, we _____ the behaviours of those around us. This copying behaviour _____ the likelihood that we will be _____ —as humans, it would seem that we do care what _____ people think of us.

Word list: certainty, change, consequence, copy, criticised, experts, informational, other, reduces, reliable.

Unit 3 Topic 2

Aggression (optional topic)

Contents

Learning objective

By the end of this topic, you should be able to explain, evaluation, apply and analyse:

- Biological influences on aggression, which must include:
    - neural and hormonal
    - genetic
    - evolutionary
    - ethological
- the aims, methods, results, evaluation and conclusions of one study into biological influences on aggression
- Social psychological explanations of aggression, which must include:
    - social learning theory
    - Sykes' deprivation model
    - dysfunctional institutions
    - the importation model
- Media influences on aggression, which must include:
    - computer games
    - disinhibition
- the aims, methods, results, evaluation and conclusions of one study into media influences on aggression

2.1 Introduction

There are many definitions of **aggression** and one is from Baron who said:

> "Aggression is any form of **behaviour** directed towards the goal of harming or injuring another living being who is motivated to avoid such treatment".

(Introduction to Social psychology, 317)

It may take the form of physical, verbal, direct or indirect harm. It may be in response to an action levied against us which makes us feel unjust or hurtful. Aggression can be provoked by a situation or another person, which makes us feel angry, frightened or hostile. We will all experience aggression at some time in our lives — aggression directed towards us or initiated by ourselves. It can be seen in the big things in life such as wars, famine and disasters. It can also be seen in normal everyday life, in small things such as the fact that you did not get the grade that you thought you would for Higher Psychology!

But why is aggression there — is it something that we are born with, is it something that is rooted in our childhood, or, rather more disturbingly, is it something that we can learn by watching others?

There are many psychological explanations for aggression and this area of study will examine a few. We will look at the role that video games and the media have over us and our response(s) to this. Near the end of this area of study, you will find some theories and methods about the **reduction of aggression** and an evaluation of them. At the very end is the end of topic test which you are advised to complete.

In the completion of this area of study, candidates are advised to look at the world around them — globally and closer to home. If you can relate a theory to reality, you will greatly enhance your understanding of this topic, e.g. is there a **conflict** happening today that might be explained by one of the theories that you will encounter? As a young person in today's society, are you aware that video games may have an effect on you? Perhaps you have encountered someone who is naturally aggressive — what techniques might they use to reduce feelings of aggression?

2.2 Biological explanations of aggression

Neural and hormonal influences on aggression

Neurotransmitters are chemicals enabling impulses within brain to be transmitted from one area to another. Neurotransmitters involved in aggression include serotonin and dopamine. Low levels of serotonin and high levels of dopamine have been associated with aggression in animals and

Serotonin is thought to reduce aggression by inhibiting responses to emotional stimuli. Low levels of serotonin are associated with increased susceptibility to impulsive behaviour.

Elevated serotonin levels tend to reduce irritability and impulsive aggression.

High levels of the neurotransmitter, dopamine, is also implicated in aggression.

- Couppis and Kennedy found that in mice, a reward pathway in the brain is activated in response to an aggressive event and concluded that dopamine evolved as a positive reinforcer, suggesting that people seek out aggressive encounters to feel rewarding sensation afterwards.

- However, increased levels of dopamine might be a consequence of aggression, not the cause.

Hormonal influences on aggression

Hormones appear to have a mediating effect on aggression related hormones, such as cortisol and testosterone, possibly because they increase anxiety and the likelihood of social withdrawal.

High levels of cortisol inhibits testosterone levels and so inhibit aggression. Virkkunen found that low levels of cortisol in habitual violent offenders and in violent schoolchildren, which suggests that although relatively higher testosterone is the primary biochemical influence on aggression, low cortisol also plays an important role by increasing the likelihood of aggressive behaviour.

The role of cortisol in aggression is supported by McBurnett et al. who studied a group of four year-old boys with behavioural problems. He found that boys that had consistently low levels of cortisol began antisocial acts at a younger age and exhibited three times more aggressive symptoms. He concluded that cortisol levels are strongly related to aggressive conduct disorders.

It is thought that high levels of the male hormone testosterone result in aggression. During puberty, levels of testosterone increase, as do levels of aggression. This hormone is also found in women; however, there is a much lower level. Also, the highest testosterone levels are found in violent criminals, and much lower levels found in those who have committed non-violent crimes. Lindman *et al.* found that young males who behaved aggressively when drunk had higher levels of testosterone.

The **challenge hypothesis** suggests that in monogamous species, testosterone levels should only rise above baseline breeding level in response to social challenges (male-to-male aggression or a threat to status). Human species are monogamous, so male testosterone levels would sharply rise in response to such a challenge. The consequence of this is increased aggression if the threat is deemed relevant.

Evaluation of neural and hormonal influences on aggression

Advantages

- Lavin found that people who use amphetamines (which increases dopamine activity) also show increased aggressive behaviour.

- Mann *et al.* gave drugs to 35 healthy participants, which reduced levels of serotonin in their bloodstream. Aggression levels were measured via a questionnaire. It was found that aggression scores were higher after taking the drug.

- Raleigh *et al.* found that Vervet monkeys who were fed on diets high in tryptophan (which increases serotonin) exhibited decreased levels of aggression but monkeys fed on diets low in tryptophan showed increased aggression.

- Popora *et al.* conducted research conducted on animals which supports the serotonin link. They found that animals selectively bred for their docile temperaments developed high levels of serotonin over generations.

Disadvantages

- The link between dopamine and aggression is not well established.

- Mann's study was conducted on males only so the findings can only be applied to males. Also, the use of questionnaires means that responses may be unreliable, due to the fact that participants might lie and say they are less aggressive than they are in order make themselves appear better to others. (Social desirability effect).

- Much of the research has been conducted with non-human animals, and it is difficult to apply the findings to humans. Also a causal link was not established, only a correlational one meaning that other factors may have reduced aggression, and in turn serotonin.

- It may not be the levels of serotonin that cause aggression but the receptors. For example, fewer receptors in the brain will result in less serotonin being taken up, therefore making less use of the serotonin. Low levels are also linked with depression and overeating, therefore aggression is not a definite consequence suggesting that serotonin levels are not solely responsible.

- The finding that there are higher levels of testosterone in violent criminals is challenged by the fact that much of the research is correlational, so it could be argued that aggression leads to high levels of testosterone, not the other way round. Plus, conducting research on a prison sample means that the sample is not representative of the population.

Activity: Neural and hormonal mechanisms in aggression Go online

Q1: Which of the following is not part of the limbic system?

a) Hippocampus
b) Amygdala
c) Parietal lobe
d) Hypothalamus

....

Q2: Which of these hormones is not associated with aggression?

a) Dopamine
b) Serotonin
c) Testosterone
d) Melatonin

Q3:

The _____ system connects to the cingulate gyrus and the _____ cortex. These areas are involved in focusing attention on emotionally significant events, forward planning and the anticipation of _____ . These areas control how we respond to _____ events or stimuli and play an important role in aggressive behaviour.

The hypothalamus regulates emotional responses, and the _____ attaches emotional significance to sensory information. Any damage to these areas could cause an inappropriate aggressive response.

Signals are passed from the lower systems of the prefrontal cortex (where our feelings are regulated) to higher systems (where feeling are monitored and interpreted), which then triggers a _____ response. If the prefrontal cortex is damaged then this reduces the _____ effect of the amygdala, leading to more aggression.

Wordlist: threatening, physical, prefrontal, amygdala, inhibiting, reward, limbic

---

2.2.1   Genetics and aggression

There is a belief that genetic factors play a role in aggressive behaviour, for which there is supporting evidence from twin studies. Psychologists have looked at twin studies to try and find evidence for a genetic basis to compare the degree of similarity of aggression between sets of monozygotic (MZ) twins (who develop from the same egg and share 100% of the same genetic makeup) and dizygotic (DZ) twins (who come from two different eggs and share 50% of the same genetic makeup). Findings in general suggest that aggressive behaviour is more highly correlated in MZ twins than DZ twins. For example, Gottesman found a concordance rate of 87% for aggressive behaviour for MZ twin pairs, compared with 72% for DZ twin pairs.

Adoption studies can help to disentangle the relative contributions of the environment and genetics. If researchers find a greater similarity in levels of aggression between adopted children and biological parents than between their adoptive parents, it suggests genetics are an important influence.

Researchers have also identified a number of genes potentially for aggression. Although no individual gene for aggression has been identified in humans, a gene responsible for the production of the protein Monoamine oxidase (MAOA) has been associated with aggressive behaviour. MAOA regulates the metabolism of serotonin in the brain. Low levels of serotonin have been associated with aggression. In the 1980s, a study of a Dutch family found that many of its male members behaved in a particularly violent manner and most convicted of serious violent crimes. These men were found to have significantly low levels of MAOA and a defect in this gene was later identified by Brunner.

Rather than either genetics or environment alone being responsible for the development of aggression, some researchers believe that interactions between genes and environment influence traits which are the diathesis-stress model. This theory is supported by research by Caspi et al. where researchers investigated a link between high/low levels of MAOA, upbringing and levels for anti-social behaviour. It was found that males who had been maltreated and had high MAOA were less likely to be aggressive and males from a non-violent home and low MAOA found no aggression. This shows that genetic influences and environmental influences on their own to not cause aggression. However, in violent homes were the participant had low levels of MAOA, they tended to be more aggressive, suggesting that individuals have a genetic disposition to be aggressive which is triggered by environmental influences, such as deprivation or provocation.

Evaluation of genes as an explanation of aggression

Advantages

- A study by Mednick reviewed over 14000 adoptions in Denmark and found a strong relationship between the number of criminal convictions for criminal violence among biological parents and their adopted sons, thus supporting the genetic role in aggression.

Disadvantages

- It is hard to disentangle nature and nurture, which is a problem for twin studies, which this explanation relies on. It has been suggested that MZ twins are treated more alike and share more similar environments than DZ twins due to them acting more like 'one' person rather than two separate people. This may affect how alike they are and how likely they both are to express aggression.

- Also, there are gender differences involved in twin studies. Button *et al.* studied 258 twin pairs and found that both aggressive and non-aggressive antisocial behaviour are subjected to significant gender differences. The heritability of aggressive antisocial behaviour was significantly higher in girls than boys, suggesting a stronger genetic effect on aggression in females than in males.

- There are also various methodological problems involved in adoption studies. For example, one problem is that in some countries such as the US, children given up for adoption showed a higher rate of antisocial behaviour at the time of adoption compared with the general population. Consequently, correlations between adoptees and their biological parents may be due to either genetic factors or environmental influences, such as antisocial behaviour as a result of feelings of abandonment, not genes.

- The role of environmental factors may have affected the findings of many studies, as the aggressive behaviour observed may have been due to shared environmental factors such as bad parenting and inappropriate role modelling.

- Brunner himself suggested that it was unlikely that a single gene was the direct cause of a specific behaviour. Rather, genes may exert some influence on behaviour, but they are not the sole cause of behaviour.

- This explanation is oversimplified as it is saying that one gene causes aggression when in reality it is several factors that can lead to aggressive behaviour.

2.2.2 Evolutionary explanations of aggression

Notebook exercise — evolutionary explanation of aggression

You will need your psychology notebook for this exercise.

In a group (or by yourself), discuss, or think about why giraffes have developed long necks. Write your thoughts and conclusions in your notebook.

You should now have a section in your notebook called *evolutionary explanations*.

Write your responses in your notebook, then show to your teacher/lecturer for checking.

- Evolution — a change over time in the inherited characteristics of a population

- Fitness — the ability to survive and reproduce

- Adaptation — changes that help an organism to survive

Questions

1. For the giraffes in the above activity, which characteristic increased fitness?

2. What would happen if the only trees in the environment the giraffes lived in became much shorter? Explain your answer in terms of evolution and fitness.

The evolutionary explanation suggests that we behave aggressively because we are born with an aggressive 'instinct', as our ancestors who behaved aggressively survived long enough to reproduce, and so to pass on these aggressive genes to us —this is called 'natural selection'. This is because the environments they lived in required aggressive behaviour in order to survive —probably because of the proximity of predators, and/or of other humans who were competition for resources, mates, etc. Aggression has evolved as it gave our ancestors a 'fitness to survive' (also known as 'survival of the fittest —although this refers to the fittest genes not the fittest person). Therefore, aggression, for our ancestors, was an adaptation to support our survival.

Some examples of aggression being used to enhance survival include the mate-retention strategy. Daly and Wilson claim that men evolved this strategy to deter their mate from leaving or cheating because without a mate, the chance of passing on his genes is reduced. This strategy therefore enhances fitness. This strategy involves *vigilance* (e.g. guarding their mate) and violence to deter infidelity. Guarding restricts their mate's freedom to prevent males gaining access: other forms may include snooping through personal belongings to look for signs of infidelity. Strategies such as this have evolved to prevent sexual infidelity on the part of the female, which may result in the male expending his resource on raising offspring that are not his own, genetically (paternal uncertainty).

Women also use mate-retention strategies, but these tend to involve verbal, rather than physical, aggression. For example, Buss and Shackleton (1997) found that females used verbal possession tactics, such as 'he's taken' or threats to leave her partner if he is unfaithful.

Notebook exercise

You will need your psychology notebook for this exercise.

Explain why mate-retention strategies are adaptive.

You should now have another section in your notebook titles *evolutionary explanations of aggression*.

Write your responses in your notebook, then show to your teacher/lecturer for checking.

2.2.3 Evaluation of evolutionary explanation of aggression

Advantages

- Helps explain why aggression increases in circumstances where resources are scarce, such as in chimpanzees whose habitats are becoming depleted.

- Research by Dobash and Dobash in 1984 supports the notion of aggression due to sexual jealousy, as victims of domestic abuse cited the extreme jealousy of their partners as the major cause of violence against them.

- A study by Wilson found evidence of guarding as mate-retention. Among women who reported partners using this tactic, 72% required medical attention after an assault by their partner.

Disadvantages

- Holttzworth-Monroe and Anglin suggest that violence in males may not be directly due to jealousy itself, but due to their inability to respond effectively to feelings of jealousy.

- Gender bias —studies tend to focus on male violence, but females also engage in violent tactics to retain a mate. For example, Archer (2002) found equal rates of violence by males and females.

- Evolutionary theories are criticised for justifying behaviours such as aggression. Most people are not aggressive —they have developed adaptive ways of dealing with the emotions that trigger aggression in others.

Notebook exercise —evolutionary explanations for aggression

You will need your psychology notebook for this activity.

If the predictions made by evolutionary theory are valid, what are the potential consequences of living in places where key natural resources (like food and clean water) are becoming scarcer? Explain your thoughts in terms of evolutionary theory.

Write your responses in your notebook, then show to your teacher/lecturer for checking.

Application activity —evolutionary explanations for aggression

Q4:
Leanne was telling her friend about her partner, Ajay. Leanne said the Ajay asked for the password for her mobile phone, and that he wasn't too keen on her going out with her workmates at the weekend.

Leanne's friend told her that she should be careful as these types of behaviours could become more extreme over time.

Using your knowledge of evolutionary explanations of aggression, explain why Leanne's friend may be right.

2.2.4   The ethological explanation of aggression

An ethologist studies behaviours of animals (including humans) in their natural environment. Like the evolutionary explanation, ethologists try to explain aggression as an adaptive behaviour that helps a species survival. Ethologists believe that studying animal behaviour can help us to understand human behaviour.

Lorenz (1966) was an eminent ethologist who proposed that aggression in animals is often ritualistic (symbolic aggression), which he argued is more adaptive than direct aggression, as symbolic aggression would help ensure the organism was not harmed, as being harmed may impair the ability to reproduce. Therefore, ritualistic aggression such as 'teeth baring' would have the effect of deterring an opponent without physical harm being caused.

Evaluation of ethological explanations of aggression

Advantages

- Ethological explanations help to explain how species adapt to their environments.

- Some research, such as that into stickleback fish by Tinbergen, does support the theory. Tinbergen found that, during mating season, male sticklebacks are highly aggressive towards other male sticklebacks who invade their territory.

Disadvantages

- Much of the research is conducted with non-human animals, which means that the results cannot be generalised to humans.

- The concepts tend to be descriptive rather than explanatory, and involve circular reasoning.

- Ethological explanations do not account for cultural differences in aggression —some cultures are more aggressive than others.

- It is a negative view of aggression, in that as it sees aggression as innate, it does not offer hope for its reduction.

Test your knowledge on ethological explanations of aggression   Go online

Q5:   Ethology is:

a) an inbuilt mechanism which his activated in response to a certain stimulus.
b) the study of animal behaviour in its natural environment.
c) behaviour that enables survival of the species.

....

Q6:   'Adaptive' means:

a) an inbuilt mechanism which his activated in response to a certain stimulus.
b) the study of animal behaviour in its natural environment.
c) behaviour that enables survival of the species.

....

Q7: Male paternity uncertainty has made it an adaptive advantage to be aggressive towards:

a) same sex rivals.
b) sexual partners.
c) neither.
d) both.

2.3 Social psychological explanations of aggression

Social learning theory (SLT) argues that we learn to become aggressive via imitation and reinforcement. This theory originated in USA in the 1940s and was an attempt to reinterpret some aspects of Freud's psychoanalytic theory in terms of conditioning theory (classical and operant conditioning).

Imagine that you are at a very posh wedding and you are faced with an array of different knives and forks. What do you do - you observe what others are doing. We do this all the time in a variety of situations - so why should aggressive behaviour be any different?

Bandura proposes that there are five main cognitive factors that mediate control of the aggressive behaviour:

- **Attention** —must be paid to the aggressor. So, a child must pay attention to an act of aggression carried out by a role model; for instance, when a child engages in a computer game or watches a violent film they are attending to the aggression.

- **Retention** —To model the behaviour, it needs to be placed into long-term memory, which enables the behaviour to be retrieved. A child needs to remember the aggression that they have witnessed.

- **Production** —The individual needs to have the physical ability to reproduce the behaviour observed. So for instance, aggression displayed by superheroes is less likely to be imitated if the child does not possess the physical capabilities to actually carry out the behaviour.

- **Motivation** —An individual must be expecting to receive positive reinforcement for the copied behaviour. A child must expect they will get some kind of reward from carrying out aggression, such as being admired by their peers.

- **Self-efficacy** —this relates to the self-belief a person has. Individuals must have confidence in their own ability to carry out the action. If a child decides aggression will be an appropriate action, they must be confident that they can carry out the behaviour and that it will end up in a positive outcome.

2.3.1 Research into aggression and SLT

Bandura, Ross and Ross (1965)

A famous study conducted into social learning theory and aggression was conducted by Bandura *et al.* in 1965

Aim:
To see if children would learn aggressive behaviours by observing and imitating an adult role model.

Method:

This study involved three groups of young children; group one (control group), group two (model-rewarded) and group three (model punished).

Group One —was shown a video which demonstrated an adult kicking and punching a BoBo doll.

Group Two —were shown the same video, but a second adult appeared near the end and commended the model's aggressive behaviour. Sweets and lemonade were offered to the model.

Group Three —were shown the same video but this time a second adult scolded the model and warned against further aggression. In other words, the only real difference between these three groups of children was the consequences of the aggressive behaviour.

After the video, the children played in a room which contained lots of toys, including the BoBo doll and a toy mallet. They were observed via a two-way mirror and the number of aggressive acts was recorded for each child.

Later, all three groups were asked to reproduce as much of the model's behaviour and were directly rewarded for this.

Results:

Group C children demonstrated significantly fewer aggressive acts than A or B. There was no real difference between the numbers of aggressive acts in groups A or B.

Conclusion:

This suggests that vicarious punishment is more powerful than vicarious reinforcement. All three groups demonstrated the same high level of aggression when they were asked to reproduce the model's behaviour for a direct reward. This means that all of the children must have observed the model's aggressive behaviour. Only after receiving direct reinforcement, did most of the children copy this behaviour. If this is true, it means that reinforcement (vicarious or direct) was not needed for learning (acquisition) but was for imitation (performance).

Evaluation:

- The Bobo doll is a non-living thing and even young children know that they do not feel pain or take revenge, so we cannot say whether they would treat a real child in the same way.

- However, Bandura carried out a study where the Bobo doll was replaced by a live clown and the same type of behaviour was observed in the children.

- The children were in a laboratory —an unfamiliar environment —so they did not behave as they would in a real-life setting.

- The participants all came from white, middle-class, American families so the results may not generalise beyond this narrow group.

The social learning theory of aggression was also supported by the following study:

Research by Sheehan and Watson

Aim:

To find out if there is a link between parental discipline and child aggression. To find out if the ethnicity of the parent made any difference in discipline.

Hypotheses:

1. A mother's use of aggressive discipline predicts an increase in later child aggression.

2. Child aggression predicts an increase in later use of aggressive discipline.

3. The use of reasoning predicts a decrease in later child aggression.

4. Child aggression predicts a later use of reasoning.

Method:

This was a longitudinal study which took place in the town of Springfield, Massachusetts, USA. It looked at mothers between the ages of 25-44 years who had children between the ages of 7- . The original sample included 242 boys and 198 girls from a variety of ethnic and social backgrounds. Interviews were completed in family homes. Mothers and children completed questionnaires about their psychological and behavioural characteristics.

Interestingly, this study also looked at the mother's level of education. A variety of different tests were completed which measured the aggression (verbal and physical) of mother and child, levels of reasoning and disciplinary practices used.

Results:

Hypothesis 1, 2 and 4 were all supported and 3 was partially supported. The results suggest that a child's early aggressive behaviour leads to an increase in their mother's use of both reasoning and aggressive discipline. In turn, this increased the use of aggressive discipline and lead to an increase in aggression during childhood and adolescence. The use of reasoning was more consistent for European Americans than African Americans and Hispanics. They also found that child aggression at younger ages predicted an increase in maternal use of aggressive discipline and the use of aggressive discipline predicted an increase in child aggression at all ages.

Implications:

If you accept that this study has some validity, it could mean that it might be possible to identify children who are aggressive at a young age and treating them via the prevention of parents using aggressive discipline in the first place. This could allow the child's aggression to be kept in check without making the problem worse. It would also be possible to educate parents about positive, less harmful forms of discipline and this could make it possible for children not to become aggressive adolescents.

2.3.2   Evaluation of Social Learning Theory

Advantages

- SLT can explain why some people are non-aggressive, i.e. the Amish. If aggression was biologically determined it would be apparent in all communities.

- SLT can explain why some people are aggressive in a context (e.g. home) where aggressive behaviour might be reinforced but not in other contexts (e.g. work) where they have seen aggressive behaviour being punished.

- Bandura (1977) found that people who live in high crime areas are more likely to commit violent crimes than people who live in low crime areas. This seems to support SLT as people are more likely to observe aggressive behaviour in high-crime areas, but it could also be due to the fact that there are other factors, such as unemployment, poverty, drug and alcohol abuse in these areas.

Disadvantages

- SLT can be described as reductionist, as it does not take into account values, morals and social norms.

- It does not take into account biological factors such as the role of hormones or genetic factors.

- SLT does not explain all types of aggressive behaviour. It does explain proactive, instrumental (behaving aggressively in order to achieve something) aggression, but not reactive aggression, which is a response to a threat or provocation.

2.3.3   SLT notebook activity

SLT notebook activity

You will need your psychology notebook for this activity.

Can you identify other behaviours that are learned by social learning? Who's behaviour do you think children will imitate in particular?

These people are **role models**. Who have been the main role models in your life?

The most important factor in whether we imitate behaviour or not is if we see that behaviour being reinforced (rewarded). In other words, if a child sees a behaviour being reinforced, it creates an expectation that they will be reinforced for the behaviour if they imitate it. It is this role model; imitates expectation that motivates the behaviour (aggression).

Describe how aggression can be learnt by using the example of a child watching a film where the hero defeats the baddie by hitting him. Use the following words in your response: *Attention; retention; production; motivation; self-efficacy; vicarious learning; role model; imitates; reinforcement.*

Write your responses in your notebook, then show to your teacher/lecturer for checking.

2.4 Institutional explanations of aggression

Research to explain aggression.

2.4.1 Sykes' deprivation model (1958)

Sykes argues that institutional aggression has causes within the institution, not from the individuals themselves. It is thought that this occurs as a result of the 'deprivations' that inmates experience on a daily basis. He outlined **5 deprivations** that inmates experience:

1. **Deprivation of Liberty:** society makes it clear that inmates cannot be trusted with freedom, therefore civil rights are lost as inmates need permission to do everyday things, such as eat and wash.

2. **Deprivation of Autonomy:** Prisoners have no independence and very few choices; being constantly controlled by prison officers can cause feelings of helplessness and frustration, leading to aggression.

3. **Deprivation of Goods/Services:** Prisoners are forced to live in near poverty conditions, bringing a sense of failure and frustration, which can lead to aggressive behaviour.

4. **Deprivation of Heterosexual Relationships:** Losing female company reduces a man's sense of self-worth.

5. **Deprivation of Security:** Many prisoners feel insecure and report fears of their safety whilst imprisoned, which can cause helplessness, leading to aggression.

All these deprivations can lead to increased stress for inmates, and as a consequence of this, some inmates act aggressively to both reduce stress and try and gain some control over the social order imposed on them.

Activity —Evaluation of Sykes' deprivation model Go online

Q8: Decide whether the evaluative points below are advantages or disadvantages.

- Research by Magargee (1976) found that aggressive incidents in prisons were related to the amount of living space available for each prisoner. This links with the deprivation theory as with overcrowding comes deprivation of many things, such as security or autonomy. Furthermore, in overcrowded prisons, strategies may be put in place to compensate (e.g. being kept in prison cells for long periods of time), which results in fewer opportunities for prisoners to interact with each other, which leads to further deprivation of relationships.

- However, this theory focuses on the external environment, so ignores other potential explanations of aggression, such as biological ones, such as higher rates of testosterone in the prison population.

- This implies that it is unlikely that the environment found in prisons is the sole explanation for aggressive behaviour.

- It does not account for phenomena such as prison riots. Why do these suddenly explode when levels of deprivation remain the same?

2.4.2   Dysfunctional institutions

The dysfunctional institutions theory argues that the organisation of power within an institution allows individuals within that institution to become aggressors. This theory places responsibility on the managers of the institution. Factors that appear to lead to abuse are based on structural faults in how an institution is organised. These faults include:

- Isolation of a group from the outside world and removal from everyday life; an inward looking group.

- A very close cohesion and agreement on ideology.

- A provocative situation with external stressors causing high stress and moral dilemmas.

- A resultant view that everyday norms and values are not seen as relevant in this workplace and alternative norms and values replace them.

- Dehumanisation of the outgroup.

This explanation is supported by the famous Stanford Prison experiment, conducted by Philip Zimbardo in the early 70s.

Aim: Zimbardo aimed to see how his participants would react when place in an institutionalized prison environment.

Method: Of the seventy-five people who applied, twenty-four males considered to be 100% fit and healthy (emotionally, physically, and psychologically) were selected to participate.

Each of the participants was told that they would be going into a simulated prison environment for two weeks and that the roles of prisoner and guard would be assigned arbitrarily. Professor Zimbardo was to act as the Prison Warden and oversee the experiment.

"Prisoners" were to be confined to the makeshift prison for the duration of the experiment, but guards were allowed to work eight-hour shift patters in teams of three.

When not "working", the guards were allowed to leave the site and resume their normal life. Wooden batons were given to the guards, although they were not supposed to be used to punish the prisoners. Prisoners were given ill-fitting garments, chains around their ankles, and assigned a number as part of a disorientation and depersonalization process.

Prior to the experiment, the guards were told they were not allowed to physically punish the prisoners, but they could reinforce the sense of powerlessness prisoners would expect to feel in a real prison environment.

Results: The first day of the experiment was uneventful, but by day two the situation inside the makeshift prison had begun to heat up.

A riot broke out and some of the prisoners barricaded themselves inside their cell. The guards used fire extinguishers to break the riot and attempted to implement various psychological tactics as a way of regaining control.

By the end of thirty-six hours, one of the prisoners was already experiencing a mental breakdown and was eventually released.

The treatment dished out to the prisoners became increasingly inhumane and interactions between the participants of the experiment were hostile and dehumanizing. More prisoners began to show signs of psychological stress and five more prisoners were released early.

Some of the guards began to exhibit genuine sadistic tendencies and even Zimbardo, acting in his role as Prison Warden, lost sight of reality as the experiment unfolded. On the sixth day the experiment was stopped after a graduate student, Christina Maslach, voiced concerns as to the morality of the experiment.

Implications: Zimbardo claimed that the experiment demonstrated the crucial role a situation can have on human behavior. Irrespective of an individual's personality, when placed in certain situations people behave in ways they would not normally act in.

Notebook exercise

You will need your psychology notebook for this exercise.

Look at the features of dysfunctional institutions, and identify features of Zimbardo's study which relate to these features. Note this down in your notebook.

You should now have an entry in your notebook titled dysfunctional *institutions*.

Show your notebook entry to your teacher/lecturer for checking.

2.4.3   The importation model

In contrast with Sykes' deprivation model, and the dysfunctional institutions explanation, which focus on the environment as the cause of aggression, the importation model focuses on the personality characteristics that prison inmates take into the prison with them. For example, inmates with values, attitudes, experiences, and social norms that tend towards violent behaviour towards other people will be more likely to be aggressive than inmates with less violent personalities and experiences. Often it is younger inmates that tend to behave violently as they are more likely to find it harder to adjust to prison life, and may therefore engage in more conflicts with others, and are more likely to view aggression as an appropriate way of dealing with conflict. The importation model argues therefore that it is not the environment of the prison that causes aggression, but rather the personalities of the individuals within it.

Evaluation of the importation model Go online

Q9: Decide whether the evaluative points below are advantages or disadvantages.

- Much of the research into institutional aggression consists of mainly male populations. This means that the findings may not generalise to females.

- There is research evidence to support the model. Adams (1981) found that in American prisons, black inmates were more likely to be associates with violent acts than white inmates. The argument for this is that black prisoners tended to come from poorer backgrounds with higher rates of crime, and so imported their cultural norms into the prison.

- Keller and Wang (2005) found that prison violence is more likely to occur in facilities with higher-security (and therefore who had committed more violent crimes) inmates, than those with lower security inmates, again supporting the idea that the inmates had brought violent behaviour into the institution with them.

- Harer and Steffensmeier (1996) found that in US prisons, black inmates were significantly more aggressive than white inmates, but that white inmates were significantly more likely to engage in alcohol and drug taking than black inmates. They argued that these behaviours reflected the cultural norms that black and white societies hold outside prison, and so the behaviours had been imported into the prison.

- This explanation does not accurately predict which inmates will behave aggressively in prison. This is because the model states that prisoners who were members of violent gangs before they were convicted will be more likely to behave aggressively in prison, however DeLisi et al (2004) found no evidence that gang membership prior to imprisonment was linked with violence once in prison.

Test your knowledge on institutional explanations of aggression Go online

Q10: According to the Importation Model, which of the following factors is not responsible for aggression within prisons?

a) lack of freedom
b) ethnicity or race
c) gender
d) personality and traits

....

Q11: Deprivation of goods, according to Sykes, is where:

a) Prisoners are deprived of freedom during their stay, they have to ask for permission to wash, eat, etc.
b) Prisoners have no power over their lives, or the ability to make their own choices.
c) Prisoners have limited ownership of material items, e.g. mobile phones or other material goods they were previously accustomed to.
d) When men cannot maintain sexual relationships with women which leads to emasculation and worries over homosexual behaviour within prisons.
e) Prisoners feel continually threatened by other inmates' aggressive behaviour.

. . . .

Q12: Deprivation of heterosexual relationships, according to Sykes, is where:

a) Prisoners are deprived of freedom during their stay, they have to ask for permission to wash, eat, etc.
b) Prisoners have no power over their lives, or the ability to make their own choices.
c) Prisoners have limited ownership of material items, e.g. mobile phones or other material goods they were previously accustomed to.
d) When men cannot maintain sexual relationships with women which leads to emasculation and worries over homosexual behaviour within prisons.
e) Prisoners feel continually threatened by other inmates' aggressive behaviour.

. . . .

Q13: Deprivation of liberty, according to Sykes, is where:

a) Prisoners are deprived of freedom during their stay, they have to ask for permission to wash, eat, etc.
b) Prisoners have no power over their lives, or the ability to make their own choices.
c) Prisoners have limited ownership of goods, e.g. mobile phones or other material goods they were previously accustomed to.
d) When men cannot maintain sexual relationships with women which leads to emasculation and worries over homosexual behaviour within prisons.
e) Prisoners feel continually threatened by other inmates' aggressive behaviour.

. . . .

Q14: Deprivation of security, according to Sykes, is where:

a) Prisoners are deprived of freedom during their stay, they have to ask for permission to wash, eat, etc.
b) Prisoners have no power over their lives, or the ability to make their own choices.
c) Prisoners have limited ownership of goods, e.g. mobile phones or other material goods they were previously accustomed to.
d) When men cannot maintain sexual relationships with women which leads to emasculation and worries over homosexual behaviour within prisons.
e) Prisoners feel continually threatened by other inmates' aggressive behaviour.

2.5   Media influences on aggression

This section deals with the role that the media plays in making us aggressive or lessening this aggression. But first, we need to be clear as to what the media includes:

"The means of communication that reach large numbers of people, such as television, newspapers, and radio" (http://www.collinsdictionary.com)

Today, it is generally accepted that media covers all forms of communication —TV, radio, newspapers, internet, games etc. We live in a society today where information is relayed instantly all over the world —we are surrounded by it. Does it have any effect on us? Can it make us violent or aggressive?

Can it be a release for our violent thoughts and actions? Some psychologists argue that the media has a bad effect on us (especially children), whilst others say that it is good for us.

But first, a question. How many forms of media have you encountered today —count them up. How many do you have? Ask your parents/grandparents —how many forms of the media have they used today? Can you see that the media is all around us for most of the time. If this is the case, then surely it must have some effect on us?

Media influences on aggression

Create a table as below, count up and describe briefly the number of aggressive or violent acts that you have heard or seen today. Report back to the class next lesson. Did you think that there would be more or less? Do you think that they had an effect on you? If a child witnessed any of these acts, what might the impact be?

Media source	Violent or aggressive acts —description

Video games discussion

Do games make you feel angry? Does it matter if you are an experienced gamer or not? What is your own experience? Relate this and other studies to your own experience. In groups of four, talk about this for about 20 minutes. Report your findings to the rest of the class.

2.5.1   Computer games and aggression

Research into computer games and aggression

Goodson and Pearson completed two similar studies into the possible effects of violent and aggressive video games; this one was in 2009.

Aims:
To find out if violent video games resulted in violent behaviour, to test out their real life stressor theory and to try to address methodological flaws in previous research.

Method:
Thirty participants were used (15 male and 15 female), some of whom were experienced gamers whilst others were not. Three different video games were used - Project Racing Gotham Racing 3 (a realistic car racing game), Perfect Dark Zero (a violent first-person shooter) and a 3D table tennis game. The games were set up so as not to be overly complicated. Each participant was randomly assigned to one of three groups and an assigned game was played for 5 minutes. The participants played the games on an Xbox 360 games console with a high definition TV and surround sound. Their heart-rates were monitored and an EEG measured the activity in different parts of their brains. These readings were taken before, during and just after playing the game. In addition, all participants completed a questionnaire which was used to measure aggression.

Results:
The EEG data demonstrated that the participants who had played the racing game had an increase in brain activity concerned with anger. There was little difference in regard to the table tennis game. Interestingly, they found that the more experienced the gamer, the greater the increase in brain activity in the brain associated with anger when playing the racing game. In fact, they found that the aggression score for these people was equal to that of an adult offender.

Conclusions:
There seemed to be little evidence to suggest that violent games caused violent feelings. There was evidence to suggest that more effects were noticed in experienced gamers.

Goodson and Pearson completed two similar studies into the possible effects of violent and aggressive video games; this one was in 2011.

Aim:
To investigate the role of video game content in inducing aggression.

Method:
For this experiment, 40 participants were recruited (20 male and 20 female). Two games were selected —Project Gotham Racing 3 (a realistic car racing game) and Gears of War 2 (an extremely violent third-person shooter). All participants were randomly assigned to one of two groups —irrespective of their gaming experience. Each participant was asked to play an assigned game for 10 minutes and, again, EEG readings and heart rate were recorded. Again, a questionnaire which measured aggression was used.

Results:
When playing the racing game, participants, regardless of experience, had a significant increase in brain activity associated with anger. There was also an increase in respiration and heart rate for each game, but particularly so for the racing game.

Implications:
Goodson and Pearson argue that both studies present evidence for their real life stressor hypothesis —the idea that, as humans, we have had everyday experience of real life stressful events. These events give rise to anger —something simple like racing to college may make us very angry. We then play a similar video game and we 'remember' our own real life experience. If this theory is to be accepted, it may mean that video game manufacturers will take advantage of this. They could manufacture games which are based around real life events. If they do this, then we may get angry but actually enjoy this experience. Goodson and Pearson do not say that these experiences are necessarily bad for us.

2.5.2 Cognitive priming

Personal factors in aggression can include things such as our individual life experiences (abuse) or cultural factors. In turn, this will 'mould' our reactions to a violent or aggressive situation or video. The theory is that we make up social scripts. These scripts will determine how we react to violence and aggression.

A **mental script** is a bit like a mental tape of how we are supposed to act in a given situation. If a young boy is raised on Tom and Jerry, Teenage Mutant Ninja Turtles, Arnold Schwarzenegger, action films and video games, such as Call of Duty, he learns to 'act like a man'. He has seen these programmes and DVDs lots of times before and subconsciously 'knows' that this is how a man would act in these circumstances. Similarly, if this young boy grows up to become a man and watches pornography, he will identify that this behaviour is acceptable male behaviour. In other words, we re-enact our own mental script.

Our scripts can be altered very subtly; Leonard Enron taught children in Chicago that TV does not portray real life —everything is exaggerated. He found that if he kept saying this to children, it had the effect of 'recalibrating' their mental script —the children learned that aggression and violence was not everywhere as TV may suggest. It even seemed to have the effect of making them see that being a man was not necessarily anything to do with violence and aggression.

2.5.3   Disinhibition

Another way to explain how media can influence aggression is disinhibition. This explanation proposes that exposure to media violence makes us loosen the normal restraints we put on our behaviour, and aggressive behaviour becomes normal. A consequence of this is that aggression is seen as a 'normal' response in certain circumstances. One aspect of aggression that is particularly believed to become normal and acceptable is an aggressive response as a result of a real or imagined wrongdoing. So if the viewed aggression is seen as a revenge response, this is deemed to be 'normal', and acceptable. This type of viewed aggression is believed to have a greater disinhibitory effect on consequential aggressive behaviour.

As we have learned, aggression can be learned through the process of social learning, as illustrated by Bandura in his Bobo doll experiment. Adult films can present role models such as James Bond which children may look up to and imitate. However, when aggression levels become perceived as 'normal' in these role models, the child can grow up with the belief that aggression is socially acceptable as a response. This process of disinhibition is more powerful if violence is rewarded. Many computer games reward the player for initiating violence and in any negative consequences from aggression are minimal.

2.6 End of topic test

End of topic 2 test Go online

Q15: The two neurotransmitters mostly associated with aggression are:

a) melatonin and dopamine
b) serotonin and dopamine.
c) dopamine and thyroxin.
d) serotonin and thyroxin.

....

Q16: Which hypothesis suggests that aggression should only occur where there is a threat to status or to access to a potential mate?

a) Frustration-aggression hypothesis
b) Neurotransmitter hypothesis
c) Evolutionary hypothesis
d) Challenge hypothesis

....

Q17: The brain centre associated with strong emotions, like aggression is:

a) limbic system.
b) cerebellum.
c) suprachiasmatic nucleus.
d) motor cortex.

....

Q18: Which researcher found a concordance rate of 87% for aggressive behaviour in MZ twins?

a) Gottesman
b) Caspi
c) Mednick
d) Brunner

....

Q19: The ability to survive and reproduce is known as:

a) evolution.
b) fitness.
c) adaptation.
d) guarding.

....

Q20: Women, more than men, tend to use:

a) physical aggression.
b) verbal aggression.
c) emotional aggression.
d) passive aggression.

. . . .

Q21: Ethological psychologists suggest that aggression often takes the form of:

a) physical aggression.
b) verbal aggression.
c) ritual aggression.
d) guarding behaviour.

. . . .

Q22: According to social learning theory, which of the following two factors are involved in learning aggressive behaviours?

a) Genes and evolution
b) Neurotransmitters and hormones
c) Dopamine and serotonin
d) Imitation and reinforcement

. . . .

Q23: Self-efficacy refers to:

a) paying attention to the aggressive behaviour.
b) placing of the aggressive event in long-term memory.
c) a child's belief in their ability to recreate the aggressive act observed.
d) the expectation of a reinforcement for producing an aggressive act.

. . . .

Q24: The aim of Bandura, Ross and Ross' bobo doll study was to see if:

a) a child would imitate behaviours observed in a role model.
b) there was a link between parental discipline and child aggression.
c) there was a link between the number of criminal convictions between adopted children and their adoptive parents.
d) there were gender differences in aggression.

. . . .

Q25: Which of the following is **not** one of Sykes' deprivations?

a) Deprivation of liberty
b) Deprivation of security
c) Deprivation of goods/services
d) Deprivation of control

. . . .

Q26: Which of the following studies found a link between cultural norms and the types of aggression found in prisons?

a) Mednick
b) Harer and Steffensmeier
c) Gottesman and Shields
d)

....

Q27: A study into the real life stressor theory was conducted by:

a) Bandura, Ross and Ross.
b) Gottesman.
c) Goodson and Pearson.
d) Lorenz.

....

Q28: The notion that media images can stimulate thoughts of aggression is called:

a) cognitive priming.
b) mental scripts.
c) social learning.
d) imitation and reinforcement.

....

Q29: A mental script is:

a) an association made between and event with something in long-term memory.
b) a schema of how we are meant to act in certain situations.
c) the idea that there are gender differences in aggression.
d) the idea that there is a link between aggression and hormones.

....

Q30: An explanation that sees aggression as being caused by repeated exposure to aggression in the media is called:

a) schema theory.
b) deprivation model.
c) disinhibition.
d) social learning.

End of Topic 2 activity

Complete your own research in a group of four, into violence and aggression in the media. Use research, facts and figures. Visit the British Crime Survey, the Scottish Government Website, charitable organisations, and, of course, psychology web sites. Use books, journals and web sites.

Complete a poster to illustrate your findings. Which studies or theories in this area of study persuade you that violence and aggression stems from the media? Could there be other explanations?

Put together a PowerPoint if you have the equipment. Video this and play back to the rest of the class. Report to the rest of the class.

Unit 3 Topic 3

Social relationships (optional topic)

Contents

Learning objective

By the end of this topic, you should be able to explain, evaluate, apply and analyse:

- theories of romantic relationships, which must include:

  - evolutionary theory
  - filter theory
  - social exchange theory
  - Rusbult's investment theory

- the aims, methods, results, evaluation and conclusions of one study into a theory of romantic relationships

- virtual relationships in social media, which must include:

  - gating
  - Sproull and Kiesler's reduced cues theory
  - Walther's hyperpersonal theory

- the aims, methods, results, evaluation and conclusions of one study into virtual relationships in social media

- parasocial relationships, which must include:

  - levels of parasocial relationships
  - the absorption-addiction model
  - attachment theory

3.1   Introduction

We all have relationships with others - some may be sexual, others not. Social relationships form the basis of our society; some relationships are 'just friends', some are just work-mates, some are just the person next door. We can love other human beings, cats and dogs, and works of art. So why do we 'choose' our friends and partners? Is it looks, personality, sex or something else that draws us to other people?

As you work your way through this topic, many questions you may already have asked yourself about human relationships will come up and hopefully be answered. You may have asked yourself:

- Why do we like particular people?

- Why do we not like particular people?

- How do we fall in love?

- Why do we sometimes fall out of love?

- Do opposites attract?

- Why do we form connections to celebrities and other people we haven't even met?

Introduction: Notebook exercise

You will need your psychology notebook for this activity.

Think of the friends and relationships that you have. Where did you meet these people? Did you grow up together? What brought you together? Are you a similar age?

On an individual basis, complete the following template - no need to talk to the rest of the class - just think about relationships, friends and acquaintances.

An example has been included for you to see the kind of information required. This example is from a girl who has a boyfriend of the same age, physical appearance and has the same musical tastes. However, the boyfriend is a different gender and has a different academic ability. They met in school 10 years ago and are still friends today. Your examples could be a school friend, a neighbour, your pet, someone you met at a bus-stop —anyone. Just think about your relationships, how long you have known this person and possible similarities and differences between the two of you. Why are you still friends?

Relationships example

Relationship	Where did you meet?	How long have you known them?	Similarities or differences	Why?
Example —boyfriend	School	10 years	Similar physical appearance (e.g. height) Same musical tastes Same age Different gender Different academic abilities	Still friends because we like the same things so we can talk to each other. Don't really know why we love each other

None of us is an island, we all interact with people every day, both in reality and virtually. This next activity is designed to make you aware of all the social relationships you are part of in your own life and the importance you attach to each of them. You are going to build up your own sociogram; this is a graphic representation of the social links that you have. Sociograms are very useful psychological tools for visually representing social relationships.

Social relationships: Sociogram

Instructions for building your own sociogram:

1. You are the central circle in your world - add your name to the circle in the centre of the page.

2. The circles round you are the spheres of relationships that you have in your life.

3. Start by looking at the relationships between you and your family members. Add the name of each of your family members (parents/guardians, siblings, aunts, uncles, cousins, grandparents, pets).

4. Once you finish inputting the name of that person you can then move on to the next member of your family.

5. When you have finished family move on to the friends, acquaintances, peripheral (this means people like teachers, lollipop man you speak to on your way to school/college, local newsagent); virtual (this means any online relation ships you may have through internet gaming sites or any other online relationships you have).

Here is an example.

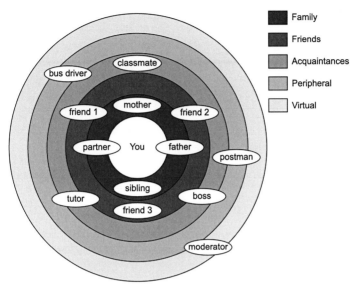

Sociogram

Once you have completed your own sociogram for the relationships in your life, you will realise that all the lines that connect you to someone else are the social relationships that occur in your life.

Social relationships: Question   Go online

Q1: Complete the following sentence using words from the list.

A social relationship involves _____ people who associate _____ over a _____ period of time and whose behaviour is _____ of each other.

Word list: daily, four or more, independent, interdependent, long-term, medium-term, regularly, short-term, three, two, weekly.

Social relationships: Notebook exercise

You will need your psychology notebook for this activity.

Copy the definitive statement for what a social relationship is into your psychology notebook: it is a typical SQA question in the exam, e.g. "Define what is meant by a social relationship."

3.2   Theories of romantic relationships

Evolutionary theory of romantic relationships

Evolutionary or sociobiological theories seek to describe social relationships in terms of evolution. Men and women, according to sociobiological theories, are attracted to very different characteristics in each other, to put it bluntly:

- men are attracted to appearance

- women are attracted to resources (money)

Evolutionary theory explains these differences in attraction by saying that both men and women seek to find the best mate who will maximise their reproductive success.

Because a man's input in sexual reproduction is so minimal (while a woman's is a time-consuming nine months), according to sociobiological theorists, it is in the man's best interests to be as promiscuous as possible to spread his chances of making as many women as possible pregnant, and thereby spreading the gene pool.

For women, the opposite is true; because human babies have such a long incubation period, women need to use the principles of natural selection to seek out the perfect mate, one who will provide resources for her and her children.

Research in this area does seem to conclude that men prefer youth and beauty, and evolutionary psychologists would suggest that this is because these are good indicators of fertility in women. Research also concludes that women select a partner who is older, and has a more stable career and money-earning potential. Again, this might indicate to women that these men are more dependable, a serious indicator when choosing a father to your children.

3.3   Evolutionary explanations of romantic relationships — Buss (1989)

Aim: Buss wanted to see if evolutionary explanations for sex differences in human mate preferences are found in cultures.

Method: This was a survey of mate preferences in a number of countries. A questionnaire was used to gather information. 37 samples were taken from 33 countries, located on 6 continents and 5 islands. The total samples size was 10,047 participants. Samples varied in size from 55 in Iran and 1,491 in mainland America. The mean age of the overall sample was 23.05 years. In countries where there was more than one ethnic group, more than one sample was taken, e.g. in Canada, Buss took a sample of French and English speakers.

Sampling Techniques varied across the different countries:

- West Germany = Newspaper advertisement.

- New Zealand = High school student taken from 3 schools.

- Estonia = Couples applying for a marriage license and high school students.

Occasionally, the questionnaire had to be altered to reflect the cultural differences. For example, in Nigeria, polygamy is practiced, so questions had to be added to reflect the possibility of multiple wives, while few couples marry in Sweden and just prefer to live together.

Questionnaires

- Part 1 —collected biographical data.

- Part 2 —mate preferences (preferred age to marry, preferred age difference)

- Part 3 —participants had to rate 18 characteristics on a 4 point scale.

Findings: The main findings of his study were:

1. across six continents, women (more than men) wanted mates who were rich in resources

2. the majority of men in the study placed far greater emphasis on physical attractiveness in their mating partner than women did

3. the majority of men in the study wanted a woman younger than themselves —Buss concluded that this was because, across cultures, younger women are perceived as being more fertile

4. there was no difference between the sexes about what personal characteristics were desired in a mate —both men and women wanted a kind, intelligent and dependable partner, all indicators, Buss concludes, of partners who would make good parents.

Conclusions: In general these findings show 1) evolutionary explanations of sex differences in human mate preferences are appropriate, 2) that mate preferences are not just explained in terms of female choosiness since both males and females showed preferences and 3) that cultural influences matter as there were cultural differences.

Evaluation:

Strengths

- Questionnaires were used, which can be easily repeated so data can be collected from large numbers of people relatively cheaply and quickly.

- Respondents may feel more willing to reveal personal/confidential information when writing their own answers than in an interview.

- Findings can be generalised to the general population there was a range of ages, cultures, education etc.

- Extensive efforts were made to ensure that all respondents understood the questions (translated to local languages, and words adapted to match local customs and read to those who could not read) however, this means the questions could have been taken out of context.

Weaknesses

- Answers may not be truthful due to leading questions and the social desirability bias (misrepresentation)

- The sample may be biased because maybe only certain types of people fill in questionnaires such as literate individuals who are willing to spend time filling in a questionnaire and returning it.

- The sample was biased, as different 'cultures' sampled were dominated by 'Westernised, industrialised nations' (26 of 37) and these samples contributed to 7,749 of the whole sample.

- Buss acknowledged that rural and less-educated people were under-represented

Professor Winston explains more about evolution and its impact on our behaviour, here: https://top documentaryfilms.com/human-instinct/

Evolutionary theory of romantic relationships

Look through the lonely hearts column and select ten 'men seeking women' and ten 'women seeking men' adverts.

- Make a list of what each is offering (i.e. which of their own characteristics do they mention?) and what they are looking for in a partner.

- Do the results support the evolutionary theory of attraction? Explain your answer.

Evaluation of evolutionary explanation of romantic relationships

Advantages

- the theory is supported by research evidence, such as that by Buss.

Disadvantages

- this theory only applies to heterosexual couples. What about the part of the population who are in homosexual relationships? This theory doesn't cover the scope and diversity of human relationships;

- there is little evidence of the link between physical attractiveness and child-bearing potential;

- it is a reductionist viewpoint — this theory assumes that all behaviour can be reduced to natural responses.

Evolutionary explanation: Notebook exercise

You will need your psychology notebook for this activity.

Make notes under the following headings:

- the evolutionary explanation of romantic relationships;

- Buss's 1989 study;

- evaluation of the evolutionary explanation of romantic relationships.

3.4 Filter theory

Filter theory

This theory was proposed by Kerckhoff and Davis in 1962, who propose that people develop relationships by applying a series of filters, such as similarity of social demography and attitudes and complementarity of needs, to narrow down the pool of available candidates, what Kerckhoff and Davis call the 'field of availables'.
The first filter is:

- **Social demography**: We are more likely to meet people who are physically close and share several demographic characteristics. Our most meaningful and memorable interactions are with people who are nearby. The key benefit of proximity is accessibility —meaning it does not require much effort to meet people who live in the same area, go to the same school etc. The field gets narrower because our choices are also limited by our social class. Anyone who is too 'different' so too far away or too middle class is discounted as a potential partner. The outcome of this filtering is *homogamy* —meaning you are more likely to form a relationship with someone who is socially or culturally similar.

The second filter is:

- **Similarity in attitudes**: this is a factor which depends on the extent to which two people share views and beliefs. If you do share views and beliefs, it is easier to communicate which will help a relationship to form. Kerckhoff and Davis found that this filter was important at the beginning of a relationship and a good predictor of whether a relationship is likely to last. People with dissimilar attitudes to yourself are likely to be 'filtered out' early on in the process. Evidence to support the importance of this filter comes from Donn Byrne, who suggests that similarity causes attraction as the law of attraction. If similarity did not exist, e.g. the partners who have little in common —they may go out together a few times, but the relationship is likely to breakdown.

The third filter is:

- **Complementarity**, which affects attraction in romantic relationships. It refers to how well two people complement each other and meet each other's needs. Two partners complement each other when one partner has a trait that the other lacks —the two halves then make a whole. For example, one partner may enjoy making the other laugh, and the other partner enjoys being made to laugh.

A short-hand way of remembering these is to use the acronym 'D.A.N.'
D = Demography
A = Attitudes
N = Needs

Filter theory

Pick three people from the sociogram you created earlier. Apply Kerckhoff and Davies' three filters to each, in order i.e.:

1. **Social demography:**

   - do they live close to you?
   - are they of the same social class?

2. **Similarity of attitudes:**

   - do they share the same beliefs and attitudes as you (mostly)?

3. **Complementarity:**

   - Does the other person have characteristics that you lack? i.e. do your two halves make a whole?

Did your findings confirm the predictions made by filter theory? Where they did not, why could this be?

To study the model, Kerckhoff and Davis conducted a study using students in a relationship for 18 months. Using self-report questionnaires, the study found that attitude similarity was the most important factor up to 18 months, where complementing each other's needs becomes the most important factor. The study used real-life couples and so has an aspect of mundane realism. The study does support the filter model by showing that there are stages to a relationship and that these stages have distinct features.

Evidence in support of the theory comes from Winch (1957) who found that similarities of personality, interest and attitudes between partners are typical characteristics of a relationship in its early stages. Winch also found that complementarity of needs is more important than similarity.

Evaluation of filter theory

Advantages

- Has some research support, such as Byrne who found that similarity was a key factor in initial attraction, like filter theory predicts.

- Kerkhoff and Davis' own study into the importance of complementarity also supports filter theory.

- Sprecher (2001) conducted a study which found that couples matched in physical attractiveness, social background, and interests were more likely to develop a long-term relationship, which is what filter theory would predict.

Disadvantages

- Levinger suggests that many studies have failed to replicate the original findings that formed the basis of filter theory, probably due to social change that has happened over time.

- The theory is based on studies that use self-report data, which can be unreliable due to social desirability.

- Filter theory suggest that people are attracted to each other because they are similar - which is the reason why their relationship is formed. However, there is evidence which undermines this. Anderson et al. found that cohabiting partners became more similar in their emotional responses over time, a phenomenon they called emotional convergence.

- Online dating has reduced the importance of some social demographic factors. Dating sites have made it easier for people to find a partner where we might have a date with someone outside the usual demographic limits such as culture or social class or proximity.

- The theory does not account for long-distance relationships, such as those found in the military.

- What about love?

Test your knowledge on the filter theory of romantic relationships   Go online

Q2:

Fill in the blanks from the word list below:

This model states that relationships go through three 'filters'. These filters can be remembered as 'DAN'. _____ , Attitudes, and Needs.

Before we begin filtering we look to the '_____'. This includes all the people we could possibly have a relationship with.

The first filter is then Socio-Demographic Variables. Such variables include similar _____, education, location etc. People with different or incompatible variables are 'filtered' out at this point.

The second filter is Similar _____. Similar attitudes help aid _____ and so the more attitudes, beliefs, and ideas the couple share the more likely they are to form and _____ a relationship. People with different or incompatible attitudes are 'filtered' out at this point.

The third filter is _____ Needs. Once the relationship is established, complementing each other's needs becomes one of the most important factors.

However, there are problems with this study. Firstly, Kerckhoff and Davis relied on questionnaires. _____ questionnaires are problematic as they are easy to lie on, or to misrepresent data, or to get wrong as they often require retrospective knowledge.

The model itself is also flawed. The _____ stage may not be as important as the model makes out, with the rise in internet dating and also long-distance relationships, especially in _____ families, not fitting in with the model.

However, _____ conducted a study and found that couple matched in physical attractiveness, social background, and interests were more likely to develop a long-term relationship. This suggests that the filter model is correct in regards to socio-demographic variables.

*Word list:*demographic; complementarity; sustain; background; attitudes; Sprecher; Field of Availables; self-report; military; socio-demographic; communication

---

3.5   Social exchange theory

The key terms in social exchange theory (SET) are reward, cost, outcome and comparison; remember, these terms may sound like economic ones, but the gains are emotional ones. Remember the mathematical equation for relationships that economic theorists believe:

$$\text{Rewards} \quad - \quad \text{Costs} \quad = \quad \text{Outcome}$$
$$R \quad - \quad C \quad = \quad O\ (p\ or\ l)$$

Rewards	Costs	Outcome
These are the positive, great parts of a relationship —companionship, etc.	These are the negative parts of a relationship —long distance relationships, annoying habits.	(profits or loss)

Those psychologists who believe in SET, believe that people in a relationship, consciously or unconsciously, weigh up the 'rewards' and 'costs' in their relationship to see if the outcome will be profitable enough for them.

Explanations of social relationships: Weighing up rewards and costs in a relationship

For each area mentioned in the list, decide if it is a reward or a cost in terms of a relationship.

1. Constant effort

2. Financial investment

3. Being cared for

4. Sharing holidays

5. Lack of privacy

6. Having to remember birthdays

7. Cooking with someone

8. Companionship

9. Shared interests

10. Having to get on with their family

11. Security

12. Annoying habits

SET and comparison level

Thibaut and Kelley also proposed that, in a relationship, everyone has a comparison level (CL). A comparison level is an individual's perceptions about the amount of rewards and costs they are likely to obtain in a social relationship.

Your comparison level is closely linked to your self-esteem: if you have a good opinion of yourself then your comparison level is likely to be high; conversely, if you have a low opinion of yourself and self-esteem, your comparison level will probably be low too.

Self-esteem discussion

With a partner, discuss each of these people who are making a speech.

1. I'm a single mum who was married to an alcoholic. My new partner doesn't come in until after 10pm most nights, but it doesn't matter because he doesn't drink and he's great with my kids.

2. I married my childhood sweetheart. I had no previous partners and I expect a lot from my partner —she must remember anniversaries and still enjoy doing romantic things.

3. My new partner is in a higher social class to me so I do a lot of the chores and menial tasks around our home.

Firstly, think about what you perceive their self-esteem to be like. Secondly, try and think about what sort of comparison levels each person might have.

SET and alternative comparison level

A related concept from Thibaut and Kelley is that everyone also has an alternative comparison level (ACL), which is the amount of rewards, and costs they're likely to obtain in an alternative relationship.

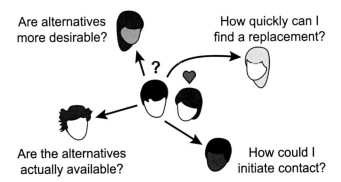

Thibaut and Kelley realised that 'no man is an island', meaning that we do not conduct our social relationships in a vacuum; we are part of society and so we therefore look to the rest of society to 'check out' our alternatives. We may not even be conscious of doing this, but Thibaut and Kelley felt that, even while we are in the 'maintenance' level of a relationship, partners are still constantly assessing the alternatives.

How attractive are the alternatives?
In a 1994 study, Duck argued that we perceive the alternative possibilities to the relationship we are in depending on how happy we are with the relationship we are in. If everything is going well, then although we perceive there are other partners, we do not find them attractive (both in the physical and emotional sense).

Conversely, if the committed relationship is slightly rocky or stale, then the alternatives seem far more attractive!

Comparison level and alternative comparison level
Again, it is best to look at a mathematical equation to understand what Thibaut and Kelley are trying to describe.

If	CL > ACL	Happy relationships
If	CL = ACL	Less stable relationship, but not unhappy
If	ACL > CL	Unhappy relationship

Thibaut and Kelley felt that, if the comparison level was greater than the alternative comparison level, then you could have a worthwhile, committed relationship. If you had an alternative comparison level that was greater than your comparison level, then your relationship could be in trouble.

SET and alternative comparison level: Notebook exercise

You will need your psychology notebook for this activity.

Make notes on the following:

- the two main divisions in explanations of social relationships;

- what is meant by economic theories;

- social exchange theory;

- SET and comparison and alternative comparison levels.

According to Thibault and Kelly, all relationships proceed through a series of stages. They are:

- **Sampling stage**, where people explore potential rewards and costs of relationships, not just romantic ones, either by direct experience or by observing others.

- **Bargaining stage**, which is the first stage of any romantic relationship. At this stage, partners exchange rewards and costs, figure out the most profitable exchanges and negotiate the dynamics of the relationship.

- **Commitment stage**, when relationships become more stable, and partners become familiar with sources of rewards and costs, and each other's expectations, so rewards increase and costs lessen.

- **Institutionalisation stage**, when costs and rewards are firmly established.

Evidence that supports Social Exchange Theory comes from Floyd et al. (1994), who found that commitment develops when couples are satisfied with, and feel rewarded by, a relationship and when they feel that equally attractive or more attractive alternative relationships are not available to them. Also, Sprecher (2001) found that comparison levels for alternatives were a strong predictor of satisfaction, especially for women.

Evaluation of Social Exchange Theory   Go online

Q3:   Decide whether the evaluative points below are advantages or disadvantages.

- SET is supported by studies, such as Sprecher (2001) and Floyd et al. (1994), from which it can be concluded that some people appear to base their evaluation of romantic relationships on rewards and costs, just as SET suggests.

- Research evidence for SET is, however, limited.

- Much of the evidence that is available is not true to how relationships work in the real world, as they are based on procedures involving game-based scenarios involving rewards and costs.

- SET concepts are difficult to define (how would you operationalise 'commitment'. If they are difficult to define, they are difficult to measure, which makes this theory unscientific.

- The theory assumes that romantic partners keep a daily score of costs and rewards, which is unlikely.

- Other research findings suggest that it is the perceived fairness of relationships, rather than a balance of costs and rewards, that keep romantic partners happy (e.g. Clark and Mills, 2011)

- The theory has useful real-life applications, such as Integrated Behavioural Couples Therapy (IBCT), where partners are trained to increase the rewards they give their partners, and reduce the costs.

3.6   Rusbult's investment model of relationships

The main rationale for the investment model was that many couples remain together despite costs outweighing rewards, so there must be other factors involved.

Caryl Rusbult (1983) extended SET by suggesting that maintenance and commitment to a relationship is also about the investment you have already put into that relationship.

> **Example:** If you have been married for 18 years, have children together, have many friends in common and share hobbies, then you have invested a huge amount of your time, energy, memories and (probably) money together. If, after 18 years, this relationship started to go stale, Rusbult felt that the previous investment in a relationship helped to stabilise it and people would therefore not give up so quickly.

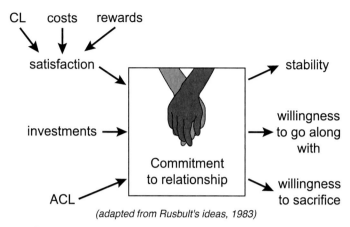

(adapted from Rusbult's ideas, 1983)

Rusbult proposed that the three major factors that maintain commitment, which are: **satisfaction level, comparison with alternatives**, and **investment size**.

You'll recognise comparison with alternatives from SET, and satisfaction levels are similar. Rusbult suggested that people will have a high level of satisfaction with relationships if they have more rewards and fewer costs. They also tend to be committed to relationships were there are no better alternatives in terms of satisfying their needs. Alternatives can include staying on their own, as well as finding someone new.

Rusbult's theory differs from SET in that he proposes that the most important factor in maintaining commitment is **investment** —it is this that make couples stay together in situations where costs outweigh rewards. Investment refers to those resources that couples will lose if they leave the relationships. These resources can be material, such as a house, or possessions, or immaterial, such as happy memories.

Rusbult proposed that types of investment fall into two categories: intrinsic and extrinsic.

- **Extrinsic investment** —what we put into relationships directly, e.g. effort, possessions, money

- **Intrinsic investment** —what we bring to the relationship indirectly, like children, shared memories, friends.

These are all factors that influence commitment, according to Rusbult, as they would be lost should the relationship end. The larger the investment, the greater likelihood of commitment.

Rusbult also identified factors that help maintain relationships, such as:

- **Accommodation** —acting in ways that promotes relationships, such as responding constructively to the destructive behaviours of your partner (you'll find an accommodation questionnaire directly after this section)

- **Willingness to sacrifice** —putting your partner's interests before your own

- **Forgiveness** —willingness to forgive your partner's mistakes

- **Positive illusions** —being positive about your partner —even when this is unrealistic

- **Ridiculing alternatives** — minimising the advantages of being with someone else, by 'putting them down'

In the Accommodation test below, answer firstly based on how you behave in your most important relationship, then for how your partner behaves.

Responses to Relationship Problems

My Responses to Relationship Problems

Please read each of the following statements concerning the manner in which you respond to problems in your relationship. Use the following scale to record a response for each item.

Response Scale:

0	1	2	3	4	5	6	7	8
Never Do This		Seldom Do This		Sometimes Do This		Frequently Do This		Constantly Do This

Response:

1. When my partner says something really mean, I threaten to leave him/her.

2. When my partner is rude to me, I try to resolve the situation and improve conditions.

3. When my partner behaves in an unpleasant manner, I forgive my partner and forget about it.

4. When my partner does something thoughtless, I avoid dealing with the situation.

5. When my partner is rude to me, I feel so angry I want to walk right out the door.

6. When my partner behaves in an unpleasant manner, I calmly discuss things with him/her.

7. When my partner does something thoughtless, I patiently wait for things to improve.

8. When my partner says something really mean, I sulk and don't confront the issue.

9. When my partner behaves in an unpleasant manner, I do something equally unpleasant in return.

10. When my partner does something thoughtless, I try to patch things up and solve the problem.

11. When my partner says something really mean, I hang in there and wait for his/her mood to change — these times pass.

12. When my partner is rude to me, I ignore the whole thing.

13. When my partner does something thoughtless, I do things to drive my partner away.

14. When my partner behaves in an unpleasant manner, I spend less time with him/her.

15. When my partner says something really mean, I talk to my partner about what's going on, trying to work out a solution.

16. When my partner is rude to me, I give him/her the benefit of the doubt and forget about it.

My Partner's Responses to Relationship Problems

Please read each of the following statements concerning the manner in which our partner responds to problems in your relationship. Use the following scale to record a response for each item.

Response Scale:

0	1	2	3	4	5	6	7	8
Partner Never Does This		Partner Seldom Does This		Partner Sometimes Does This		Partner Frequently Does This		Partner Constantly Does This

Response:

1. When I say something really mean, my partner threatens to leave me.

2. When I am rude to my partner, he/she tries to resolve the situation and improve conditions.

3. When I behave in an unpleasant manner, my partner forgives me and forgets about it.

4. When I do something thoughtless, my partner avoids dealing with the situation.

5. When I am rude to my partner, my partner feels so angry he/she wants to walk right out the door.

6. When I behave in an unpleasant manner, my partner calmly discusses things with me.

7. When I do something thoughtless, my partner patiently waits for things to improve.

8. When I say something really mean, my partner sulks and doesn't confront the issue.

9. When I behave in an unpleasant manner, my partner does something equally unpleasant in return.

10. When I do something thoughtless, my partner tries to patch things up and solve the problem.

11. When I say something really mean, my partner hangs in there and waits for my mood to change —these times pass.

12. When I am rude to my partner, he/she ignores the whole thing.

13. When I do something thoughtless, my partner does things to drive me away.

14. When I behave in an unpleasant manner, my partner spends less time with me.

15. When I say something really mean, my partner talks to me about what's going on, trying to work out a solution.

16. When I am rude to my partner, my partner gives me the benefit of the doubt and forgets about it.

Scoring

Add up and average your score across Exit and Neglect, and reverse your scores for Voice and Loyalty, then add them together to find your overall Accommodation score. The lower the better.

Response:

Exit —
1. When my partner says something really mean, I threaten to leave him/her.
5. When my partner is rude to me, I feel so angry I want to walk right out the door.
9. When my partner behaves in an unpleasant manner, I do something equally unpleasant in return.
13. When my partner does something thoughtless, I do things to drive my partner away.

Voice —
2. When my partner is rude to me, I try to resolve the situation and improve conditions.
6. When my partner behaves in an unpleasant manner, I calmly discuss things with him/her.
10. When my partner does something thoughtless, I try to patch things up and solve the problem.
15. When my partner says something really mean, I talk to my partner about what's going on, trying to work out a solution.

Loyalty —
3. When my partner behaves in an unpleasant manner, I forgive my partner and forget about it.
7. When my partner does something thoughtless, I patiently wait for things to improve.
11. When my partner says something really mean, I hang in there and wait for his/her mood to change —these times pass.
16. When my partner is rude to me, I give him/her the benefit of the doubt and forget about it.

Neglect —
4. When my partner does something thoughtless, I avoid dealing with the situation.
8. When my partner says something really mean, I sulk and don't confront the issue.
12. When my partner is rude to me, I ignore the whole thing.
14. When my partner behaves in an unpleasant manner, I spend less time with him/her.

Evaluation of Rusbult's Investment Model   Go online

Q4:   Decide whether the evaluative points below are advantages or disadvantages.

- There are numerous studies which support the model, such as that by Le and Agnew (2003) who found that satisfaction, comparison with alternatives and investment did contribute to commitment.

- Rusbult provides an explanation for why people stay in abusive relationships, where the costs are high and the rewards low. It is because of the investment they have made, as found by Rusbult and Maltz. This means that the investment model can account for a wider range of relationships than other models, such as the Social Exchange Theory.

- Cause and effect relationships are difficult to establish (does investment cause commitment, or is there just a relationship between the two?), as many studies into the model are correlational.

- Were you honest when you completed the Accommodation test?   A problem with questionnaires is the social desirability bias, which means that you may have answered in ways that make you appear in a good light. Questionnaires were used a lot to study the Investment Model, so this means that the results may not be valid.

Rusbult's Investment Model: Notebook exercise

You will need your psychology notebook for this activity.

Make notes on the following:

- The three main factors, that according to Rusbult, are most important in maintaining commitment.

- Intrinsic and Extrinsic Investment.

- The 5 factors that Rusbult suggests help maintain relationships.

3.7   Explanations of virtual relationships

Much of the research conducted into social relationships assumes that they are based predominantly around face-to-face communication.   The emergence of electronically mediated relationships through the Internet —email and chat —has forced us to rethink our assumptions.

Virtual relationships are those where people are not physically present but communicate exclusively using online methods such as emails, social media, or texting. Initial research suggests that the nature of online communication is distinctly different from traditional types of social interaction.

One key difference between traditional and virtual relationships is the fact that **self-disclosure** happens much faster.   Self-disclosure is the revealing of personal information about oneself to another person. The anonymous nature of virtual relationships means that individuals can reveal personal information with less fear of being socially embarrassed as information is less likely to be leaked to mutual friends.

Self-disclosure in virtual relationships is also often based on a person's true self rather than their publically presented false self. As well virtual relationships ae more meaningful as they are based on shared attitudes and interests which therefore enables self-disclosure to happen more quickly.

The **hyperpersonal model** of virtual relationships was developed in 1996 by Walther. This model proposes that, as self-disclosure in virtual relationships happens earlier that in face-to-face ones, closeness and intimacy are believed to develop more quickly compared to in face-to-face relationships which leads to a more intense relationship. Walther suggests that this is because participants online have more time to 'edit' their responses to present themselves in a 'good' light, which he called '**selective self-presentation**'. Presenting a positive image will then make an online partner want to disclose more personal information, increasing the intensity of the relationship.

Reduced cues

Imagine you have established a virtual relationship with Andrew and you agree to meet face-to-face. He is late in arriving at the pub where you have agreed to meet. He is dressed in a hooded jacket (the hood stays up), his speech is slurred and it is clear that he hasn't been near a bar of soap for a while.

What information have you gained about Andrew based on what you see or hear?

Sproull & Kiesler (1986) suggested that self-disclosure happens less in virtual relationships due to the idea of **reduced cues**. This is the idea that virtual relationships have a lack of nonverbal cues such as facial expressions and tone of voice compared to face-to-face relationships.

The lack of these nonverbal cues can create deindividuation (having a reduced sense of identity) which leads to disinhibition which can reduce the constraints people would normally place on their behaviour, and cause them to behave in a more extreme way, such as aggressively. This leads to people being less likely to self-disclose.

Absence of gating is another key difference between virtual and traditional interactions. In face-to-face interaction, we are greatly influenced by visual characteristics, such as appearance, habits, age and ethnicity. Each of these act as 'gates', which limit our choice of potential romantic partners. When these gates are absent, it allows those who are more shy and less attractive access to a wider pool of romantic partners. Even when a person's physical characteristics are discovered later, they are unlikely to decrease the bond that has been created due to the sense of intimacy that self-disclosure has brought.

Virtual relationships — applying filter theory

Pick three people that you interact with through social media. Choose people who are not immediate family or close friends. Apply Kerckhoff and Davies' three filters to each, in order i.e.:

1. **Social demography:**
   - Do they live close to you?
   - Are they of the same social class?

2. **Similarity of attitudes:**

   • Do they share the same beliefs and attitudes as you (mostly)?

3. **Complementarity:**

   • Does the other person have characteristics that you lack? i.e. do your two halves make a whole?

Did your findings confirm the predictions made by filter theory? Where they did not, why could this be?

3.8   Study of virtual relationships — Zhao, Grasmuck & Martin (2008)

Aim: to investigate identity construction on Facebook.

Method: The Facebook accounts of 63 students of differing genders and ethnicities were downloaded. The contents were analysed using content analysis, which focused on:

• the user's profile

• contact information

• social networks

• self-description

Findings: Only 15 of the 63 participant completely blocked their accounts to non-'Friends, indicating that the majority of users saw Facebook as a way of getting to know others online. Most participants were also happy to let the public see a wide range of photos of themselves in the context of their friends, having fu , being affectionate and socialising. Zhao et al. call this 'self as social actor', projecting an image of themselves as a desirable social entity.

The second 'self' is the cultural self, as shown in the interests and preferences section of their profile.

The least populated section of the profiles were the 'About Me' section, with only one or two short sentences being the norm. Zhao et al. concluded from these findings that, on Facebook, people prefer to 'show' rather than 'tell' information about themselves.

Conclusions: Zhao et al. concluded that identities created on Facebook are different from the identities created offline. The 'Facebook selves' were highly socially desirable, which the user is not in real life. The anonymity of Facebook does tend to make people more realistic and honest in how they present themselves, but the absence of gating online enables users to 'stretch the truth' a bit, in terms of making themselves appear more socially desirable. This means that they are creating an online identity which is appreciated by others which enhances their overall self-image and increases the quality of their face-to-face, as well as their online, relationships.

Evaluation: The Facebook accounts of students from only one university were looked at, which means that the findings may not generalise to other universities, or other settings. Students are not typical of the general population, so the results may not generalise to other types of people.

Content analysis, which was used by Zhao et al., is a method which has strengths and weaknesses.

It is a reliable way to analyse qualitative data as the coding units applied to the qualitative data are not open to interpretation and so are applied in the same way over time and with different researchers. It is an easy technique to use and is not too time consuming. The coding of descriptive data allows a statistical analysis to be conducted if required as there is usually quantitative data as a result of the procedure. However, cause and effect relationships cannot be established as it merely describes the data. As it only describes the data it cannot extract any deeper meaning or explanation for the data patterns arising.

Evaluation of virtual relationships   Go online

Q5: Decide whether the evaluative points below are advantages or disadvantages.

- Research support from Mishna found that most 16-24 year olds considered virtual relationships to be as real as their physical ones and the internet played a large role in sexual and romantic experiences of adolescents which illustrates the importance of social media in virtual relationships.

- Most of the research looking at virtual relationships was conducted in the late 1990s and early 2000s. This means that psychological research in this area is outdated, as technology is changing so rapidly. This means that research findings in this area may not apply to the current situation.

- The way that virtual relationships form and are conducted will continue to evolve as different forms of social media emerge e.g. Facebook replacing MySpace. This means that the importance of virtual relationships will continue.

- It must be considered that even face-to-face relationships have a virtual side e.g. texting, which means that it is not a straightforward case of either or.

- Online interactions often take longer than face-to-face ones as individuals can create the perfect response which therefore improves the quality of interactions.

3.9   Parasocial relationships

A **parasocial relationship** is one-sided. It is the kind of relationship that we might have with our favourite soap star. We watch the programme each week and 'know' his or her character. Not only that, we can follow their lives outside of the soap on news channels, the internet etc. In this way, we know their persona (their on-screen self), but also think that we know the real person. This persona creates an intimacy, perhaps with thousands of people. This person has no idea who we are at all.

An example might be Billy Connolly — we all know him via his comedy, charity work, TV appearances and movies. If you met him, would you call him Mr. Connolly or Billy? Probably the latter because we feel that we know him well and this has created an intimacy. Unfortunately, he knows nothing at all about us.

> **Parasocial investigation**
>
> In groups of no more than four, think of celebrities, soap stars or singers. Write down everything that you know about them. This could be an acting role that they were in or something that you discovered about them on the internet.
>
> Try to sort out their persona from their real selves. This can be achieved by writing down persona characteristics and real characteristics on a piece of paper. Are there any similarities? If this theory is correct, it will be difficult for you to complete this task for several reasons.

You will learn about two ways in which psychologists have tried to explain parasocial relationships:

- the absorption-addiction mode (including *levels of parasocial relationships*)
- attachment theory

The Absorption-Addiction model

This model, put forward by McCutcheon, says people seek parasocial relationships with celebrities to fill the dissatisfaction they feel in their own lives. For example, someone might feel like they haven't achieved much in their lives, so by becoming fanatical about a 'successful' celebrity, the fan 'absorbs' some of the success.

McCutcheon said that this fanaticism will normally stay at a healthy level. However, sometimes this can lead to addiction. Giles and Maltby (2006) identified three levels of parasocial relationships using the Celebrity Attitude Scale in a large scale survey. He suggested that parasocial relationships can progress in 3 stages:

1. **Entertainment-social level**, where the person keeps up with their celebrity and finds out information about them in order to entertain themselves.

2. **Intense-personal level**, where the person develops intense feelings for the celebrity and you may describe them as obsessed.

3. **Borderline-pathological**, is where the person has over-identified with celebrity and their fantasies and behaviour may have become uncontrollable, like an addiction.

McCutcheon explains that looking for satisfaction in parasocial relationships can be so rewarding that people are motivated in the first level to become more intensely attached to the celebrity —this is the first stage of the model - absorption.

This sense of fulfilment then becomes addictive, leading the person to engage in more risky behaviour, such as stalking.

Attachment theory of parasocial relationships

Celebrity worship has been explained using **Bowlby**'s attachment theory and Mary **Ainsworth**'s types of attachment.

Bowlby's attachment theory suggests that we have an instinct to form a bond with a caregiver in infancy, and when this doesn't happen, we try to find a substitute attachment figure in adulthood, and celebrities can provide.

Ainsworth described different attachment types that develop with caregivers in infancy, dependent on how the caregiver interacts with the infant. Hazan and Shaver (1987) found that the attachment type you develop infancy can extend into the attachment type you form with others in adulthood.

Ainsworth found that infants with an **insecure-resistant** type of attachment were very clingy to their mothers and showed less exploratory behaviours than children with secure attachments, as they did not feel secure enough to leave their parent, and showed great distress when their mother left the room. This type, in adulthood, will be more likely to form parasocial relationships, as they are too afraid of criticism and rejection from real life partners, and haven't developed the social skills to avoid these. Hazan and Shaver suggest that adults who have this attachment type will become clingy and jealous in adulthood, making it difficult to develop lasting romantic relationships. Celebrity worship allows the insecure-resistant person to fulfil an attachment need without the risk of heartbreak and rejection.

Those with a secure attachment style, according to Hazan and Shaver, are confident in their adult relationships, so are unlikely to feel the need to look to celebrities to fulfil the need for attachment. They are secure enough to form lasting attachments to real people.

The attachment explanation of parasocial relationships was supported by research from Cole and Leets (1999). They found that individuals with an insecure-resistant attachment style were most likely to enter into parasocial relationships, and those with insecure-avoidant type were least likely (as those with an insecure-avoidant attachment style tend to avoid relationships altogether).

This suggests that parasocial relationships may serve a different function for different people, where the purpose for insecure-resistant individuals is to satisfy their unrealistic and unmet needs.

You can find out your own attachment style in romantic relationships by completing the test found here: https://www.verywellmind.com/how-do-you-behave-in-romantic-relationships-2796098

Evaluation of parasocial relationships   Go online

Q6:

Decide whether the evaluative points below are advantages or disadvantages.

- Research has suggested that the formation of parasocial relationships has positive effects.

- Perse and Rubin (1989) found that people who are exposed to the same characters over again from soap operas benefit from parasocial interactions as there is a reduction in uncertainty about social relationships.

- Maltby et al (2005) found that the parasocial relationship with celebrities who are perceived as slim and with a good body shape may lead to a poor body image in female adolescents and a predisposition to eating disorders (e.g. anorexia or bulimia nervosa). This suggests that parasocial relationships provide models of social behaviour and provide opportunities to learn cultural values. This suggests that there is a relationship between attitudes to celebrities and body image which can result in low self-esteem.

Test your knowledge on parasocial relationships   Go online

Fill in the blanks with the words found in the Word List below:

Q7:

The absorption-addiction model

The celebrity Attitude Scale (CAS was used by _____ to identify three levels of parasocial relationships. It asses celebrity attraction. The first level is '*entertainment-social level*'. This is the _____ intense level where celebrities are viewed as sources of entertainent and fuel for social interaction. The second level is ' _____ ', an intermediate level where someone becomes more personally involved with a celebrity and may include _____ thoughts. The third level is '*borderline pathological level*', the _____ level of celebrity worship where _____ are uncontrollable and behaviour is more _____ .

Attachment theory

_____ 's attachment theory suggests that early difficulties in attachment may lead to difficulties in forming _____ relationships later in life. Such difficulties may lead to a _____ for parasocial relationships to replace those within one's own social circle as parasocial relationships don't require the same _____ .

Ainsworth identified 2 attachment types associated with unhealthy emotional development: insecure- _____ and insecure-avoidant.   Insecure-resistant types are more _____ to form parasocial relationships because they want to have their unfulfiled needs met in a relationship where there is no real threat of _____ . Insecure-_____ types prefer to avoid the pain and rejection of any type of relationship, either social or parasocial.

Word list: successful; Maltby et al.; obsessive; least; social skills; extreme; likely; Bowlby; strongest; resistant; intense-personal; fantasies; preference; rejection; avoidant

3.10 End of topic test

End of topic 3 test   Go online

Q8: The different behaviours that humans exhibit in order to increase their reproductive success is known as:

a) sexual selection.
b) evolution.
c) human reproductive behaviour.
d) investment.

. . . .

Q9: According to the evolutionary theory of romantic relationships, the strategy used by males to ensure the survival of their genes is:

a) to find a mate who will provide resources to support their offspring.
b) to be as promiscuous as possible.
c) to have a long incubation period.
d) by applying a series of filters to narrow down the pool of available candidates.

. . . .

Q10: Kerckhoff and Davis' first filter is called:

a) social demography.
b) similiarity in attitudes.
c) complementarity.
d) child-bearing potential.

. . . .

Q11: Complementarity refers to:

a) sharing different views and beliefs.
b) how well two people fit together.
c) where someone lives in relation to us.
d) having a kind, dependable partner.

. . . .

Q12: A theory of romantic relationships that suggests that people weigh up the costs and rewards of that relationship.

a) Reorganisational theory
b) Restoration theory
c) Filter theory
d) Social exchange theory

. . . .

Q13: According to Thibault and Kelley, which of the following is closely tied to your self-esteem?

a) Comparison level
b) Constant level
c) Costs
d) Rewards

. . . .

Q14: The third stage of relationship formation, according to Thibault and Kelley, is:

a) institutionalisation stage.
b) bargaining stage.
c) commitment stage.
d) sampling stage.

. . . .

Q15: A feature common to both Social Exchange theory and Rusbult's Investment model is:

a) satisfaction.
b) bargaining stage.
c) comparison with alternatives.
d) investment.

. . . .

Q16: According to Rusbult, which of the following is the term used for what we bring to relationships?

a) Extrinsic investment
b) Intrinsic investment
c) Accommodation investment
d) Emotional investment

. . . .

Q17: One of the factors that Rusbult suggests helps maintain relationships is:

a) intrinsic investment.
b) accommodation investment.
c) positive illusions.
d) perceptual illusions.

. . . .

Q18: Being able to use physical features as potential barriers to forming a relationship is known as:

a) virtual relationships.
b) gating.
c) reduced cues.
d) deindividuation.

....

Q19: Sproull and Kiesler notion that a feeling of reduced identity can occur in virtual relationships is known as:

a) absence of gating.
b) reduced cues.
c) deindividuation.
d) disinhibition.

....

Q20: A parasocial relationship is:

a) one-sided.
b) two-sided.
c) three-sided.
d) many-sided.

....

Q21: McCutcheon's stage of parasocial relationships that is characterised by intense feelings and obsession is known as:

a) entertainment-social.
b) borderline-pathological.
c) entertainment-intense.
d) intense-personal.

....

Q22: The attachment theory of parascocial relationships suggests that they form due to:

a) a person having an insecure-resistant attachment style.
b) a person having an insecure-avoidant attachment style.
c) a person having a secure-resistant attachment style.
d) a person being deprived of attachment in infancy.

....

Q23: The psychologists who found that the attachment style developed in infancy can extend into adulthood are:

a) Bowlby and Ainsworth.
b) Sproull and Keisler.
c) Hazan and Shaver.
d) Giles and Maltby.

End of Topic 3 activity

To help with your understanding of the topic of social relationships, as well as to help you develop the skills of explanation, evaluation and analysis required for Higher Psychology, think about the following in relation to social relationships.

Explain: Describe what is meant by 'social relationships' and explain what function they serve.

Explain: In no more than three paragraphs in total (i.e. one paragraph for each explanation of virtual relationships), summarise:

- gating;

- Sproull and Kiesler's reduced cues theory;

- Walther's hyperpersonal theory.

Evaluate: Give an evaluation of both filter theory and social exchange theory of romantic relationships. Remember to say why each evaluative point is a strength or a weakness.

Analyse:

- Give one implication of the evolutionary explanation of romantic relationships. (If the explanation is true, what does this say about the reasons why we develop romantic relationships?)

- Give one application of Rusbult's investment model of romantic relationships. (How can it be used to enhance the health and/or well-being of people?)

Unit 3 Topic 4

Prejudice (optional topic)

Contents

Learning objective

By the end of this topic, you should be able to explain, evaluation, apply and analyse:

- Types of discrimination, which must include:
  - direct and indirect
  - racial
  - age
  - gender
- Explanations of prejudice, which must include:
  - authoritarian personality
  - stereotyping
  - realistic conflict theory
  - scapegoat theory
  - social identity theory
- The aims, methods, results, evaluation and conclusions of one study into an explanation of prejudice
- Ways of reducing prejudice, which must include:
  - the jigsaw technique
  - media's ability to challenge stereotypes
  - education
  - affirmative action
- The aims, methods, results, evaluation and conclusions of one study into ways of reducing prejudice

4.1 Introduction

We are all prejudiced towards or against someone or something in society —whether we like to admit it to ourselves or not. If you are young you may feel that society judges you in a negative way —you are all stupid, lazy, uneducated and not polite. But what is your perception of the elderly? Could you say honestly that you judge older people in a positive or negative fashion? Probably the latter —they are 'old fogies', forgetful, child-like and cost the country a lot of money. These prejudices may contain a grain of truth but this truth may be exacerbated by media coverage, our contact with the elderly/youth and our experiences of life in general. This area of study looks at possible reasons why we become prejudiced and ways that can reduce it. But first it is important to define what we are talking about.

Stereotyping —a fixed, sometimes simplistic, generalisation about a group or type of person, e.g. a 'typical' man (simplistic), all fat people are slow (exaggeration or distortion); all Muslims are terrorists (generalisation) or the Irish are all warmongers (cultural attributes). Do stereotypes sometimes contain a grain of truth? Stereotypes change over time, e.g. homosexuality is immoral.

Prejudice —an unjustified, usually negative attitude towards an individual solely based on their membership of a particular category or group, or forming an evaluation of someone. We have formed a judgement with reference to an existing bias that may be based on our social stereotypes and may result in discrimination. We may, therefore, develop the idea that all people from that group are the same, e.g. all women are the same, and therefore sexism may develop.

Discrimination —a way of behaving towards members of a categorised group that is unfair in comparison with behaviour towards members of another group. Racism, sexism, ageism.

4.2 Aspects of prejudice

All prejudices can be thought as being made up of three aspects —the **affective**, the **behavioural** and the **cognitive**.

The affective aspect of prejudice —this part involves the feelings experienced in response to the group: possibly angst, fear, hate, revulsion etc. These feelings occur when we encounter members of this group.

The behavioural aspect of prejudice —this part consists of the actions towards the object of prejudice. Behaving differently towards people based on their being part of a group is called discrimination.

The cognitive aspect of prejudice —this involves the beliefs held about the group. These beliefs will be in the form of stereotypes.

Research by LaPierre

The following case study was published in 1934. It is important to contextualise the year because the study should not be applied to modern America, but should be seen in its own context - 1930's America. The vast majority of Americans in the 1930s would have been of white, European heritage; people of an Asian descent would have been in a tiny majority.

Aim

LaPierre wanted to discover if people who had various prejudices/negative attitudes towards the members of various social groups would actually demonstrate these behaviours in observable discriminatory behaviour.

Method

For approximately two years, LaPierre travelled around the USA with a young Chinese couple. They stopped at 184 restaurants and 66 hotels. They were refused service only once and generally received a better than average standard of service from the establishments they stayed in.

Results

On returning from travelling, LaPierre wrote to all the businesses where he and the Chinese couple had dined/stayed. In a letter, which gave no suggestion of his previous visit, he enquired whether they would offer service to Chinese visitors. Most said they would not serve the Chinese visitors.

Conclusion

The results demonstrate a gap between the attitudes expressed and the actual behaviour when the Chinese guests were present in the flesh. LaPierre believed that the results showed people sometimes acted inconsistently with their attitudes.

Evaluation

- The Chinese visitors were attractive and were easy to understand.

- It is unclear if the businessmen were the same individuals as the businessmen who were originally contacted.

- Only 50% of people completed the mail questionnaire.

Research by LaPierre: Questions   Go online

The methodology used for this study was a mixture of naturalistic observation and questionnaire.

Q1:   Define naturalistic observation.

....

Q2:   Explain *two* strengths of naturalistic observation.

....

Q3:   Explain *two* weaknesses of naturalistic observation.

4.3   Protected characteristics (Equality Act, 2010)

In the UK, it is against the law to to discriminate against anyone because of:

- age
- being or becoming a transsexual person
- being married or in a civil partnership
- being pregnant or on maternity leave
- disability
- race including colour, nationality, ethnic or national origin
- religion, belief or lack of religion/belief
- sex
- sexual orientation

Direct and indirect discrimination

Go to: https://www.gov.uk/discrimination-your-rights/how-you-can-be-discriminated-against

Take a note of what is meant by 'direct' and 'indirect' discrimination.

Show your notes to your teacher/lecturer to check for understanding, or find the response here.

Spot the difference between direct and indirect discrimination   Go online

Identify which of the following scenarios illustrate direct discrimination, and which illustrate indirect discrimination.

Q4: Apolinario has come from the Philippines to work on a Scottish fishing boat, but is paid less than the rest of the (Scottish) crew.

a)   direct
b)   indirect

....

Q5: Marta has come to the UK from Lithuania where she qualified as a dental assistant. When she applied for a job at a local dental practice, she was denied an interview as she did not have UK qualifications.

a)   direct
b)   indirect

....

Q6:   Fahmida goes to a nightclub with a group of her (also Asian) friends. The doorperson tells them that the nightclub is full, but as they walk away, they see another group of white people walking in.

a) direct
b) indirect

....

Q7:   Tomas, a Czech national living in the UK, applies for a security position at a local shopping mall. The job advert gives "native English speaker" as a requirement, but Tomas is bilingual and meets all the other requirements. After interview, he is rejected as a non-native English speaker.

a) direct
b) indirect

....

Q8:   Nicky prefers to wear trousers to school, but the headteacher insists that all pupils conform to the school policy regarding what they can wear, which stipulates that girls wear a skirt.

a) direct
b) indirect

....

Q9:   Patience, a person of Nigerian ethnicity, applies to work as a receptionist at a car dealership in a predominantly white area. She meets all of the job requirements, but following an interview the employer tells Patience "you wouldn't fit in here". A white person with similar skills and experience is hired instead.

a) direct
b) indirect

....

Q10:   David has asked for management training, as he is keen to progress in his career, but his boss has refused this on the basis that he is too young.

a) direct
b) indirect

4.4   Types of discrimination

The behavioural aspect of prejudice consists of the actions towards the object of prejudice. Behaving differently towards people based on their being part of a group is called discrimination.

When prejudice takes a particular form of discrimination it can become:

- racist —prejudice towards individuals of a particular race;
- sexist —prejudice towards individuals of a particular sex;
- ageist —prejudice towards individuals of a particular age.

Racism

Racism can take various forms, from talking about or avoiding certain people, to extreme prejudice such as ethnic-cleansing massacres.

Research by Skellington

Skellington (1995) aimed to discover the extent of racial attitudes in Britain.

Participants

959 white British people.

Method

Participants were given a questionnaire asking them to rate their views on various aspects of race relations. Questions included whether they would object to living next door to a non-white person, their perceptions of race relations in Britain etc.

Results

- 75% said that race relations in Britain were 'fair' or 'poor'.
- 25% said that they thought that race relations were good.
- 25% said that they would object to a non-white person living next door.
- 10% wanted anti-racism laws abolished.
- 40% wanted anti-racism laws strengthened.

Research by Skellington: Questions

Q11: Briefly describe the questionnaire method of research.

....

Q12: Discuss two weaknesses of the use of questionnaires in the above study.

....

Q13: Which results did you find the most depressing and why?

The Stephen Lawrence case

Read an extract from an article about a famous case of racism in Britain, that of the murder of Stephen Lawrence, a black teenager from London.

Stephen Lawrence, an eighteen year old from London, was stabbed to death in April 1993. The crime was reported through the national press as a murder motivated by racism.

The murder was so controversial, because of the way the case had been handled by the police authorities. The police were unable to gain conviction against five youths allegedly involved in the murder. This lack of conviction was seen by the press, and through a public enquiry, as a revelation of the extent of the corruption in the police force handling the case. It was also see as a reflection of the degree of the racism in the police force at the time.

At the public enquiry, and through the press, the following insinuations were made:

- dubious police practice;
- incompetence with police methods;
- corruption in the ranks;
- unreliable compilation of evidence;
- poor surveillance techniques with inefficient follow up work.

The Justice System too was publicly put under the microscope and seen to be inefficient. This view was constructed by the public at large around the double jeopardy rule concerning re-trials, with the five suspects being acquitted.

The high profile Macpherson inquiry into the Stephen Lawrence affair sited *institutional racism* within the police force. The report also attempted to extend the findings to consider other forces such as the armed forces and the immigration service.

After a retrial in 2012, two of the original suspects were found guilty of Stephen Lawrence's murder.

Stephen Lawrence case: Notebook exercise

Using the information about the Stephen Lawrence case, try to complete the following table which looks at:

- the behavioural aspects of racism in this case;
- the cognitive aspects of racism in this case;
- the affective aspects of racism in this case.

Remember that there are two aspects of racism at work in this case - the racism against Stephen Lawrence and the racism from the police.

Aspect of racism in this case	Racism against Stephen Lawrence	Racism by the police
Behavioural		
Cognitive		
Affective		

Check your understanding of this task by showing your article to your teacher or tutor and/or by consulting the expected answer.

In the Stephen Lawrence case, the Metropolitan Police Force were accused in the Macpherson Report as being institutionally racist.

Institutional racism

Institutional racism is racism that is endemic in an institution such as the police force, the army or a country such as Nazi Germany. It refers to practices in social institutions that favour one group over another.

Institutional racism is "the collective failure of an organisation to provide an appropriate and professional service to people because of their colour, culture or ethnic origin. It can be seen or detected in processes, attitudes and behaviour which amount to discrimination through unwitting prejudice, ignorance, thoughtlessness and racist stereotyping which disadvantage minority ethnic people." (Macpherson Report, 1999)

Extreme racism: Genocide

Racism is never a good thing, but when there is violence and propaganda to fuel it, it can have very serious consequences.

Genocide is defined as the deliberate and systematic destruction, in whole or in part, of an ethnic, racial, religious or national group.

The most infamous example of genocide was the Holocaust of WWII, but, more recently, it has occurred in the genocide in Bosnia of 1992-1995 and in Rwanda in 1994.

The eight stages of genocide

In 1996, Gregory Stanton, the president of Genocide Watch, presented a paper called "The 8 Stages of Genocide" at the US Department of State. In it, he suggested that genocide develops in eight stages.

1. Classification —people are divided into 'us and them'.

2. Symbolisation —when combined with hatred, symbols may be forced upon unwilling members of pariah groups.

3. Dehumanisation —one group denies the humanity of the other group; members of it are equated with animals, vermin, insects or diseases etc.

4. Organisation —genocide is always organised; special army units or militias are often trained and armed.

5. Polarisation —hate groups broadcast polarising propaganda.

6. Preparation —victims are identified and separated out because of their ethnic or religious identity.

7. Extermination —it is 'extermination' to the killers because they do not believe their victims to be fully human.

8. Denial —the perpetrators deny that they committed any crimes.

Genocide in Rwanda   Go online

Use the following link to find out more about the genocide on Rwanda: http://en.wikipedia.or g/wiki/Rwandan_Genocide

Eight stages of genocide: Notebook exercise

You will need your psychology notebook for this activity.

In a group, if possible, try to match Stanton's eight stages of genocide to what occurred in either:

- Rwanda;

- The Holocaust.

Make some notes about your thoughts.

Check your understanding of this task by showing your article to your teacher or tutor.

Gender discrimination

Sexism is a negative attitude towards someone based on their gender and often includes discriminatory behaviour. We hear it frequently levelled against men about their views of women but it works both ways.

Ambivalent sexism is a type of discrimination which consists of both a 'hostile' and a 'benevolent' prejudicial discrimination towards woman.

Hostile sexism

- Antagonistic attitude towards women.

- Women are viewed as trying to control men so need to be belittled by comments or actions.

Benevolent sexism

- A chivalrous attitude towards women.

- Feels favourable, but is actually sexist because it casts women as weak creatures who need a man's protection.

How is ambivalent sexism measured?

Ambivalent sexism is measured with a paper-and-pencil or computer-based questionnaire known as the Ambivalent Sexism Inventory (ASI). It was developed by Glick and Fiske in 1996. The ASI is composed of two 11-item sub-scales that measure hostile sexism and benevolent sexism. In the sample items below, agreement with a statement indicates a more sexist response.

Hostile sexism items:

- most women fail to appreciate all that men do for them;

- women seek to gain power by getting control over men;

- most women interpret innocent remarks or acts as being sexist.

Benevolent sexism items:

- women should be cherished and protected by men;

- many women have a quality of purity that few men possess;

- a good woman ought to be set on a pedestal by her man.

Ambivalent sexism: Discussion

In a group if possible, discuss and answer these questions:

Q14: Which do you feel is worse - hostile or benevolent sexism?

....

Q15: How easy would it be for a woman to distinguish between chivalrous behaviour (old fashioned manners - holding the door open etc) and benevolent sexism?

Forms of prejudice: Notebook exercise

You will need your psychology notebook for this activity.

Make notes about the following and then show these to your teacher or tutor:

- discrimination —racism;

- discrimination —the Stephen Lawrence case;

- institutional racism;

- extreme racism —genocide;

- the eight stages of genocide;

- discrimination —sexism.

At this stage, you should be able to demonstrate a knowledge and understanding of, and analyse and evaluate the nature of, prejudice including stereotyping and discrimination; cognitive, affective and behavioural aspects.

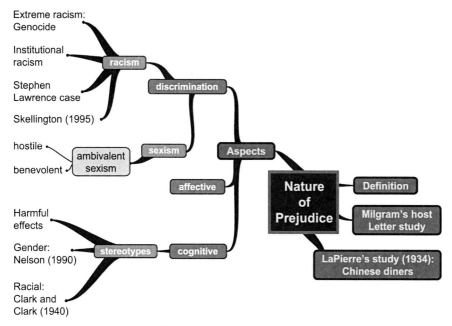

Forms of prejudice - mind map

Age discrimination

In 2002, Fiske *et al* found that pity was the emotion that college students were most likely to feel towards older people.

In 2000, Zebrowitz found that only 1.5% of characters on TV are elderly. In 2006, The Commission for Social Care Inspection found that there was explicit discrimination in the care of the elderly.

Heterosexism

Some out-groups are viewed as negative or deviant. In a public opinion survey in the 1960s, homosexuals were viewed as the third most dangerous group in USA. In 1973, the American Psychiatric Association removed homosexuality from its list of mental disorders. In 2006, Cowan and Valentine monitored 168 hours of TV on BBC1 and 2 and found that lesbian and gays were only portrayed realistically and positively for a mere 6 minutes.

Hegerty argues that some people do express more tolerant views towards lesbian and gay people because of a belief in immutability (fixed and unchangeable). Participants who believed that homosexuality was more biological than personal expressed more tolerant views.

4.5   Explanations of prejudice

Learning objective

Authoritarian personality theory

The authoritarian personality theory of prejudice was proposed by Theodor Adorno in 1950. Adorno refers to someone with an authoritarian personality a being extremely obedient to, and dependent upon, authority figures, but being prejudicial and tyrannical over those they perceive as being inferior in rank, weaker, or more vulnerable to themselves.

Adorno believed that people develop an authoritarian personality because of their childhood. If their parents were overly strict and punitive and show little love, the child grows up being resentful and hostile towards their parents. This hostility is directed towards members of minority groups (who they perceive as being inferior and weaker to them) through a process of displacement.

He created the F-scale (F = Fascist) with which to measure the degree to which someone has an authoritarian personality. You can have a go yourself, here http://www.anesi.com/fscale.htm , but don't take the results too seriously! This theory of prejudice has been soundly criticised, as you will find later.

There are nine variables in the F-scale:

1. **Conventionalism**: strict following of conventional, middle-class values.

2. **Authoritarian submission**: submissive, uncritical attitudes towards idealised authorities of the ingroup.

3. **Authoritarian aggression**: condemnation and rejection of those who violate conventional values, and request for their severe punishment.

4. **Anti-intraception**: opposition to everything subjective, imaginative, not dealing with their own inner psychic life and experience.

5. **Rigid thinking, superstition and stereotypy**: tendency to think in rigid categories and belief in mystical causes of the individual's fate.

6. **Power and 'toughness'**: identification with those in power, exaggerate the importance of strength, toughness and discipline.

7. **Destructiveness and cynicism**: rejection of compassion and empathy. Being generally hostile.

8. **Projectivity**: projection of inner unconscious impulses onto the outer world, and the belief that the world is dominated by secret and dangerous forces.

9. **Sex**: overemphasised interest in sexual deviations, false morality.

Evaluation of the authoritarian personality theory Go online

Q16: Decide which of the following items in bullet points are advantages and which are disadvantages.

- Situational and sociocultural factors are underemphasised. For example, more racism is found in cultures like South Africa and the southern states of America, but no differences have been found in the frequency of authoritarian personalities.

- The theory does not explain why prejudice within a society can change very quickly; for example, the US became largely anti-Japanese immediately after Pearl Harbor, which is not consistent with Adorno's proposal that prejudice always goes back to early childhood.

- It does not account for prejudice affecting large groups or whole societies, such as South Africa under apartheid.

Stereotyping

A stereotype is a widely shared and simplified evaluative image of a social group and its members (Vaughan and Hogg, 2002).

A stereotype is an exaggerated belief, which assumes that whatever is believed about a group is characteristic of the entire group. Stereotypical thinking is unavoidable in social life and it is not automatically bad. Indeed, it may be useful in allowing quick judgements that inform us about how to interact with an individual. The essence of prejudicial thinking, however, is that the stereotype is not regularly checked against reality. It is not modified by any encounters that don't fit with the stereotypical ideas (Farley, 2000).

Stereotyping is when you judge a group of people who are different from you based on your own and/or others opinions and/or encounters.

- Person 1: I met someone from Auchterturra yesterday.

- Person 2: Everyone from Auchterturra are thieves, I met one yesterday who stole my credit card.

- Person 3: You're just stereotyping. How can you judge an entire group of people based on one person?

The process of turning stereotyping into prejudice and discrimination works like this:

- *Stereotype*: Everyone from Auchterturra is a thief.

- *Prejudice*: You have never had anything stolen from you by someone from Auchterturra, but you still believe that everyone from there will steal from you.

- *Discrimination*: When you found out about people from Auchterturra, you probably started asking people from Auchterturra whether or not they had stolen their possessions. Some of you may have held on tightly to your bags and wallets. An employer may not hire someone from Auchterturra as a cashier because of the stereotype.

> Stereotyping can lead to prejudice; prejudice leads to discrimination, discrimination can lead to harassment and even violence.

Stereotypes can be very resistant to change, due to a number of factors, including:

- avoiding members of groups we stereotype, which means that we do not encounter the many ways in which members of that group do not behave in stereotypical ways.
- we tend to ignore or 'explain away' behaviour that does not conform with our stereotypes.
- we may be hostile or rude to members of stereotyped groups, which may influence them to behave in ways that reinforce our stereotypes.

How stereotyping can lead to discrimination

Using the process of turning stereotyping into prejudice and discrimination, explain how the following examples of stereotypes could lead to discrimination.

- People with mental health problems are very disabled and unable to lead normal lives.
- People from Afro-Caribbean origin are lazy.
- Women are emotionally unstable.
- All Asian people are good at maths.

You are moving on to learn about another explanation of prejudice, called Realistic Conflict Theory, and the famous study that inspired it: The Robbers Cave Study. This is a study you will need to know well.

The Robbers' Cave — Muzafer Sherif (1954)

Aim: to find out if intergroup conflict occurs when there is competition for resources.

Method: 22 eleven-year-old boys were taken to summer camp at Robbers Cave State Park in Oklahoma and split into two camps:

- Stage 1: (in-group formation) Teams are named the Eagles and the Rattlers. They are unaware of the other group and proceed to stencil their group name on shirts and bonded as a group.

Results

- Stage 2: (friction stage) Both groups met each other and competed in a number of games. Rivalries and outgroup prejudice occurred: name-calling, flags burned, cabins ransacked, etc.

- Stage 3: (Integration stage) Eagles and Rattlers were brought together to solve problems, like fixing their water supply that was 'vandalised', and eventually outgroup prejudice turned into all of the boys being a part of the same ingroup and resolving most of their differences through mutual cooperation.

Evaluation: As this was a field experiment, so carried out in a real-life situation, it has high ecological validity. As the study was experimental, cause and effect relationships can be established —i.e. we can be sure it was the competition for resources (the IV) that created the competition and conflict (the DV). However, the groups did not occur naturally: they were created by the experimenters, so the groups may not have behaved the way real groups do. The sample were also very similar in that they were all white, middle-class boys —would the findings generalise to groups of girls, or to rival football supporters? The study also has questionable ethics: the boys were not informed of the true nature of the experiment, and were all under the age of 16 —parental consent was not sought. Neither were the boys protected from physical or psychological harm. Finally, evidence from Sherif's own writings about the experiment indicate that the groups of boys were becoming hostile towards each other before the introduction of organised competitive events. So, perhaps the mere presence of another group was sufficient to bring about prejudice, as social identity theory suggests.

Conclusion: Sherif found evidence to support his aim that competition for resources was the cause of conflict (at least in this example). The implication of this is that if people are in competition for resources, the group they belong to (ingroup) will become a highly cohesive one, and that an outgroup stereotype will be created that will become prejudice and then discrimination. Examples of this happening in the real world can be seen, for example, when there is competition for jobs, outgroups are formed from migrants who are then blamed for 'taking our jobs'.

Realistic conflict theory (RCT) states that whenever there are two or more groups that are seeking the same limited resources, conflict, negative stereotypes and beliefs, and discrimination between the groups will follow. The conflict can lead to increasing animosity toward the groups and can lead to the development of a long-lasting feud.

However, another implication of Sherif's findings are that conversely, conflict, negative stereotypes and beliefs, and discrimination between groups can potentially be reduced in situations where two or more groups are seeking to obtain some superordinate goals. **Superordinate goals** are mutually-desirable goals that cannot be obtained without the participation of two or more groups.

Evaluation of Realistic Conflict Theory	Go online

Q17: Decide whether the evaluative points below are advantages or disadvantages.

- Similar studies have suggested that when populations expand and land becomes in short supply conflict and violence increase.
- Sherif's robbers care experiment found that competition increases hostility between the two groups of 12-year-old boys.
- Sherif supports this as he also found a reduction in intergroup conflict as a result of the removal of competition. Therefore, RCT can be applied to real life by helping reduce prejudice between groups in society through the use of superordinate goals.

- RCT can be used to explain real life situations such as the Rwandan genocide. The Tutsi tribe settled peacefully and intermarried with the Hutu tribe of Rwanda, until political rivalry between the groups caused the mass genocide of almost one million Tutsi.
- Conflicting results: Tyerman and Spencer (1983) didn't obtain the same results
- Suggests ways in which prejudice can be reduced (see the jigsaw technique).

Scapegoat theory

Scapegoat theory derives from the frustration-aggression hypothesis, which is the theory that all frustration leads to aggression, and all aggression comes from frustration. Dollard et al. (1939) argued that if goal achievement is prevented **psychic energy** rises and frustration is experienced (**disequilibrium**) which can only be alleviated by aggression.

> *Example of frustration as a result of prevention of goal achievement:* supposing you faced a problem at work, which you couldn't solve —your **psychic energy** increases and you feel a sense of being out of balance (**disequilibrium**). On the way home, you may find -yourself driving more aggressively —your **psychic energy** decreases and your frustration disappears.

The target of aggression is usually the perceived cause of the frustration, but sometimes the target is not easy to identify, such as bureaucracy, or the economy; or too powerful, e.g. your boss or teacher; or someone you love. In these instances, the aggression is displaced onto a **scapegoat**.

> **Displacement:** a defence mechanism whereby aggression is moved from an unsafe object to a safe one.

If a group is frustrated in its goals by another group that is too powerful, the aggression is displaced onto a weaker group = scapegoat.

An example would be the rise of anti-Semitism in Germany during the 1920s and 1930s.

Theoretical principle	Historical events
Personal goals	Political and economic dominance of Germany
Psychic energy activated	Each and every German in a state of arousal, because of WWI.
Frustration of goal achievement	Defeat and Treaty of Versailles (1919)
Disequilibrium. Instigation to aggress.	Economic and political crisis (postwar to early 1920s)
Location of scapegoat	Anti-Semitism of 1920s and 1930s

Scapegoating has benefits for the ingroup. The origin of the term 'scapegoat' is biblical. Tribes would identify a goat onto which all of the sins of the tribe would be ascribed. The goat would then be sacrificed in a ritual act to rid the tribe of its sins. Therefore, targeting scapegoats, such as those from other cultures, ethnicities, genders, sexuality, increases the confidence of those doing the scapegoating, particularly in times of trouble, such as high unemployment, or social strife. It relieves the ingroup's responsibility for their own wrongdoings.

Scapegoating occurs when there are certain conditions within a society that make life difficult, such as poverty, overcrowding, low income and high unemployment. A source of these difficulties is hard to find, let alone displace frustration onto, so other, easily identifiable, social groups become scapegoated. Destructive ideologies can become attractive during these times, as those experiencing the difficulties feel powerless and without a voice. These destructive ideologies can offer up suitable groups to scapegoat, and can encourage active discrimination (Staub, 1996).

Evaluation of scapegoating

Advantages

- The theory seems plausible: we have all taken our aggression out on someone or something other than the original cause of our frustration Therefore, the theory has **face validity**.

- Research has found supporting evidence for scapegoating as an explanation of prejudice. For example, Weatherly (1961) got students frustrated and then asked them to write stories based on given pictures. Where the people in the pictures were given Jewish names, students with anti-Semitic tendencies wrote stories that included aggression towards the Jewish characters.

Disadvantages

- Scapegoating theory suggests that aggression always follows frustration. However, this is not always the case. An alternative consequence of frustration is depression, or anxiety.

Social Identity Theory (SIT)

This is a theory developed by Tajfel and Turner, two British psychologists, in 1979. The theory proposes that we identify strongly with the groups to which we belong, such as football team supporter groups, our family, our country, etc. As you have seen when you learned about Sherif's Realistic Conflict Theory, when we perceive ourselves as part of a group, this becomes an ingroup for us (it forms part of our social identity), and other groups that we do not identify with become outgroups. This creates an 'us and them' way of thinking.

Tajfel and Turner propose three processes that create this ingroup/outgroup mentality:

- **Social Categorisation.** The process of deciding which group you or "another person or persons" belongs to. This group will have 'norms' which help you know how to behave when in the company of others in that group. We categorise, therefore understand a bit about, people who belong to groups (ourselves included), such as Canadians, Muslims, students, affiliation to sports teams, etc.

- **Social Identification.** We adopt the identity of the group that we belong to, and we act in ways that we perceive members of that group act. For example, if you identify as a Scottish Nationalist, you will most likely behave within the norms of that group. As a consequence of your identification with that group, you will develop emotional significance to that identification, and your self-esteem will be dependent on it.

- **Social Comparison.** After we categorise ourselves within a group and identify ourselves as being members of that group, we tend to compare our group (the ingroup) against another group (an outgroup). To maintain your self-esteem, you and your group members will compare your group favourably against other ones. This helps explain prejudice and discrimination, since a group will tend to view members of competing groups negatively to increase self-esteem.

Intergroup Comparisons

There are a couple things that tend to happen in the process of comparing an ingroup to an outgroup, as mentioned above. Members of an ingroup will tend to:

1. favour the ingroup over the outgroup

2. magnify the differences between the ingroup and the outgroup

3. minimise the perception of differences between ingroup members (this increases the cohesion of the ingroup)

4. remember more positive information about the ingroup and more negative information about the outgroup.

So, in a nutshell, members of ingroups will always look for, and remember, the negative aspects of outgroups in order to enhance their self-image. This, in effect, is prejudice, and can lead to conflict, e.g. such as the 'Troubles' in Northern Ireland between Catholics and Protestants.

Test your knowledge on explanations of prejudice   Go online

Q18: According to Realistic Conflict Theory, which of the following statements are true?

a) Whenever there are two or more groups that are seeking the same limited resources, this will lead to conflict, negative stereotypes, and discrimination between the groups.
b) Whenever there are two or more groups that are seeking the same limited resources, this will lead to cooperation.
c) Whenever there are two or more groups that are seeking the same limited resources, this will lead to an exploration of group beliefs and norms.
d) Both a and b.

. . . .

Q19: What are superordinate goals?

a) Mutually desirable goals that cannot be obtained without the participation of two or more groups.
b) Mutually desirable goals that can be obtained without the help of another group.
c) Goals that none of the involved groups care about achieving, but are necessary for group cohesion.
d) None of the above.

. . . .

Q20: What is the F-Scale used for?

a) to identify those who feel weaker to most other people.
b) to identify the different components that make up an authoritarian personality.
c) to identify those who are hostile to authority figures.
d) to test for knowledge about Freud.

. . . .

Q21: When does the authoritarian personality type develop?

a) infancy
b) childhood
c) adolescence
d) adulthood

....

Q22: What does conventionalism mean?

a) having aggressive feelings towards people who violate society's norms.
b) uncritical submission to authority.
c) sticking to society's norms and values.
d) the belief that the world is dominated by secret and dangerous forces.

....

Q23: What does authoritarian aggression mean:

a) having aggressive feelings towards people who violate society's norms.
b) uncritical submission to authority.
c) sticking to society's norms and values.
d) the belief that the world is dominated by secret and dangerous forces.

....

Q24: Realistic Conflict Theory states that conflict between groups is a result of:

a) categorisation
b) a person's upbringing
c) having similar beliefs
d) competition for scarce resources

....

Q25: Frustration can be defined as a feeling of irritation or annoyance when something or someone is preventing you from:

a) becoming stressed
b) achieving a goal
c) fighting
d) calming down

....

Q26: According to which theory does membership of an ingroup bolster our self-esteem:

a) Authoritarian personality
b) Realistic Conflict Theory
c) Scapegoating
d) Social Identity Theory

....

Q27: According to the Scapegoating explanation of prejudice, frustration at being blocked from achieving a goal results in an increase in:

a) displacement
b) social categorisation
c) hostility
d) psychic energy

....

Q28: According to the Stereotyping explanation of prejudice:

a) prejudice leads to discrimination, discrimination can lead to violence.
b) discrimination leads to violence which can lead to prejudice
c) violence leads to violence, which can lead to discrimination
d) displacement leads to an increase of psychic energy which leads to prejudice

4.6 Prejudice reduction

Ways of reducing prejudice

Prejudice, unfortunately, is universal - however, this does not mean that there is no means of conquering it.

Jane Elliot —education

One method that can be used to reduce prejudice and conflict is education. Giving people information concerning the cause and effects of prejudice may help reduce it. This is because education can help prevent society developing prejudice attitudes as the accepted social norm (Bem and Bem, 1970).

The us of education to help reduce prejudice is particularly effective on young people, but Hill (2001) states that if adults are forced to listen to information incompatible to their deep-seated attitudes, they will reject it, twist it, or pay no attention to it. So the idea then is to get young, impressionable minds and educate them to prevent perpetuation of prejudicial attitudes.

Jane Elliott (1968) is a key contributor to the idea of promoting education as a classroom tool to prejudice reduction. She confirmed that it can be used effectively to teach us to be more considerate of others.

The historical background to Elliott's study

American civil rights leader Martin Luther King Jr. was assassinated in Memphis Tennessee on 4th April 1968. The United States at this time was rife with prejudicial attitudes and discrimination against all colours except whites, especially in the Southern states of America.

Immediately before Martin Luther King's murder, Elliot had attempted to introduce her young pupils to the concept of racial equality. She had made Martin Luther King her class 'hero of the month', but had found it difficult to communicate what racism was and how unpleasant racism really could be. The children in her class were all white and had never seen people of a different colour before.

A class divided: Brown and blue eyes

Jane Elliott was not a psychologist, she was a thoughtful primary school teacher who carried out a study as a psychologist would. She started her study by gaining parental permission to teach her class about the realities of racism. She then told her Primary 4 class a lie.

She told them that people with blue eyes were cleverer, faster, and more likely to achieve in life than people with other eye colours - they were better than people with brown eyes, who were described as being not to be trusted, lazy and unintelligent.

Elliott then separated her class into two groups on the basis of whether they had brown eyes or blue eyes. On the first day of the study, she told the blue-eyed children they were smarter, nicer, neater and better than those with brown eyes. For the first day, she praised the blue-eyed children and gave them extra playtime. Her brown-eyed children were made to wear collars identifying them as 'different'. The brown-eyed children were not allowed to drink from the same water fountain. Elliott criticised their work in the classroom.

On day two, Elliott reversed roles. She made the brown-eyed children feel superior by praising them and giving them treats. The blue-eyed children were now made to wear the ribbons, and their behaviours and class performance were ridiculed by her and the other children.

Elliott noticed that when the groups were made to feel inferior, they adopted the behaviours expected of that label. Their body language became defensive and their academic performance dropped.

She noted that those pupils who had been kind and tolerant of others before the study, when assigned to the superior group became mean and discriminatory towards those in the inferior group.

Results of Elliott's study

At the end of her study, Elliott asked her pupils what it felt like to be thought of as inferior. The children reported feeling angry and confused. They talked of their frustration and loneliness, especially when those in the superior group were treated as being better and rewarded with extra treats.

Repercussions of Elliott's study

50 years later, many of the pupils who took part in the original study are still influenced by it. They learned that judging people as superior or inferior on the basis of the colour of their skin is an especially insidious form of prejudice.

Criticisms of Elliott's study

This study can be criticised in that it caused distress to its participants. As Jane Elliott has never claimed to be a psychologist, she is not bound by the strict ethical guidelines when conducting research. Since the study took place, she has spent her time promoting tolerance and teaching people that everyone has a right to respect and to feel valued.

Jane Elliott's work: Documentary   Go online

There is an excellent television documentary about Jane Elliott's work and its implications.

Follow the link and then choose to either view the full programme or excerpts from it: http://www.pbs.org/wgbh/pages/frontline/shows/divided/

Jane Elliott's work: Discussion

In groups, discuss the following questions about Elliott's study.

1. Do you feel this study would work with students of your age? Why/why not?

2. This is not a psychological study, but it is a very thought-provoking one. How would you adapt Elliott's study nowadays to make it into a psychological study? (Think about how you should structure a study with aims, participants, IV, DV etc.)

Consult your tutor or teacher and/or the *expected answer*.

Evaluation of Jane Elliott's study

Advantages

- She demonstrated that we become prejudiced very quickly.
- She demonstrated that prejudicial feelings can be reversed.
- She demonstrated that education can play a part in the reduction of prejudice.

Disadvantages

- The study was conducted in America, a Western society, so results may not generalise to other cultures.
- This study was conducted in the 1970s, when prejudice may have been much more prevalent than it is now. The study may therefore be outdated.
- Ethics —the children may have remained prejudiced.
- Ethics —the parents gave their permission, but the children did not know they were part of a research study.

Research by Weiner and Wright

Weiner and Wright were psychologists who imitated Elliott's study years later (1973) to see if the same effects would occur.

Method

White American children aged between 9 and 10 years were put at random into an orange or green group. Each group wore coloured armbands to identify their group membership. On the first day, the 'orange' children were told they were cleverer and cleaner than the 'green' children, and they were given privileges that were denied to the 'orange' children. The situation was reversed on the second day.

Results

On each day, the group that was discriminated against showed reduced self-confidence and did less well in their school work. In order to see whether the experience of these children has made them less prejudiced, they were asked whether they wanted to go on a picnic with some black children, nearly all (96%) agreed. In contrast, only 62% who had not been exposed to prejudice agreed to go on the picnic.

Conclusion

Experiencing prejudice at first hand can reduce prejudice towards other people.

Elliott, and Weiner and Wright: Notebook exercise

You will need your psychology notebook for this activity.

Make notes about Jane Elliott's study under the heading of "Prejudice Reduction: Education: Elliott and Weiner and Wright".

Remember to outline the studies, its results, repercussions and any criticisms.

Check your understanding of Elliott and Weiner and Wright by showing your notebook entry to your teacher or tutor.

Show racism the red card

Show Racism the Red Card (SRTRC) is an anti-racist charity which was established in January 1996. The aim of this organisation is to produce anti-racist educational resources, which use the high profile nature of professional footballers to help school pupils to combat racism.

The SRTRC achieve their Prejudice reduction message by means of:

- producing educational resources;

- developing activities to encourage people, particularly school students, to challenge racism;

- challenging racism in the game of football and other sports in parts of the UK.

The Educational Institute of Scotland and SRTRC have run a national competition in Scottish primary and secondary schools since 2002.

The competition asks Scottish pupils and their teachers to consider racial discrimination and how to combat it using art, poetry and films.

The results of the students efforts can be seen at http://www.srtrc.org/scotland under *Schools and Education*.

Reducing prejudice through education: Discussion

In groups, discuss the following question.

Elliott, Weiner and Wright and SRTRC aim to reduce prejudice through education - which study do you feel is more effective and why?

Report your answers to your teacher or tutor.

The jigsaw technique

The jigsaw technique is a classroom teaching method that improves relationships between students who may typically not associate with each other because of racial divides.

Each student is held accountable to being an expert of a certain topic and interacting with multiple groups of students to share and assess information:

- Group 1 —individually become expert in a topic, and share that expertise with the group

- Group 2 —meet with people who studied the same topic, synthesise information and discuss

- Group 3 —share with their original group the new things they have learned about their topic

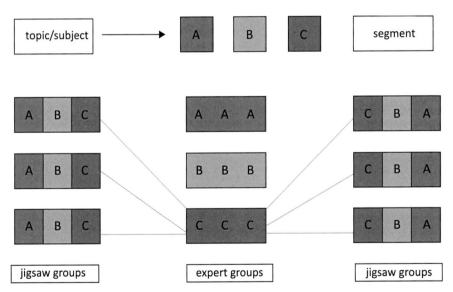

Like with the boys in the Robbers' Cave study, the jigsaw technique reduces prejudice by having groups work cooperatively towards achieving superordinate goals.

Without co-operation, the task cannot be completed. The child's mark is based on the group's overall knowledge of the topic (Aronson et al, 1978).

The Jigsaw Classroom is a cooperative learning technique which effectively reduces conflict. Just as in a jigsaw puzzle, each piece, or each student's part, is essential for the completion and full

---

understanding of the final product.

The jigsaw process encourages listening and empathy by giving each member of the group an essential part to play in an academic activity. Group members must work together as a team to accomplish the task; each person depends on all the others. Cooperation facilitates interaction among all students in the class, which encourages them to value each other as contributors to their common task.

The jigsaw technique: Internet Go online

For further information about the jigsaw technique, including the ten steps for implementing the jigsaw technique in a classroom, have a look at this website: http://www.jigsaw.org

---

Evaluation of the jigsaw technique

Advantages

- Other studies support the effectiveness of cooperative learning techniques in reducing prejudice.

- This study confirms the findings of Tajfel (Realistic Conflict Theory) that the use of superordinate goals can and does reduce conflict between groups.

Disadvantages

- The study was conducted in America, an individualistic culture (one where the individual is valued over the group), so the findings may not generalise to collectivist cultures (such as Japan or some African cultures, where the group is valued over the individual).

- It is simplistic to say that the use of superordinate goals will always reduce conflict —conflict can arise for many different reasons.

- Ethics —parental consent was granted, but the boys did not know they were part of a psychology experiment.

The media's ability to challenge stereotypes

We learn stereotypes from lots of different places. The media is very influential in shaping how we think and often spreads gender stereotypes.

Stereotypes in the media

Watch this TED video talk on how the media creates stereotypes and reinforces them here: https://youtu.be/kMS4VJKekW8 —sexual objectification of women, and here: https://youtu.be/ueOqYebVhtc —how movies teach manhood.

Using the media as an approach to tackle prejudice is quite common, through TV, radio, and the internet. The media can tackle prejudice through providing information or through changing society's norms that maintain stereotypes and prejudice, using, for example, storylines in soaps.

Anti-prejudice campaigns tend to fall into three categories:

- general awareness raising;

- encouraging of reporting discrimination/abuse, and;

- campaigns targeting certain groups (e.g. Show Racism the Red Card —tackling racism in the context of football).

The media can increase contact between diverse groups, particularly when actual contact is not feasible. Aboud et al (2012) carried out a review of 32 studies (a meta-analysis) of various types of interventions to reduce prejudice in early childhood, across various different countries. They found that media forms of interventions had a 47% success rate in terms of improvements in prejudiced attitudes, but to a lesser extent on prejudiced behaviours. They found that using the media to increase indirect contact between diverse groups worked much better than providing information alone.

Aboud et al.

Aboud et al found that media interventions were successful in reducing prejudiced attitudes, but less so prejudiced behaviours.

In groups, discuss the implications of this finding. Do they actually show a reduction in prejudice? What is an alterative explanation for these findings?

Media campaigns are often used to promote change through raising awareness and challenging prejudice, such as *Show Racism the Red Card, and One Scotland, Many Cultures.*

The evidence for the success of these campaigns is scarce, however. One of the few studies conducted in the effect of media campaigns on prejudice reduction was conducted by Sutton et al. in 2007, who found that there is little evidence of their effectiveness, despite the frequency with which people encounter them.

An example of an unsuccessful media campaign is the 'One Scotland, Many Cultures' campaign launched by the Scottish Government in 2002. An evaluation of this campaign was carried out by Sutton et al. in 2007. The found that the campaign failed as it included the portrayal of Asian shopkeepers and doctors, and Black footballers. The campaign, therefore, conformed to racial stereotypes rather than tackling them. Plus, the campaign backfired as it was seen to favour certain groups, which also alienated audiences.

Some media campaigns, such as those for charities and health promotion, focus on the provoking of fear, anger, guilt, etc. Campaigns that use this strategy for prejudice reduction, however, may be ineffective, says Abrams (2010). He suggests that inducing feelings of guilt in this case will result in the person using defensive strategies to reduce these feelings, rather than reducing prejudicial attitudes and behaviour themselves.

A conclusion from the findings described above suggest the following about how to run an effective media campaign to reduce prejudice:

- longer-term strategies are more successful than short-term ones in attitude change;

- the content of the campaign is important, e.g. providing opportunities for indirect contact are better than providing information about different cultures alone;

- the messenger needs to be credible and we need to be able to identify with them (i.e. tackling prejudice with football supporters should include ordinary football supporters, not people from far-right groups);

- inducing empathy and compassion is more successful as a strategy than inducing guilt.

Media campaigns to reduce prejudice   Go online

You can find an example of how the media was influenced to change prejudiced attitudes here: https://youtu.be/LOdyhEeYnJI

Once you have watched the video, identify which of the bullet points above were used successfully, and which were not used at all.

Q29: Long-term strategy?

a) Used
b) Not used

....

Q30: Content of campaign?

a) Used
b) Not used

....

Q31: Credible and identifiable messenger?

a) Used
b) Not used

....

Q32: Inducing empathy and compassion?

a) Used
b) Not used

Media campaign to reduce prejudice

You could run a media campaign of your own to reduce prejudice, perhaps in conjunction with your Student Association. Use the strategies given above to ensure the success of your campaign.

Affirmative (positive) action

Affirmative action policies are those in which an institution or organisation actively engages in efforts to improve opportunities for historically excluded groups in society. Affirmative action policies often focus on employment and education. In universities, affirmative action refers to admission policies that provide equal access to education for those groups that have been historically excluded or underrepresented, such as women and minorities.

In the UK, the term *positive action* is used. Positive action is when an employer takes steps to help or encourage certain groups of people with different needs, or who are disadvantaged in some way, access work or training.

Positive action is lawful under the Equality Act (2010). For example, an employer could organise an open day for people from a particular ethnic background if they're under-represented in the employer's workforce. This wouldn't be unlawful discrimination under the Act.

An employer can take positive action when someone who is characterised as having a protected characteristic, if:

- they're disadvantaged in some way in relation to work,
- their participation in employment or training is particularly low, or
- they have particular needs which are different from other people who don't share their protected characteristic.

A reminder that protected characteristics under the Equality Act (2010) are:

- age
- disability
- gender reassignment
- marriage and civil partnership
- pregnancy and maternity
- race
- religion or belief
- sex
- sexual orientation.

An example of positive action is WiSETI (Women in Science, Engineering and Technology Initiative), which aims to improve the underrepresentation of women in these fields. The Initiative holds seminars, lectures and other events that are specifically targeted at women in, or hoping to be employed in, one of the STEMM (Science, Technology, Mathematics and Medicine).

Positive action has also been taken by the football league, who have set a target of between 10% and 20% of recruitment from Black, Asian or Minority (BAM) backgrounds to youth development jobs by 2019.

Positive action is more than just changing policies. It involves actively targeting and empowering those who may be disadvantaged by having a protected characteristic. For example, the WiSETI programme will go into schools, youth organisations, colleges, etc., to actively seek out, empower and recruit young women to careers in STEMM.

Evaluation of positive action

Advantages

- In the US, Affirmative action programmes have resulted in doubling or tripling the number of minority applications to colleges or universities, and have made colleges and universities more representative of their surrounding community.

- Graduates who benefited from affirmative action programs say that they have received better jobs, earned more money, and ultimately are living better lives because of the opportunity they received.

Disadvantages

- Critics argue that positive and affirmative action causes a form of reverse discrimination by favouring one group over another. This preference, they argue, is based on whichever characteristic they have, rather than suitability for the job/place at university.

- This preferential treatment may result in further prejudice and discrimination by those who do not have a protected characteristic.

- Those who gain jobs/university places through positive action may be perceived as undeserving of the job/place.

- Affirmative/positive action can be seen as condescending to the underrepresented groups since it is implied that the groups need affirmative action in order to succeed.

Positive action

You could interview your school/college's HR Manager to ask about what positive action they take in relation to recruitment of staff and pupils/students.

Test your knowledge on ways to reduce prejudice   Go online

Q33: All of the following are elements of a jigsaw classroom except:

a) students are separated by ethnicity and/or gender.
b) students depend on each other.
c) students work in small groups.
d) students work equally together.

. . . .

Q34: Examples of positive action include:

a) SRTRC
b) One Scotland, Many Cultures
c) WiSETI
d) The jigsaw technique

. . . .

Q35: A criticism of the jigsaw technique is:

a) Preferential treatment may result in further prejudice and discrimination by those who do not have a protected characteristic.
b) May not apply to collectivist cultures.
c) It is too simplistic to say that superordinate goals will reduce conflict.
d) Parental consent is needed.

....

Q36: A protected characteristic under the Equality Act (2010) does not include:

a) pregnancy and maternity.
b) race.
c) religion or belief.
d) paternity.

....

Q37: Ways of improving the effectiveness of media campaigns include:

a) long-term strategy.
b) content of campaign.
c) credible and identifiable messenger.
d) all of the above.

....

Q38: Hill (2002) states that in order for education to work as a way of reducing prejudice:

a) the message has to induce feelings of guilt.
b) the message has to be given to children, as adults will distort or ignore any message that contradicts their own view.
c) there must be contact between the groups affected.
d) it has to be given by teachers, not parents.

4.7   End of topic test

In the question paper, you may be asked to give an analysis of any theory, study or explanation. A good way to help you prepare for this type of question is to use a Venn diagram as it allows you to compare aspects of theories, studies and explanations. Making comparisons is a key analytic skill to develop.

Consider the Realistic Conflict Theory (RCT) and Social Identity Theory (SIT) explanations of prejudice. Identify whether the following items fall under RCT, SIT or both.

You may wish to use a Venn diagram using:

- the outer section of the Venn for items that are specific to that explanation alone;

- the intersection of the circles where the item is common to both explanations.

Q39: Assumes that people join groups to increase or maintain their self-esteem

....

Q40: People have different social identities, depending on which group they belong to, which are different from those of outgroups

....

Q41: Conflict comes about through competition for scarce resources

....

Q42: Conflict comes about because of a need to establish an identity

....

Q43: Conflict can be reduced through cooperation to achieve superordinate goals

....

Q44: Research into this explanation includes *The Robbers' Cave*

....

Q45: Claims that prejudice happens immediately after you categorise yourself as belonging to an ingroup

Glossary

Acquiescence response

a tendency to give socially desirable answers

Acronym

created by combining the first letters of words to be learned into a new word (or word-like) area of study

Acrostic

uses the first letters of words to create a meaningful sentence

Affective prejudice

involves the feelings experienced in response to the group - possibly angst, fear, hate, revulsion etc.

Aggression

behaviour whose intent is to hurt - verbal, physical, mental or emotional

Alternative hypothesis

like the experimental hypothesis, this is the hypothesis that sample observations are influenced by non-random causes; this term is used when the hypothesis relates to non-experimental studies

Ambivalent sexism

a type of discrimination which consists of both a hostile and a benevolent prejudicial discrimination towards woman

Anti-Semitism

anti-Jewish feelings

Apparent non-conformity

occurs when someone seems to be a non-conformist, but is in fact conforming to a different set of group's norms

Artificial Intelligence

the science of creating computers to perform processes that imitate human cognition

Asch Paradigm

(or The Asch conformity experiments) a series of studies that starkly demonstrated the power of conformity in groups

Attachment

a close bond that we form with our mum/teacher/friend and is an emotional attachment

Atypical behaviour

abnormal behaviour

Authoritarian personality

an individual theory from Adorno, associated with the F-scale, which says that prejudice stems from an authoritarian upbringing during childhood

Autism

a mental health illness where sufferers have difficulty in recognising emotions and understanding emotions, sometimes failing to know right from wrong - they may also have obsessional behaviours

Autokinetic effect

a perceptual illusion in which the observer imagines movement of a stationary spot of light

Average

a number that represents the middle region of a set of data; usually a mean, median or mode is calculated to find an average

Behaviour

actions by which we adjust to our environment

Behavioural prejudice

consists of the actions towards the object of prejudice

Behaviour modification

the systematic use of principles of learning to increase the frequency of socially desirable behaviour

Biological psychology

the study of the biological basis of behaviour

Blind obedience

occurs when people carry out orders without questioning whether these orders should be carried out or not

Capacity

the maximum number of items that can be recalled from memory after a single presentation, e.g. for digits it usually about 7

Case history

comprises of records or case notes obtained from a school, college, doctor, social worker, police etc.

Case study

a non-experimental research method used in psychology which is a detailed, in-depth investigation of a single case happening concerning a person, a family, an organisation, or an event

Catharsis

a process of expressing strongly felt, but usually negative, emotions

Central nervous system

(CNS) the part of the nervous system that contains the brain and the spinal cord

Chunks

organising stimuli, such as words or numbers, into manageable memory 'lots', e.g. it is difficult to store the number 35242140591, but a 'telephone number' of 35242 140 591 is easier to remember

Classism

prejudicial behaviour towards someone because of their social class

Closed question

a question that only offers restricted answers

Cognitive prejudice

involves the beliefs held about a group - these beliefs will be in the form of stereotypes

Compliance

a change in our behaviour, but not our opinion, as a consequence of a request from someone; it often relies on rewards or coercion by someone in power

Confederate

a person who assists in a psychology experiment and is an accomplice of the psychologist

Conflict

perceived incompatibility of goals

Conformity

the process of giving in to real or imagined pressure from a group and going along with them, acting in the same way that they do

Confounding variable

a variable which has an unintentional effect on the dependent variable

Content analysis

a methodology that is used to detect the content of TV, radio, newspapers to uncover information

Correlation

refers to a measure of how strongly two or more co-variables are related to each other

Correlational hypothesis

a statement to be tested: predicts that there will be a relationship between two covariables

Counterbalancing

this involves alternating the order in which participants do the conditions of the experiment to avoid order effects

Covert

hidden

Declarative coding

coding in memory that is usually associated with exciting, important, emotional or traumatic events

Defence mechanisms

keeps us 'sane' in order to help us cope with something

Denial

a defence mechanism deployed by the ego to protect the person from anxiety by an outright refusal to admit or recognise that something has occurred or is currently occurring

Dependent variable

(DV) a variable that is measured by the researcher

Diary

daily or chronological record of events, happenings etc.

Directional hypothesis

(one-tailed hypothesis) a statement to be tested: predicts which set of scores will be better/faster (difference) or positively/negatively associated (correlation); previous research (a literature review) suggests the direction

Discrimination

a way of behaving towards members of a categorised group that is unfair in comparison with behaviour towards members of another group, e.g. racism, sexism and ageism

Disobedient models

(rebellion) occur when a group, or individual, refuses to submit to the authority of the larger group

Displacement

a defence mechanism whereby there is a transference of an undesirable emotion from one object to another, safer, one, e.g. when a worker is humiliated by his boss, he comes home and kicks the cat (the boss may retaliate, the cat won't)

Ecological validity

refers to how well a study can be related to, or how well it reflects everyday, real life

Ego

this is like a referee between the id and society

Electroencephalogram

(EEG) a technique for recording brain activity

Elliot, Jane

a psychologist who carried out the brown eyes blue eyes experiment

Empirical data

factual, objective measurable information

Encoding

the process of locating new information into the memory

Episodic memory

concerns memory of events that have happened

Ethics

rules, values and principles

Ethnocentrism

looking at the world from our nationality and culture only

Ethological approach

looks at the scientific and observable nature, and has a focus on animals in their natural environment - it believes that biology, evolution and our environment can have an effect on us and also that our experiences of life can, and do, have a lasting effect on us and our behaviours

Experiment

a scientific procedure that adheres to the experimental method of research

Experimental hypothesis

a statement to be tested: predicts a relationship between the Independent Variable (IV) and the Dependent Variable (DV)

Experimental method

a type of research method in which the investigator manipulates one or more independent variables to determine the effect(s) on some behaviour (the dependent variable), while controlling other relevant factors - there are three types of experiment: laboratory, field and quasi; this is the only method that can give cause and effect

Experimenter bias

a bias towards achieving the aims of an experiment on the part of an experimenter, which may influence the objectivity of the research (this affects validity)

Experimenter effect

where an experimenter unconsciously effects the behaviour of participants (this affects validity)

Extraneous variable

a variable which could affect the dependent variable but which is controlled

Field experiment

an experiment that takes place in a natural setting, e.g. a classroom

Frequency distribution

a breakdown of how all the scores fell into the different categories or ranges that the overall score was broken into

Frustration-aggression hypothesis

this theory argued that aggression is always the result of frustration

F-scale

(Facist-scale) a questionnaire that helps indicate the degree of authoritarianism an individual may have

General adaptation syndrome

(GAS) our body's defence mechanism against both the short- and long-term effects of stress

Generalisation

being able to apply the results of a piece of research to those other than the original participants, or to situations beyond a laboratory

Generic norm

a tendency to categorise people in terms of in-groups and out-groups

Genocide

the deliberate and systematic destruction of an ethnic, racial, religious or national group

GIGO

('garbage in garbage out') a particular criticism of poorly constructed surveys

Hawthorne effect

changes in behaviour resulting from the attention that participants believe they are getting from researchers, and not the variable(s) manipulated by the researchers (thereby reducing validity)

Heinz's dilemma

to further understand Kohlberg's six stages of moral reasoning, he devised a dilemma that he felt showed all the stages - this became know as Heinz's dilemma, which related to a man stealing medicine for his sick wife

Histogram

a graph in which each bar represents some class or element (for example, a score on an IQ test) - the primary difference between a bar graph and a histogram is that the bars in the histogram actually touch each other to show that there are no gaps in between the classes; the bars in a bar graph have space in between them

Homeostasis

refers to the body's tendency to maintain a balanced or constant internal state that is optimal for functioning, e.g. if you get too hot, your homeostatic mechanisms will make you sweat in an attempt to reduce your temperature to normal levels

Hypothesis

a clear, testable statement that is made at the beginning of an investigation, which aims to predict the outcome of that investigation

Hypothetical construct

a concept that we have an idea of, but which cannot be measured directly because it does not exist in reality, e.g. anxiety or unconscious

Id

present from birth, consists of inherited instincts and is entirely unconscious

Identification

occurs when we change our behaviour and/or opinion when we want to identify with a particular group

Idiographic

unique to the individual

Imprinting

a primitive form of learning in which some infant animals physically follow and form an attachment to the first moving object that they see/hear

Independent measures

(between subjects design) an experimental design where two or more groups/conditions consist of different individuals

Independent variable

(IV) the variable that is manipulated by the researcher

Informational influence

refers to changing behaviour as a consequence of information gained from 'experts' whose views are considered both valid and reliable

Institutional racism

the collective failure of an organisation to provide an appropriate and professional service to people because of their colour, culture or ethnic origin

Intellectualisation

avoiding unacceptable emotions by focussing on the intellectual aspects

Intelligence

the ability to problem-solve

Interference

occurs when one set of information competes with another in memory processing

Internalisation

a change in our behaviour and in our opinion, internalisation of others' views or opinions are more likely to affect how we think, feel, and behave; it often stems from knowledge and credibility

Interviewer bias

describes a situation where the interviewer influences responses from participants

Interview method

a non-experimental research method used in psychological research - the interview method of research is a conversation with a purpose

Jigsaw classroom

involves dividing the class into small groups where each group member has to learn a different piece of information - this information is then passed on to the other members of their group to reach a superordinate goal

The jig-saw technique

associated with Aronson and says that the use of superordinate goals has the effect of reducing prejudice

Kohlberg's theory of moral reasoning

Kohlberg felt that moral reasoning could be broken into six stages which were grouped into three levels: pre-conventional, conventional, and post-conventional - as people grew up, both physically and morally, he felt they would move through these stages

Koluchová

a Czech psychologist famous for her case study into 'wild children' JM and PM

Learning

a process based on experience that results in a relatively permanent change in behaviour

Levels of processing model of memory

a model about information processing and connectivity pathways

Likert scale

adds up responses to statements representative of a particular attitude

Longitudinal

research that is conducted for more than one year

Matched-pairs

an experimental design where every participant in one group/condition is matched with a very similar person in the other group(s)

Maternal deprivation

when a child is separated from their mother

Maternal privation

a lack of an attachment between a mother and child

Mean

the arithmetical average which is calculated by adding all of the values and then dividing by the total number of values - can be affected by extreme scores

Media

all forms of TV, radio, newspapers, internet, games etc.

Median

the middle score in a data set which is calculated by placing all of the values in order and finding the mid-point

Memory

the faculty by which the mind stores and remembers information

Mental script

learned behaviour of how to deal with people or situations

Minority Influence

when a group that is perceived to be in a minority, or less powerful, is able to change the minds of the majority of a more powerful group

Mode

the most frequent score in a data set

n

used to denote the number of items in a sample

Nationalism

the feeling of pride we get at being Scottish, English, Irish, American etc. - this feeling can spill over into prejudice

Nationality

a legal partnership between a person and the state; it means that it gives the state legal jurisdiction over the person, but also provides the person with protection - sometimes nationality is used when we really mean ethnicity

Naturalistic observation

the planned watching and recording of behaviours as they occur within a natural environment; an example would be naturalistic observation of animals in their natural habitat

Nature

what we are born with (genetics)

Non-conformity

occurs when someone has made independent decisions and resisted social influences

Non-directional hypothesis

(two-tailed hypothesis) a statement to be tested: predicts there will be a difference or a relationship, in either direction

Non-experimental method

this is termed 'non-experimental' because there is no independent variable involved

Non-participant observation

the researcher has no involvement with recordings of observed behaviours being taken from afar

Normal distribution

describes how characteristics are distributed amongst a population, graphs of which are referred to as "bell curves" because the shape looks like a bell; it tracks rare occurrences of a trait on both the high and low ends of the 'curve', with the majority of occurrences appearing in the middle section

Normative influence

the ability that others have to influence an individual to conform to the social norms

Norms

standards based on measurements of a large group of people, e.g. "it is wrong to kill" or "we should wear clothes when outside"

Null hypothesis

a statement to be tested: predicts there will be no difference or relation between two conditions or variables

Nurture

environmental impacts on our behaviours (parenting)

Obedience

a form of social pressure in acting in response to an order from a person in authority; obedience is behaving as you're told, but not necessarily changing your opinion

Observational learning

the process of learning new responses by watching the behaviour of others

Observational method

a non-experimental design in psychology where the researcher plans, observes, and later analyses behaviours as they occur in a natural setting

Observation schedule

a pre-prepared checklist used in observational studies to record observed behaviours

Observer bias

an example of a confounding variable in observational research which can occur in that the observer, and thus their results may be influenced by prior knowledge, or experience of the situation / subject(s) / participant(s) under investigation

Observer effect

a confounding variable in observational research; an observer effect occurs where any change in the participant's behaviour is a result of the observer's presence

Oedipus complex

boys at the age of 3 - 12 years old (the phallic stage) desire their mother and see their father as a threat to the fulfilment of this desire, fearing that their father will castrate them (castration anxiety) if he finds out about this, thus developing an intense hatred of him and wanting to kill him - however, this is unrealistic, so they overcome this complex by identifying (taking on the male characteristics of) with their father, hence learning the male role

Open question

a question that can have many different answers

Order effects

when people behave differently because of the order in which the conditions are performed - this is a problem in repeated measures designs

Overt

open

Participant observation

the researcher sets up and takes part in the observation of the behaviour under investigation

Peripheral nervous system

    (PNS) the part of the nervous system that relays information from the brain and spinal cord (CNS) to the rest of the body and vice versa, including the somatic nervous system (SNS) and the autonomic nervous system (ANS)

Personal factors

    many, but can include our life experiences and the use of mental scripts

Personality

    your particular temperament, characteristics, traits etc.

Physiology

    how the nervous system and hormones work, how the brain functions, how changes in structure and/or function can affect behaviour

Pie chart

    a circular chart which, like a pie, is divided up, in this case into percentages

Pilot study

    (or pilot survey) a smaller version of a study carried out before the main research to test that the procedures work; essentially a 'dummy run' of your research

Population

    a group of people from whom the sample is drawn

Post-traumatic stress disorder

    (PTSD) an anxiety disorder characterised by persistent experiences of a traumatic event, e.g. war or a car crash - symptoms include nightmares, hallucinations, flash-backs and feelings of insecurity

Prejudice

    an unjustified, usually negative, attitude towards an individual solely based on their membership of a particular category or group or forming an evaluation of someone

Procedural coding

    coding in memory which has become automatic as a result of repetition, e.g. riding a bike

Procedural memory

    is about learning of skills

Projection

    placing unacceptable impulses in yourself onto someone else

Psychiatrist

    someone who has obtained an MD Degree and has completed post-doctoral speciality training in mental and emotional disorders; they can prescribe medications

Psychodynamic model

    argues that all behaviour, including our personality, is understood through internal/mental processes which are often unconscious

Psychometric test

the measurement of knowledge, abilities, attitudes, and traits

Qualitative data

data that describes meaning and experiences

Quantitative data

data that focusses on numerical information

Questionnaire

a set of questions seeking information and opinions

Random variable

something that varies due to chance

Range

a measure of dispersion which involves calculating the difference between the highest and lowest scores

Rationalisation

supplying a logical or rational reason as opposed to the real reason

Reaction formation

taking the opposite belief because the true belief causes anxiety

Realistic conflict theory

emphasises that prejudice stems from direct competition between social groups over valued resources (land, money, jobs etc) - in this theory, often the out-group becomes a scapegoat for any problems occurring, e.g. Sherif and the robbers cave experiments, use of superordinate goals reduces prejudice

Recency

the words last called out during a free recall memory test are usually remembered well

Reconstructive memory

memory changed by circumstances/influences around the event being recalled

Reduction of aggression

many, but include finding the cause, anger management, cognitive behavioural therapy, catharsis, not smacking, education, parents, socialisation etc.

Regression

returning to a previous stage of development

Reliability

the extent to which a piece of research can be repeated using the same procedures and gain similar results

Repeated measures

(between subjects design) an experimental design where two groups/conditions consist of the same participants:

Replication

where something is done again

Representativeness

the degree to which a sample contains those that are typical of the target population

Repression

pulling into the unconscious

Research

the process of gaining knowledge through the examination of data derived empirically

Retrieval

the process of getting information back out of the memory system through recall or recognition

Retrospective

in, or from, the past

Sample

the group of participants taking part in the research

Scapegoat

a person, often innocent, who is blamed and punished for the crimes of others, generally as a way of distracting attention from the real issues

Scattergram

a graphical way of presenting data, to display the relationship between two variables

Schema

cognitive framework or concept that helps organise and interpret information

Semantic memory

involves language and other cognitive concepts and general knowledge

Situational factors

can include things such as the media, the opportunity to engage in aggressive actions, acute arousal or disinhibiting events and situations etc.

Situational variable

a factor in the environment that can unintentionally affect the results of a study; such variables include noise, temperature, smells, and lighting - experimenters should try to control for situational variables so that they don't throw off research results

Social identify theory

(SIT) associated with Tajfel and say that membership of a group gives us the feeling of superiority

Socialisation

starts in the family (primary socialisation) and continues in school (secondary socialisation), this process teaches us social norms and beliefs, including right from wrong, but also allows us to adapt to life in general (the skills of life)

Socialisation process

starts at birth and lasts a life-time; primary socialisation starts in the family and then is added to by secondary socialisation in schools - it teaches us the rights and wrongs of society, gender roles and ways of dealing with life

Social learning theory

(SLT) stresses the role of observation and imitation of others

Standard Deviation

a measure of dispersion that uses the mean in its calculation and which illustrates how scores in a data set are spread about the mean

Standardisation

given the same instructions establishing norms for the population being researched

Stereotyping

a fixed, sometimes simplistic, generalisation about a group or type of person, e.g. blonds are stupid

Storage

refers to the maintenance of information in the memory over time

Stress

a state of mental or emotional strain or tension resulting from adverse or demanding circumstances

Structured observation

the planned watching and recording of behaviours as they occur within a controlled environment; used particularly with infants and young children

Sublimation

acting out unacceptable impulses in a socially acceptable way

Super-ego

tells us what we should and shouldn't do

Superordinate goal

a goal that helps people from opposing sides to come together and work towards a common end result

Suppression

the act of pushing into the unconscious

Survey method

a non-experimental method of research which asks a representative sample of people either oral or written questions to find out about their attitudes, behaviours, beliefs, opinions, and values

True independence

occurs when someone follows their conscience rather than social norms

Unethical

not conforming to approved standards of ethical behaviour

Unstructured observation

the unplanned, informal watching and recording of behaviours as they occur in a natural environment

Validity

refers to whether a study measures what it claims to measure

Variance

the average of the squared differences from the mean

Working memory

short-term memory is working memory and is important in our everyday mental work - 'working' is meant in terms of storing and processing information

Answers to questions and activities for Unit 1

Topic 1: Stages in the research process

Introduction: Questions (page 5)

Q1: Basing decisions on evidence, rather than on private emotions, beliefs or experiences.

Q2: The tendency to base conclusions on private emotions, beliefs or experiences, rather than on objective evidence.

Q3: Psychologists, like all scientists, would adopt an objective approach; they need their research and their research findings to be as free of their own personal values as possible.

Directional and non-directional hypotheses: Questions (page 10)

Q4: a) Directional

Q5: b) Non-directional

Q6: a) Directional

Q7: b) Non-directional

Q8: a) Directional

Q9: a) Directional

Q10: a) Directional

Q11: a) Directional

Examining the data: Calculating the range (page 14)

Q12: 7

Q13: 746

End of Topic 1 test (page 16)

Q14:

1	Choose topic
2	Review literature
3	Form hypothesis
4	Design study
5	Collect data
6	Examine data
7	Reach conclusion
8	Report findings

Q15:

- Improves the researcher's understanding of the topic that they have chosen to study.
- Demonstrates their knowledge to others.
- Brings the reader up-to-date with findings in the topic area.

Q16: d) Null

Q17:

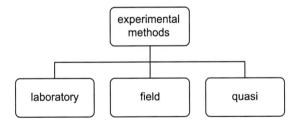

Q18: b) Observation, Case Study and Survey

Q19:

The most accurate measure of central tendency, which uses all of the values in a data set:	mean.
A measure of central tendency, calculated by ranking all values and finding the middle value:	median.
A measure of central tendency, determined by the most frequently occurring value:	mode.
A measure of dispersion, calculated by ranking values and subtracting the lowest value from the highest:	range.
A very accurate measure of dispersion, which uses all of the values in a data set:	standard deviation.

Q20:

1	Title
2	Contents
3	Abstract
4	Introduction
5	Methods
6	Results
7	Discussion
8	Conclusions
9	References
10	Appendices

Topic 2: Experimental methods

Independent and dependent variables: Questions (page 22)

Q1: Sometimes it is easier to start with the variable that is being measured, the dependent variable. Two factors are involved:

- accidents;
- mobile phones.

The variable that will be measured in this case will be the incidence of accidents, therefore:

1. independent variable: mobile phones;
2. dependent variable: accidents.

Q2:

1. Independent variable: classical music playing in background/no music playing in background.
2. Dependent variable: how many stacks of papers each group has made.

Smithers' conclusion would be that playing classical music in the factory will not increase the productivity of workers.

The experimenter effect: Questions (page 26)

Q3: To investigate a confounding variable that they later called the experimenter effect.

Q4: Experimental

Q5: Having two groups of students:

1. one of whom were told that they had bright rats to train;
2. the other being told that they had dull rats to train.

Q6: Reported maze running times.

Q7: They asked students to train rats to run through a maze. They told one group of students that they had been given particularly smart rats that would learn to run the maze quickly. The other group were told that they had dull rats that would be slow to learn to run the maze.

Q8: The smart rat group produced data showing a better maze running performance in comparison to the dull rat group.

Q9: Their students' false expectations about whether a rat was smart or dull had had an effect on the results. The group with the smart rats concluded the result they did either because they put more effort into training their rats to run the maze or because their recording of the rats maze running abilities was affected by expectations.

The Hawthorne effect: Questions (page 27)

Q10: They were interested in the relationship between factory pollution and productivity levels at the Hawthorne electrical generating plant in America. The aim was to investigate participant expectancy. A confounding variable associated with the participant in an experiment, they later renamed it The Hawthorne Effect.

Q11: Field experiment

Q12:

1. Changing the lighting on the factory floor.
2. The times the five female workers could take their breaks.

Q13: Output, or productivity.

Q14: Changing the lighting conditions in the factory, and the times the five female workers could take their breaks they assessed their output for two years.

Q15: They found that when they manipulated their independent variable of worsening working conditions, the women's productivity actually increased rather than decreased.

Q16: On investigation, they discovered that the women had worked harder because they wanted to please the psychologists. It was this 'wanting to please the psychologist' effect that produced their strange results. Knowing that you are taking part in an experiment, and therefore wanting to please, can create The Hawthorne Effect.

Experimental designs: Questions (page 31)

Q17: c) Independent measures

Q18: c) Independent measures

Q19: c) Independent measures

Q20: a) Repeated measures

Q21: c) Independent measures

Q22: b) Matched pairs

Q23: a) Repeated measures

Q24: a) Repeated measures

Samples and populations: Question (page 36)

Q25:

A group of participants who responded to an advertisement in the student newsletter	self-selected.
134 air force cadets comprising percentages reflecting all air cadets in Scotland in terms of ethnic origin, and selected randomly:	stratified.
153 air force cadets comprising 20% from each ethnic origin known to represent all air cadets in Scotland:	quota.
210 air force cadets who have been selected from all air force cadets in Scotland by using a random number table:	random.
100 air force cadets who have been selected as their names appeared fifth or tenth on a troop roster:	systematic.

Types of experiment: Questions (page 37)

Q26: Exposure to testosterone in adult female rats will increase the amount of aggressive behaviours.

Q27: Whether or not adult female rats were injected with testosterone.

Q28: The number of aggressive acts shown.

Q29: Laboratory experiment. It took place in controlled conditions, an IV was manipulated, and a DV measured.

Evaluation of the experiment: Questions (page 38)

Q30:

Advantages of the laboratory experiment	Disadvantages of the laboratory experiment
Control of extraneous variables	Artificial situation, so lacks ecological validity
Cause and effect can be easily established	Experimenter bias can influence behaviours, results conclusions
Procedures can be replicated easily, meaning it is high in reliability	Demand characteristics can give away the aim of the experiment, affecting behaviour, results, conclusions
DV can be measured precisely	Impossible to control for all extraneous variables

Q31:

Advantages of the field experiment	Disadvantages of the field experiment
Situation true to life, so high ecological validity	Low reliability
Participants less influenced by demand characteristics	Reduced validity
Participants less influenced by experimenter effects	Control of extraneous variables
Less stressful than being manipulated in a laboratory	Participants unaware they are being observed (ethics)

Q32:

Advantages of the quasi experiment	Disadvantages of the quasi experiment
Ecological validity	Little control over IV
Participants less influenced by demand characteristics	Establishing cause and effect
Participants less influenced by experimenter effects	Reliability

End of Topic 2 test (page 40)

Q33: All participants take part in all conditions of the independent variable.

Q34: Either of:

- fewer participants are required;
- less affected by differences between participants.

Q35: Either of:

- participants can suffer from order effects, or fatigue, which in turn will affect results;
- if a gap is left between conditions, participants may drop out.

Q36: Participants are split into groups, and each group takes part in a different condition of the independent variable.

Q37: Either of:

- not affected by order effects or fatigue;
- there is no need to leave a gap between conditions as there are different participants for the different conditions.

Q38: Either of:

- can be affected by individual differences between participants (e.g. dyslexia, sight problems, ADHD, high IQ);
- requires more participants.

Q39: Participants are matched in terms of key features, for example age, intelligence, social class etc.

Q40:

Type of experiment	Laboratory	Field	Quasi
Setting	Artificial	Real life	Real life
Replicability	High	Low	Low
Ecological validity	Low	High	High
Control	High	Control only over IV	IV already occurring
Validity	High	Less	Less

Q41: a) A participant variable.

Q42: c) An experimental variable.

Q43: Opportunity sampling consists of taking the sample from people who are **available** at the time the study is carried out and who fit the criteria you are looking for. It is a popular sampling technique as it is relatively **cheap** and quick to do. For example, the researcher may use friends, family or colleagues. However, opportunity sampling can produce a **biased** sample as it is easy for the researcher to choose people from their own social and **cultural** group. This sample would therefore not be **representative** of your target **population** as your friends may have different qualities to people in general.

Q44: Random sampling is a technique which is defined as a sample in which every **member** of the population has an **equal** chance of being chosen. This involves identifying everyone in the target population and then selecting the number of participants that you need in a way which gives everyone in the population an equal chance of being picked. For example, you could get details of all students in your school or college and pick names using a random **number** table or a computer **program**. This is the best technique for providing an **unbiased** representative sample. However, this technique can be very time consuming and is often **impossible** to carry out, particularly when you have a large target population.

Q45: Stratified sampling involves classifying the population into **categories** and then choosing a sample which consists of participants from each one in the same **proportions** as they are in the population. A strength of this technique is that the sample should be representative of the population. However, stratified sampling can be very time consuming as the categories have to be identified and **calculated**. As with **random** sampling, if you do not have details of all of the **people** in your target **population** you would struggle to conduct a stratified sample.

Q46: Self-selected sampling consists of participants becoming part of a study because they **volunteer** when asked or they **respond** to an advert. This technique is useful as it is **quick** and relatively easy to do. It can also reach a **wide** variety of participants. However, the **type** of participants who volunteer may not be representative of the **target** population for a number of reasons.

Topic 3: Non-experimental methods

Observational techniques: Questions (page 48)

Q1:

Advantages of participant observation	Disadvantages of participant observation
behaviours are less prone to misinterpretation because researcher was a participant	observer effect
gives an 'insiders' view	possible lack of objectivity on the part of the observer
opportunity for researcher to become an 'accepted' part of the environment	

Q2:

Advantages of non-participant observation	Disadvantages of non-participant observation
avoidance of observer effect	observer is detached from situation so relies on their perception which may be inaccurate

Q3:

Advantages of structured observation	Disadvantages of structured observation
allows control of extraneous variables	lack of ecological validity
provides a safe environment to study contentious concepts	observer bias
reliability of results can be tested by repeating the study	observer effect
	the implementation of controls may have an effect on behaviour

Q4:

Advantages of unstructured observation	Disadvantages of unstructured observation
gives a broad overview of a situation	only really appropriate as a "first step" to give an overview of a situation/concept/idea
useful where situation/subject matter to be studied is unclear	

Q5:

Advantages of naturalistic observation	Disadvantages of naturalistic observation
particularly good for observing specific subjects	replication due to standardised procedures (designs/instructions)
provides ecologically valid recordings of natural behaviour	
spontaneous behaviours are more likely to happen	

Interview types: Questions (page 51)

Q6:

Advantages of a structured interview	Disadvantages of a structured interview
allows generalisation of results/conclusions to the population from which the sample was drawn	insensitivity to participants' need to express themselves
data is more reliable as the issue is being investigated in a consistent way	restrictive questioning leads to restrictive answers
replication	validity of questions asked - are they the right ones?
standardisation of all questions can give quantifiable data	

Q7:

Advantages of a semi-structured interview	Disadvantages of a semi-structured interview
ability to ask some spontaneous questions is sensitive to participants need to express themselves	its use of an occasional spontaneous question makes these answers difficult to quantify and analyse
data is reasonably reliable	spontaneous questions asked of some and not others can be seen as unfair especially in personnel selection
replication	
standardisation of most questions gives quantifiable data	

Q8:

Advantages of a clinical interview	Disadvantages of a clinical interview
core questions and responses should be reliable and analysed easily	as a result an inability to generalise your findings to a wider population
flexible, responsive and sensitive to participants	difficult to replicate
preparation of core questions should ensure validity	possible interview bias in their use of leading spontaneous questions

Q9:

Advantages of an unstructured interview	Disadvantages of an unstructured interview
flexible, responsive and sensitive to participants	as a result, an inability to generalise your findings to a wider population
highly detailed and ecologically valid qualitative data	difficult to replicate
relaxed and natural for those taking part	possible interview bias in 'selective' use of leading and spontaneous questions

Advantages and disadvantages of the survey method: Question (page 54)

Q10: a) advantage

Q11: b) Disadvantage

Q12: a) Advantage

Q13: a) Advantage

Q14: b) Disadvantage

Q15: b) Disadvantage

Q16: a) Advantage

Q17: a) Advantage

Advantages and disadvantages of the case study method: Question (page 57)

Q18:

Advantages of the case study method	Disadvantages of the case study method
detailed in-depth information got of a single case concerning a person, a family, an organisation or an event	cannot generalise results
high ecological validity	interviewer/observer bias
sensitive to the individual, and sensitive issues concerning the individual	reliability of information collected by self-report
	replication impossible, to confirm earlier results

End of Topic 3 test (page 59)

Q19: c) There is no independent variable involved.

Q20: b) Observational method

Q21: c) a covert observation.

Q22: a) Survey method

Q23: c) Interview method

Q24: a) survey method.

Q25: b) A case study

Q26: a) high ecological validity.

Topic 4: Calculating/presenting data using descriptive statistics

Scattergrams: Notebook exercise (page 68)

Q1: To discover whether there is a correlation between the number of hours spent socialising and assessment scores, you would tabulate the data as shown in the question and then plot the pairings onto a scattergram.

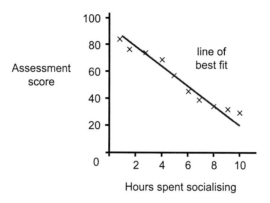

A scattergram illustrating the statistical relationship between hours spent socialising and marks scored in an assessment

What type of correlation is shown; is it positive or negative? Why is this the case? Would you assess the correlation as weak, moderate, strong or perfect?

The patterns that our plots form indicate whether a correlation exists. Number of 'hours spent socialising' is the x-axis value, plotted on the horizontal, and 'assessment score' is the y-axis value, plotted on the vertical.

Our research is investigating the correlational or alternate hypothesis H_A:

There is a negative relationship between the number of hours a student spent socialising and their subsequent assessment score.

Consequently, our null hypothesis is H_O:

That there will not be a negative relationship between the number of hours a student spent socialisingand their subsequent assessment score.

Our alternate (or research) hypothesis, H_A, is *one-tailed*. This is because it is predicting the direction of expected relationship, i.e., as the number of hours spent socialising increases, a student's assessment score should comparatively decrease. It is predicting a *negative correlation* or relationship.

However, correlations can only infer a positive or negative relationship between its covariates. No cause-effect conclusions can be reached. This is the province of the experimental method. A correlation scale is sometimes useful in analysis. A scale of +1 to 0 to -1 is often used where the scale shows the strength of relationship from very positive (+1), through to no relationship (0), to very negative (-1).

Overlapping data curves: Questions (page 74)

Q2: Something like H_1: *altruism in children can be encouraged as a consequence of observing it in others.*

Q3: The control condition of the IV was one group watching neutral videos; the experimental condition of the IV was the other group watching altruistic videos.

Q4: Recorded observations of helping behaviour seen in the children over a four-week period.

End of Topic 4 test (page 75)

Q5: c) Descriptive statistics

Q6: a) central tendency.

Q7: c) 12.6

Q8: b) 12

Q9: a) Range

Q10: c) A correlation

Q11: a) One-tailed

Q12: b) Scattergram

Q13: a) Raw data

Topic 5: Choice of method and ethical guidelines

Experimental methods: Questions (page 78)

Q1: The laboratory experiment is the one with the most **control** over extraneous variables, so cause and effect are easier to establish. This also increases the **validity** (ability to measure what is intended to be measured) and **reliability** (ability to repeat study and obtain very similar results). However, the close proximity of the researcher may result in experimenter **bias**, and the procedures and apparatus used may result in **demand** characteristics. These may both interfere with the validity and reliability of results. The biggest issue with the laboratory experiment is its artificiality, which means it is low in **ecological** validity.

Q2: A field experiment is an experiment that is conducted in a natural setting. In field experiments, the participants are not usually **aware** that they are participating in an experiment. An independent variable is still **manipulated**. Field experiments are usually **high** in ecological validity and may avoid demand characteristics as the participants are unaware of being studied. However, in field experiments, it is much harder to control confounding variables and they are usually time consuming and **expensive** to conduct. In field experiments, it is not usually possible to gain **informed** consent from the participants and it is difficult to **debrief** the participants.

Q3: A quasi experiment is where the independent variable is not manipulated by the researcher but occurs **naturally**. These experiments are often called **natural** experiments. In a quasi experiment, the researcher takes advantage of pre-existing conditions, for example an **event** that the researcher has no control over such as a participants' occupation. A strength of some quasi experiments is that participants are often unaware that they are taking part in an investigation and they may not be as **artificial** as laboratory experiments. However, it is argued that the use of quasi experiments means that it is harder to establish **causal** relationships because the independent variable is not being directly manipulated by the researcher.

Non-experimental methods: Questions (page 79)

Q4: These are investigations where the researcher observes a situation and **records** what happens but does **not** manipulate an independent variable. Observational studies therefore tend to be high in ecological validity as there is no intervention and if the observation is **covert**, the method avoids problems with demand characteristics. A main **strength** of observational studies is that they get to see how participants actually behave rather than what they say they do. A further strength of observational studies is that they offer ways of studying behaviour when there are **ethical** problems with manipulating variables. On the other hand observational studies are difficult to **replicate**, so are low on reliability. Cause and effect relationships **cannot** be established because of low control over extraneous variables. There is also the problem of observer **bias** with observational studies. A number of ethical issues can arise with observational studies including problems with a lack of informed **consent** and invasion of **privacy**.

Q5: Surveys use questionnaires, usually in a highly structured written form. Questionnaires can contain both open and **closed** questions and participants record their own answers. Surveys allow a large **sample** of people to be studied, and can obtain information about **attitudes** and opinions.

Interviews are usually **one-to-one** and the interviewer records the responses. Interviews can be structured with a **predetermined** set of questions or **unstructured**, whereby there is opportunity for more detailed information to be provided.

However, in both surveys and interviews, participants may not respond **truthfully**, either because they cannot remember or because they wish to present themselves in a **socially** acceptable manner. Social **desirability** bias happens when participants answer to portray themselves well. Furthermore, questions must be unambiguous, clear and should not **lead** respondents to answer in a particular way.

Closed questions are questions which provide a **limited** choice. Such questions provide **quantitative** data which is easy to analyse. However, these questions do not allow the participant to give such in-depth insights. **Open** questions are those questions which invite the respondent to provide more detail and provide **qualitative** data. Although these types of questions are more difficult to analyse they can produce more in-depth responses, provide the 'why' of behaviour.

Q6: These are forms of qualitative, **descriptive** research that is used to look at individuals or a small **group**. Researchers collect data about participants using observations, interviews, protocols, tests, examinations of records, and collections of writing samples. This is called the compilation of a case **history**. However, case studies cannot be **generalised** beyond the person or small group being studied, and they can be biased due to the close relationship that can build up between researcher and researched. They are often the only way to study very rare, or **unique** cases, like multiple personality disorder, but **retrospective** data can be unreliable.

Matching topic to method: Question (page 81)

Q7:

1. e - laboratory
2. a and d
3. b - extra marks if you identified 'covert'!
4. c

Possible ethical concerns could include:

1. Causing distress to animals.
2. Dale has to ensure no breach of confidentiality when reporting on Tara's behaviour. Plus, can Tara, given her illness, give informed consent?
3. Participants cannot give informed consent. Participants will be under 16 (vulnerable group) and parents may not have been asked for their consent.
4. David is asking respondents to give information about illegal activities, which may cause distress. Given that they are under 16 years of age, he will have needed to ask permission from the respondents' parents prior to conducting the survey.

Ethical Guidelines and Code of Conduct: Questions (page 83)

Q8:   1. Risk, 2. Valid consent, 5. Deception, 6. Debriefing

Q9:   1. Risk, 2. Valid consent, 5. Deception, 6. Debriefing

Q10: 4. Giving advice

Q11: 1. Risk, 2. Valid consent, 5. Deception, 6. Debriefing

Q12: 1. Risk, 2. Valid consent, 5. Deception, 6. Debriefing

End of Topic 5 test (page 85)

Q13: a) Experimental

Q14: Field experiment

Q15: b) Quantitative

Q16: Frequencies (quantities) of helping behaviour.

Q17: The experimental situation needs to be natural so that people behave naturally, i.e. they cannot be aware they are being experimented on. However, an IV (drunk or ill) needs to be controlled and a DV (helping behaviour) measured.

Q18: a) Experimental

Q19: Field or quasi experiment

Q20: b) Quantitative

Q21: Scores on reading tests.

Q22: Field experiment: children will behave more naturally in their normal classrooms (increasing validity) than they would in a laboratory while the experimenter still has control of the IV (increasing reliability).
Quasi-experiment: where the researcher takes advantage of phonics-based reading programmes being introduced in one school while other schools are using other methods (these are the conditions of the IV occurring naturally).

Q23: b) Non-experimental

Q24: Survey and/or interview

Q25: a) Qualitative

Q26: Survey or interview responses.

Q27: Survey: can gain superficial data on opinions quickly and to a large sample. Note that a survey would use primarily quantitative data if using only closed-questions.
Interview: can gain detailed information on opinions and the reasons for them.

Q28: a) Experimental

Q29: Laboratory experiment

Q30: b) Quantitative

Q31: Scores on short-term memory tests.

Q32: Memory tests can be administered in a controlled environment, with minimal interference from possible confounding variables.

Q33: a) Experimental

Q34: Laboratory experiment

Q35: b) Quantitative

Q36: Measures of cognitive ability.

Q37: A controlled environment where length of time asleep can be accurately measured using appropriate apparatus (IV) and cognitive tests administered (DV).
Participants could also be interviewed on their views of their own cognitive ability after sleep which would involve collecting some qualitative data as well.

Q38: b) Non-experimental

Q39: Case study

Q40: a) Qualitative

Q41: Interview data

Q42: This is a study of one individual, so this is the best method to use so that rich, descriptive, idiographic information can be gathered. However, the results cannot be generalised beyond this person.
The participant could also undergo IQ tests, or other tests of conginition, which would involve collecting some quantitative data as well.

Q43: b) Non-experimental

Q44: Observation (covert)

Q45: b) Quantitative

Q46: Quantities of aggressive behaviours will be counted.

Q47: Observing children in the playground after they have played Minecraft would be more ethical than experimenting with this vulnerable group. Aggressive behaviours displayed in the playground could be recorded on an observation checklist which has been drawn up before the observation. Using covert observation will increase the ecological validity of the research as children will not be aware they are being observed (although permission from parents should be sought beforehand).

Q48: Risk, valid consent.

Q49: Risk

Q50: Risk, valid consent, debriefing.

Topic 6: Research investigation

Introduction: Question (page 98)

Q1:

1. Always begin with the psychological approach your research belongs in. . .
2. . . . then the area. . .
3. . . . then the specific topic.
4. Note format of in-text referencing. Plus, these should ALL appear in a References page.
5. The first background studies contextualise the general background to your study. You then move to research that is more like your own, ending with the study you are replicating.
6. Link between your own research and background research.

Possible marks	Included in example	Actual marks
Research set in its theoretical context. Background studies. *Up to 8 marks*	• Approach, topic and specific topic outlined and defined. • Six background theories and studies explained, all relevant to the topic. (only 5 marks left, so 5/5)	• 3 • 5
Aim and hypothesis *Up to 2 marks*	• Aim and clear link to background research. • Accurately stating the experimental or alternative hypothesis including clear expression of variables.	• 1 • 1

Total marks for Introduction section: 10/10

Method: Question (page 100)

Q2:

1. This student used a correlation, which you do not need to do.
2. This is where the writer of this report has outlined control of variables.
3. Please note that the marker will check Appendices to see that all materials have been included. If not, marks may be deducted.

Possible marks	Included in example	Actual marks
1 mark for identifying your method and justifying why you have chosen this method, including identification of design (where appropriate).	Yes	1
1 mark for describing research variables.	Yes	1
1 mark for describing extraneous / confounding / controlled variables.	Yes	1
1 mark for identifying the sampling method you have chosen, with a justification for your choice; and a description of your participants.	Yes	1
1 mark for identifying the materials you used, as well as where these can be found in appendices (to allow for replication).	Yes	1
1 mark for fully describing your procedure.	Yes	1

Total marks for Method section: /6

Results: Question (page 104)

Q3:

Possible marks	Included in example	Actual marks
2 marks for justifying your choice of statistical procedure(s).	**Yes**	2
1 mark for accurately carrying out appropriate statistical procedures, as demonstrated in your calculations (which must be included in appendices).	**Yes** (the calculations would be in the Appendices, but we will assume they are correct)	1
2 marks for presenting your data in an appropriate format(s). To gain full marks, a table and graph must be included, with appropriate title and accurate labels and legend (if appropriate). These must provide enough information to enable interpretation.	**Yes**	2
1 mark for an accurate statement on whether the results support or refute your hypothesis.	**Yes**	1

Total marks for Results section: 6/6

Discussion: Question (page 107)

Q4:

Possible marks	Included in example	Actual marks
1 mark for explaining the ways in which they confirm or refute the research hypothesis, or are inconclusive.	Yes	1
1 mark for explaining relationships between research variables.	Yes	1
1 mark for explaining the possible effect of variables other than the research variables.	Yes	1
1 mark for explaining the ways in which your results are the same or different from other research results.	The results are only related to one theory (Craik and Lockhart's), but to no other research. 1 mark in total	1/2
1 mark for explaining the relationship between your own research results and the results of previous research.	The results are only related to one theory (Craik and Lockhart's), but to no other research. 1 mark in total	1/2
1 mark for drawing out and relating the implications of your own research findings in terms of further research or real world applications.	Yes	1
1 mark for drawing conclusions about points of analysis.	Yes	1
1 mark for giving any other acceptable response.	Yes	1
1 mark can be awarded for each relevant point of evaluation that includes evidence of a reason for the judgement. Evaluate must be specific to your own research study and supporting reasons must be given for evaluative points made, e.g. "this is unreliable because...", or "this is a strength because...".	• Ethical strengths with reasons; • sampling technique with reasons; • sample size with reasons; • strength of design, with reasons.	• 1 • 1 • 1 • 1

Total marks for Discussion section: 11/12

Topic 7: Research test

Research test (page 112)

Q1:

1. *Choose topic* - This is where the researcher identifies an area of interest from which they would like to find some answers. This leads to the desire to learn more about the topic, and to...

2. *Review the literature* - Here, other studies in the area of interest are read to improve understanding of the area and to bring the researcher up-to-date with the current research. This should help narrow the focus of the area of interest, enabling the researcher to...

3. *Formulate a hypothesis* - In other words, to make a prediction about what may be expected to happen as a result of carrying out the research. It is the null hypothesis that is tested: this is the prediction that the research will result in no change happening between the variables. When the variables have been established, the researcher can then...

4. *Design the study* - The choice is between experimental designs: laboratory, field or quasi; or non-experimental designs: case study, survey, correlational, interview or observational. Once this has been established, the researcher can...

5. *Collect data* - This can be in numerical form (quantitative) or in descriptive form (qualitative). If the data that is collected is numerical, the researcher can...

6. *Examine the data* - This may be achieved by using descriptive statistics, including measures of central tendency (averages) and measures of dispersion (how the data is spread). Inferential statistics will often be calculated to test for significance. Once the data has been calculated, the researcher can...

7. *Reach a conclusion* - In other words, they will try to explain the implications of the data to real life. Finally, the researcher will...

8. *Report the findings* - The researcher compiles a report about their research procedures and findings in a specified format. It can then be published, understood and replicated by peers, who may potentially discover an area of interest of their own, so the research process begins anew.

Q2: This was a **field experiment**.

Its key features are that it is carried out in a natural environment and people are often unaware that they are taking part in an experiment. However, the IV is still controlled by the experimenter. In this instance the IV was the two conditions: student-centred and teacher-centred teaching methods.

Advantages are that people behave naturally, as the environment is not artificial; in other words, it has high ecological validity. There is a reasonable amount of control of the IV and DV, but not as much as there is in a laboratory, so the results are less reliable (unlikely that the same results could be found if the study was to be repeated) and valid (the researcher can be less certain that it is the IV that is causing changes to occur to the DV: it may be the effect of extraneous/confounding environmental variables). If participants are unaware that they are taking part in research, then the ethical principle of informed consent is being breached.

Q3: The sampling method is **opportunity sampling**.

This has the advantage that participants are easy to find because they are chosen from those that are readily available to the researcher, but it is always biased because not everyone in the population has an equal chance of being selected. The sample is therefore unlikely to be representative of the target population.

Q4: Any one from:

- risk - this relates to 'doing no harm' to participants, psychologically or physically;
- valid consent - all research participants should be aware of the research aims and implications;
- confidentiality - information obtained from and about a participant during an investigation is confidential;
- giving advice - advise participants to speak with someone who is qualified to deal with any concerns;
- deception - research should always be designed to maintain the dignity and autonomy of participants as far as is possible;
- debriefing - it is important for participants to be given the chance to discuss the research process when procedures are complete.

Q5: Condition 1:

Mean: $(78 + 32 + 42 + 53 + 32 + 78 + 98 + 67 + 87 + 67) / 10 = 634 / 10 = 63.4$

Median: 32, 32, 42, 53, 67, 67, 78, 78, 87, 98 - the middle two values are both 67 so the median is 67

Modes: 32, 67, 78 - all occur twice each so this data set is said to be multi modal

Condition 2

Mean: $(65 + 65 + 78 + 86 + 87 + 97 + 67 + 75 + 57 + 88) / 10 = 765 / 10 = 76.5$

Median: 57, 65, 65, 67, 75, 78, 86, 87, 88, 97 - the middle two values are 75 and 78 so the median is $(75+78) / 2 = 76.5$

Mode: 65 - this is the only value to occur more than once in the data set

Q6: The survey method can collect a lot of information from a large sample because it is cheap to administer and distribute.

It collects mainly quantitative data which is easy to analyse.

It does this by means of the use of closed questions that are quick and easy to answer, ...

... but which do not provide much, if any, detail.

A big problem with surveys is the rate of attrition which means that many people do not respond, especially when a survey is conducted by post.

You will be awarded marks for any other valid expanded evaluative point.

Answers to questions and activities for Unit 2

Topic 1: Sleep and dreams (mandatory topic)

Circadian rhythms (page 133)

Q1: **Circadian** rhythms have a cycle of about 24 hours, such as the **infradian**. There are five stages of sleep, one of which is **REM** sleep. **Endogenous** rhythms are those located within the body. The main human exogenous pacemaker is the **suprachiasmic**nucleus. External factors, such as light, **noise**, clocks, etc., are known as exogenous **zeitgebers**.

Suprachismic nucleus (page 133)

Q2: **Circadian** rhythms have a cycle of about 24 hours. Rhythms which have a cycle of longer than 24 hours are called **infradian** rhythms, e.g. the menstrual cycle. Cycles of less than 24 hours are controlled by **ultradian** rhythms, e.g. the 90 minute sleep cycle. There are five stages of sleep, one of which is **REM** sleep. Research into ultradian rhythms include the REM and dreaming study by Dement and **Kleitman** in 1957.

Endogenous rhythms are those located within the body. The main human endogenous pacemaker is the **suprachiasmic** nucleus. External factors, such as light, **noise**, clocks etc., are known as exogenous **zeitgebers**. **Insomnia** and sleep deprivation are both examples of sleep disorders associated with disruption of biological rhythms. Effects include deficits in health, task performance and **memory**.

Q3: The SCN obtains information about **light** from the optic nerve in the eye: in the morning, there is more light; in the evening, there is less light. The SCN then sends a **signal** to the pineal gland.

When there is lots of light, the pineal gland **inhibits** the production of **melatonin** ('sleepy hormone'). When a decrease in light is detected, the pineal gland **stimulates** the production of melatonin (usually at night). Melatonin induces sleep by inhibiting brain mechanisms responsible for **wakefulness**.

The SCN therefore controls the **sleep-wake** cycle by inhibiting the production of melatonin during the day.

Test your knowledge on the biology of sleep and dreams (page 134)

Q4: c) the suprachiasmic nucleus.

Q5: c) body temperature continues to fluctuate when it is removed.

Q6: a) Increase

Q7: b) Decrease

Q8: a) People have reduced sleep quantity after the spring time change, and increased sleep quantity after the autumn time change.

Q9:

Sleep efficiency:	ratio of total sleep time in bed compared with amount of actual sleep.
Ultradian rhythms:	occur more than once in a 24 hour cycle, including sleep-wake cycle.
Light and temperature:	types of exogenous zeitgebers.
Suprachiasmic nucleus:	part of the brain responsible for our biological clock.
Melatonin:	a hormone, derived from serotonin, which plays a role in sleep.
Pineal gland:	a pea-sized organ in the brain that secretes the hormone melatonin.
Circadian rhythms:	daily cycle of biological activity influenced by environmental variation.
Insomnia:	a sleep disorder that results in feeling sleepy at all times of the day.

Introduction to sleep and dreams: Dement and Kleitman questions (page 135)

Q10:

Strengths	Weaknesses
Ecologically valid studies have confirmed Dement and Kleitman's findings.	Some participants dreamt in NREM sleep.
Has led to the development of other research into the purpose of sleeping and dreaming.	Low ecological validity.

Cognitive approach to sleep and dreams: Information processing question (page 144)

Q11:

Perception:	the internal process by which an organism becomes aware of and interprets external stimuli.
Attention:	the ability to 'tune out' irrelevant information, and focus only on the relevant.
Language:	a formal system of communication which uses a combination of words and/or symbols, whether written or spoken.
Memory:	the ability to take in and store information, as well as to retrieve it when required.
Thinking:	the process of using knowledge and information to make plans, interpret, and constructively interact with and make predictions about the world in general.

End of topic 1 test (page 151)

Q12: d) 90 minutes.

Q13: c) 7.5 hours.

Q14: Rapid Eye Movement

Q15: Any two from:

- disorientation;
- memory difficulties;
- hallucinations;
- paranoia.

Q16: b) There is a link between family conflict in childhood and insomnia in adulthood.

Q17: c) Both of the above.

Q18: Secondary insomnia is associated with stress, age or **medical** conditions. Primary insomnia has no obvious **cause** so appears to be an illness in its own right. It is by far the most **common** form of insomnia.

Q19:

Cognitive behavioural therapy:	tries to restore restorative sleep by changing faulty cognitions.
Medicine:	can help regulate the sleep-wake cycle (no restorative sleep).
Stimulus control therapy:	creates positive associations with sleep cues and other advice.

Q20: b) input > information processing > output

Q21: a) senses > perception, attention, language, memory, thinking > behaviour

Q22: c) a pre-existing mental structure acquired on the basis of experience.

Q23: b) the function of sleep is to process information acquired during the day.

Q24: d) All of the above

Q25: c) what the mind is doing while we sleep.

Q26: b) condensation.

Q27: d) All of the above.

Q28: b) False

Q29: c) the unconscious content of the dream.

Q30: a) the actual content of the dream.

Q31: d) secondary elaboration.

Q32: b) False

Q33: b) in-depth data is gained over a period of time - the data is valid.

Q34: a) where information is pushed into the unconscious mind.

Q35: a) a stimulant drug

Q36: c) 6 hours after consumption

Q37: d) melatonin

Q38: a) adrenaline

Q39: b) suprachiasmic nucleus

Q40: c) blue light

Q41: c) melatonin

Topic 2: Memory (optional topic)

End of Topic 2 test (page 182)

Q1: a) information

Q2: a) encoding.

Q3: b) retrieval.

Q4: c) storage.

Q5: d) 1 second

Q6: c) 7

Q7: b) Baddeley and Hitch

Q8: c) sound

Q9: a) long-term

Q10: a) trace decay

Q11:

2 answers:

- a) trace decay
- b) interference
- c) context-dependent
- d) state-dependent

c) and d)

Q12: b) interference

Q13: c) context-dependent

Topic 3: Stress (optional topic)

Biological approach to stress: GAS questions (page 192)

Q1: a) True

Q2: b) False

Q3: b) False

Q4: a) True

Q5: a) True

Q6: b) False

Q7: a) True

Q8: a) True

Activity on immunosuppression (page 198)

Q9:

The HPA axis is the body's "stress system" which controls levels of cortisol and other important stress related hormones, as well as the **immune system**. Any stress lasting longer than a few minutes results in increased levels of **cortisol** being released from the adrenal cortex. This happens as a result of activation of the pituitary gland which causes the release adrenocorticotrophic hormone (ACTH), which in turn causes the adrenal cortex to release cortisol.

Prolonged release of ACTH causes the **adrenal cortex** to increase in size (presumably to cope with a greater need for cortisol production), whereas long-term ACTH deficiency causes it to shrink.

This system is referred to as the hypothalamic-pituitary-adrenal axis (or HPA axis). The ultimate result of the HPA axis activation is to increase levels of cortisol in the blood during times of stress. Cortisol's main role is in releasing glucose into the bloodstream in order to facilitate the **"fight-or-flight"** response. It also suppresses and modulates the immune system, digestive system and reproductive system.

Stress causes an increased overall cortisol output. During **chronic** stress, changes occur to areas in the brain resulting in increased sustained activation of the HPA axis. Whether or not chronic stress results in high or low cortisol output depends on the nature of the threat, the time since onset, and the person's response to the situation.

Long-term stress can lead to exhaustion, due to the **suppression** of the HPA axis in the brain.

Sources of stress questions (page 205)

Q10: A life event is something that rarely happens while a daily hassle happens every day.

Q11: Parents, health, teachers, workload, smoking, appearance, weather etc.

Q12: A list of 43 items that are considered significant life changes.

Q13: The study was androcentric, as it included only male participants and findings cannot be generalised to women —is one weakness —you may have come up with another. Remember to explain your weakness —say why it is a weakness.

Q14: Rahe et al

Q15: Daily hassles have more of an effect on health than life events.

Q16:

A weakness of this study is that it used the self-report method of questionnaires. This means that participants may answer in ways that make them appear in a good light, which makes results invalid.

A strength would be that using a questionnaire allowed the collection of quantifiable data, which means that results can be analysed statistically.

Q17: Because both studies found the same thing —that there is a link between daily hassles and the development of health problems.

SIT: Turning negatives into positives activity (page 214)

Q18:

Focusing on the problems —we dwell on the problem, instead of the situation.	Always assume that most problems have a solution, and ask 'How could I make this situation better?
Expecting the worst —we always expect the worst, which only promotes anxiety.	Always give yourself a more positive thinking outcome. 'What can I do to prevent myself from thinking the worst?'
Thinking in absolutes —we often exaggerate reality.	Replace the exaggerations with more accurate and positive words. 'I often expect the worst to happen, but I can change that.'

End of Topic 3 test (page 218)

Q19: b) emotional

Q20: a) angry

Q21: c) given to the positive effects of stress.

Q22: a) physical and psychological illness.

Q23: b) chronic stressor.

Q24: a) Yes

Q25: Any four from:

- chronic heart disease;
- type II diabetes;
- stroke;
- depression;
- anxiety;
- asthma;

- respiratory problems;
- cancer;
- digestive problems;
- etc.

Q26: d) internal

Q27: c) faulty thinking and poor perceptions.

Q28: Cognitive behavioural therapy

Q29: b) Meichenbaum

Q30: b) Conceptualisation, skill acquisition and application.

Topic 4: Depression (optional topic)

Major Depressive Disorder (page 225)

Q1: Jessica shows all of the symptoms of MDD, except for weight loss and loss of appetite.

Persistent Depressive Disorder (page 227)

Q2: John shows all of the diagnostic criteria for PDD. The diagnosis is likely to be PDD, and not MDD, because the symptoms have lasted for over 2 years.

MDD and PDD compare and contrast activity (page 227)

Q3:

MDD only	Both MDD and PDD	PDD only
All of the symptoms of MDD are present in PDD, but in PDD they have persisted for at least 2 years.	• Depressed mood most of the day, nearly every day, as indicted by either subjective report (e.g. feels sae, empty, hopeless) or observation made by others (e.g. appears tearful. • Markedly diminished interest or pleasure in all, or almost all, activities most of the day, nearly every. • Significant weight loss when not dieting or weight gain (e.g. a change of more than 5% of body weight in a month) or an increase in appetite nearly every day. • Insomnia or hypersomnia nearly every day. • Feelings of worthlessness or excessive or inappropriate guilt (which may be delusional) nearly every day. • Diminished ability to concentrate, or indecisiveness, nearly every day. • Recurrent thoughts of death (not just fear of dying), recurrent suicidal ideation without a specific plan, or a suicide attempt or a specific plan for committing suicide.	• During the two year period, the symptoms have not been absent for less than two months at a time. • The criteria for a major depressive order may be continuously present for the two years. • The individual has never experienced a manic or hypomanic episode. • The criteria for cyclothymic disorder has never been met. • The criteria for schizoaffective disorder, schizophrenia, delusional disorder or other psychotic disorder does not better explain the disorder. • Drug abuse or another medical disorder do not explain the symptoms.

Evaluation of the role of neurochemistry in depression (page 230)

Q4:

Strengths	Weaknesses
• • SSRIs, which are medication given for depression and target serotonin, are successful in treating the symptoms of depression, supporting the idea that there is a link between serotonin and depression.	• There is no way to measure serotonin levels in the living brain. Therefore, there have not been any studies supporting the serotonin explanation of depression. • Blood levels of serotonin are measurable —and have been shown to be lower in people who suffer from depression —but researchers don't know if blood levels reflect the brain's level of serotonin. • It is not known whether the dip in serotonin causes the depression, or the depression causes serotonin levels to drop. • Medications that work on serotonin levels —SSRIs (selective serotonin reuptake inhibitors) and SNRIs (serotonin and norepinephrine reuptake inhibitors) —reduce symptoms of depression, but exactly how they work is not fully understood.

Evaluation of role of noradrenaline in depression (page 231)

Q5:

Strengths	Weaknesses
• People who take medication for anxiety, which lower levels of noradrenaline, sometimes develop depression.	• Drugs which treat levels of noradrenaline increase these levels very quickly, but the symptoms of depression can take two to three weeks to decrease.

Evaluation of SSRIs (page 233)

Q6:

Strengths	Weaknesses
	• Treat the symptoms of depression, not the cause.
	• Are unsuccessful in 10-20% of cases.
	• They can have side effects, such as:
	○ Insomnia
	○ Headaches
	○ Rash
• Have fewer side effects than other medications for depression.	○ Blurred vision
	○ Drowsiness
• Are effective in 80-90% of cases.	○ Dry mouth
	○ Agitation or nervousness
• Some people experience no side effects and others find they disappear after a few weeks.	○ Feeling dizzy
	○ Pains in the muscles or joints
• The majority of SSRIs are not physically addictive (see exception for Paroxetine).	○ Upset stomach, nausea or diarrhoea
	○ Reduced sexual desire
• Not dangerous if overdose is taken.	○ Problems with erection or ejaculation
	• The SSRI, Paroxetine, is associated with withdrawal effects, such as nausea, insomnia, agitation and dizziness.
	• Treats the symptoms, not the causes of depression.
	• Some people (especially children or young adults) can have increased thoughts of suicide

Evaluation of SNRIs (page 234)

Q7:

Strengths	Weaknesses
<ul><li>Have fewer side effects than other medications for depression</li><li>Are effective in 80-90% of cases</li><li>Some people experience no side effects and others find they disappear after a few weeks.</li><li>SNRIs are not physically addictive</li><li>Not dangerous if overdose is taken.</li></ul>	<ul><li>Treat the symptoms of depression, not the cause</li><li>Are unsuccessful in 10-20% of cases</li><li>They can have side effects, such as:<ul><li>Insomnia</li><li>Headaches</li><li>Rash</li><li>Blurred vision</li><li>Drowsiness</li><li>Dry mouth</li><li>Agitation or nervousness</li><li>Feeling dizzy</li><li>Pains in the muscles or joints</li><li>Upset stomach, nausea or diarrhoea</li><li>Reduced sexual desire</li><li>Problems with erection or ejaculation</li><li>Excessive sweating</li></ul></li></ul>

Evaluation of tricyclics (page 235)

Q8:

Strengths	Weaknesses
	• Cause side effects, which although similar to those found with SRRIs and SNRIs, are more severe and more likely, such as:
	○ Blurred vision
	○ Dry mouth
	○ Constipation
	○ Weight gain or loss
	○ Low blood pressure on standing
• Useful in cases where other anti-depressants have failed.	○ Rash
	○ Hives
• Helps 65% of patients	○ Increased heart rate
	○ Reduced sex drive
	○ Difficulty with urinating
	• Associated with withdrawal symptoms, such as nausea, headache and dizziness
	• Interacts with blood pressure medication
	• Is not effective with 35% of patients
	• Associated with heart problems in some

Evaluation of MAOIs (page 236)

Q9:

Strengths	Weaknesses
	• MAOIs also affect other neurotransmitters in the brain and digestive system, causing side effects, which include:
	◦ Dry mouth
	◦ Nausea, diarrhoea or constipation
	◦ Headache
	◦ Drowsiness
	◦ Insomnia
	◦ Dizziness or lightheadedness
	◦ Involuntary muscle jerks
	◦ Low blood pressure
	◦ Reduced sexual desire or difficulty reaching orgasm
	◦ Weight gain
	◦ Difficulty starting a urine flow
• Can be useful in cases where other anti-depressants have not worked.	◦ Muscle cramps
	◦ Prickling or tingling sensation in the skin (paresthesia)
	• As well as side effects, there are safety concerns associated with MAOIs, which need careful monitoring by the person taking them and their GP, for example:
	◦ Dangerous interactions with certain food and drinks containing high levels of tyramine (an amino acid that regulates blood pressure, found in cheese, sauerkraut, cured meats, draft beer and soy products. The interaction of tyramine with MAOIs can cause dangerously high blood pressure, which means that those taking them should exclude these products from their diets.
	◦ Can cause serious reactions when taken with other medication, such as other antidepressants, pain-killers, cold and flu treatments, allergy medication and some herbal treatments.
	• Takes two to three weeks for it to affect the symptoms of depression.
	• Treats the symptoms, not the causes of depression.

Evaluation of ECT as a treatment for depression (page 238)

Q10:

Strengths	Weaknesses
• Studies have shown that ECT works for many people who have treatment-resistant depression. One study of 39 people with treatment-resistant depression compared the effects of an antidepressant with ECT. After two to three weeks, 71% of people who received ECT had a positive response to treatment. But only 28% who received the antidepressant had a positive response after four weeks of treatment (Acta Psychiatrica Scandinavia 1997). • ECT can often work quickly, which can be lifesaving.	• ECT is associated with side effects, the most common of which is short-term memory loss. However, some people report that they have long-term memory loss, as well. ECT also causes a brief rise in heart rate and blood pressure during the procedure, so it may not be recommended in people with unstable heart problems. • 50% or more of the people who receive this treatment will relapse within several months if there is no subsequent treatment (for example, antidepressants) to prevent relapse.

Cognitive biases —name that bias! (page 240)

Q11: b) Overgeneralisation

Q12: e) Minimisation

Q13: f) Personalisation

Q14: c) Catastrophising

Q15: d) Magnification

Q16: a) Polarised thinking

Change the negative to a positive activity (page 242)

Q17:

Negative thought	Bias involved	Rational, Positive Thought
"I got into trouble at school today. I just know they are going to exclude me tomorrow."	Catastrophising	"I did something at school today that I'm not proud of, but everyone makes mistakes and it's not the end of the world! I'll try harder tomorrow not to make the same mistake again."
"My friend looked at her watch when I was talking today. She must think I'm boring."	Personification	"I can't know for certain why she looked at her watch when I was talking. If she thought I was boring, she probably wouldn't come over to talk to me everyday!"
"I got an award at assembly yesterday, but that's no big deal. I'm not really that good a student."	Minimisation	"I worked really hard to get that award! My work definitely paid off."
"I only got a B in my psychology test. I always fail. I shouldn't even have tried."	Polarisation	"Even though a B isn't what I was hoping for on that test, it's still pretty good! Next time I could study even more and see if I can do even better!"
"I can't believe I ate that Mars bar! I'm so fat and ugly."	Maximisation	"Eating one Mars bar isn't the end of the world, and is not going to make any difference to what I look like, or my worth as a person. As long as I eat healthily most of the time."
"Another student called ma a name once today. People are always making fun of me."	Overgeneralisation	"A student teased me today, but that's his problem! Lots of other people are friends with me. I don't need to dwell on one negative experience."

Evaluation of Beck's cognitive theory of depression (page 246)

Q18:

Strengths	Weaknesses
• Results of study by Alloy et al support Beck's theory that depression is caused by faulty thinking styles. • There is much other research evidence supporting Beck's theory. For example, Brown et al (1995) found that their sample of university students who received poor exam scores were having negative thought about themselves (they felt they did not deserve to be at university), their future (they may not pass the course), and the world (they no longer enjoyed the course). • The effectiveness of Cognitive Behavioural Therapy (CBT) supports Beck's theory. CBT is just as effective at treating depression as anti-depressants, which supports Beck's assertion that depression is a cognitive disorder.	• It is difficult to establish a cause and effect relationship between negative thinking and depression. This is because it is not known if the negative thinking is the cause of depression, or as a result. • Beck's theory has been criticised as reductionist, as it does not account for other, non-cognitive factors which may be responsible for depression, such as biological ones.

End of Topic 4 test (page 246)

Q19: b) mood disorder

Q20: d) all of the above

Q21: d) all of the above

Q22: a) 2020

Q23: a) with PDD, the symptoms have lasted for over 2 years

Q24: c) both of the above

Q25: d) neurotransmitter

Q26: d) all of the above

Q27: d) all of the above

Q28:

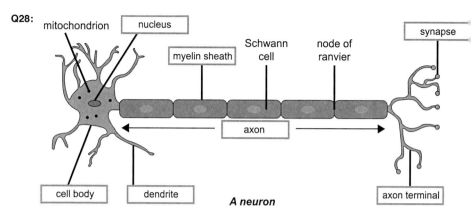

A neuron

Q29: b) genetic predispositions

Q30: b) blocking the reuptake of serotonin and noradrenaline

Q31: b) blocking the reuptake of serotonin and noradrenaline

Q32: c) stopping the enzyme monoamine oxidase from removing serotonin, noradrenaline and dopamine

Q33: d) creating a brain seizure to relieve the symptoms of depression

Q34: c) both a & b

Q35: c) negative views about the future

Q36: c) negative views about the future

Q37: b) faulty information processing

Q38: c) Alloy et al (1999)

Answers to questions and activities for Unit 3

Topic 1: Conformity and obedience (mandatory topic)

Introduction: Questions (page 256)

Q1: b) identification

Q2: c) internalisation

Q3: c) internalisation

Q4: a) compliance

Q5: a) compllance

Q6: b) identification

Sherif (1936): Questions (page 259)

Q7:

- Representative of the whole population.
- Group avoids bias.
- A good age range.
- Etc.

Q8: Yes and no!
Yes, because the experimenters did not include knowledgeable participants (psychology students) who would know about the effect.
No, because there were no women, the age range was narrow and the social range was narrow (all participants were university students).

Q9: Any two from:

- psychologist can control variables more easily;
- psychologist can see the cause-effect relationship;
- it is easy to replicate.

Q10: Any one from:

- it is an artificial situation;
- subjects always know they are part of an experiment;
- there are many ethical considerations - informed consent is not always possible;
- the results cannot be generalised to real-life as it was not a real-life situation.

Asch (1952): Questions (page 263)

Q11:

- Make it more representative of the population - include women.
- Increase the age range of the participants.
- Test participants from different social backgrounds.
- Etc.

Q12: Bar graph

Q13: c) Laboratory

Milgram (1963): Questions (page 277)

Q14: 40 male participants with a range of careers (professionals, white collar and unskilled workers), all of whom were aged between 20 and 50.

Q15: No. All were male, so there was no balance of the genders. There was a reasonable range of careers, but the age range did not fully encompass a representative sample.

Q16: Embarrassment, shock, anger etc.

Q17:

- Deception - participants were deceived into thinking they were being tested for their learning skills.
- Lack of informed consent - participants agreed to be tested for learning and not for obedience.
- Right to withdraw - participants may not have been fully aware that they had the right to withdraw at any stage.
- Psychological trauma - participants could have been stressed by the realisation of what they were prepared to do. This could have a long-term adverse effect on them.

Q18: Any one from:

- easy to control variables, especially if it is in a laboratory situation;
- it allowed the psychologist to see the cause-effect relationship;
- easy to replicate.

Variations on Milgram's study: Questions (page 279)

Q19: 30% - less. Far less than Milgram, as the teacher had to touch the learner's hand.

Q20: 21% - less. The teachers often pretended that they had given an electric shock but 21% still continued to obey.

Q21: 47.5% - less

Q22:

- More educated: No actual figures available - but it was less.
- Military personnel: No actual figures available - but it was more.

End of topic 1 test (page 282)

Q23: a) be accepted by others.

Q24:

- The difficulty of the task
- Gender
- Group size
- If you have low self-esteem

Q25: Mori and Arai carried out a study about **conformity** in 2010. They decided to try to update the study by Asch. Their aims were to find out if similar results could be obtained without the use of confederates, and whether or not **culture** or **gender** made any difference to the overall results.

The **method** used was as follows: 104 undergraduate participants, who knew each other, took part (40 men and 64 women). They used the fMORI technique so participants wore filter glasses. All participants had normal **eyesight**. Groups of four were tested - one participant in each group was given a different type of filter in the glasses without knowing. This filter made them perceive lines of a different **length** to the others in the group. Each participant stated which lines matched out loud. By using this technique it meant that everyone was a true **participant**, unlike the Asch study.

Mori and Arai used a **questionnaire** to ascertain if participants noticed anything odd or if they were confident in their judgements of the length of the lines. **Female** participants conformed to the majority in about a quarter of cases while **male** participants did not conform to the majority.

Q26: Informational influence is when we **change** our behaviour as a **consequence** of information from people we regard as **experts**. To us, their views are valid and **reliable**. This demonstrates a need for **certainty**. When we are not sure how to behave in a certain situation, we **copy** the behaviours of those around us. This copying behaviour **reduces** the likelihood that we will be **criticised** - as humans, it would seem that we do care what **other** people think of us.

Topic 2: Aggression (optional topic)

Activity: Neural and hormonal mechanisms in aggression (page 289)

Q1:   c) Parietal lobe

Q2:   d) Melatonin

Q3:

The **limbic** system connects to the cingulate gyrus and the **prefrontal** cortex. These areas are involved in focusing attention on emotionally significant events, forward planning and the anticipation of **rewards**. These areas control how we respond to **threatening** events or stimuli and play an important role in aggressive behaviour.

The hypothalamus regulates emotional responses, and the **amygdala** attaches emotional significance to sensory information. Any damage to these areas could cause an inappropriate aggressive response.

Signals are passed from the lower systems of the prefrontal cortex (where our feelings are regulated) to higher systems (where feeling are monitored and interpreted), which then triggers a **physical** response. If the prefrontal cortex is damaged then this reduces the **inhibiting** effect of the amygdala, leading to more aggression.

Application activity — evolutionary explanations for aggression (page 293)

Q4:

Leanne's friend believes that Ajay will become more extreme as he is employing mate retention strategies. Ajay is currently using aggressive guarding strategies, such as wanting the password so he can check Leanne's phone or preventing her from going out and potentially talking with other men. Evolutionary theory states that males will use these strategies to prevent their partner from cheating or from leaving them. Males do not want this to happen, as the woman may get pregnant by another man. This means the males might not be certain when it comes to paternity and may end up using resources to bring up this child that does not carry his genes.

His behaviour may become more extreme as, due to his sexual jealousy, he may progress from using aggressive guarding strategies using physical violence towards Leanne to her engaging with or showing interest in other males. This is why Leanne's friend tells her to be careful.

Test your knowledge on ethological explanations of aggression (page 294)

Q5:   b) the study of animal behaviour in its natural environment.

Q6:   c) behaviour that enables survival of the species.

Q7:   d) both.

Activity — Evaluation of Sykes' deprivation model (page 299)

Q8:

Advantages	Disadvantages
• Research by Magargee (1976) found that aggressive incidents in prisons were related to the amount of living space available for each prisoner. This links with the deprivation theory as with overcrowding comes deprivation of many things, such as security or autonomy. Furthermore, in overcrowded prisons, strategies may be put in place to compensate (e.g. being kept in prison cells for long periods of time), which results in fewer opportunities for prisoners to interact with each other, which leads to further deprivation of relationships.	• However, this theory focuses on the external environment, so ignores other potential explanations of aggression, such as biological ones, such as higher rates of testosterone in the prison population. • This implies that it is unlikely that the environment found in prisons is the sole explanation for aggressive behaviour. • It does not account for phenomena such as prison riots. Why do these suddenly explode when levels of deprivation remain the same?

Evaluation of the importation model (page 302)

Q9:

Advantages	Disadvantages
• There is research evidence to support the model. Adams (1981) found that in American prisons, black inmates were more likely to be associates with violent acts than white inmates. The argument for this is that black prisoners tended to come from poorer backgrounds with higher rates of crime, and so imported their cultural norms into the prison. • Harer and Steffensmeier (1996) found that in US prisons, black inmates were significantly more aggressive than white inmates, but that white inmates were significantly more likely to engage in alcohol and drug taking than black inmates. They argued that these behaviours reflected the cultural norms that black and white societies hold outside prison, and so the behaviours had been imported into the prison. • Keller and Wang (2005) found that prison violence is more likely to occur in facilities with higher-security (and therefore who had committed more violent crimes) inmates, than those with lower security inmates, again supporting the idea that the inmates had brought violent behaviour into the institution with them. • Keller and Wang (2005) found that prison violence is more likely to occur in facilities with higher-security (and therefore who had committed more violent crimes) inmates, than those with lower security inmates, again supporting the idea that the inmates had brought violent behaviour into the institution with them.	• This explanation does not accurately predict which inmates will behave aggressively in prison. This is because the model states that prisoners who were members of violent gangs before they were convicted will be more likely to behave aggressively in prison, however DeLisi et al (2004) found no evidence that gang membership prior to imprisonment was linked with violence once in prison. • Much of the research into institutional aggression consists of mainly male populations. This means that the findings may not generalise to females.

Test your knowledge on institutional explanations of aggression (page 302)

Q10: a) lack of freedom

Q11: c) Prisoners have limited ownership of material items, e.g. mobile phones or other material goods they were previously accustomed to.

Q12: d) When men cannot maintain sexual relationships with women which leads to emasculation and worries over homosexual behaviour within prisons.

Q13: a) Prisoners are deprived of freedom during their stay, they have to ask for permission to wash, eat, etc.

Q14: e) Prisoners feel continually threatened by other inmates' aggressive behaviour.

End of topic 2 test (page 307)

Q15: b) serotonin and dopamine.

Q16: d) Challenge hypothesis

Q17: a) limbic system.

Q18: a) Gottesman

Q19: b) fitness.

Q20: b) verbal aggression.

Q21: c) ritual aggression.

Q22: d) Imitation and reinforcement

Q23: c) a child's belief in their ability to recreate the aggressive act observed.

Q24: a) a child would imitate behaviours observed in a role model.

Q25: d) Deprivation of control

Q26: b) Harer and Steffensmeier

Q27: c) Goodson and Pearson.

Q28: a) cognitive priming.

Q29: b) a schema of how we are meant to act in certain situations.

Q30: c) disinhibition.

Topic 3: Social relationships (optional topic)

Social relationships: Question (page 315)

Q1:   A social relationship involves **two** people who associate **regularly** over a **long-term** period of time and whose behaviour is **interdependent** of each other.

Test your knowledge on the filter theory of romantic relationships (page 321)

Q2:

This model states that relationships go through three 'filters'. These filters can be remembered as 'DAN'. **Demographic**, Attitudes, and Needs.

Before we begin filtering we look to the '**Field of Availables**'. This includes all the people we could possibly have a relationship with.

The first filter is then Socio-Demographic Variables. Such variables include similar **background**, education, location etc. People with different or incompatible variables are 'filtered' out at this point.

The second filter is Similar **Attitudes**. Similar attitudes help aid **communication** and so the more attitudes, beliefs, and ideas the couple share the more likely they are to form and **sustain** a relationship. People with different or incompatible attitudes are 'filtered' out at this point.

The third filter is **Complementary** Needs. Once the relationship is established, complementing each other's needs becomes one of the most important factors.

However, there are problems with this study. Firstly, Kerckhoff and Davis relied on questionnaires. **Self-report** questionnaires are problematic as they are easy to lie on, or to misrepresent data, or to get wrong as they often require retrospective knowledge.

The model itself is also flawed. The **socio-demographic** stage may not be as important as the model makes out, with the rise in internet dating and also long-distance relationships, especially in **military** families, not fitting in with the model.

However, **Sprecher** conducted a study and found that couple matched in physical attractiveness, social background, and interests were more likely to develop a long-term relationship. This suggests that the filter model is correct in regards to socio-demographic variables.

Evaluation of Social Exchange Theory (page 325)

Q3:

Advantages	Disadvantages
• SET is supported by studies, such as Sprecher (2001) and Floyd et al. (1994), from which it can be concluded that some people appear to base their evaluation of romantic relationships on rewards and costs, just as SET suggests. • The theory has useful real-life applications, such as Integrated Behavioural Couples Therapy (IBCT), where partners are trained to increase the rewards they give their partners, and reduce the costs.	• Research evidence for SET is, however, limited. • SET concepts are difficult to define (how would you operationalise 'commitment'. If they are difficult to define, they are difficult to measure, which makes this theory unscientific. • The theory assumes that romantic partners keep a daily score of costs and rewards, which is unlikely. • Other research findings suggest that it is the perceived fairness of relationships, rather than a balance of costs and rewards, that keep romantic partners happy (e.g. Clark and Mills, 2011)

Evaluation of Rusbult's Investment Model (page 330)

Q4:

Advantages	Disadvantages
• There are numerous studies which support the model, such as that by Le and Agnew (2003) who found that satisfaction, comparison with alternatives and investment did contribute to commitment. • Rusbult provides an explanation for why people stay in abusive relationships, where the costs are high and the rewards low. It is because of the investment they have made, as found by Rusbult and Maltz. This means that the investment model can account for a wider range of relationships than other models, such as the Social Exchange Theory.	• Cause and effect relationships are difficult to establish (does investment cause commitment, or is there just a relationship between the two?), as many studies into the model are correlational. • Were you honest when you completed the Accommodation test? A problem with questionnaires is the social desirability bias, which means that you may have answered in ways that make you appear in a good light. Questionnaires were used a lot to study the Investment Model, so this means that the results may not be valid.

Evaluation of virtual relationships (page 333)

Q5:

Advantages	Disadvantages
• Research support from Mishna found that most 16-24 year olds considered virtual relationships to be as real as their physical ones and the internet played a large role in sexual and romantic experiences of adolescents which illustrates the importance of social media in virtual relationships. • The way that virtual relationships form and are conducted will continue to evolve as different forms of social media emerge e.g. Facebook replacing MySpace. This means that the importance of virtual relationships will continue. • Online interactions often take longer than face-to-face ones as individuals can create the perfect response which therefore improves the quality of interactions.	• Most of the research looking at virtual relationships was conducted in the late 1990s and early 2000s. This means that psychological research in this area is outdated, as technology is changing so rapidly. This means that research findings in this area may not apply to the current situation. • It must be considered that even face-to-face relationships have a virtual side e.g. texting, which means that it is not a straightforward case of either or.

Evaluation of parasocial relationships (page 335)

Q6:

Advantages	Disadvantages
• Research has suggested that the formation of parasocial relationships has positive effects. • Perse and Rubin (1989) found that people who are exposed to the same characters over again from soap operas benefit from parasocial interactions as there is a reduction in uncertainty about social relationships.	• Maltby et al (2005) found that the parasocial relationship with celebrities who are perceived as slim and with a good body shape may lead to a poor body image in female adolescents and a predisposition to eating disorders (e.g. anorexia or bulimia nervosa). This suggests that parasocial relationships provide models of social behaviour and provide opportunities to learn cultural values. This suggests that there is a relationship between attitudes to celebrities and body image which can result in low self-esteem.

Test your knowledge on parasocial relationships (page 336)

Q7:

The absorption-addiction model

The celebrity Attitude Scale (CAS was used by **Maltby et al** to identify three levels of parasocial relationships. It asses celebrity attraction. The first level is *'entertainment-social level'*. This is the **least** intense level where celebrities are viewed as sources of entertainent and fuel for social interaction. The second level is **'intense-personal level'**, an intermediate level where someone becomes more personally involved with a celebrity and may include **obsessive** thoughts. The third level is *'borderline pathological level'*, the **strongest** level of celebrity worship where **fantasies** are uncontrollable and behaviour is more **extreme**.

Attachment theory

Bowlby's attachment theory suggests that early difficulties in attachment may lead to difficulties in forming **successful** relationships later in life. Such difficulties may lead to a **preference** for parasocial relationships to replace those within one's own social circle as parasocial relationships don't require the same **social skills**.

Ainsworth identified 2 attachment types associated with unhealthy emotional development: insecure-**resistant** and insecure-avoidant. Insecure-resistant types are more **likely** to form parasocial relationships because they want to have their unfulfiled needs met in a relationship where there is no real threat of **rejection**. Insecure-**avoidant** types prefer to avoid the pain and rejection of any type of relationship, either social or parasocial.

End of topic 3 test (page 337)

Q8: c) human reproductive behaviour.

Q9: b) to be as promiscuous as possible.

Q10: a) social demography.

Q11: b) how well two people fit together.

Q12: d) Social exchange theory

Q13: a) Comparison level

Q14: c) commitment stage.

Q15: c) comparison with alternatives.

Q16: a) Extrinsic investment

Q17: c) positive illusions.

Q18: b) gating.

Q19: c) deindividuation.

Q20: a) one-sided.

Q21: d) intense-personal.

Q22: a) a person having an insecure-resistant attachment style.

Q23: c) Hazan and Shaver.

Topic 4: Prejudice (optional topic)

Research by LaPierre: Questions (page 344)

Q1:   The study of human (or animal) behaviour in a typical, everyday environment.

Q2:

- It has a high ecological validity - meaning that it can be generalised to other situations.
- It is a good way to collect data which would usually be difficult, or unethical, to engineer.

Q3:   Any two from:

- researchers have no control over the environment so cannot use this method to establish causal relationships;
- there is an ethical issue involved, in that subjects being observed did not consent to be part of an experiment;
- there can be an observer bias, in that the observer is watching for particular behaviours and, therefore, may miss other interesting behaviours.

Direct and indirect discrimination (page 345)

Model answer:

Direct discrimination occurs where an employer or organisation treats someone less favourably because of their age, disability, gender, sexual orientation, marital status, pregnancy or maternity, race, religion or belief, or sex. These attributes are known as protected characteristics.

Indirect discrimination occurs where a policy of an employer or organisation applies to everybody but results in people with certain protected characteristics (e.g., race or gender) being put at a disadvantage.

Spot the difference between direct and indirect discrimination (page 345)

Q4:   a) direct

Q5:   b) indirect

Q6:   a) direct

Q7:   b) indirect

Q8:   b) indirect

Q9:   a) direct

Q10: a) direct

Research by Skellington: Questions (page 347)

Q11: These are conducted in person, through the post/email or over the phone and they inquire into the ways people think and act.

Q12: Any two from:

- participants may feel that they have to answer in a particular way because the researcher wants to hear a certain answer;
- results can be generalised only to the population from which the sample was drawn;
- participants written/spoken answers to questions may be not be completely honest.

Q13: This is a purely personal matter, but you should try to justify it by using the statistic and saying why it is depressing.

Stephen Lawrence case: Notebook exercise (page 348)

Expected answer

Aspect of racism in this case	Racism against Stephen Lawrence	Racism by the police
Behavioural	Lawrence was stabbed to death, seemingly because be was black.	It was found that the police did not follow the case up properly.
Cognitive	Those who murdered Lawrence possibly held the stereotypical belief that black people did not have the same rights as white people.	The police allegedly held the belief that this murder was not worth investigating properly.
Affective	The feelings of those who murdered Lawrence must have been hatred towards someone because of their colour.	The feelings of the police working on this case may have been that a black murder victim was not as important to investigate as that of a white person.

Ambivalent sexism: Discussion (page 351)

Q14: This is a personal opinion but answers should deal with examples of why you feel one type is worse than the other. For example, "I believe hostile sexism is worse as women are possibly left feeling threatened whereas with benevolent sexism women would not."

Q15: This is a personal opinion, but should be justified through an example.

Evaluation of the authoritarian personality theory (page 354)

Q16:

Advantages	Disadvantages
	• Situational and sociocultural factors are underemphasised. For example, more racism is found in cultures like South Africa and the southern states of America, but no differences have been found in the frequency of authoritarian personalities. • The theory does not explain why prejudice within a society can change very quickly; for example, the US became largely anti-Japanese immediately after Pearl Harbor, which is not consistent with Adorno's proposal that prejudice always goes back to early childhood. • It does not account for prejudice affecting large groups or whole societies, such as South Africa under apartheid.

Evaluation of Realistic Conflict Theory (page 356)

Q17:

Advantages	Disadvantages
• Similar studies have suggested that when populations expand and land becomes in short supply conflict and violence increase. • Sherif's robbers care experiment found that competition increases hostility between the two groups of 12-year-old boys. • Sherif supports this as he also found a reduction in intergroup conflict as a result of the removal of competition. Therefore, RCT can be applied to real life by helping reduce prejudice between groups in society through the use of superordinate goals. • RCT can be used to explain real life situations such as the Rwandan genocide. The Tutsi tribe settled peacefully and intermarried with the Hutu tribe of Rwanda, until political rivalry between the groups caused the mass genocide of almost one million Tutsi. • Suggests ways in which prejudice can be reduced (see the jigsaw technique).	• Conflicting results: Tyerman and Spencer (1983) didn't obtain the same results

Test your knowledge on explanations of prejudice (page 359)

Q18: a) Whenever there are two or more groups that are seeking the same limited resources, this will lead to conflict, negative stereotypes, and discrimination between the groups.

Q19: a) Mutually desirable goals that cannot be obtained without the participation of two or more groups.

Q20: b) to identify the different components that make up an authoritarian personality.

Q21: b) childhood

Q22: c) sticking to society's norms and values.

Q23: a) having aggressive feelings towards people who violate society's norms.

Q24: c) having similar beliefs

Q25: b) achieving a goal

Q26: d) Social Identity Theory

Q27: d) psychic energy

Q28: a) prejudice leads to discrimination, discrimination can lead to violence.

Jane Elliott's work: Discussion (page 363)

Expected answer

1. This is an opinion, but your answer could deal with some of the following points:

   - older children may be more cynical and so changing their views could be more difficult;
   - older children could be more perceptive about how they're being manipulated into separate groups and so the study may not work so well etc.

2. A psychological study, similar to Elliott's, would need to be structured in the usual way.

   - Aims:
     - to see if prejudice can be introduced where it wasn't present before;
     - to see if participants can reduce an existing prejudice by being made aware of it.
   - Participants - they would need to be from both genders, a wider age group than Elliott's study and they would need to be more representative of the whole of society, in terms of class, colour etc..
   - Method - three groups would have to be established:
     i. blue-eyed;
     ii. brown-eyed;
     iii. control group of blue-eyed and brown-eyed participants.

   The method would be similar to Elliott's original design, but a more thorough approach to assessing feelings would be needed. Individual questionnaires for students or one-to-one interviews would work well to assess whether prejudice had occurred and then whether prejudice reduction had occurred in the longer term.

Media campaigns to reduce prejudice (page 368)

Q29: a) Used

Q30: a) Used

Q31: a) Used

Q32: a) Used

Test your knowledge on ways to reduce prejudice (page 370)

Q33: a) students are separated by ethnicity and/or gender.

Q34: c) WiSETI

Q35: b) May not apply to collectivist cultures.

Q36: d) paternity.

Q37: d) all of the above.

Q38: b) the message has to be given to children, as adults will distort or ignore any message that contradicts their own view.

End of topic 4 test (page 372)

Q39: both RCT and SIT

Q40: SIT only

Q41: RCT only

Q42: both RCT and SIT

Q43: both RCT and SIT

Q44: RCT only

Q45: both RCT and SIT